# SAINT FRIDESWIDE'S MONASTERY AT OXFORD

# SAINT FRIDESWIDE'S MONASTERY AT OXFORD

## Archaeological and Architectural Studies

Edited by
**JOHN BLAIR**

ALAN SUTTON

First published in the United Kingdom in 1990 by Alan Sutton Publishing Ltd · Brunswick Road · Gloucester

First published in the United States of America in 1990 by Alan Sutton Publishing Inc · Wolfeboro Falls · NH 03896–0848

**British Library Cataloguing in Publication Data**
St. Frideswide's Monastery, Oxfordshire.
  1. Oxfordshire. Oxford. Monasteries. Sites. Archaeological investigation
  I. Blair, John
  942.574

  ISBN 0-86299-773-9


**Library of Congress Cataloging in Publication Data applied for**

NA
5471
.O9
S25
1991

These articles first appeared in *Oxoniensia* Volume LIII

Typeset in 10/11 Baskerville
Typesetting and origination by Alan Sutton Publishing Limited
Printed in Great Britain by Dotesios Printers Limited

# FOREWORD

This collection of essays was first printed in *Oxoniensia* Volume LIII (1988), the journal of the Oxfordshire Architectural and Historical Society. Its publication coincides with the one hundred and fiftieth anniversary of the foundation of the Society in 1839 in its first guise as the 'Oxford Society for Promoting the Study of Gothic Architecture'. This Society was to develop into the Oxford Architectural and Historical Society, which in turn combined in 1972 with the Oxfordshire Archaeological Society (itself founded in 1852) to form the present Society. The Society, as it exists today, aims to further the study of the archaeology, architecture and history of Oxford and Oxfordshire by means of lectures, excursions and the publication of *Oxoniensia*. *Oxoniensia* is published annually; intending subscribers should communicate with the Honorary Assistant Treasurer, Oxfordshire Architectural and Historical Society, Department of Museum Services, Fletcher's House, Woodstock OX7 1SN.

Although these essays have a single theme, that of the foundation and development of St Frideswide's monastery, they faithfully reflect the range of our Society's interests. Furthermore, they continue a tradition of scholarly interest in St Frideswide, Oxford's patron saint. This interest began with the publication by our sister society, the Oxford Historical Society, of the *Cartulary of the Monastery of St Frideswide* edited by S.R. Wigram (O.H.S. xxviii, 1895 and xxxi, 1896). The interest was further stimulated in 1936 when Professor F.M. Stenton published a seminal article in our own journal ('St Frideswide and her Times', *Oxoniensia* I (1936), 103–112). Stenton's article was based on a lecture given, appropriately, on 19 October 1935, the 1200th anniversary of St Frideswide's death. He established then the authenticity of the saint and provided the context for her life. Stenton also laid the foundation on which later research has been based, notably John Blair's essay 'St Frideswide Reconsidered' (*Oxoniensia* LII (1987), 71–127), which is the essential companion to this present volume.

T.G. HASSALL
President
The Oxfordshire Architectural
and Historical Society

# Notes on Contributors

JOHN ASHDOWN, Conservation Officer, Oxford City Council.

MAVIS BATEY, West House, 151 Barrack Lane, Aldwick, West Sussex, PO21 4ED. Publications include *The History of Oxford Gardens*.

MARTIN BIDDLE and BIRTHE KJØLBYE-BIDDLE, 19 Hamilton Road, Oxford.

JOHN BLAIR, Editor, *Oxoniensia*. The Queen's College, Oxford, OX1 4AW.

CATHERINE COLE, Oxford. Research interests include 17th-century craftsmen working in Oxford.

IAN FISHER, Royal Commission on Ancient and Historical Monuments, Scotland.

JAMES GRAHAM-CAMPBELL, Department of History, University College, London; currently British Academy Research Reader.

JULIA GREEN, Field Officer, Hertford Archaeological Unit.

RICHARD HALSEY, former Inspector of Ancient Monuments, now in Historic Buildings Division, English Heritage. Research interests include Romanesque architecture in Oxfordshire.

T.A. HESLOP, School of Art History and Music, University of East Anglia, Norwich, NR4 7TJ. Lecturer in the history of medieval art and architecture; research interests include English medieval seals.

J.R.L. HIGHFIELD, Merton College, Oxford.

RICHARD K. MORRIS, Senior Lecturer, Department of the History of Art, University of Warwick, Coventry.

JULIAN MUNBY, 28 Alexandra Road, Oxford, OX2 0DB.

CHRISTOPHER SCULL, Department of Archaeology, The University of Durham, 46 Saddler St., Durham, DH1 3NU.

DAVID STURDY, 47 Ulfgar Road, Wolvercote, Oxford.

# SAINT FRIDESWIDE'S MONASTERY AT OXFORD: ARCHAEOLOGICAL AND ARCHITECTURAL STUDIES

*Edited by* JOHN BLAIR

*The Society is deeply indebted to Christ Church for its generous support of this publication.*

# Prefatory Note

The remains of St. Frideswide's Priory have received the detailed attention of architectural historians from J.C. Buckler onwards, but have been little discussed in print. Buckler's voluminous notes and sketches of the 1870s have remained unpublished, as have David Sturdy's 1963 excavation and Richard Halsey's comprehensive analysis of the Romanesque building. In 1985, Christopher Scull's excavation in the cloister provided the occasion and the stimulus to bring this material together to form, in conjunction with other studies, an integrated series of reports presenting the data which have been gathered to date and the hypotheses which have been formulated.

These papers are the result of collaboration and fruitful dialogue between the main contributors; the numerous cross-references demonstrate how much they have enriched each other. Nonetheless, they offer diverse and sometimes conflicting interpretations. While a broad consensus has emerged as to the Romanesque phases and the development of the north-eastern chapels, the mid-Saxon origins of the minster, the site of Æthelred II's church and the first buildings of the Augustinian community remain matters of dispute. Prior Robert of Cricklade is the hero of these pages: his architectural transformation of the canons' church and cloister was as thoroughgoing as his literary transformation of their founder-saint's legend, and is even harder to get behind. More excavation must take place before reliable facts can replace informed conjecture, and for elucidating the Anglo-Saxon history of the site these papers are merely a starting-point.

My foremost thanks as editor are to the Dean and Chapter of Christ Church, and to the treasurer Mr. R.P. Benthall, for their financial and moral support, without which the project would certainly have foundered; to Sarah Blair for her unfailing help during this arduous and sometimes stressful task; to Pat Lloyd (as always) for her speedy and accurate typing; and to David Sturdy for generously making available the results of his work of more than two decades ago. All the contributors have assisted my own analysis and interpretation of the evidence, and Roger Ainslie, John Cherry, Brian Durham, Derek Keene, John Maddicott and Christopher Young helped in various ways.

JOHN BLAIR

## RECURRING ABBREVIATIONS

| | |
|---|---|
| B.L. | British Library, Dept. of MSS. |
| Blair, 'St.F.' | J. Blair, 'St. Frideswide Reconsidered'. *Oxoniensia*, lii (1987), 71–127. |
| *Cart.Frid.* | *The Cartulary of the Monastery of St. Frideswide*, ed. S.R. Wigram, i–ii (O.H.S. xxviii, xxxi, 1894, 1896). |
| *R.C.H.M. Oxford* | *An Inventory of the Historical Monuments in the City of Oxford* (Royal Commission on Historical Monuments, 1939). |
| *RG* | *Regesta Regum Anglo-Normannorum*, i–iii, eds. H.W.C. Davis etc. (1913–68). |
| *V.C.H. Oxon.* | *The Victoria History of the County of Oxford*. |
| Wood, *City* | A. Wood, *Survey of the Antiquities of the City of Oxford*, ed. A. Clark, i–iii (O.H.S. xv–xvii, xxxvii, 1889–90, 1899). |

# Thornbury, Binsey: A Probable Defensive Enclosure associated with Saint Frideswide

By JOHN BLAIR

With a contribution by MAUREEN MELLOR

SUMMARY

*A large sub-oval earthwork enclosure at Binsey, associated with St. Margaret's chapel and its graveyard, is identified with* Thornbiri *('thorny fortress'), named in the late 12th-century Life of St. Frideswide as one of her places of refuge. It was regarded as a holy spot from the 12th century onwards, and the canons of St. Frideswide's may have maintained a cell there. Until 18th-century changes in the road-pattern it lay directly on the main route between Eynsham and Oxford. Excavations in 1987 identified a series of boundary features. A ditch on the N.W. side, its fill containing material dated by a radiocarbon determination to the Roman or sub-Roman period, was either preceded or succeeded by a revetted rampart. On the S.W. side, the earliest identified ditch had an early Anglo-Saxon potsherd stratified under its primary fill. The earthwork seems to have remained conspicuous until the early 18th century, and is still defined by an eroded bank and field-ditch. It remains uncertain whether the original enclosure is of Iron Age or post-Roman date; it may possibly belong to the series of small Iron Age forts on terrace-edge and island sites on the Thames gravels. The stratified sherd, however, suggests that the ditch was being kept clean at some date in the early Anglo-Saxon period. The legend of Frideswide at Binsey, and the fact that it was an old-established possession of her monastery by the early 12th century, suggest a possibility that the earthwork may have been used during her life as an ancillary monastic enclosure or retreat-house.*

ACKNOWLEDGEMENTS

The excavation, by kind permission of Christ Church and its tenant Mr. D.J. Parris, was carried out in 1987–8 by Roger Ainslie, Michelle Armstrong, John Blair, Richard Hornsey, Edward Impey, Joszef Laszlovszky, Sally Oatley, Nicholas Palmer, Christine Peters and Christopher Whittick. Radiocarbon dating was financed by the Historic Buildings and Monuments Commission for England, and carried out at the Isotope Measurement Laboratory, AERE Harwell. I am also very grateful to Maureen Mellor for her contribution; to George Lambrick for advice on valley-forts; to David Haddon-Reece and Tony Fleming for help with the radiocarbon samples; to Bruce Levitan for identifying the bones; and to Mark Robinson for examining a soil sample.

HISTORICAL EVIDENCE

The early 12th-century Life of St. Frideswide relates how the princess, fleeing from the lecherous King Algar, hid at Bampton in 'a wood called Binsey', where she worked miraculous cures on a blind girl of Bampton, a young man of Seacourt and a demoniac fisherman. Although Binsey is in fact near Oxford, and nowhere near Bampton, the reference to its neighbour Seacourt suggests that the author had access to older material associating Frideswide with miracles in and around Binsey.[1]

When Robert of Cricklade, prior of St. Frideswide's, came to re-write the Life of his monastery's founder-saint around 1160, the confusion perturbed him.[2] In his own version he resolved it by inserting, between the first two miracles, a new chapter which transports Frideswide from Bampton to Binsey in time to cure the young man of Seacourt. Frideswide and her companions set out for Oxford, but when their boat reaches 'the possession called Binsey near the city' they decide to stay there for a further spell of solitude:

> On that possession (*predium*) was a place (*locus*) entangled with various kinds of trees, called *Thornbiri* in the Saxon tongue because of the many different species of thorns there, lonely and most suitable for devotion. Here she straightway built an oratory, and many buildings well-suited to the needs of holy people. And since the branch of the river was some way away, and she felt it inconvenient for the sisters to go there to draw water, she obtained by her prayers a well which remains to this day, and performs healing works for many who drink from it [*or* who pray there]. Here she hoped to hide, here devote herself to sweet tranquillity and shun the crowds.[3]

Beyond the existence of some sort of traditional link between Frideswide and Binsey, it is impossible to say how much of this story is based on anything other than Prior Robert's imagination. There is, however, independent evidence that Binsey was regarded in the early 12th century as a holy place, appropriate for the religious life. The foundation narrative of Godstow nunnery recounts that in Henry I's reign there lived a lady of Winchester named Edith, wife of Sir William Lancelin. After her husband's death

> a vision often came to her that she should go near the city called Oxford and wait there for a sign from the Almighty King, by which she would know how to do God's service. She came, as a vision commanded her, to Binsey, where she dwelt in prayer and lived a most holy life. One night she heard a voice which told her what to do: 'Edith', it said, 'arise, go without delay to the place [i.e. Godstow] where a light descends to earth from heaven, and establish nuns there to serve God.' Thus in truth was this Abbey first founded.[4]

Binsey is not mentioned in Æthelred II's charter for St. Frideswide's minster (1004), which does not, however, claim to list all properties.[5] In Domesday Book (1086), the canons' 'four hides near Oxford', which never paid geld nor belonged to any hundred, probably included both Walton and Binsey; it is even possible that the 8 ac. of

---

[1] Blair, 'St. F.', 83–4, 98–9.

[2] Ibid. 80 for Robert's authorship of the second Life.

[3] Ibid. 84–5, 110.

[4] The narrative survives as a late 14th-century French verse version (P.R.O. E164/20, f. 1 of main text): '. . . Souent luy vient par avisiun/ Ke ele alast pres de la citee/ Que Oxenford fust apele,/ E la demorast desk' ataunt/ Quele veit signe del Rey pusaunt/ Desk'ele eit oy en quele guise/ Estoit fere la Dieux service./ A Benseye est pus ale/ Cum en auisiun fut maunde,/ Entes oraisuns iluske demora,/ E mult seinte vie demena./ Une voiz oist par un nuit,/ La quele dist quy fere luy estust./ 'Ediz', fet il, 'fus levez,/ E saunz demorance yalez/ Au lu qu lumer desent/ Au tere del firmament,/ E la fetes ordeynir/ Noueines a Dieu servir.'/ En ceste manere par verite/ Fust cest albeie primes trouve./ . . .' This may well be a translation of an earlier Latin narrative. The Middle English version (*The English Register of Godstow Nunnery*, ed. A. Clark, i (.E.E.T.S. orig. ser. cxxix, 1905), 26) is simply a translation of the French.

[5] *Cart.Frid.* i, 2–9

'thorn-scrub' or 'spinney' (*spineti*), a rare item of Domesday terminology, represents the placename *Thornbiri*.[6] Henry I's re-foundation charter (*c.*1122) includes 'the whole place (*locus*) called Binsey'; this text may have been tampered with, but 'the possession (*predium*) called Binsey' appears in the more reliable confirmation of Pope Honorius II (1124×30).[7] Property returned to the canons by Roger of Salisbury in 1139 included the 'whole place (*locus*) called Binsey', and in the same year the burgesses of Oxford acknowledged that 'from the land which pertains to one hide in Walton and from the land which pertains to Binsey the said canons have yearly rent and service of their peasants and their hundred in all things'.[8] In 1279 St. Frideswide's was said to have a hamlet (*hamelot*) called Binsey in the suburbs of Oxford, assessed at half a hide.[9] The Priory's 15th-century cartulary asserts that 'the possession (*predium*) called Binsey, with the hundred and its other liberties, was given to the said monastery from the time when St. Frideswide was alive in the body', and lists the customary dues of the tenants as *sant'* (sandgavel?), landgavel, ingavel, churchscot and tollsester.[10]

The impression conveyed by these texts is not only that Binsey was an ancient, presumably pre-Augustinian, possession of St. Frideswide's monastery, but also that the house's proprietorship of it was of a somewhat unusual character. The 'four hides near Oxford' are the only holding in the Oxfordshire Domesday which is claimed to be extra-hundredal, a claim evidently re-asserted in 1139 and again in the 15th-century cartulary passage.[11] The Binsey men seem to have been unique among the Priory's tenants in the exotic customary renders which they owed, notably churchscot with its connotations of ancient parochial jurisdiction. And the terms 'possession' (*predium*) and 'place' (*locus*), if commonplace enough in themselves, are not standard legal designations like *manerium, terra, hida* or *acra*: the persistence with which they are applied to Binsey is curious. There may be an implication that Binsey was a *special* place: small and part of a larger entity, yet worth mentioning because it had some significance of its own.

The original Binsey ('Byni's island') which gave the estate its name was presumably the small gravel outcrop on which the village now stands. Since Prior Robert attributes to Frideswide the chapel and holy well, both of which still exist, he clearly identified *Thornbiri* with the area around the chapel, as distinct from the village site (Fig. 1). Binsey chapel is mentioned in the cartulary texts of Henry I's foundation charter and later royal confirmations, but there are strong reasons to suspect a systematic interpolation;[12] an episcopal confirmation of 1203×6 may provide the first genuine charter reference.[13] Nonetheless, the fact that Prior Robert could claim so ancient an origin for the chapel must mean that by *c.*1140–70 it had existed from beyond living memory. The absence of any references to it in the 12th-century charters may be precisely because it was bound so closely to its mother house as to be regarded as an extension of the Priory.

---

[6] Domesday Book f. 157a. This was evidently the belief of the later medieval canons, who rubricated their transcript of the Domesday entries as 'faciens mensionem de Wynchendon' et Bunseye': *Cart.Frid.* ii, 206.

[7] *Cart.Frid.* i, 11, 14.

[8] Ibid. i, 18, 20; *Regesta Regum Anglo-Normannorum* iii, No. 640.

[9] *Oxoniensia*, xxxvii (1972), 173.

[10] *Cart.Frid.* ii, 18.

[11] Binsey was, however, said to be part of Northgate hundred (probably a 12th-century creation) at various times from the late 13th century onwards: see *V.C.H. Oxon.* iv, 265, 270; *Oxoniensia*, i (1936), 122.

[12] The suspicious fact is that although Binsey chapel is mentioned, along with immunity from episcopal visitation, in charters of Henry I and Matilda (*Cart.Frid.* i, 10, 23), both are conspicuously absent from the otherwise comprehensive lists in papal and episcopal confirmations of 1124×30, 1141, 1158, 1154×9 and *c.*1155×60 (Ibid. 13–15, 20–22, 27–9, 29–30, 31–2). It looks as though a shameless tamperer with royal charters has baulked at falsifying papal bulls.

[13] *Cart.Frid.* i, 46.

Binsey had no burial rights, bodies being taken to Oxford for burial as late as 1552.[14] In 1341 the chapel was said to be attached to St. Edward's parish,[15] which had absorbed St. Frideswide's parish in 1298 on the suppression of its altar in the Priory church (below, p.256); a direct parochial dependence on St. Frideswide's before 1298 is therefore likely. Although post-medieval sources generally speak of St. Margaret's chapel, a reference in 1323 to 'the chapel built at Binsey in honour of St. Frideswide and St. Margaret' makes this the only reliably-attested dedication to Oxford's patron saint.[16]

Whether the Priory ever had a monastic cell at Binsey is uncertain. Edith Lancelin, who must have stayed there soon before or soon after St. Frideswide's was re-founded c. 1122, may have lived as a recluse, but the narrative does not actually say so; it is equally possible that she chose Binsey because there was a cell of canons, or even nuns, which could house her. In the 17th century, Anthony Wood believed that the Augustinian canons

> instituted and ordained it to be a cell or place of retirement . . . , and therin not only at some times enjoyed themselves in great repose and devotion, but also sent their stubborn monks to be punished for crimes committed against the prior or his brethren, and that commonly was either by inflicting on them confinement in a dark roome or else by withdrawing from them their usuall repast and the like. Here it was alsoe that several preists appointed by the prior of St. Frideswid's had habitation, purposely to confesse and absolve pilgrims of all sorts that flocked hither to receive remidy for their malidies from the water of St. Margarett's Well.[17]

Given Wood's habit of extrapolating beyond his sources this should probably not be taken too seriously, though he may have seen documents now lost. Firmer evidence that Binsey was a place of resort for the community comes with the temporary seizure of St. Frideswide's by the Crown in 1374: the prior and one fellow-canon were allowed to retain as their dwelling a place near Oxford called Binsey chapel.[18] There was no formal vicarage, and no medieval curates are recorded (with the possible exception of one 'Simon chaplain of Thornbury' mentioned in 1293); in 1423 a canon of St. Frideswide's served Binsey, and apparently lived there with one servant.[19] These intimations that the canons controlled Binsey directly, and perhaps maintained a cell or rest-house there, reinforce the impression conveyed by the land-holding records that it was a place to which they ascribed special significance.

## TOPOGRAPHY AND COMMUNICATIONS[20] (Fig. 1)

Much of Binsey township consists of poorly-drained alluvium, and human settlement has probably always concentrated on the three small gravel islands in the floodplain: Langney to the S., the area around Binsey village and Green, and the northernmost island on which the chapel stands. The edges of these islands have not been defined exactly, but the chapel probably marks the N. edge of an oval gravel outcrop encircled

[14] *V.C.H.Oxon.* iv, 270–1.

[15] *Inquisitiones Nonarum* (Rec.Comm., 1807), 142.

[16] Lincoln Archives Office, Bishops' Reg. V, f.340. Pre-Victorian evidence for the dedication of Frilsham church (Berks.) to St. Frideswide has not been found.

[17] Wood, *City*, ii, 42–3.

[18] *Cal.Close Rolls 1374–7*, 48.

[19] *V.C.H.Oxon.* iv, 271.

[20] See also Ibid. 268–9.

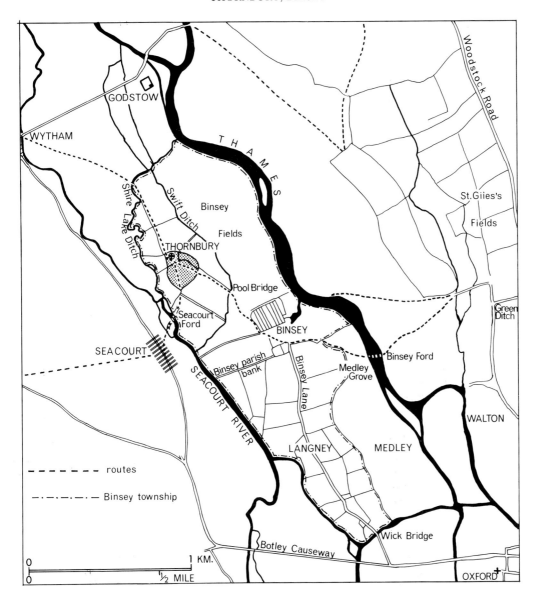

Fig. 1. Sketch-map of the environs of Thornbury, incorporating detail from the 18th-century maps (Christ Church Maps Binsey 1 and 2). The paths across Port Meadow are as shown on Cole's map of 1695 (Bodl. (E)70 Oxford (121)).

by the recently-discovered earthwork.[21] Seen from the air, the land thus defined appears slightly raised above the old enclosures, bounded W. by Shire Lake Ditch and E. by Swift Ditch, which surround it.

Binsey Green is now approached from the Botley Road causeway (built in the 16th century) by a lane crossing a branch-stream at Wyke Bridge,[22] or from North Oxford by a footpath across Port Meadow. From the Green a lane running north-westwards, laid out in 1821 to replace an earlier field-path,[23] provides the only access to St. Margaret's chapel. For modern visitors it is a place of almost perfect seclusion, disturbed only by the traffic on the western bypass.

In the middle ages Binsey may have been much less remote. Until the 18th century, the normal routes into Oxford from Eynsham and the Berkshire villages around the foot of Wytham Hill crossed the Seacourt and Shire Lake streams near the chapel. One came by the now-deserted village of Seacourt, which Anthony Wood believed to have been 'a thorough fare towne from Einsham and the westerne parts to Oxon (long before the other way by Botley was thought upon)', with a bridge at the crossing of the Seacourt stream indicated by stones 'lying in great abundance in the river'.[24] Thomas Hearne wrote of Seacourt in 1728: 'The highway passed through it, and so over the water through Binsey Ford, and so to Oxford. There is a hardway now to be seen, and at Binsey the said way (which comes over the . . . [Seacourt stream]) is called in one or two Places the King's Swarth.'[25] Prior Robert must have had this in mind when he pictured distraught suppliants from Seacourt crossing the river and beating on Frideswide's door at Binsey.[26]

A more northerly route from Wytham was used by Hearne in 1716: 'From Wightham I went to Oxford by Binsey. But the Bridge, before we come to Binsey, being broke down lately by some Young Scholars . . . I was forced to be carryed over upon a Man's Back. I stop'd in Binsey Church Yard on purpose to read the Inscriptions.'[27] This route appears on a map of 1792 (Fig. 2): a footpath runs north-westwards from Binsey Green, over Swift Ditch at Pool Bridge, into the graveyard, between the chapel and well, and across the N. boundary ditch of the graveyard by a small bridge; from there it continues northwards to meet Shire Lake Ditch (presumably where the bridge had been broken by the 'young scholars'), and its onwards direction is labelled 'to Wytham'. At one point S.E. of the chapel, this line is still marked by a hollow-way (Fig. 4).

The most direct line to Seacourt from Binsey Green would run due W., avoiding the chapel; but the road did not in fact follow it. In 1783, Thomas Warton described what he imagined to be a minor Roman road:[28]

> [It] perceptibly slants from the brow of Shotover-hill near Oxford, down its northern declivity; bisects Marston-lane, crosses the Charwell north of Holywell-church with a stone-pavement, is then called KING'S SWATH, or Way, goes over saint Giles's field, and Port-meadow, has an apparent trajectus over the Isis, now called Binsey-ford, being a few yards north of Medley-grove, runs through Binsey

[21] Geological Survey Map 1″, drift, sheet 236 (1972 edn.). The 1982 edition of this map shows the gravel island as much smaller, but observations of natural gravel at several points within the enclosed area indicate that the earlier map is more correct.

[22] V.C.H.Oxon. iv, 284, 268.

[23] Ibid.

[24] Wood, City, i, 324–5 (with editorial note that 'the ruins of this bridge are still seen in the water, 1888').

[25] Hearne's Collections, ix (O.H.S. lxv, 1914), 399.

[26] Blair, 'St. F.', 111.

[27] Hearne's Collections, v (O.H.S. xlii, 1901), 188–9.

[28] T. Warton, Specimen of a History of Oxfordshire: Kiddington (2nd edn., 1783), 57n.

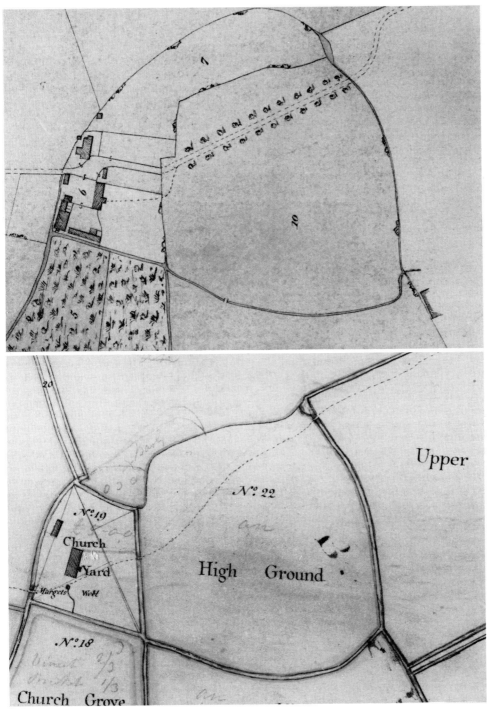

Fig. 2. Thornbury in 1792 and c.1850 (Christ Church Maps Binsey 2 and 5).

church-yard, in which are the signatures of large buildings, winds up the hill towards the left, where stood the antient village of Seckworth [i.e. Seacourt] . . . ; and from thence either proceeds to Gloucester, or falls into the AKEMAN about Witney.

The only possible interpretation of this account is that the Seacourt road from Binsey Green was identical with the Wytham road as far as the graveyard, and then turned sharply south-westwards to enter Seacourt on its N.E. side. Archaeological support for this circuitous route comes from the excavations at Seacourt in 1958–9, which identified a track and sunken way fording the river and entering the village in exactly the position required. From there the road would have continued up Seacourt Hill to join the Eynsham coach-road 1 km. W. of Seacourt.[29]

The road E. from Binsey Green across Port Meadow, which formed the main approach to Oxford via the Woodstock Road, seems to have continued as a through-route towards Shotover. It was evidently known both at Binsey and in St. Giles's Fields as the 'King's swath' (i.e. 'way' or 'track'), and may have been identical with the 'green ditch' (now St. Margaret's Road) which formed the N. boundary of the City liberty.[30]

Far from being isolated, Binsey chapel stood at a junction of routes between Oxford, Wytham and Seacourt. The late medieval traveller from Oxford or Headington to Eynsham, Witney or Bampton would have passed the chapel and well (perhaps actually between them), and would have deviated from the shortest route in order to do so. This accords ill with Prior Robert's description of *Thornbiri* as *solitarius*; it may be that the road via the chapel was established in the 12th century or later as a consequence of the cult, replacing a more direct route from Seacourt to Binsey Green along 'Binsey parish bank'.[31]


## THE CHAPEL AND WELL

The chapel and graveyard, together with the farmhouse to the N.E. and farm buildings to the N., occupy a rectilinear enclosure (Figs. 2–4) defined by wide boundary ditches (noted by Hearne in 1718).[32] The site has all the appearance of a moated manor-house, and must surely represent the establishment of the later medieval canons. A 'court' with the chapel and well is pictured in the 15th-century metrical Life of St. Frideswide:[33]

> Thre ȝer with hir' felawes. heo bilevede there,
> And to servy Ihesu Crist. a chapel heo let rere.
> Ther is ȝut a vair court. and a chirche vair and suete,
> Arered in honour of hir'. and of S' Margarete.
> . . . . . . . . . . . . . . . .
> So sprong ther up awel vair welle. crer inou and clene.
> That fond hem alle water inouȝ. that hi ne dorste noȝt hem bymene.
> That biside the chirche ȝut is. alute in the west side,
> That mony mon hath bote ido. and that mony mon sech' wide.

[29] M. Biddle, 'The Deserted Medieval Village of Seacourt, Berkshire', *Oxoniensia*, xxvi/xxvii (1961/2), 75, 77 n.35, 78 and n.44, Pl.IIA.

[30] For the crossing from Binsey to Port Meadow, and its use by Binsey commoners, see *V.C.H. Oxon.* iv, 281–2. The main medieval exit from the Meadow on the Oxford side was not, as now, at Walton Well Road, but at Brooman's well near the line of Green ditch (Ibid.). The names 'King's swath' and 'Green ditch' both suggest a track running along a grassy baulk.

[31] So named on the early 18th-century map (Christ Church Maps Binsey 1).

[32] *Hearne's Collections*, vi (O.H.S. xliii, 1902), 264; *Guilielmi Neubrigensis Historia*, ed. T. Hearne, iii (1719), 762.

[33] Bodl. MS Ashmole 43 ff.156ᵛ-157.

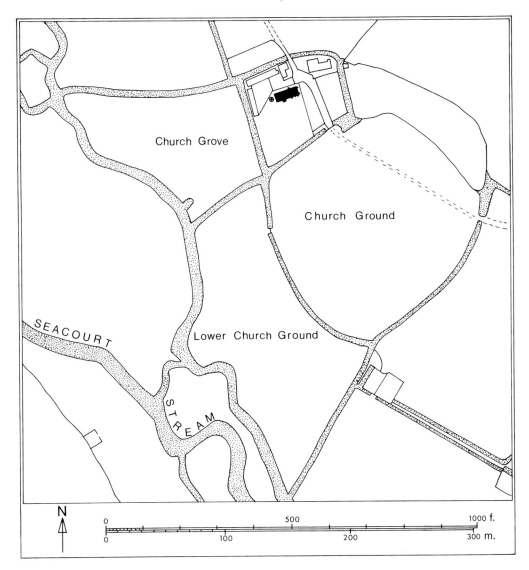

Fig. 3.   Thornbury in the late 19th century (after O.S. 25″ 1st edn.).

The chapel itself is a simple rectangular building, its earliest datable features the S. door and porch of c.1180–1200.[34] Irregularities in the external face of the N. wall suggest that the present square E. end may have replaced an apse, which implies a date rather earlier than the late 12th century for the oldest standing fabric. Fifteenth-century glass in the E. window may include fragmentary figures of St. Margaret and St. Frideswide;[35]

[34] R.C.H.M.Oxford, 148; V.C.H.Oxon. iv, 271.
[35] Cf. P.A. Newton (ed.), Corpus Vitrearum Medii Aevi: the County of Oxford (1979), 35–7.

Wood believed that the tabernacle in the S. wall of the chancel contained Frideswide's image, with the pavement before it worn hollow by 'those superstitious people that came somtimes barefoot to this place, using cringes and adorations on their knees'.[36]

Wood also notes an 'old and small building joyning to the north side of the chapple', which 'doth [not resemble] (as formerly it did) a court'; in another place he describes it as a 'house with arched windowes and arched dore, joyning to Binsey Chapel, pulled downe July 1678'.[37] In 1718 Hearne wrote: 'tho' there be no Houses now by the Chapell, yet in those Times [i.e. Frideswide's] there were several . . . . I have heard of Foundations of Buildings which confirm this Assertion';[38] Warton saw 'signatures of large buildings' in the churchyard in 1783 (above, p.10). The windowless N. wall of the chapel, with various joints and scars still visible in its outer face, suggests that buildings were indeed 'joined' to it. The traditions of the place, the residence there of regular canons, and Wood's use of the word 'court' (by which he probably meant 'courtyard' or 'cloister') all suggest the possibility of a simplified claustral layout, created perhaps in the 12th century.

The well is, as noted by Wood, 'at the west end of this chappel about three yards distant',[39] though now in a Victorian setting. According to Wood it was 'almost to the last frequented by superstitious people, and especially about 100 years before the dessolution. Soe much that they were forced to enclose it (as in old time before, they had defended it) with a little house of stone over it, with a lock and a dore to it'.[40] This building had 'on the front the picture of St. Margaret (or perhaps of St. Frideswyde)', and was pulled down in 1639; by Wood's time the well was 'overgrowne with nettles and other weeds and harbouring froggs snails and vermin'.[41] Wood probably knew the characteristics of late Perpendicular architecture, so his description suggests that the well-house was indeed of the late 15th or early 16th century.

THE OVAL EARTHWORK ENCLOSURE (Figs. 2–4)

A large, roughly oval area defined by narrow drainage ditches, with Binsey chapel and graveyard on its N.W. perimeter, appears on estate maps of 1792 and c.1850 (Christ Church Maps Binsey 2 and 5) and on late 19th-century Ordnance Survey maps.On the S.W. and S.E. sides of the enclosure the ditches were filled in during the 1960s, but the boundary remains conspicuous as a spread and eroded bank now c.15–20 metres wide, standing well above the low-lying field on the S.W., with traces of a ditch around its outer side.

There are no clear remains of the bank on the N. and E. sides of the enclosure, and its position must be inferred from field-boundaries. Skirting the area around the N.E. are two curving ditch-lines, either of which may reflect the original perimeter. The outer ditch is rather more substantial, and connects the two straight field-ditches which drain into the Shire Lake ditch on the N.W. and the S.W. The 1792 map creates an unfortunate ambiguity (Fig. 2): the outer ditch is omitted from the scale drawing in ink,

[36] Wood, *City*, ii, 43; cf. Ibid. i, 578.
[37] Ibid. i, 329, 324n; cf. ibid. i, 577, 578 and ii, 42.
[38] *Guil.Neub.* op.cit. note 32, iii, 757–8.
[39] Wood, *City*, i, 323.
[40] Ibid. 328–9. Cf. ibid. 577: 'The inhabitants here will tell you that there have bin many miracles wrought at this well and people hung up their crutches.'
[41] Ibid. 324n, 329.

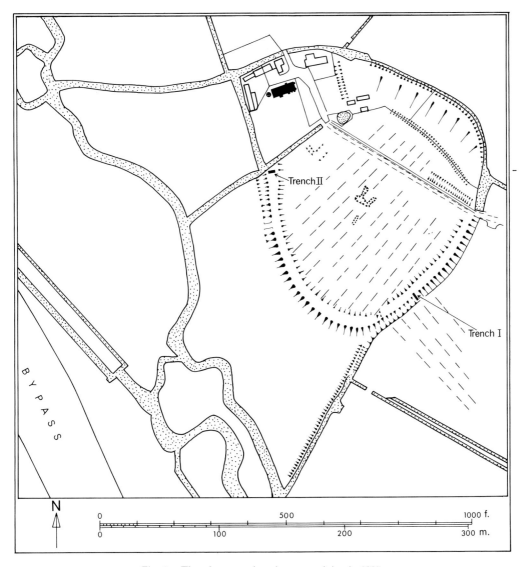

Fig. 4.  Thornbury: earthworks as remaining in 1987.

but is indicated by a very sketchy pencil line. An early 19th-century copy of this map (Christ Church Map Binsey 3) also shows the ditch in pencil, but much more clearly and accurately, the area enclosed by it being labelled 'garden'. The only other boundary which the 1792 map treats in this way is the wall dividing the graveyard from the farm to its N.E. The ditch looks most unlike a 19th-century boundary, and if the pencil lines are intended to record changes after 1792 it is odd that none of the other new inclosures are shown in this way. It is therefore a reasonable hypothesis, though no more, that the ditch was omitted accidentally by the original surveyor and added as a correction.

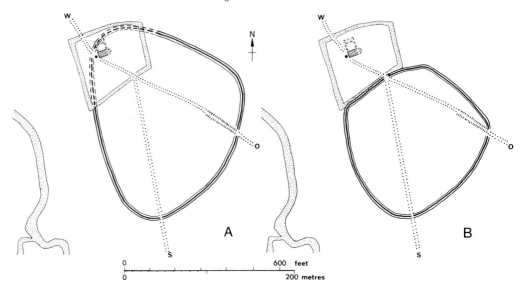

Fig. 5. Thornbury: alternative reconstructions of the early enclosure and routes leading into it. (**W** = Wytham, **S** = Seacourt, **O** = Oxford.)

This interpretation of the map evidence suggests the reconstruction shown in Fig. 5A: a large oval enclosure with the rectilinear moated area containing the chapel and farm superimposed on its N.W. sector, the original perimeter ditch having presumably been straightened out to form the N. and W. sides of the moat. Fig. 5B shows the alternative reconstruction, required if the 1792 map is accepted as reliable: a smaller oval excluding the chapel enclosure, which appears as a later addition to its N. side. Further excavation is needed to decide between these alternatives.

Ridge-and-furrow, crossed by the 1821 path to the chapel, occupies much of the interior. The hollow-way of the old road to Binsey Green only survives to the S.E., beyond the limits of the ridge-and-furrow (Fig. 4); the obliteration of the rest by ploughing had probably occurred by 1792, when the route was a mere footpath across the field (Fig. 2).

THE EXCAVATION

*Trench I* (Fig. 6)

A trench 7.5 by 1.5 m. was excavated at on the S.E. perimeter of the enclosure (see Fig. 4), bisecting the course of the field-ditch shown on the first edition of the 25″ O.S. map. The outer edge of the present low bank proved to overlie a sequence of shallow, gravel-cut ditches, evidently moving progressively outwards from the interior of the enclosure, and a phase possibly involving a stone wall. Successive layers sloping down from the inner (N.W.) end of the trench are interpreted as bank material, and the existence of substantial, continuously eroding banks seems the most likely explanation for the outwards advance of the ditch line.

The first ditch contained fill layers of grey clayey gravel (L11c) and dark-grey silt (L11b). A grass-tempered sherd lay on the clean ditch floor under L11c, securely sealed by the clayey gravel; L11b contained a sandy sherd. A wedge of dark-grey silt (L9c), left isolated by the cutting of the second and third ditches, is likely to have been part of the fill of the first ditch and identical with L11b, though it could also be interpreted as the fill of an independent re-cut. Layers of brown sandy gravel (L11a) and sticky brown clay (L5f) overlay L11b. A deposit of brown silty clay loam with manganese flecking (L5d) formed an ambiguous interface with L5f, but certainly overlay LL11a–c. L16 was identical with L5d and may have been part of the same layer, though it could also be interpreted as old ground-surface (L5d being the same material redeposited). Bedded in L5d were two rows of small blocks of corallian ragstone rubble (F8, F12), running on the alignment of the ditch, which might have been the remains of a footing. A grass-tempered sherd was found among the stones of F8. Under L5d, a small patch of orange-brown subsoil (L13) survived on the inner (N.W.) lip of the ditch, showing that the natural surface of the gravel was intact at this end of the section. LL5d/16 and F8 were cut by a pit (F14), perhaps created by robbing of the footing, containing brown silty clay loam (L7) and several stone lumps, and were overlain by a layer of brown silt loam with *c.*40% gravel (L5c); one sandy sherd was found in F14, and bones (7 cattle, 1 sheep or goat) in L7.

## TABLE 1: RADIOCARBON DETERMINATIONS

| *Site*<br>*Reference* | *Harwell*<br>*Reference* | *Years b.p.* | *Calibrated ranges*<br>*(data of Stuiver & Reimer 1986)* | |
|---|---|---|---|---|
| | | | *68% confidence* | *95% confidence* |
| L32 | Har-8921 | 1740±90 | AD 190–390 | AD 80–530 |
| L10c | Har-8922 | 220±60 | – | – |
| L5a | Har-8923 | 960±70 | AD 1000–1140 | AD 900–1220 |
| L3 | Har-8935 | 590±90 | AD 1290–1430 | AD 1260–1470 |

The surviving stratigraphy left the order of the second and third ditches uncertain, but the outermost, which was evidently open into modern times, must be the later of the two. What is therefore interpreted as the second ditch cut L11b, L9c and L5f. It had fill layers (involving at least one re-cut) of grey silty gravel (L17), grey silt with preserved organic material (LL9a–b), and brown silty clay loam (L5e); there were bones in L9b (2 cattle, 1 pig) and 5e (1 horse, 3 probably cattle).

The third ditch, which cut L9c, contained fill layers of very dark-grey silt with preserved organic material (LL10c–b), and grey silt with *c.*3% gravel (L10a). L10c contained bones (2 of cattle and 5 of cattle or horse, mostly butchered or dog-gnawed), some lying on the bottom of the ditch; this material produced a radiocarbon date of AD 1670–1790 (Table 1), indicating that the third ditch remained open until the 18th century.

Over L5c, L9a, L5e and L10a were layers of brown clay with yellowish-brown mottling (L5b) and light-grey silty clay with *c.*3% gravel (L5a), possibly derived from the slighting and spreading-out of the bank in the 18th or 19th century. A bank of brown silt loam with *c.*50% gravel (L3), containing limestone rubble and large pebbles, overlay L5b, L5a and L7; it produced 3 sheep or goat and 2 dog bones. Calibrated radiocarbon dates were obtained from bone material in L5a (AD 900–1220) and L3 (AD 1260–1470) (Table 1). It is possible

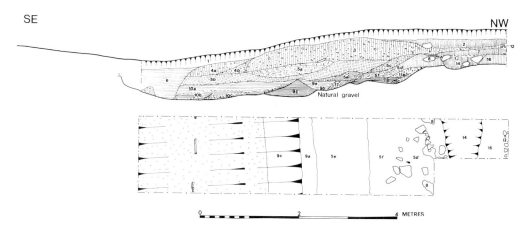

Fig. 6.   Thornbury, Trench I, plan and S.W. section.

that the high proportion of rubble in this deposit represents the robbing of a substantial footing (i.e. F8) incorporated in the pre-existing bank.

Later layers (L2, L4a–b) contained modern pottery, as did a final re-digging of the boundary as a narrow field-ditch (F6). The topsoil (L1) post-dated the filling-in of this ditch during the 20th century.

## Trench II (Fig. 7)

A trench 5.0 by 1.5 m. was excavated on the W. perimeter of the enclosure (see Fig. 4), bisecting the bank just inside the line of the late field-ditch. This revealed a sequence of boundary features comparable to those in Tr. I, except that the outermost and latest major ditch lay outside the trench area.

The earliest ditch was shallow, flat-bottomed, and cut the natural gravel. A straight baulk of gravel c.0.8 m.wide (F37), running transverse to the axis of the ditch, had been left standing proud from the ditch bottom; this is interpreted as a boundary between two work-gangs. On the E. side of the ditch, a layer of buff clay loam of ashy appearance with many flecks of charcoal and burnt daub (L42) may represent an old ground-surface. The ditch contained three successive fill-layers: redeposited gravel (L40) against the inner slope, perhaps the product of rapid erosion; dark blue-grey silt with c.6% gravel, flecks of burnt daub and organic material (L36); and sticky yellow-brown clay interspersed with small lenses of gravel and loam (L32), containing flecks of burnt daub and a group of bones (1 human humerus fragment; 11 bones and 3 teeth of horses, from at least two individuals aged 4+ years, all dog-gnawed; 1 cattle bone). The horse bones, which were a homogeneous group, produced a calibrated radiocarbon date of AD 80–530 (Table 1).

A deposit of grey-brown clay with flecks of burnt daub (L41), overlying L42, formed an interface with L32. Bedded in L41 was a footing of corallian ragstone rubble (F38), surviving to a height of between one and three courses (Fig. 8). It was built mainly of small stones bonded with clean blue clay, but included two large blocks. At the core of the footing was a sub-rectangular void, the fill of which (L39) was identical with the underlying L42.

Unfortunately the relationship between the first ditch and the footing could not be established, since the interface between L32 and L41 left the sequence of these layers ambiguous. One possible interpretation is that L41 cut L32 – in other words, that the wall was built after the first ditch had silted up. But the reverse sequence is also possible: the first ditch could have been dug up against the face of an already-existing wall, removing all trace of older ditches associated with it. This is a major difficulty which can only be resolved by further excavation.

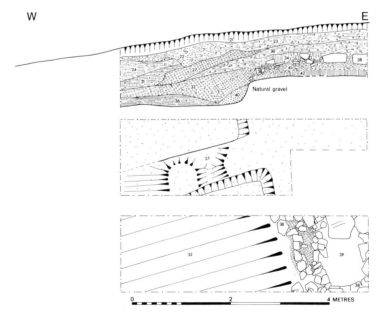

Fig. 7.   Thornbury, Trench II, plans and N. section.

Over the footing F38 were a patch of ashy grey loam with burnt daub flecks (L34), a dump of rubble (F35), and then a slump-layer of red-brown silt loam containing gravelly patches and numerous lumps of burnt daub (L30), which also overlay L32. Two layers overlying the downwards slope of L30 are best ascribed to successive ditch phases: blue-grey clay with numerous red daub flecks (L27), and gravelly buff-grey clay silt (L31). A layer of red-brown silt loam containing many large lumps of burnt daub (L23), virtually identical with L30, overlay L30 and L27; cutting its surface was a post-hole (F26) of *c*.30 cm. diameter and *c*.20 cm. deep, with three packing-stones and a light-brown clay fill. L23 was truncated at its lower end by another probable ditch cut, with fills of brown clay silt (L24) and gravelly buff-yellow clay silt (L22); L24 produced a whetstone fragment. The topsoil (L21) contained modern pottery.

*Interpretation of the excavated evidence*

The potsherd sealed by the fill of the primary ditch in Tr. I (L11c) is probably 5th- or 6th-century (below, p.18); it is thus not wholly incompatible with the radiocarbon date-range from bones in the fill of the primary ditch in Tr. II (L32): AD 190–390 at 68 per cent confidence, or AD 80–530 at 95 per cent confidence. It is therefore a reasonable hypothesis that the ditch was dug, or was still being kept clean, in the sub-Roman or early Anglo-Saxon period, though the material in L11c provides little more than a *terminus post quem* for the silting-up of the ditch. But whereas the possible footing in Tr. I (F8) definitely post-dated the primary ditch, the relationship between the footing in Tr. II (F38) and the primary ditch there was ambiguous. It remains perfectly possible (assuming no connection between F8 and F38) that the rampart and ditch were both in origin Iron Age, the latter being scoured out in the early Anglo-Saxon period, or that an

Fig. 8.   Thornbury, Trench II: stone footing (F38), looking N.

early Anglo-Saxon ditch was dug against the face of an Iron Age rampart. Alternatively, F8 and F38 could both belong to a rampart post-dating the filling of the primary ditch. The likelihood of an Anglo-Saxon presence on the site is in all cases strong, and is strengthened by the fact that all four potsherds recovered are of that date.

The construction of the footing or revetment has some distinctive features. The portion of F38 within the area of Tr. II comprised a much-damaged outer face towards the ditch, and the four inner faces of the box-like cavity at the core of the wall. The outer face included five small stones in line, which were in-set in relation to the larger blocks surviving at the two sections and should probably therefore be interpreted as a second row from which larger facing-stones had been robbed away. Assuming that the inwards-facing skin of walling (mainly outside the trench area) was of similar width to that on the ditch side, the total thickness of the wall at its base would have been some 2.2m. The filling of the cavity (L39) was identical to the underlying layer (L42), and may have originated as turves cut from the ground-surface. Unless the cavity is an abnormality it must be concluded that this massive footing consisted of two parallel faces, linked by transverse walls set at *c*.1.5m. centres, with the voids filled with earth or turves. There is no evidence that the stone facing continued to a significant height above ground-level (indeed, the general lack of rubble in later ditch-fills suggests that it did not); a timber-revetted bank on a stone footing is perhaps more likely.

Finally, the burnt daub spread through nearly all layers and features in Tr. II deserves comment. The material might derive from the firing of a timber-laced rampart, though the burning of scrub on an old ground-surface would have similar results.

THE POTTERY by MAUREEN MELLOR

Four early Saxon sherds were excavated. Two, from L11b and F14, were in predominantly sandy fabrics (fabric III); the other two, from L11c and F8, were grass-tempered (fabric IV) and possibly from one pot, with the same admixture of other detritus and laminated in the same way. The grass-tempered sherd in F8, from the shoulder of a large burnished storage-jar, was decorated with a raised band between two rows of small dots. A similar vessel with the same style of decoration was found in a sunken-feature building at Barrow Hills near Abingdon,[42] though its fabric was predominantly sandy and it was exceptionally well-made, possibly being finished on a slow wheel. The Barrow Hills example came from what is believed to be the early focus of the site, possibly 5th-century; this context produced little or no organic-tempered material, however, and the Binsey sherd may be rather later, perhaps 6th century. Grass-tempered pottery is also reported from the nearby deserted village site of Seacourt.[43]

CONCLUSIONS

The name recorded as *Thornbiri* comprises the elements *þorn* and *burh*, 'thorn' and 'fortified place';[44] it would be perverse to suggest that the 'thorn-grown fortress' was anything

---

[42] No. 185, Fig. 16 from SFB F3307, Fabric 24; typescript at Oxford Archaeological Unit.

[43] Not published; pers. comm. M. Biddle. (These sherds have not been located among the Seacourt material in the Ashmolean. I am grateful to Arthur MacGregor for his help with this.)

[44] The final element is undoubtedly *burh* (Margaret Gelling, pers. comm. 1987); the etymology 'thorn-tree hill' proposed in *Place-Names Oxon.* i, 26 was based on the 1293 spelling *Thorneberg*, the earliest form then available.

other than the oval defensive enclosure identified in 1987–8. It remains to consider what the *burh* actually was, and what its discovery contributes to our understanding of St. Frideswide's legend.

The best local parallels for the shape and location of the enclosure are Iron Age, and while the stratigraphical and radiocarbon evidence does not especially support such a date, it certainly does not exclude it.[45] The long island of gravel within the floodplain immediately E. of Binsey church and adjacent to the present main stream of the river has revealed cropmarks of ring ditches, pit alignments and enclosures of Bronze Age, Iron Age and probably Roman date,[46] and fieldwalking by David Wilson has produced Iron Age and Roman pottery.[47] Small late Bronze Age to Iron Age valley forts, on both the floodplain and the terrace-edge, can almost be described as a feature of the Upper Thames basin, Thornbury being potentially the seventh such site to be identified.[48] The footing of 'box' construction would be appropriate in an Iron Age context: the forts at Cherbury and Bladon had stone revetments, in the case of Bladon with a soil infill.[49] The burnt material found distributed through all layers in Tr. II may be significant in this context: evidence of extensive burning on Iron Age defensive enclosures is common in southern England,[50] and has been identified locally at Bladon, Cherbury and Burroway.[51] Burroway had a timber 'box' rampart with soil infill, fired during the burning episode, and a similar source is possible for the burnt clay at Binsey, where the absence of rubble in the ditch fills suggests that the rampart above foundation level was of timber rather than stone.

Alternatively, the fort could be sub-Roman or early Anglo-Saxon, and so far as it goes the very limited dating evidence supports this conclusion. The 5th- and early 6th-century colonisation of the Upper Thames must have involved the use of fortified places, and there seems a serious possibility that Thornbury was one of them.

Thus any religious occupation of the site may have involved re-using an already ancient fortress. It is worth notice in this context that *burh* has a well-attested secondary meaning of 'monastic enclosure'. Tetbury (*Tettan byrig*) occurs as *Tettan monasterium* in the late 7th century, and Westbury-on-Trym (*Uuestburg*) as *Westmynster* in 804.[52] It seems likely that many -*burh* placenames denote monastic sites, especially those compounded with female names; an example not far afield is Bibury ('Beage's monastery'?), where five hides were leased to the thegn Leppa and his daughter Beage in 718×45.[53] The first element *þorn* would be apposite to this meaning if it denoted not a cover of undergrowth but an enclosing hedge, such as the 'great thorn hedge' which surrounded St. Wilfred's monastery at Oundle.[54]

It could be argued that such parallels are made superfluous by the archaeological evidence, which suggests that the earthwork, whether Iron Age, sub-Roman or early

[45] This paragraph is based entirely on material supplied by George Lambrick, who has in preparation a more detailed discussion of valley-forts in the Upper Thames.

[46] P.P. Rhodes, 'New Archaeological Sites at Binsey and Port Meadow, Oxford', *Oxoniensia*, xiv (1949), 81–4.

[47] Pers.comm. D. Wilson esq.

[48] The others are Salmondsbury, Burroway, Cherbury, Cassington, Dyke Hills and ?Goring.

[49] R. Ainslie, 'Bladon Round Castle, 1987', *South Midlands Archaeology (CBA Group 9 Newsletter)*, xviii (1988), 94.

[50] R.J. Bradley, *The Social Foundations of Prehistoric Britain* (1984), 134–6.

[51] G.H. Lambrick, 'Clanfield, Burroway', *South Midlands Archaeology (CBA Group 9 Newsletter)*, xiv (1984), 104–5; Ainslie op. cit. note 49.

[52] For the examples in this sentence and the next, with others, see F.M. Stenton, 'The Place of Women in Anglo-Saxon Society', in *Preparatory to Anglo-Saxon England* (1970), 320–1.

[53] W. de G. Birch, *Cartularium Saxonicum*, i (1885), No. 166.

[54] Eddius Stephanus, *Vita Wilfridi*, ch. 67.

Anglo-Saxon, was at all events in existence before St. Frideswide's time. But the 'monastic' usage of the term is important as a reflection of the fact that Iron-Age and Dark-Age forts, like Roman walled enclosures, were places normally and naturally selected for the new monasteries of the 7th and 8th centuries. Many early English minsters were *burga* in the sense of being pre-Anglo-Saxon fortified places, such as the Iron Age hillforts enclosing minster churches at Aylesbury and Hanbury.[55] If Thornbury was still a conspicuous earthwork it would have been a prime candidate for monastic re-use, especially perhaps as a cell or retreat-house dependent on the main monastery at Oxford.[56]

Finally, the possibility remains that the stratified material is residual, and that Thornbury was constructed at the outset as an Anglo-Saxon monastic enclosure. Since this category of site has received little archaeological notice it is hard to find close parallels, but enclosures of a similar general shape and size can be identified surrounding known minster churches.[57]

From the written legends and traditions, centuries later than Frideswide's time, the existence of an early monastic settlement at Binsey can only be inferred as a tenuous possibility. The importance of the newly-discovered earthwork is that its evidence, so independent and so different, points in the same direction: Binsey chapel stands in just the kind of place that mid-Saxon monastic founders did in fact favour. Any further advances must be through archaeology, following the leads suggested by the scraps of pottery in the ditches and the 8th-century *sceat* found somewhere nearby.[58] An extensive excavation within the earthwork might add significantly to our knowledge of the Oxford region in both the Iron Age and the Anglo-Saxon period.

---

[55] For these and other examples see J. Blair, 'Minster Churches in the Landscape' in D. Hooke (ed.), *Anglo-Saxon Settlements* (1988), 41–7; D. Hooke, *The Anglo-Saxon Landscape: the Kingdom of the Hwicce* (1985), 219, 91.

[56] As argued by Blair, 'St. F.', 92.

[57] Cf. the examples illustrated in Blair, op. cit. note 55, Fig. 2.3. Other cases are Bampton, Oxon. (J. Blair in *South Midlands Archaeology*, xviii (1988), 90, Fig. 1) and Tetbury, Glos. (*V.C.H. Glos.* xi, 260).

[58] Blair, 'St. F.', 92.

# Excavations in the Cloister of St. Frideswide's Priory, 1985

By CHRISTOPHER SCULL

With contributions by JOHN BLAIR, NIALL DONALD, DEBORAH DUNCAN, ALISON R. GOODALL, IAN H. GOODALL, MARY HARMAN, ARTHUR MACGREGOR, N.J. MAYHEW, MAUREEN MELLOR and SUE STALLIBRASS

SUMMARY

*Excavation in the cloister garth revealed burials, almost certainly belonging to the cemetery of the Anglo-Saxon minster church. Many graves had been destroyed or damaged by medieval pits, probably associated with construction of the Augustinian priory buildings after A.D. 1122 and subsequent episodes of building. Exposed masonry in the garth was shown to be part of a rectangular, corner-buttressed foundation, dated to the second quarter of the 16th century and interpreted as the footing of a timber belfry.*

INTRODUCTION

Upon completion of renovation work in the cathedral cloister, Christ Church, in 1985, the College proposed to improve the appearance of the garth by replacing the grassed area with a formal garden. This involved reducing and burying the stone foundation which had been exposed in a cross-of-Lorraine shape on the cloister lawn since the 19th century.

The foundation was uncovered in 1871, when the level of the garth was lowered during George Gilbert Scott's restoration work.[1] It had apparently been buried since the 17th century, when alterations were made to the cloister which included raising the level of the garth (below, p. 73). A small trench dug against the northern end of the foundation by David Sturdy in 1958 revealed that its rubble fabric incorporates fragments of late 15th- or early 16th-century window cusping,[2] demonstrating that it is not part of a medieval monastic building, as had been suggested previously,[3] but that in all probability it post-dates Cardinal Wolsey's suppression of the Augustinian priory in 1524.[4] It has most often been assigned to the period 1524–9, when the buildings of

---

[1] H.L. Thompson, *College Histories: Christ Church* (1900), 240; S.A. Warner, *Oxford Cathedral* (1924), 38.

[2] D. Sturdy, 'Recent Excavations in Christ Church and Nearby', *Oxoniensia*, xxvi–vii (1961–2), 29.

[3] E. Venables (ed.), *Handbook to the Cathedrals of England: Eastern Division* (1881), 40–1; E.W. Watson, *The Cathedral Church of Christ in Oxford* (1935), 44.

[4] H.E. Salter, 'Priory of St. Frideswide, Oxford', *V.C.H. Oxon.* ii (1907), 100–1; *R.C.H.M. Oxford* (1939), 29; M. Maclagan, 'Christ Church', *V.C.H. Oxon.* iii (1954), 228–9; J. Cooper, 'St. Frideswide's Priory', *V.C.H. Oxon.* iv (1979), 364–5.

Fig. 9.    Renovation and excavation in St. Frideswide's cloister, 1985.

Wolsey's secular college were being erected on the site of the suppressed priory, and has been interpreted as the western foundation of an unfinished free-standing stone bell-tower, whose completion would have entailed demolishing the eastern cloister range.[5] However, neither the exact date of the foundation nor its full plan were known, nor its purpose properly understood; so the College invited the Oxford Archaeological Unit to examine and record the foundation before its partial demolition and burial with a view to elucidating these problems. This also afforded an opportunity to investigate earlier pits and burials in the cloister garth, first revealed by Sturdy's 1958 excavation,[6] which it was hoped might reflect the development of adjacent priory buildings and the history of the site before conversion of the Anglo-Saxon minster to an Augustinian priory in the first half of the 12th century.[7]

EXCAVATION AND STRATIGRAPHY

Two weeks' preliminary trenching under the supervision of Peter McKeague in April and May was followed in July and August by five weeks of more extensive excavation

    [5] *R.C.H.M. Oxford*, 29; J.G. Milne and J.H. Harvey, 'The Building of Cardinal College, Oxford, *Oxoniensia*, viii–ix (1943–4), 152; N. Doggett, 'Footings in the Cathedral Cloisters, Christ Church College' (1982), unpublished MS at Oxford Archaeological Unit.
    [6] Sturdy, op. cit. note 2.
    [7] See below, pp. 90–2, 227–8, 236–40.

(Fig. 9) supervised by Christopher Scull. Brian Durham, who was responsible for overall direction of the project, observed builders' work when the paving of the garth was renewed in September.

The preliminary excavation revealed two burials to the E. of the exposed N.–S. foundation wall and a sunken internal floor to its W., demonstrating that the visible masonry was not complete in itself, nor the western part of an unfinished project, but the eastern half of a building foundation situated in the centre of the cloister garth and partially concealed beneath the paving. For the main excavation the trench was extended to allow complete excavation of the accessible interior of the building and examination of burials and deeper stratigraphy down the E. side of the cloister garth (Trench One). Flagstones were also lifted in two places to confirm the presence of foundations beneath the paving (Trenches Two and Three). All the work between April and August was recorded as a single excavation. The results are described as a series of excavation stages which correspond inversely to the phases in which the site is interpreted. These are integrated in Fig. 10.

The excavated material is housed at the Ashmolean Museum. The original site records are at the Oxford Archaeological Unit, site code OX:CCL 1985.

### STAGE A (PHASE 6: 19TH & 20TH CENTURIES)

The modern cement capping of the foundation (F6/1) was removed to expose the original masonry (F6/2). Beneath the turf, set into the topsoil (L1) around the foundation and along the W. edges of the lawn, was a border of orange-brown sandy clay (L2), presumably originally intended to offset the foundation as a garden feature. Below the topsoil were modern disturbances, land drains and service features F4–5, F11/12, F42, F44–6, F76–7. Baulks were left to support the functioning water pipe in F11/12 and the ground-water drain in F77. The most recent feature uncovered was Sturdy's 1958 trench (F152).

### STAGE B (PHASE 5: 17TH CENTURY) FIG. 12

To the E. and S.E. of the foundation the modern features overlay or cut a layer of disturbed brown gravelly loam (L3, L41) which, to judge by the thin and discontinuous traces overlying the fill of F78 and the dump layers within the foundation, had been truncated during lowering of the garth in 1871 (below, p. 242 n.95). This contained pottery of the late 17th century and earlier, a single mid 18th-century sherd, and a few intrusive fragments of 19th- and 20th-century ceramics. Below L41 in the angle between the S.E. buttress foundations was a thin spread of hard white mortar (L43) which petered out to the S. and S.E. into a compacted earth surface with inclusions of mortar, sand and clay (L47), which also extended S. of the foundation. Both these surfaces lipped-up against the foundation. Traces of a similar earth surface (L51), presumably the same as L47, survived below L3 to the E. of the foundation: although encountered at this stage, both L51 and L47 appear to have been formed by compaction of, and accumulation on, a surface exposed for a considerable time (see below, Stage D). L43 did not appear to be an intentional surface, and most probably resulted from mortar-mixing against the angle of the buttresses. L47 was cut by a small pit filled with powdered mortar and fragments of masonry rubble (F57).

Beneath a very thin and discontinuous layer corresponding to L3 between the N.E. buttress foundations was a shallow rectangular pit filled with a silty loam containing inclusions of powdered mortar and masonry rubble (F78), overlain by a localised layer of ash (L80). It had cut earlier burials, and charnel from these (L103) had been redeposited neatly against the S. side of the pit before it was backfilled.

### STAGE C (PHASE 4: 16TH CENTURY) FIG. 12

Beneath the modern levels and a very thin and discontinuous layer corresponding to L3, the interior of the foundation was filled with a dump-layer of sandy silt and powdered mortar (L8/9) containing much decorated floor tile and freshly-broken fragments of ornamental masonry, some painted and gilded. Sealed by this, and lipping-up against the masonry, was a surface of compacted silty material incorporating lenses of charcoal and mortar (L15, L18, L20, L27), interpreted as the floor of the building. Post-hole F14 cut L15, and so must either

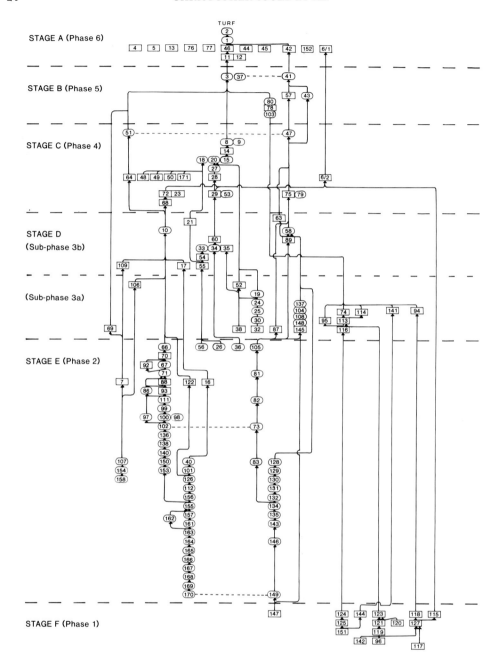

Fig. 10.   Excavated stratigraphy (Trench One).

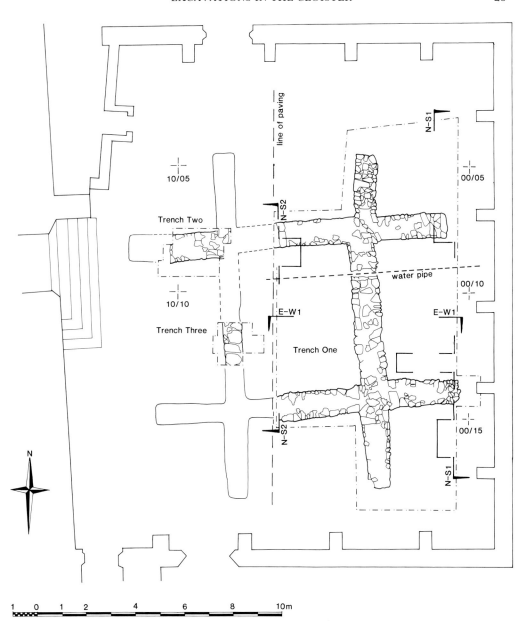

Fig. 11.   Location of trenches and sections.

post-date accumulation of part, if not all of the floor, or else have held a post around which the floor levels accumulated.

Sealed by the floor levels were post-holes F48–50, shallow trenches F28 and F171, and the foundation construction trench (F29, L53), which was also detected externally along the E. wall (F23) and around the S.E. buttresses (F72, F75, L79). Post-hole F38 cut the fill of construction trench F29 and was only partially sealed by L20 in a manner suggesting that the floor levels had accumulated around a standing post. F28 also cut F29. F72 cut F68, a feature only detected in the section. The shallow pit F64 contained human bone, presumably re-buried after being disturbed during construction of the foundation.

## STAGE D (PHASE 3: SECOND HALF OF THE 12TH CENTURY – EARLY 16TH CENTURY) FIG. 13

Externally, the foundation was cut into a layer of gravelly loam containing no pottery later than the late 15th or early 16th century (L10, L58), the surface of which, compacted over a considerable time, formed L47 and L51. Internally, this layer had been dug away to form the sunken floor, but the bottom of a shallow pit (F21) containing pottery contemporary with this horizon survived. In the area between the S.E. buttress foundations a shallow pit (F63) containing worked masonry was defined below L58, but may have been cut through it, or from a level within it, as some of the masonry protruded through L58. It cut the fill of a grave containing an unaccompanied supine inhumation, orientated W.–E. (F89), which was sealed beneath L58 and had been cut by construction trench F75.

The fills of intercutting medieval pits were exposed below the late 15th- and 16th-century levels. The density of pits was greatest towards the centre of the garth. Part of pit F35, and of pit F38, and a sequence of pit fills and other contexts in the N.W. corner of the trench, were excavated within the foundation during trial-trenching. It was often difficult to distinguish between the fills of different features, and this exacerbated the problem of relating newly-exposed stratigraphy to excavated contexts when the trench was extended. In addition, some relationships were obscured by the water-pipe baulk. It was never intended to investigate the medieval layers within the foundation during the main excavation, and from this stage work concentrated on the east side of the garth, the interior of the building being backfilled and used for dumping soil. However, sufficient artefactual and stratigraphic evidence was recovered to date and phase the medieval features sealed by L20 and associated contexts. Where they survived, L10 and L58 sealed all contexts of Stage D which had been cut into the backfill of earlier extraction features.

The later medieval pits, F35, F54–5 and F60, clustered towards the centre of the garth. Only F35 was excavated: the others were defined by trowelling over, and dating material was obtained from this cleaned surface. F35 was cut by F60 and cut F54, which appeared to cut F55.

Pits of the later 12th and 13th centuries were more dispersed. Within the foundation, contexts L19, L24–5, and L30 overlay pits F32 and F38. The relationship between F52, F74 and F106 had been destroyed by the foundation, but they may all have been part of the same large pit. In the area between the N.E. buttress foundations a series of shallow features containing charnel (F113–4, F116, F141), and a possible infant burial (F95), were cut into the upper fills of earlier burials, and were themselves cut by pit F74. The upper fills of pit F145, at the S.E. of the site, were cut by construction trench F75.

Pits F69 and F87, post-holes F109 and F17, and shallow trench F94 were also excavated at this stage but contained no datable artefacts and cannot be closely dated stratigraphically.

## STAGE E (PHASE 2: FIRST HALF OF THE 12TH CENTURY) FIGS. 14–15

Construction trench F72 cut into the fill of a broad **V**-sectioned gully (F140) sloping away under the E. cloister range. The lowest levels within this were dark sticky fills L140, L138, L136 and L102. These were overlain around the E. margins by a thin intermittent layer of gravel and clay (L98/100), and towards the E. by a dark sticky fill apparently contemporary with L98/100 (L97). A probable turf line (L99) overlay L98/100. The horizon L97–100 appears to represent an attempt to consolidate the partially infilled gully. L99 was overlain around the N. and E. sides of the gully by a dump-layer of sandy loam (L111). This was cut by a small pit (F93) and overlain by three distinct layers of gravelly loam (L86, L71, L67). Cut into L86 and F93, but sealed by L71, was an unaccompanied supine inhumation, orientated W.–E., with a stone at either side of the skull (F88). Only four gully fills, L73, L81–2 and L105, were discerned S. of the construction trench. L73 appeared to correspond to L102. L105, which directly underlay L58, appeared to be a turf line.

L86 and L71 were cut by a shallow pit, F92. This also cut L67, but the relationship between them had been destroyed by another shallow pit, F70, which cut both. L67 and F70 were overlain by a thin localised spread of clean yellow sand (L66), which formed the interface between this horizon and the overlying L10.

North of the gully, sealed by later medieval and post-medieval levels, were two supine inhumations, oriented W.–E., in mortared stone cists (F7, F16). The right leg and lower left leg of inhumation F7 had been

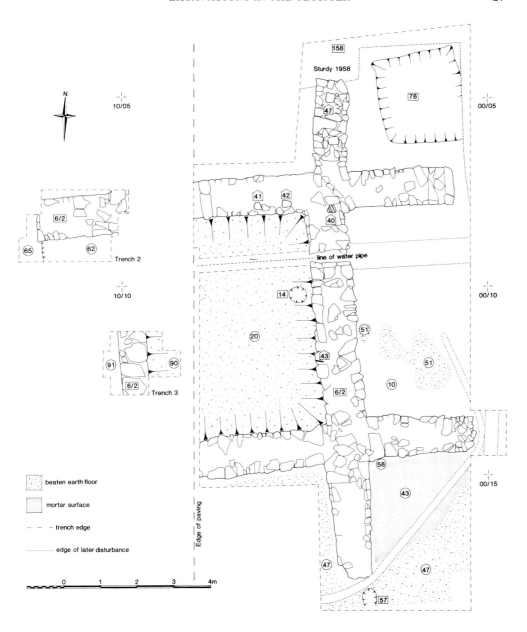

Fig. 12.   Excavation Stages B and C.

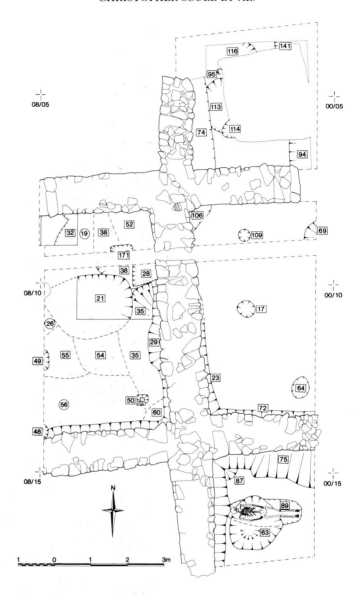

Fig. 13.   Excavation Stage D.

Fig. 14.   Excavation Stages E and F (upper stratigraphy).

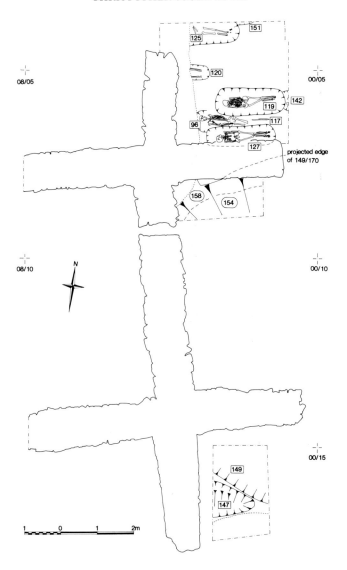

Fig. 15.   Excavation Stages E and F (lower stratigraphy).

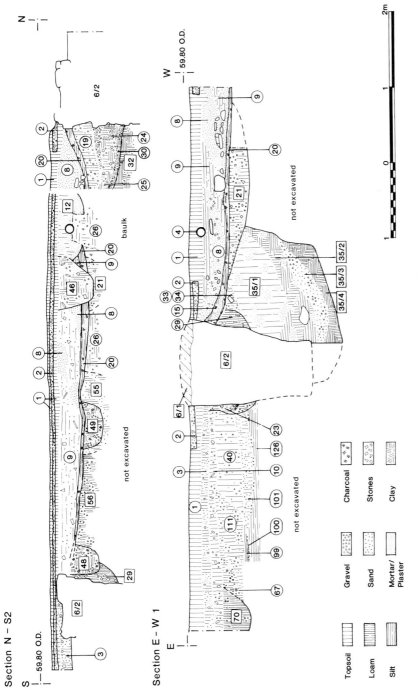

Fig. 16. Sections N.–S. 2 and E.–W. 1.

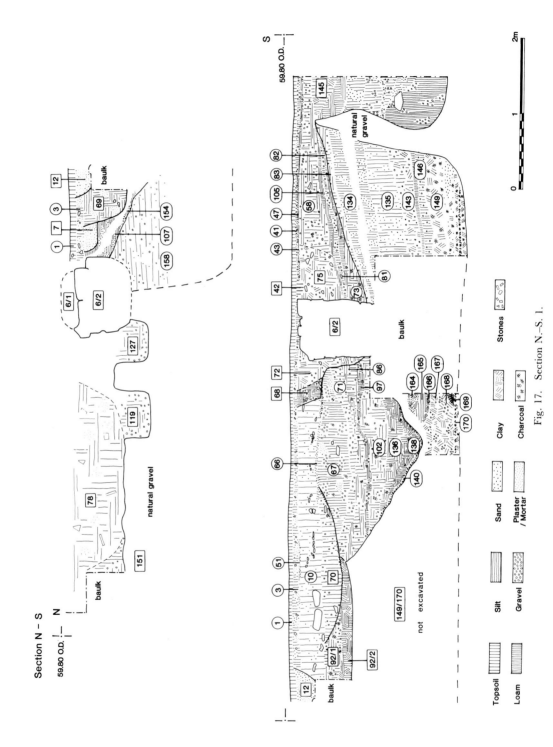

Fig. 17.  Section N.–S. 1.

cut away by pit F69; redeposited human skeletal material was recovered from the fill of F7. A third cist (F122), also orientated W.–E., lay beneath the water-pipe baulk and so was not excavated.

The gully F140 was formed by a depression in the backfill of a large pit (F149/170), into which most of the medieval features within the foundation, as well as burials F7, F16 and F122, had been cut. This feature was c. 10m. from N. to S. and over 2m. deep where excavated, and extended beneath the E. cloister range. Like pit F145, it appears to have been backfilled shortly after excavation, before any erosion or collapse of the sides could occur. Covering the bottom was a thin layer of burnt clay covered with charcoal and compacted ash (L170, L149/2–3), which was overlain by a localised layer of burned pebbles (L169), and by layers of silt and burned clay with lenses of charcoal, ash, sand and unburned clay (L162–8, L149/1). Above this, the pit was filled with a series of interleaved dump layers of sandy silt, loam, gravel and rubble (L40, L83, L101, L107, L112, L126, L128–36, L143–6, L154–8, L161–2). L26, L36 and L56, exposed within the foundation, may also be part of the backfill of this feature.

## STAGE F (PHASE 1: PRE-CONQUEST) FIGS. 14–15

Between the N.E. buttress foundations the surface of the natural gravel survived at a depth of c. 0.6m. below the modern level of the garth. It was capped by a disturbed layer of red-brown gravelly loam (L139). Cut into this horizon were fourteen inhumations (F96, F115, F117–21, F123–5, F127, F142, F144 and F151). These cut each other to a considerable extent (see site matrix, Fig. 10), and some had been partially destroyed by later features; their condition consequently varied greatly, from the in situ bones of a single limb (F115, F117) to complete skeletons in intact grave pits. Charnel from earlier burials was recovered from the fills of F96, F118, F119, F124 and F127. So far as could be ascertained, all burials were unaccompanied, supine and orientated W.–E. Two were in grave pits lined with charcoal, with a layer of charcoal over the body also (F121, F123). Another appeared to be within the remains of a stone cist (F144). Nails from the fills of F96 (SF116, 123) and F144 (SF131) suggest that they may have been coffined; however, the possible nail-shank from F124 seems too large to come from a coffin. No other coffin traces were detected.

Features cut into the capping loam or the surface of the natural gravel survived only in this area of the site. Elsewhere, they had been destroyed by features of the 12th century or later. The density of burials here, where the gravel had not been quarried, suggests that most of them antedate pit F149/170.

At the S. end of the site, the upper fill of F147, a pit, or possibly a ditch terminal, was cut by F149/170.

## TRENCHES TWO AND THREE

Beneath the bedding of the flagstones (L59, L84), Trenches Two and Three revealed a W. buttress at the projected N.W. corner of the foundation and a N.–S. return wall, suggesting a rectangular plan with angle buttresses at each corner. This was confirmed by Brian Durham's subsequent observations.

Of the contexts exposed in these trenches, L61 and L91 appeared to correspond to L3, L85 to L8/9, L65 to L10, and L90 to the pit fills sealed by L20. The foundation appeared to have been robbed-out just S. of the N.W. corner and the resulting trench backfilled with building debris (L62).

## THE FINDS

### POTTERY by MAUREEN MELLOR (Figs. 18–19)

736 sherds were recovered from stratified contexts.

### Phase 1

Only one sherd was recovered, from F147, an Oxford Early Medieval Ware (Fabric AC, Group IB) which would not be expected before the mid 11th century.[8]

---

[8] B.G. Durham, 'Excavations at All Saints Church, Oxford', Oxoniensia (forthcoming): 5% AC in Phase 3b, associated with a coin of Edward the Confessor dated 1044.

*Phase 2*

A much larger assemblage is associated with Phase 2. Oxford Early Medieval Ware (Fabric AC, Group IB) is dominant (Fig. 18, Nos. 2 and 4), but sandy wares (Oxford Medieval Ware, Fabric Y, Nos. 3 and 6; Abingdon Medieval Ware, Fabric AG, No. 1) are in strong competition. Continental imports include a Pingsdorf type (Fabric BV); regional imports include glazed Stamford-type pitchers (Fabrics Z and AT).

The contemporary pots in Oxford Early Medieval Ware are cooking/storage vessels (Nos. 2 and 4). The sandy wares from the group have rather larger vessels (Nos. 1 and 3), but probably served similar functions. A glazed sherd in Oxford Medieval Ware (Fabric Y, from F138) probably represents a pitcher. One small unglazed sherd (No. 6) with incised decoration and an applied finger-pressed strip may also represent a smaller jug.

This group can be paralleled with an assemblage from 79–80 St. Aldates, dating to the first half of the 12th century.[9] It is consistent with the date of *c.* 1125–1150 for the contexts of Phase 2 proposed by the excavator (below), but accumulation nearer the earlier rather than the later date, or *vice versa*, cannot be ruled out.

Some residual Saxon sherds, including grass-tempered sherds, were found in F16 and F67. St. Neots-type ware (Fabric R, Group IA) was also recovered from the latter context. Residual Late Saxon wares (Fabrics B and R, Group IA), were recovered from F16 and F138. One sherd of Oxford Late Saxon Ware (Fabric B, Group IA) was decorated with an applied thumb-pressed strip (No. 5). This style of decoration has not been noted on this fabric previously in Oxford, and may indicate a new form type: a storage jar.

TABLE 1: SHERD NUMBERS IN EACH FABRIC SHOWN AS A PERCENTAGE OF THE TOTAL IN EACH PHASE

| FABRIC | | Ph1 | % | Ph2 | % | Ph3a | % | Ph3b | % | Ph4 | % | Ph5 | % | TOTAL |
|---|---|---|---|---|---|---|---|---|---|---|---|---|---|---|
| IA | A | | | | | | | | | | | | | |
| | B | | | 2 | 0.9 | | | 1 | 0.5 | 2 | 1 | | | |
| | R | | | 7 | 3 | | | 2 | 1 | | | | | |
| IB | AC | 1 | 100 | 109 | 48 | 17 | 20 | 40 | 21 | 22 | 14 | 2 | 3 | |
| | BR | | | 1 | 0.4 | | | | | | | | | |
| II | AQ | | | | | 3 | 3 | | | 3 | 2 | 1 | 1 | |
| | BF | | | 10 | 4 | | | 2 | 1 | 2 | 1 | | | |
| III | Y | | | 40 | 18 | 39 | 45 | 18 | 9 | 12 | 8 | 1 | 1 | |
| | Z | | | 2 | 0.9 | | | | | | | 1 | 1 | |
| | AG | | | 37 | 16 | 3 | 3 | 4 | 2 | 2 | 1 | 2 | 3 | |
| | AH | | | | | 4 | 5 | 1 | 0.5 | | | | | |
| | AM | | | 1 | 0.4 | 15 | 17 | 19 | 10 | 13 | 8 | 8 | 12 | |
| | AP | | | | | | | | 1 | 0.5 | | | | |
| | AT | | | 1 | 0.4 | | | | | | | | | |
| | AW | | | | | 1 | 1 | 1 | 0.5 | | | | | |
| | BV | | | 1 | 0.4 | | | | | | | | | |
| | BN | | | | | | | 4 | 2 | | | | | |
| | BX | | | 1 | 0.4 | | | 73 | 37 | 61 | 39 | 7 | 10 | |
| | ST | | | | | 1 | 1 | 4 | 2 | 14 | 9 | 25 | 36 | |
| | DA | | | | | | | | | 4 | 3 | | | |
| | DB | | | | | | | | | | | 1 | 1 | |
| | DE | | | | | | | | | 4 | 3 | | | |
| | DF | | | | | | | 5 | 3 | | | 2 | 3 | |
| | DG | | | | | | | 1 | 0.5 | 1 | 0.6 | 7 | 10 | |
| | DH | | | | | | | | | 1 | 0.6 | | | |
| | DI | | | | | | | | | 1 | 0.6 | | | |
| | DT | | | | | | | | | 1 | 0.6 | | | |
| | DX | | | | | | | 2 | 1 | 2 | 1 | | | |
| | ZZ | | | 15 | 7 | 4 | 5 | 17 | 9 | 12 | 8 | 12 | 17 | |
| TOTAL | | 1 | | 227 | | 87 | | 195 | | 157 | | 69 | | 736 |

[9] B.G. Durham, 'Archaeological Investigations in St. Aldates, Oxford', *Oxoniensia*, xlii (1977), 133: associated with a coin of Stephen *c.* 1141.

## Phase 3A

In the earlier contexts of this sub-phase (F32, F38, F104, F106, F108, F137 and F148) Oxford Medieval Ware (Fabric Y, Group III) dominates, with only a few regional imports represented (Fabrics AG and AH). An early 13th-century date is suggested.[10]

Oxford Late Medieval Ware (Fabric AM, Group III, Brill/Boarstall types) dominates in the later contexts (F24, F25, F30 and F74). The underglaze plastic decoration and the use of copper oxide in the glazes suggests a mid 13th-century date.[11]

Oxford Medieval Ware included cooking/storage vessels, a dish with combed decoration (No. 8),[12] and 8 glazed sherds, probably from pitchers. Glazed sherds, probably of ovoid jugs[13] or small pitchers with strap handles (No. 7),[14] in Fabric AH were present in both the earlier and later contexts of this sub-phase.

## Phase 3B

Pottery from beneath the belfry floors and the contemporary external surface includes a considerable element of residual material (Oxford Early Medieval Ware, Fabric AC, Group IB, from F21, F33 and F54/55, and from L10, L58, L65 and F89).

Brill types dominate (Fabric BX), but small amounts of Raeren-type Rhenish stonewares, and white and red earthenwares, are also present. Vessel types include jars, both plain (No. 10) and partially glazed (No. 12); deep-sided pans (Nos. 13 and 14); and jugs (Nos. 18 and 19), some with rod handles (No. 11), others with wedge-sectioned strap handles (No. 21). Decoration is confined to deep horizontal grooves (No. 15) and partial glazing in clear or mottled dark-green glazes. Cups (Nos. 9 and 20) and drinking tankards (Nos. 16 and 17) were also present. A similar assemblage can be paralleled at the Hamel Phase E4(2), dated to the early or mid 16th century,[15] and this would complement the preferred dating of the latest contexts of this sub-phase to the end of the 15th century and the first quarter of the 16th (below, p. 66).

## Phase 4

Pottery from the infill of the belfry continues to be dominated by the Brill-type coarsewares, and a slightly wider range of red and white earthenwares were also present. The vessel forms associated with Brill show no evidence of development from those of Phase 3b. A few other vessel-types were recovered from the post-holes within the foundation: a dripping pan with a thick carbon deposit on the exterior (No. 30), and a skillet-handle (No. 32). Jars (No. 27), some with knife-trimmed bases (No. 31), and jugs, partially glazed in mottled green (No. 29), continue in use. One vessel contained a thick deposit of calcium carbonate on the internal surface (No. 28), suggesting that water had been heated in it. It also had evidence of frost-pitting externally.

Smaller cups or tankards with internal and external glaze were found (No. 22), one a Cistercian type with purplish glaze (No. 23, Fabric 126), obviously a 'second' since it had a small hole in its base.

Rhenish stonewares accounted for 9 per cent of the assemblage, an increase over the previous phase. Plain stonewares included Raeren-type drinking vessels (Nos. 24–6) and a single sherd of a Raeren copy of a Cologne oak jug or drinking mug, from L9.[16] Their *floruit* is *c.* 1500–50. One drinking vessel was clearly a 'second', the handle having fractured prior to or during firing and the glaze having trickled into the fracture, leaving the handle very insecure! There is nothing amongst this assemblage which would not conform to the date of 1545–6 proposed for the infilling of the belfry (below, p. 72).

[10] N. Palmer, 'A Beaker Burial and Medieval Tenements in The Hamel, Oxford', *Oxoniensia*, xlv (1980), 161, Fig. 8, Phase D3b.

[11] G. Lambrick, 'Further Excavations on the Second Site of the Dominican Priory, Oxford', *Oxoniensia*, l (1985), 177: south-western area Phase 1, dated *c.* 1250, with a coin of Henry III (1216–72) probably deposited 1230–50. Palmer, op. cit. note 10, 161, 176–8: Phase B10b, dated 1250–65.

[12] Palmer, op. cit. note 10, Fig. 10(18): dated late 12th/early 13th century.

[13] R.L.S. Bruce-Mitford, 'Archaeology of the Site of the Bodleian Extension in Broad Street, Oxford', *Oxoniensia*, v (1940), Fig. 10(4).

[14] Palmer, op. cit. note 10, Fig. 10(23): mid 13th century. Bruce-Mitford, op. cit. note 13, Pl. 10(4) for pitcher with tubular spout and strap handle: 12th/early 13th century.

[15] Palmer, op. cit. note 10.

[16] I am grateful to John Hurst for identifying this rare copy. For examples of oak-leaf only see *Steinzeug* (Cologne, 1971), 267.

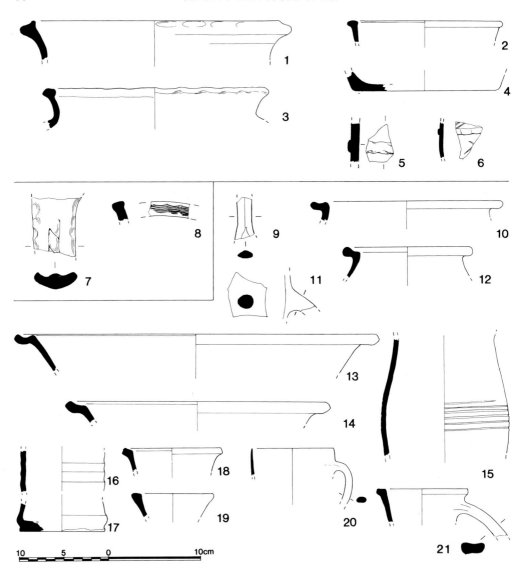

Fig. 18.   Pottery. *Scale 1:4.*

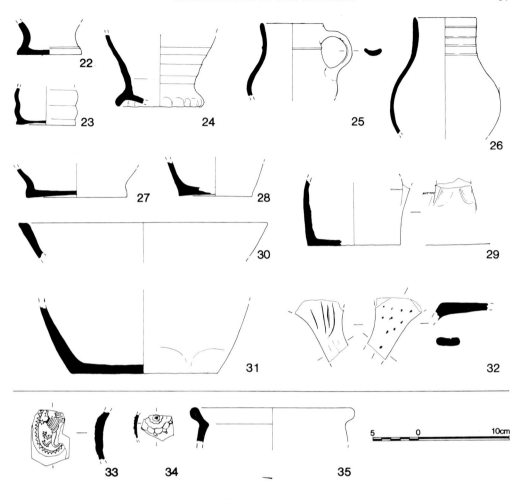

Fig. 19. Pottery. *Scale 1:4.*

## Phase 5

This phase yielded a smaller assemblage of pottery, which was largely from one context, the fill of F78. It is clear from this material that the medieval Brill-type fabric was no longer so popular and had been replaced by another fabric (Fabric 124), also believed to have been made at Brill: a red earthenware, often glazed orange internally (No. 35).[17]

Rhenish stonewares appear to dominate, a characteristic not noted on tenement sites in Oxford. Raeren types were present, but Frenchen flagons and globular tankards dominate, some with bellamine masks, with fake heraldic medallions.[18] A Nuremburg jetton of Hans Krauwinckel gives a *terminus post quem* of *c.* 1580–1610 for the deposition of the assemblage from F78 (below, p. 38); the stonewares suggest a mid 17th-century date.

[17] T.G. Hassall, C.E. Halpin and M. Mellor, 'Excavations in St. Ebbes, Oxford, 1967–1976: Part II: Post-Medieval Domestic Tenements and the Post-Dissolution Site of the Greyfriars', *Oxoniensia*, xlix (1984): Red Earthenware Fiche II E4–E6.

[18] See Hassall et al., ibid., Fig. 65(5), for a similar, though not identical, medallion.

A fine rosette from a Jackfield jug (No. 33), glazed black both internally and externally, was recovered from L3, and dates to the mid 18th century. However, given the modern disturbance of L3, this piece, like the 19th- and 20th-century ceramics, may well be intrusive.

## Conclusions

The earlier medieval sequence is useful, as little or no late Saxon contamination was present. It is, however, significant that a few sherds of early Saxon type were found in association with ceramics of recognisably 10th-century traditions. This may indicate that local middle Saxon ceramics included grass-tempered and shelly limestone fabrics.

However, the Christ Church pottery is most interesting for the 16th-century material. The assemblages from beneath the floor of the belfry, from the floor itself, and from the infill are not large (indeed, 16th-century assemblages within the City have always been meagre in comparison with groups of the 12th, 13th and 14th centuries, and those from the mid 17th century onwards). There is nevertheless sufficient to show that the predominating Brill-type fabric was similar to the medieval fabric, but with less quartz and varying amounts of iron ore. It is hard-fired and breaks to a smooth fracture. The vessel forms show little or no stylistic development over half a century (c. 1500–50), despite considerable religious upheavals and changes in fashion of dress. But a stylistic development does occur over the next 50 to 70 years, and we need further well-stratified groups for this period in order to fit the earliest excavated post-medieval Brill kiln into the sequence.[19]

## COINS AND JETTONS by N.J. MAYHEW

Four of this group of six items may be dated securely to the 16th century, all jettons. The earliest combines a typical French écu-type obverse (shield of France modern) with a typical Nuremburg reverse of Reichsapfel within a tressure of three curves alternating with three angles. It is of larger diameter than the other jettons, and it is this feature, together with the combination of typical French 15th-century obverse with typical Nuremburg 16th-century reverse, which suggests that it is the earliest of the jettons found. This piece is pierced. The other three jettons are all of the same type, Barnard No. 84,[20] with varying legends. Two name the famous Nuremberg jetton maker Hans Krauwinckel (c. A.D. 1580–1610), while the third has a garbled legend. The two coins are a very worn and clipped French douzaine or blanc of the 15th or 16th century, and a Roman piece of Valens. The latter, and the jetton No. 5, are clearly residual.

1. Roman coin of Valens, A.D. 369–378. *Securitas Reipublicae.* SF125 L134 Ph 2.
2. Uncertain French *douzaine* or *blanc*, 15th or 16th century. Very worn and clipped. SF59 F50 Ph4.
3. Nuremberg jetton with French-type obverse. Perhaps early 16th century. SF39 topsoil.
4. Nuremberg jetton, Krauwinckel type, though illegible. SF1 L8 Ph4.
5–6. Nuremberg jettons of Hans Krauwinckel. 5, SF87 L3 Ph5; 6, SF101 F78 Ph5.

## LEAD *BULLA* by ARTHUR MACGREGOR (Fig. 20)

Lead *bulla* of Pope Innocent IV (1243–1254).
Obv. *SPASPE*; conventional heads of SS Paul and Peter within dotted pear-shaped outlines and in the centre a Latin cross, all within a dotted border.
Rev: *INNO/CENTIVS/·PP·IIII.* within a dotted border.
Vertical string-hole. Diameter (max.) 38 mm., Thickness 5 mm., Weight 45.9 g.
SF103 L84 modern.

A lead sealing of the standard type from a papal document.[21] The issues of Innocent IV are among those most commonly found in England. This find is from the bedding of the cloister garth paving.

[19] M. Farley, 'Pottery and Pottery Kilns of the Post-Medieval Period at Brill, Buckinghamshire', *Post-Med. Arch.* xiii (1979), 127–52.
[20] F.P. Barnard, *The Casting Counter and the Counting Board* (1916), Pl. 33.
[21] cf. C. Serafini, *Le Monete e le Bolle Plumbee Pontificie del Medgliere Vaticano* i (Milan, 1910), 29.

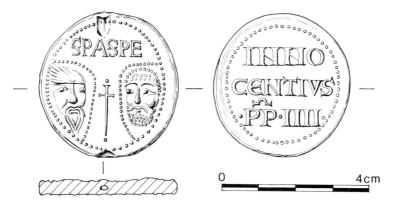

Fig. 20 Lead *bulla*. Scale *1:1*.

NON-FERROUS METAL OBJECTS by ALISON R. GOODALL (Figs. 21–3)

Monastic and ecclesiastical sites typically produce few copper-alloy finds related to costume and personal ornament, except in the case of graveyard excavations. No. 8 is probably a buckle-plate and the strap-end, No. 9, could have come from a belt. The wire eye, No. 10, and the many lace-ends, represented by Nos. 12–14, are also from costume. However, these sites often provide evidence for the presence of books, which is less frequently found on town and village sites. The cathedral cloister is no exception: Nos. 1–5 are clasps from book-bindings.

Most of the lead fragments are from window leads, and all but two of these are of the type made by drawing a cast rod or came through a vice.[22] The other two fragments appear to have been made by the earlier method of casting.

*Copper-alloy Objects (Figs. 21–2)*

1–3. Hooked book-clasps. All are of typical late medieval to early post-medieval form. Nos. 1 and 2 have incised decoration and No. 3 is plain. No. 2 retains some leather between the plates. Similar book-clasps have been found, for instance, at Basing House, Hants., dating perhaps from before the building of the house in 1531,[23] and on book-bindings of the 15th and 16th centuries.[24] 1, SF48 L8 Ph4; 2, SF34 L9 Ph4; 3, SF56 F12 modern.

4–5. Eyes from book-clasps. These would probably have been used with hooks similar to Nos. 1–3. Comparable examples have been found at the Carmelite Friary, Newcastle-upon-Tyne,[25] and the Austin Friars, Leicester, where it was identified as a buckle-plate.[26] 4, SF79 L10 Ph3b; 5, SF151 L8 Ph4.

6–7. Perforated plates, possibly from book-bindings or from belts. No. 7 (not illustrated) is incomplete. 6, SF66 L35 Ph3b; 7, SF81 L58 Ph3b.

8. Probably a buckle-plate. The upper surface has a *repoussé* hump and there appear to be a pair of spacers between the plates. SF6 L33 Ph3b.

9. Strap-end with two rivets and retaining leather between the plates. SF31 L9 Ph4.

[22] I. Davies, 'Window Glass in Eighteenth-Century Williamsburg', in I. Noël Hume et al., *Five Artifact Studies* (Colonial Williamsburg Occasional Papers in Archaeology i, 1973), 82.

[23] S. Moorhouse, 'Finds from Basing House, Hampshire (*c.* 1540–1645): Part II', *Post-Med. Arch.* v (1971), 59, Fig. 24(162).

[24] For example, a book on display at Sudeley Castle, Gloucestershire, dated 1429, with an embossed leather binding: it is not clear if the date also refers to the binding. Also a book of *c.* 1600 in Bayntons' Museum of Bookbinding, Bath.

[25] B. Harbottle, 'Excavations at the Carmelite Friary, Newcastle-upon-Tyne, 1965 and 1967', *Archaeologia Aeliana* 4th ser. xlvi (1968), 222, Fig. 18(154).

[26] P. Clay, in J.E. Mellor and T. Pearce, *The Austin Friars, Leicester* (C.B.A. Research Report xxxv, 1981), 133, Fig. 48(35).

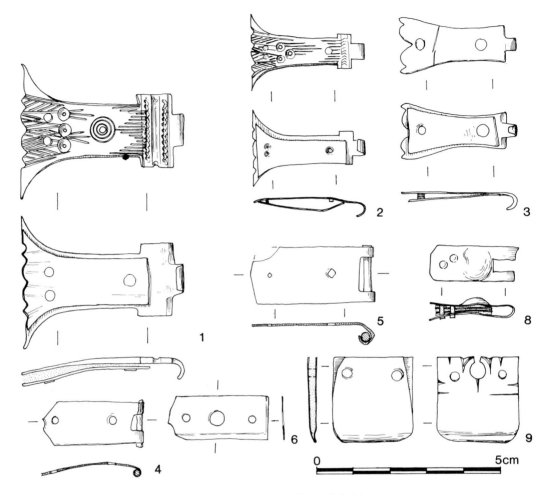

Fig. 21.   Copper-alloy objects. *Scale 1:1.*

10. (Not illustrated) Wire eye from a hook-and-eye. SF62 L20 Ph4.
11. Hinged manicure set, attached to a suspension loop. It consists of a curved nail-cleaner, scoop, pointed implement, and another curved implement which possibly did not always belong to the set since it has a decorated surface and lacks the cast moulding of the other pieces. Other manicure sets come from Hull,[27] dating from the late 13th to early 14th century, and from a late 15th century context at Lyveden, Northants;[28] but these examples, although similar to each other, do not resemble this one from Christ Church closely. SF138 L10 Ph3b.
12–14. Lace-ends. No. 12 is unusually narrow and has been bent through 90 degrees, but otherwise resembles a lace-end. Nos. 13 and 14 have been made from rolled sheet and were secured by a rivet. 12, SF71 L58 Ph3b; 13, SF20 L18 Ph4; 14, SF32 L9 Ph4.

[27] A.R. Goodall, 'Objects of Copper Alloy' in P. Armstrong and B. Ayers, 'Excavations in High Street and Blackfriargate', *East Riding Archaeology*, viii (1987), 206, Fig. 117(225).
[28] J.M. Steane and G.F. Bryant, 'Excavations at the Deserted Medieval Settlement at Lyveden. Fourth Report', *Jnl. of the Northampton Museum and Art Gallery*, xii (June 1975), 114, Fig. 43(49).

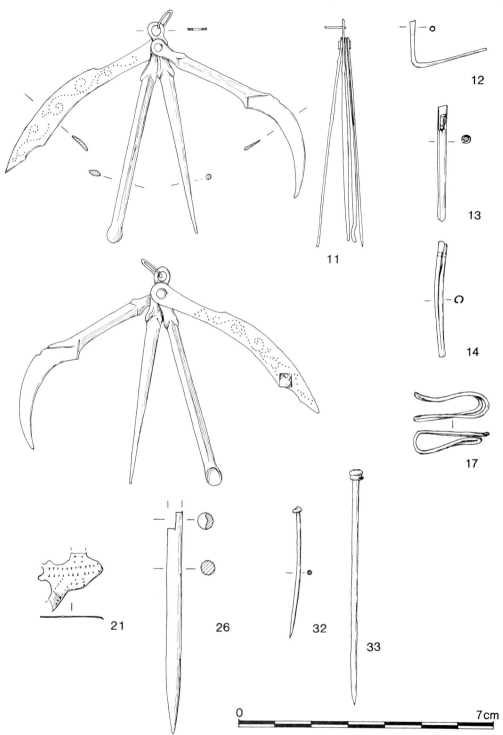

Fig. 22. Copper-alloy objects. *Scale 1:1.*

There are a further 38 lace-ends of this type, 25 of which appear to have rivets; two of these have a black coating on them. None comes from a context earlier than Phase 3b. Phase 3b: SF74, 102, 106, 171. Phase 4: SF2, 9, 37, 60. Phase 5: SF14, 25, 58, 68, 99, 148. One lace-end has been made from folded rather than rolled sheet. It has been suggested that lace-ends of this type are later than the rolled ones.[29] SF65 F49 Ph4.

15–16.  (Not illustrated) Lower halves of sheet-metal bells, with dumbell-shaped openings. No. 15 has a diameter of 16.5 mm. and No. 16 of approximately 28 mm. 15, SF33 L9 Ph4; 16, SF95 F77 modern.

17.  Chain link, apparently cast rather than of drawn wire. SF157 L38 Ph3a.

18.  (Not illustrated) Roughly cast ring with file marks on surface; diameter 22 mm. SF76 L58 Ph3b.

19.  (Not illustrated) Probably a fragment from a vessel rim. SF28 L45 modern.

20.  (Not illustrated) Strip of thin sheet with rivet holes; possibly a patch. SF86 L3 Ph5.

21.  Small decorative fragment. SF167 L100 Ph2.

22.  (Not illustrated) Rolled strip with rivet holes; width 7.5 mm. but broadening at one end. SF175 L21 Ph3b.

23.  (Not illustrated) Fragment of round plate with remains of two nail holes with countersinking for heads. Surviving width 31 mm. SF158 topsoil.

24.  (Not illustrated) Rounded fragment with two holes, possibly a sequin; width 10 mm. SF70 L58 Ph3b.

25.  (Not illustrated) Strip of wood covered with leather which has been attached with a row of six, closely spaced, gilt-headed studs; head diameter 10 mm. Probably from furniture. SF73 F45 modern.

26.  Pointed object with a rebate at the blunt end. SF121 L98 Ph2.

27–31.  (Not illustrated) Sheet fragments and off-cuts; 27, SF118 F109 Ph3b; 28, SF57 L9 Ph4; 29, SF176 L8 Ph4; 30, SF47 L3 Ph5; 31, SF91 L80 Ph5.

32–33.  Pins. No. 32 has a head made from coiled wire and a relatively thick shank. No. 33 is similar but, as with most post-medieval pins, the head has been attached to the shank by stamping it between moulds, giving it a more regular shape than No. 32. 32, SF75 L58 Ph3b; 33, SF144 L3 Ph5. Two more pins resemble No. 32 (SF35 and SF61, both Phase 4), while there are a further 12 pins of the same type as No. 33, of which four show evidence of white-metal plating. Phase 3b: SF82. Phase 4: SF3, 61, 82, 94, 104 (8 specimens). A further pin, SF65 (F49 Ph4) is of indeterminate type.

34–35.  (Not illustrated) Wire. No. 34 is a roll of fine wire; No. 35 is a piece of thick, 2.5 mm., wire. 34, SF4 L18 Ph4; 35, SF98 F78 Ph5.

36–38.  (Not illustrated) Lumps, possibly from metalcasting. 36, SF109 F74 Ph3a; 37, SF97 F78 Ph5; 38, SF105 F78 Ph5.

*Lead Objects (Fig. 23)*

1.  Piece of cut sheet. SF26 L9 Ph4.

2.  Sheet, possibly from roofing or flashing. SF72 L10 Ph3b.

3.  Pieces of window lead, probably from rectangular or diamond-shaped panes. Nearly all of the leads have been made from cast bars or cames which have been drawn out and shaped in a glazier's vice. SF177 L8 Ph4.
There are 15 similar pieces of lead: Phase 3a: SF113. Phase 3b: SF162. Phase 4: SF13, 18–19, 21, 38, 44, 55, 114, 180. Phase 5: SF67, 147. Modern: SF43, 163. Two pieces of lead appear to have been made simply by casting, without being drawn through a vice: SF30 L9 Ph4; SF152 L85 Ph4.

4.  (Not illustrated) Narrow strip, probably a tie used to secure a window to iron cross-bars. SF63 L20 Ph4.

5–6.  (Not illustrated) Probably caulking. 5, SF52 L9 Ph4; 6, SF120 L85 Ph4.

7.  Fragment with longitudinal grooves. SF7 topsoil.

8–10.  (Not illustrated) Strips. 8, SF85 topsoil; 9, SF161 L21 Ph3b; 10, SF155 F28 Ph4.

11.  Iron nail wrapped in lead sheet. SF166 F12 modern.

12–13.  (Not illustrated) Fused lead. 12, SF50 L9 Ph4; 13, SF77 L58 Ph3b.

---

[29] G.E. Oakley, 'The Copper-Alloy Objects', in J.H. Williams, *St. Peter's Street, Northampton: Excavations 1973–1976* (1979), 262–3.

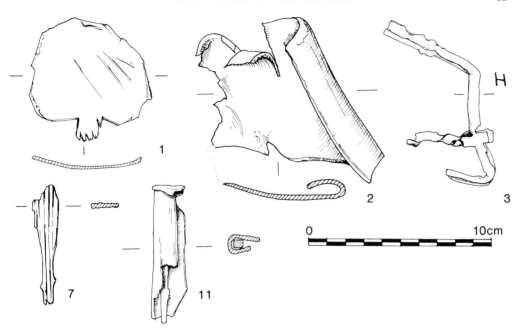

Fig. 23.   Lead objects. *Scale 1:2.*

## IRON OBJECTS by IAN H. GOODALL (Fig. 24)

1–4.   Knives. No. 1, with a whittle tang, was probably lost soon after manufacture since its cutler's mark is not inlaid, the practice followed from about the mid 16th century.[30] Nos. 2–4 are late medieval scale-tang knives, 4 (not illustrated) a 37 mm. long blade fragment with the stub of the tang. 1, SF36 L8 Ph4; 2, SF49 L9 Ph4; 3, SF181 L8 Ph4; 4, SF64 F28 Ph4.

5.   Shears blade with cusped top. SF53 L9 Ph4.

6–7.   Hinge or strap terminals with projecting tips. Such shaping is rare on most hinges, and these may be from a door or chest. Some indication of the elaborate form of hinges and fittings on some 12th-century doors is given by that at Stillingfleet, North Yorkshire, and some of its contemporaries.[31] 6, SF128 L101 Ph2; 7, SF160 F21 Ph3b.

8.   (Not illustrated) Strap fragment, 31 mm. long, 17 mm. wide. SF11 L8 Ph4.

9.   Tip of a stapled hasp, commonly used in conjunction with a lock fixed to a chest. The lock bolt passed through the staple, the two together thereby securing the chest, while the projecting scrolled tip enabled the hasp to be easily removed from the lock when free. SF142 L3 Ph5.

10–11.   Arrowheads, both of the blunted type used in medieval and later times for target practice and found in considerable numbers both at Baile Hill, York,[32] and in Coventry.[33] 10, SF185 F29 Ph4; 11, SF117 F78 Ph5.

[30] J.F. Hayward, *English Cutlery, Sixteenth to Eighteenth Century* (1957).
[31] P.V. Addyman and I.H. Goodall, 'The Norman Church and Door at Stillingfleet, North Yorkshire', *Archaeologia*, cvi (1979), 75–105.
[32] P.V. Addyman and J. Priestly, 'Baile Hill, York: a report on the Institute's Excavations', *Archaeological Jnl.* cxxxiv (1977), 121, 140, Fig. 10 (29–49).
[33] C. Woodfield, 'Finds from the Free Grammar School at the Whitefriars, Coventry, *c.* 1545–1547/8', *Post-Med. Arch.* xv (1981), 87, Fig. 3(1–9).

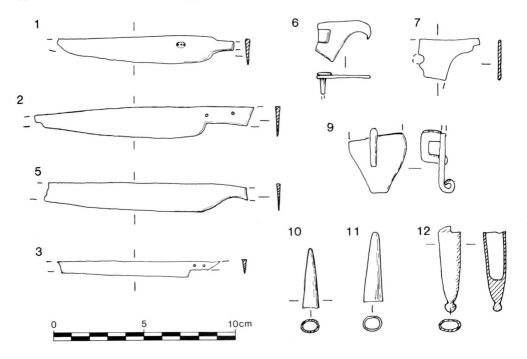

Fig. 24.   Iron objects. *Scale 1:2.*

12.   Chape with knobbed tip. Iron chapes are not common, but other, probably late, examples are known.[34] SF164 L3 Ph5.

13–17.   (Not illustrated) Timber nails from graves. Nos. 13–15, all from F96, are complete, 59 mm., 69 mm., and 72 mm. long respectively, with flat circular heads 21 mm. in diameter. Nos. 16 and 17 are nail shanks. 13 and 14 SF123, 15, SF116, F96 Ph1; 16, SF131 F144 Ph1; 17, SF136 F89 Ph3b.

18.   (Not illustrated) Possible shank of large timber nail, square-sectioned, 155 mm. long. SF122 F124 Ph1. Many other complete nails and fragments, representing at least 192 nails in addition to Nos. 13–18, were recovered. The great majority, a minimum of 147, were from post-medieval contexts, 68 from Phase 4. 32 were recovered from Phase 3b, 12 from Phase 3a, and 1 from Phase 2.

## BONE OBJECTS by ARTHUR MACGREGOR

1.   Antler connecting plate from a composite comb, parallel-sided and **D**-shaped in section; broken at either end, both breaks running through rivet holes. One edge is marked by repeated transverse saw cuts. 45 × 12.5 × 3.5 mm. SF126 L136 Ph2. It is unclear whether this piece comes from a single-sided or double-sided comb: the thin cross-section and straight edges are more appropriate for a double-sided comb; the transverse saw-cuts (from cutting the teeth) on one edge only might be taken to indicate a single-sided comb, although instances are known of double-sided combs with single opposing edges marked in this fashion.

2.   Bone gouge, made from sheep or goat metatarsal. Length 44 mm., diameter 14 mm. SF88 F78 Ph5. Possibly from an unfinished 'apple-scoop', a well-known post-medieval implement type, often made from sheep metatarsals. The distal end is usually left intact while the shaft is cut through to form a

[34] I.H. Goodall in P. Wade-Martins, *Excavations in North Elmham Park* (East Anglian Arch. ix, 1980), 516, Fig. 267(129); I.H. Goodall in C.M. Cunningham and P.J. Drury, *Post-Medieval Sites and their Pottery: Moulsham Street, Chelmsford* (C.B.A. Research Report liv, 1985), 57, Fig. 34(84).

gouge. Although usually identified as scoops with which toothless ancients ate their apples, other functions have also been attributed to them, including taking core samples from cheeses to test for ripeness.[35]

## WINDOW GLASS by NIALL DONALD (Fig. 25)

223 stratified fragments of glass were recovered, 63 of them painted. Most seem to be 14th-century, although fragment No. 19 could be early or mid 15th-century. Nearly all came from post-medieval contexts, but five fragments were recovered from medieval contexts (F74, L94). None of these is painted and, apart from one clear glass fragment, any colour is indistinguishable. These fragments, from Phase 3a, are the earliest glass from the site.

The illustrated fragments show the range of recognisable patterns and motifs. There are geometric patterns (Nos. 1, 6–7, 17, 18), several of which are backpainted. Background (Nos. 2–4, 8, 19, 26) and border (Nos. 5, 9–12, 25) designs occur: No. 19 has a characteristic seaweed foliage design; Nos. 25 and 26 have been picked out of a matt wash, and No. 25, like No. 20, is part of a quarry design with no clear parallels in the *Corpus Vitrearum Medii Aevi* for Oxfordshire.[36] Nos. 13 and 14 are fragments of *grisaille*, and No. 21 is a large fragment from a *grisaille* quarry with a foliage of daisies similar to glass excavated in the Latin Chapel. Nos. 15, 16, 22 and 23 have architectural details: 22 has been picked out of a matt wash to give the effect of masonry; No. 23 is unlikely to be drapery due to the narrowness of the design.

The majority of the glass comes from the floor of the belfry and the dump layers which sealed it: 86 fragments, of which 22 are painted, came from the dump, and 46 fragments from the floor, of which 25 were painted. The similarity between the glass fragments from the floor (Nos. 1–5) and the dump (Nos. 6–16) suggests that they share a common source. It is clear that some glass was dropped on the floor, and other fragments dumped on a builders' dump which was then used to backfill the belfry. In the main report it is argued that this material is the result of work carried out in the church in 1545–6; it seems likely, therefore, that this included destruction of, or alterations to, at least some of the glass. The character of the assemblage, composed of borders, backgrounds and *grisaille* without any definite fragments of drapery or figural pieces, suggests the stripping of lead or the replacement of old windows in new frames; the glass and lead from the floor suggests that this may have been done in the belfry before its demolition and infilling.

## BRICK AND TILE by DEBORAH DUNCAN (Fig. 26)

928 stratified pieces of ceramic tile and brick were recovered, of which 425 were too fragmentary to classify as either roof or floor tile. One Romano-British box or half-box tile (No. 1), with a roller relief pattern (Lowther W-chevron type),[37] was recovered from Phase 3b.

## Brick

8 pieces of brick were recovered, including one corner-piece from Phase 2. There is no archaeological reason to think that it is intrusive, and it has the same fabric as two floor tiles from contexts of the same phase.

## Roofing Material

197 fragments of roof tile were recovered. The majority were ordinary tiles, but 9 were identifiable as peg-tiles and 7 as spurred ridge-tiles. The coarse red sandy fabric with a few white clay inclusions indicates a local source.

---

[35] A. MacGregor, *Bone, Antler, Ivory and Horn: the Technology of Skeletal Materials since the Roman Period* (1985), 180, Fig. 97. For another example excavated from Oxford, see A.G. Hunter and E.M. Jope, 'Excavations on the City Defences in New College, Oxford, 1949', *Oxoniensia*, xvi (1951), 28–41.

[36] P.A. Newton and J. Kerr, *The County of Oxford: a Catalogue of Medieval Stained Glass (Corpus Vitrearum Medii Aevii* i, 1979).

[37] A.W.G. Lowther, *A Study of the Patterns on Roman Flue Tiles and their Distribution* (Research Papers of the Surrey Archaeological Society i). I am grateful to Leigh Turner for this identification.

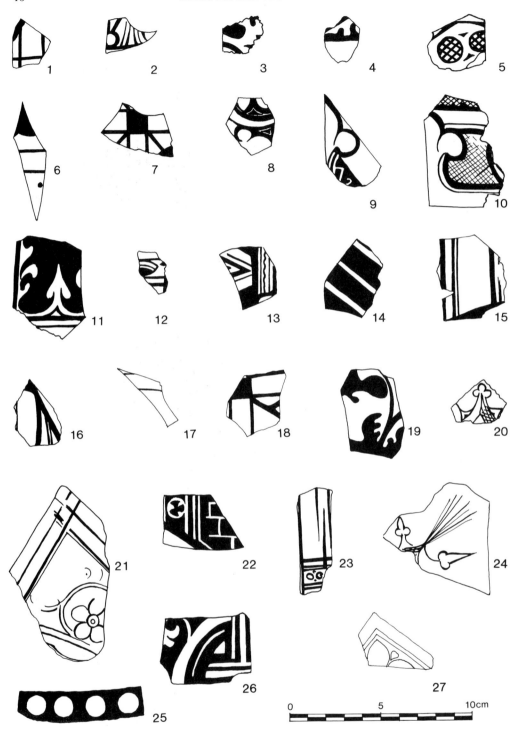

Fig. 25.　Painted window glass. *Scale 1:2.*

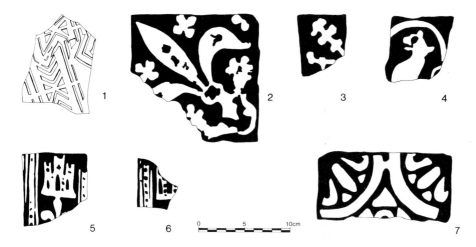

Fig. 26.   Tile. *Scale 1:4.*

## Floor Tile

Most of the floor tile was recovered from post-medieval contexts, the majority, including much decorated tile originally from the Priory church, from the infill of the belfry. Two tile fragments were recovered from contexts of Phase 2. These are plain, thicker than usual (32 mm.), and dark grey in colour with a high iron content and rounded calcareous inclusions. The fabric is identical to that of a roof tile from Mount House, Witney.[38]

Post-medieval material included 32 pieces of large paving slabs, 4 green-glazed, the rest yellow-glazed, identified as Flemish.[39] The 1528–9 building accounts for Wolsey's college record payments to one John Norton for yellow and green paving tiles.[40]

Of the decorated medieval fragments, 169 are inlaid 'Stabbed Wessex' types, 16 are printed. Identifiable designs are listed below, where possible by Haberly's serial number;[41] an asterix denotes types not previously known from Christ Church. Also found was one dark green, almost black, glazed border tile of a different fabric from the rest.[42]

## Inlaid Tiles

### 'STABBED WESSEX' TYPES

| | | | |
|---|---|---|---|
| XI* | | XXXVI* | 2 fragments |
| XXII | | XXXVIII | |
| XXIII* | 2 fragments | XLIX* | 2 fragments |
| XXV | | LI* | |
| XXVI | | LII | |
| XXXI | | LV* | |
| XXXII/LIII | 2 fragments | LXI | |
| XXXIII | 4 fragments | CCIX*[43] | |

[38] D. Duncan, 'The Tiles', in B.G. Durham, 'Witney Palace', *Oxoniensia* (forthcoming).

[39] Initial identification by Sarah Jennings.

[40] *V.C.H. Oxon.* iii, 231.

[41] L. Haberly, *Medieval English Paving Tiles* (1937).

[42] See M. Mellor, 'The Tiles', in T. Hassall and C. Halpin, 'Excavations in St. Ebbes, Oxford, 1967–1976: Part I', *Oxoniensia* (forthcoming).

[43] *cf.* A.B. Emden, 'Medieval Floor Tiles in the Church of St. Peter in the East, Oxford', *Oxoniensia*, xxxiv (1969), 39–40, Fig. 12(11).

*Possibles*

| | | | |
|---|---|---|---|
| XVI | | LI or ? variant of L | 3 fragments |
| XXIV *or* | | | |
| XXIVa *or* XXV | 5 fragments | LII | 2 fragments |
| XXXI | | LV | |
| XXXVI | | LXV *or* LXVI | |
| LI *or* L | | | |

*Variants*

L[44]
XXXII/LIII (No. 2)
?XLII (No. 3)

*Others*

Reverse of a similar tile found at the Dominican priory, Oxford (No. 4).[45]
Two fragments of border designs with castles and *fleurs-de-lis* (Nos. 5 and 6). These may be described as 'Chertsey type' since, although they are local 'Stabbed Wessex' types, they are copies of designs originating from Chertsey in the 1290s.[46]

*Printed Tiles*

CX*
CLXVII
CCXXIX*

*Variant*

Two fragments of a combination of CLXVI and CLXVII (No. 7).

## CLAY PIPES by CHRISTOPHER SCULL

17 stem fragments and a single bowl were recovered, from contexts of the 17th century or later. The bowl, from L47, is of local form B, dated *c.* 1650–90.[47]

## WORKED STONE FROM THE CLOISTER, LATIN CHAPEL AND PRIORY HOUSE by JOHN BLAIR (Figs. 27–9)

Of greatest intrinsic interest are the fragments of St. Frideswide's shrine (Nos. 19–28), all recovered from the infill of the belfry except for one canopy fragment from the Priory House; detailed discussion of these is reserved for a future publication. The other material from the cloister and Latin Chapel is not usefully stratified, and most of the former is late. It is, however, of interest that the W. part of the Latin Chapel produced three fragments (Nos. 2–4) from a Romanesque structure which had been heavily burnt and subsequently painted several times, on one occasion in red and black. These suggest that some part of the northern chapels existed before 1190, was damaged in the fire of that year, but survived thereafter through several repaintings.

[44] Ibid., 36–7, Fig. 11(1).
[45] G. Lambrick and M. Mellor, 'The Tiles', in Lambrick, op. cit. note 11, 181, Fig. 20(5).
[46] E. Eames, *English Medieval Tiles* (1985), 46.
[47] A. Oswald and J. Rutter, 'Clay Pipes', in Hassall et al., op. cit. note 17, 251–62.

The three groups of material are listed and illustrated together, arranged by date and type. Items from the 1985 cloister excavation are referenced 'CCL' followed by the layer or feature number and the worked stone number. Items from the 1962–3 Latin Chapel excavation are referenced 'LC' with Sturdy's cutting number (below, pp. 77–86). The two items found among rubble during renovation of the Priory House in 1986 are referenced 'CPH'. All pieces are in local oolitic limestone except where otherwise stated.

## 12th and 13th Centuries

1. Part of a small block worked on one face with a chevron; possibly the outer edge of a voussoir. (LC unstrat.)
2. Fragment from end of shaft of *c.* 11 cm. diameter. Heavily fire-stained, with traces of (i) white and (ii) black paint-layers over the staining. (LC, cutting 2W)
3. Obtuse-angled edge of block. Heavily fire-stained, with at least three layers of white paint over the staining. (LC, cutting 2W)
4. Fragment from corner of block with quarter-hollow moulding and quirk. Fire-stained, with paint layers over the staining: (i) white; (ii) quarter-hollow red, quirk black; (iii) yellow; (iv–vi) white. (LC, cutting 2, from rubble layer)
5. Straight 12-cm. length of attached keeled shaft. (LC, cutting 2)
6. Small fragment of shaft. (LC unstrat.)
7. Straight 17-cm. length of attached round shaft or string. (CCL, F6/2 WS41)

## Late Medieval and Indeterminate

8. Trefoiled finial from some elaborate structure with ogee cusping, probably mid 14th century. (LC unstrat.)
9. Straight 12-cm. length of window mullion with bulbous filleted roll. (CCL, F63 WS44/1)
10. Straight 17-cm. length of window mullion with bulbous filleted roll; small incised cross on end of block. (CCL, F6/2 WS40)
11. Fragment of standard window mullion; small incised cross on end of block. (CCL, F63 WS44)
12. Straight 13-cm. length of mullion from unglazed structure. (CCL, L7 WS25)
13. Straight 12-cm. length of ?polygonal shaft with slightly concave faces. (CCL, L8 WS3)
14. Straight 9-cm. length of bulbous fillet. (CCL, L9 WS20)
15. Straight 12-cm. length of beaked moulding. (CCL, L9 WS11)
16. Fragment of small block with concave face. (CCL, F78 WS46)
17. Corner of parapet of elaborate late Gothic structure with crenellated top and frieze of blind quatrefoils. Probably from a tomb, shrine or something similar. (CCL, L8 WS5)
18. Carved block with a fleuron on one side and ?a wimpled female face on the other, forming the junction of two lengths of upwards-pointing bulbous filleted moulding. This strange object is perhaps best interpreted as one corner of a polygonal or coffin-shaped trough or basin. The moulding and the fleuron suggest a 15th-century date. (CPH, WS5)

## Fragments from the Late 13th-Century Shrine-Base of St. Frideswide

19–23. Five fragments of moulding and cusping from the canopy; hard shelly limestone. (CPH, WS6; CCL, L9 WS12, L3 WS48, L8 WS28, L9 WS10)
24–5. Two fragments of shaft bases; Purbeck marble. (CCL, L9 WS9, F12 WS4)
26–7. Two fragments of quatrefoil-section shafts; Purbeck marble. (CCL, L9 WS15, L9 WS17)
28. Fragment of pinnacle or detached buttress; Purbeck marble. (CCL, L9 WS14)

## Not illustrated

Block with flat plastered face and traces of red pigment. (CCL, L9 WS27)
Indeterminate fragments. (CCL, WS9, 12, 13, 16, 18, 19, 21–4, 30, 32–9, 42–4, 47)

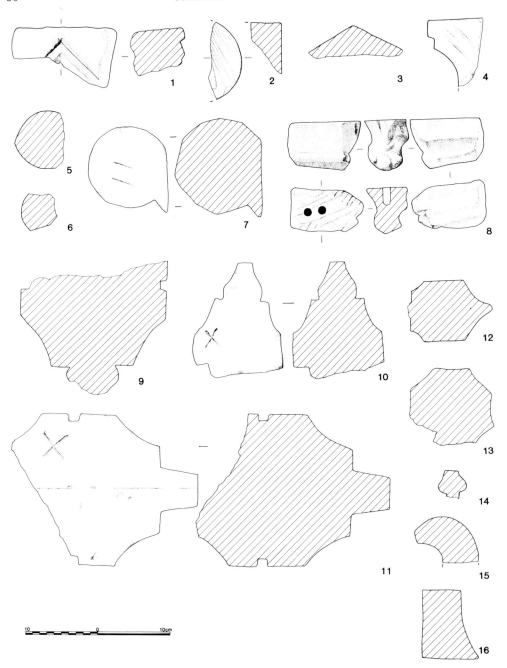

Fig. 27.   Worked stone. *Scale 1:5.*

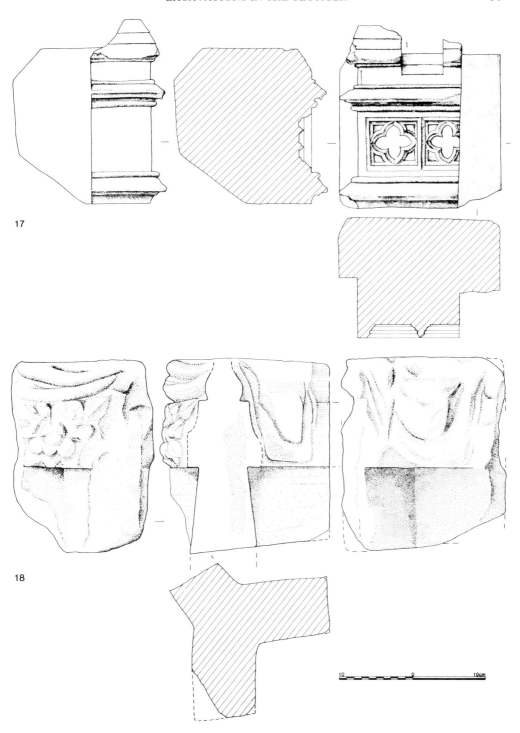

Fig. 28. Worked stone. *Scale 1:5.*

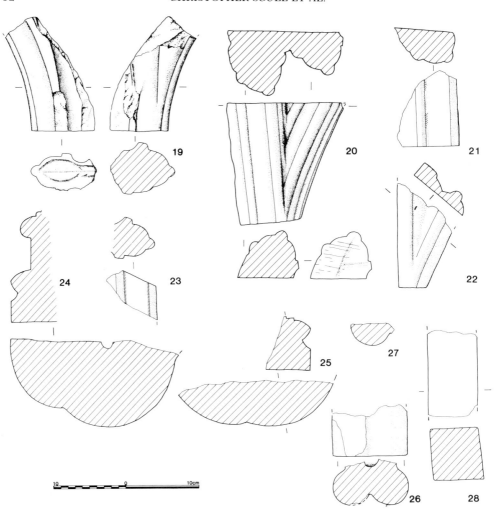

Fig. 29.    Fragments from the shrine-base of St. Frideswide. *Scale 1:5.*

## HUMAN SKELETAL MATERIAL AND FAUNAL REMAINS

### THE HUMAN BONES by MARY HARMAN

All of the bones recovered were examined. Most were in good condition, but some from the lowest levels were poorly preserved, and many, particularly those which had been redeposited, were broken. Unfortunately, owing to extensive re-use of the site, many graves were disturbed and the majority of bones recovered had been redeposited, there being only seven virtually complete skeletons, and thirteen partially complete despite having been disturbed in antiquity. Three of the latter, from F87, F118 & F127, and F127 respectively, had been entirely redeposited, but there were enough bones of the right size and conformation to be confident that, although they were amongst charnel, they belonged together. The skeletons were recorded as units, and the disturbed bones listed under the number of the context in which they were found. Copies of the basic records are in the site archive.

In the case of skeletons, the sex of adults was decided where possible from the relevant features of the skull and the pelvic girdle, using the criteria recommended by Ferembach et al.,[48] and if possible the sex of individual skulls and pelves from the charnel was also recorded. The age of adults was assessed where possible from the degree of wear on the teeth, using Miles's chart,[49] while the age of children was assessed from the state of tooth eruption and of epiphysial fusion and from the length of the diaphyses, though this was more difficult when the bones were broken: the ages are based on information given in Ferembach et al.[50] The height of adults was calculated where possible from the total length of long bones using the formula of Trotter and Gleser as published by Brothwell.[51]

The amount of information which can be derived from a small number of skeletons and a mass of jumbled bones is limited, but the charnel, representing minimum numbers of 28 adults and 22 children (based on the number of skulls), can in some areas augment the more intact burials to provide information based on a larger sample. This group is important in being the only middle or late Saxon human material extant from Oxford, and thus provides the nucleus for information on the population of the area between the early Saxon and high medieval periods, for both of which larger samples are already available.

Table 2 shows the basic details of each identifiable individual; Table 3 presents the remainder of the skeletal material recovered as total numbers of fragments of each bone from adults and from children of different ages. Both men and women are represented, and while there is only one possible child's grave among the more intact burials, new-born babies and children of various ages are represented among the charnel, though their bones are not as numerous as those of adults. Table 4 shows the age at death, based on the skeletons and the maxillae and mandibles from the charnel. The gap in the 25–30 age group probably results from the smallness of the sample; otherwise the table shows a high mortality among children under 10 years, and also that a high proportion, about a quarter, survived beyond 40 years, and severe tooth wear in some individuals suggests an age considerably greater than this. Table 5 shows the state of dental health; generally this became worse with increasing age, though the number of carious teeth is proportionately greater in the 30–40 year age group, and dental health was generally remarkably good, particularly compared with the modern British population.

The incidence of normal variations in the skull is as follows: coronal wormian bones: 0 of 20 possible occurrences; parietal wormian bones: 1 of 20; lambdoid wormian bones: 5 of 17; inca bones: 1 of 19 (this is an asymmetric bipartite inca bone); open metopic suture: 2 cases of 20 possible. These frequencies are not unusual.

Some of the individual skeletons exhibit unusual variations and evidence of disease and injury. No. 2, a man of 40–45 years, has cervical vertebrae 2, 3 and 4 joined at the arch and body: this is probably an unusual developmental anomaly. No. 11, a man of the same age, has a very unusual spinal anomaly; the neural arches of the first three thoracic vertebrae have not completely joined so that there is a narrow gap: on the first two, the gap is on the right side; on the third, it is on the left side. The third and fourth vertebrae are joined by the arch. The gaps in the neural arches are narrow and the person is unlikely to have been aware of any abnormality. Spina bifida occulta of this sort is not uncommon in the sacrum, and the first and last vertebrae of the spinal column, but is rare in other parts of the spine. No. 2 also has a separate acromion process on the right scapula, and possibly on the left. This is probably a growth anomaly, and is unusual.

Several individuals have some degeneration in the spine; all were over 35 years of age: four women, Nos. 3, 7, 14 and 15, and one man, No. 4, had minor osteophytes mostly on the thoracic and lumbar vertebrae, and another man, No. 2, had small osteophytes on the bodies of nearly all the vertebrae, and also irregular hollows in the articular surfaces of the bodies of several thoracic vertebrae and the first lumbar vertebra. This man was an unfortunate individual: in addition to the above he had small areas of growth around the left femur head and a patch of eburnation and extra bone growth on the right first metatarsal and its first phalanx; he was also one of those who had a healed fracture of the lower arm, and this was unusual in that the broken ends of the ulna had not united, though the radius was not broken. No. 6, an adult of whom only the right arm survives, has a slight swelling towards the distal end of the ulna, possibly a healed fracture. This may be related to an area of eburnation on the distal end of the radius, where it articulates with the ulna. Among the redeposited material there is a left ulna from F96 which may have a healed fracture towards the distal end, and a right radius from F127 which quite clearly has a healed fracture just below the mid shaft, which mended at an angle; the ulna must have been broken.

[48] D. Ferembach, I. Schwidetzky and M. Stloukal, 'Recommendations for Age and Sex Diagnoses of Skeletons', *Jnl. Human Evolution*, ix (1980), 517–549.

[49] A.E.W. Miles. 'Assessment of the Ages of a Population of Anglo-Saxons from their Dentitions', *Proc. Royal Soc. Medicine*, lv (1962), 881–6.

[50] Ferembach et al., op. cit. note 48.

[51] D.R. Brothwell, *Digging up Bones* (1981).

TABLE 2: DETAILS OF INDIVIDUAL IDENTIFIABLE SKELETONS. Nos. 16, 17 and 18 are redeposited, No. 19 probably so.

| No. | Context | Bones present | Sex | Age | Height | Caries, abcess, loss in remaining teeth and tooth sockets | Other comments |
|---|---|---|---|---|---|---|---|
| 1 | F7 | Upper half. | M | 30–35 | | 00/22 00/25 00/25 | 4 lambdoid womian bones. Periostitis on R. clavicle. |
| 2 | F16 | Virtually complete. | M | 40–45 | 1.64 m | 04/22 07/31 01/32 | 2 lambdoid womian bones. Cervical vertebrae 2, 3 & 4 joined. Separate acromion process on scapula. Fracture of L ulna. L femur and R toe pathological. |
| 3 | F88 | Virtually complete. | F | 45+ | 1.67 m | 02/29 02/29 23/32 | Spondylosis on mid thoracic and lumbar vertebrae. |
| 4 | F96 | All except L arm, lower legs. | M | 35–45 | 1.72 m | 00/25 00/22 01/26 | Inca bone. Spondylosis on lower thoracic and lumbar vertebrae. |
| 5 | F115 | L leg, feet. | ? | 16–22 | | | |
| 6 | F117 | R arm. | ? | Adult | | | Fracture of R Ulna. R radius pathological. |
| 7 | F118 | Head, chest, upper arms. | ?F | 40–45 | | 01/32 00/32 00/32 | |
| 8 | F119 | Virtually complete. | F | 30–35 | 1.58 | 01/25 00/27 00/30 | |
| 9 | F120 | Lower legs. | ? | Adult | | | |
| 10 | F121 | Lower legs. | ?F | Adult | | | |
| 11 | F123 | Head, upper chest and arms. | M | 40–45 | | 02/30 03/32 00/32 | Thoracic vertebrae 1, 2 & 3 cleft arches. |
| 12 | F124 | Lower legs. | ? | Adult | | | |
| 13 | F125 | Lower L arm, legs. | ?F | Adult | 1.59 m | | |
| 14 | F127 | Virtually complete. | F | 35–40 | 1.66 m | 01/27 04/32 01/32 | ?R ulna fractured. |
| 15 | F144 | Lower jaw, body, arms. | F | 25+ | | 00/05 01/12 01/12 | Spondylosis on thoracic and lumbar vertebrae. |
| 16 | F118/127 | Parts. | ? | 3–4 | | | |
| 17 | F127 | Arms, thighs. | M | Adult | 1.69 m | | |
| 18 | F87 | Most post-cranial. | M | 25+ | 1.59 m | | |
| 19 | F95 | L arm and chest. | ? | c.2.5 | | | |
| 20 | F89 | Virtually complete. | ? | 18–23 | | 02/28 00/28 00/28 | Lumbar vertebrae 5 has cleft neural arch. R tibia pathological. |

TABLE 3: REDEPOSITED HUMAN SKELETAL MATERIAL. Numbers are given for fragments of each bone, except for skulls, for which the minimum number of skulls represented is given. Numbers of complete maxillae (detached from skulls) and mandibles are given in the centre of the columns. Other numbers in centre columns are not attributable to either right or left.

| Bone | ADULT | | | CHILD Age not known | | | 10–15 | | | 5–10 | | | 0–5 | | | 0 years | | |
|---|---|---|---|---|---|---|---|---|---|---|---|---|---|---|---|---|---|---|
| | R | | L | R | | L | R | | L | R | | L | R | | L | R | | L |
| Skull | | 28 | | | 18 | | | | | | 1 | | | 1 | | | 2 | |
| Maxilla | 3 | 4 | 1 | | | | | | | | | 1 | | | | | | |
| Mandible | 4 | 23 | 4 | | | | 2 | | | 5 | | 2 | 8 | | | | | |
| Vertebra | | 141 | | | 9 | | | | | | | | | | | | | |
| Clavicle | 17 | 3 | 23 | 3 | | 2 | | | | 1 | | | 2 | | | 1 | | |
| Scapula | 14 | 2 | 14 | 5 | | 6 | | | | | | | | | | | | 2 |
| Humerus | 32 | 10 | 38 | 3 | | 3 | | | 4 | 8 | | 6 | 5 | | 8 | 1 | | 2 |
| Radius | 27 | 9 | 20 | | | 4 | 1 | | | | 1 | 1 | 2 | | 1 | | | 1 |
| Ulna | 16 | 8 | 20 | 2 | 2 | 4 | 1 | | 1 | 1 | 1 | 1 | 6 | | 2 | 1 | | 3 |
| Metacarpal | | 85 | | | 2 | | 6 | | | | | | | | | | | |
| Pelvis | 31 | 1 | 36 | 12 | | | 11 | | 2 | | | | | | | | | |
| Femur | 37 | 30 | 50 | 5 | 8 | 5 | 1 | | 3 | 5 | 1 | 4 | 8 | 2 | 8 | 3 | 1 | 6 |
| Tibia | 44 | 12 | 46 | 2 | 4 | 2 | 2 | | 2 | 4 | | 3 | 6 | | 8 | 4 | | 3 |
| Fibula | 10 | 37 | 12 | 9 | | | | | | 1 | 1 | 1 | | 1 | | 1 | | |
| Astragalus | 12 | 1 | 6 | | | | | | | | | | | | | | | |
| Calcaneum | 21 | | 12 | | | 2 | | | | | | | | | | | | |
| Metatarsal | | 10 | | 10 | | | | | | | | | | | | | | |
| Phalanx | | 59 | | | | | | | | | | | | | | | | |

TABLE 4: AGE OF INDIVIDUALS AT DEATH, BASED ON WHOLE SKELETONS, AND REDEPOSITED MAXILLAE AND MANDIBLES (EXCLUDING MATERIAL FROM F87, F89 AND F95).

| Age in years: | 0–5 | 5–10 | 10–15 | 15–20 | 20–25 | 25–30 | 30–35 | 35–40 | 40+ | Adult |
|---|---|---|---|---|---|---|---|---|---|---|
| No. of individuals: | 10 | 7 | 2 | 2 | 5 | 0 | 4 | 15 | 21 | 13 |

TABLE 5: DENTAL HEALTH; SHOWING TOTAL NUMBERS OF CARIOUS TEETH IN TEETH FOUND, AND ABSCESSES AND TEETH LOST BEFORE DEATH IN TOOTH SOCKETS FOUND, ARRANGED BY AGE GROUP

| Age in years | No. of people and jaws | Caries | | Abscess | | Loss | |
|---|---|---|---|---|---|---|---|
| 20–30 | 4 | 00/17 | 0% | 00/51 | 0% | 00/52 | 0% |
| 30–40 | 19 | 23/187 | 12% | 09/276 | 3% | 03/284 | 1% |
| 40+ | 21 | 15/255 | 6% | 24/338 | 7% | 22/363 | 6% |

No. 1, a man of 30–35 years, has severe periostitis on the left clavicle; there are small areas on the right clavicle also, but none of the other bones is affected.

The late medieval or post-medieval burial, F89, was that of a young person between 18 and 20 years of age. The lowest lumbar vertebra has a cleft neural arch, and the shaft of the right tibia is swollen with a spongy appearance on the medial and lateral aspects of the shaft, though the posterior aspect is unaffected. There is no evidence to suggest why this person should have been buried in what at that time would appear to be an irregular place.

Some of the redeposited bones, besides those lower arm bones showing fractures already described, had some evidence of disease. A pair of clavicles from F7 have bony growth at the sternal end, with very rough and uneven articular surfaces, the right clavicle showing eburnation on both the sternal and scapular ends. A group of vertebrae from F119 consist of the lowest four thoracic and the first three lumbar vertebrae, of which the upper two and lower five are joined by a smooth-surfaced bony growth covering most of the bodies, and are joined also at the arches, so that the whole group has a slight inward curve. Two further lumbar vertebrae from an unstratified deposit are joined by a single large lump of extra bony growth on the right side. Part of a left femur from F54–5 has a growth on the greater trochanter, mostly on the lateral aspect, and a right femur from F96 has on the distal end an area of severe degeneration and eburnation on the patellar surface.

Minor spondylosis in the spine is normal with increasing age; further comments on abnormalities would depend on diagnosis from a pathologist, but the frequency of fractures of the lower arm is interesting and may be the result of brawling.


## THE ANIMAL BONES by SUE STALLIBRASS

The animal bones recovered are very well preserved and show few signs of mixing due to residuality. Although the assemblage is small, it provides an interesting span of material from early medieval to late post-medieval times.

The bones from all contexts were scanned for a quick listing of identified species. These are recorded in a table of frequency of occurrence (Table 6). In addition, all fragments from selected contexts were identified and recorded in Table 7. A context was selected either because it was a well-sealed pit and/or because it produced a comparably large group of animal bone fragments.

Table 6 shows that sheep/goat and cattle are the two most common species represented throughout the six phases of the excavated area. Sheep/goat always occur slightly more frequently than do cattle (78–100 per cent occurrence per phase, but 44–89 per cent for cattle). Within each context, sheep/goat fragments also appear to be more common than those of cattle, and this observation is supported by the more detailed figures recorded for the selected contexts (Table 7). The third most frequently occurring species in all phases is pig. However, pig is never the dominant species in a context, and its frequency of occurrence varies greatly between phases, probably due to the great ranges in sample sizes from different contexts. Bird bones are present in *c.* 24–50 per cent of contexts in all phases excepting Phases 1 and 2, in which they are sparse. Other identified species are: dog, cat, horse, fallow deer and red deer. These are always rare, even when present. Rabbit and fish are also occasionally present, but only in Phases 4, 5 and 6, the 16th–20th centuries. The bird and fish bones have not been identified to species but, amongst the bird bones, it was noticed that those from domestic fowl appear to be dominant. One of the fragments from L8 and L9 (Phase 4, 16th century) is very large and probably comes from a peacock or swan.

Almost all of the bones appear to be food refuse. There are almost no fragments from skulls nor bones from the foot. These are likely to have been removed during primary butchery at another location, and only the dressed carcasses brought to the site. One possible exception to this observation concerns Phases 2 and 3, from some contexts of which some sheep/goat metapodials and horncores were recovered. However, none of these was from large groups that could be compared with the selected contexts of Phases 3, 4 and 5. Butchery marks are common, both those incurred during jointing and those due to meat removal. In the selected contexts, 43 per cent of Phase 5 and 35 per cent of Phase 4 bones show cutmarks. Only 15 per cent of the Phase 3 bones studied show cutmarks, however, and this difference is probably significant since the Phase 3 bones also have a different level of chewing (Phase 3: 10 per cent; Phase 4: 4 per cent; Phase 5: 6 per cent) indicating different patterns of bone disposal.

It is interesting that animal bones were recovered from the fill of some graves of Phase 1, suggesting that these had been cut through earlier deposits containing domestic refuse.

The only bones that do not fit the interpretation of food refuse are horncores from sheep and goats. Most of these are particularly large (the sheep horncores appear to be from rams). Although these horncores are never particularly common, they do appear to occur more frequently than do the concomitant skull fragments, and it is possible that they were deposited at the site as a result of horn-working rather than food consumption. They occur only in contexts of Phases 2 and 3. Sheep horncores were recovered from L126, L138, L140 and L150 (Phase 2) and F21 (Phase 3b); goat horncores from F16 and L86 (Phase 2), L104 (Phase 3a) and L10

## TABLE 6: FREQUENCIES OF OCCURRENCE OF IDENTIFIED SPECIES OF ANIMAL BONE

| PHASE | DATE RANGE | contexts with ID ANIMAL BONE N | contexts with CATTLE N | % | contexts with SHEEP/GOAT N | % | contexts with PIG N | % | contexts with BIRD N | % | contexts with DOG N | % | contexts with CAT N | % | contexts with HORSE N | % | contexts with FALLOW DEER N | % | contexts with RED DEER N | % | contexts with RABBIT N | % | contexts with FISH N | % |
|---|---|---|---|---|---|---|---|---|---|---|---|---|---|---|---|---|---|---|---|---|---|---|---|---|---|
| 6 | 19th/20th C | 5 | 3 | 60 | 4 | 80 | 4 | 80 | 1 | 20 | | | | | | | | | | | 1 | 20 | 1 | 20 |
| 5 | 17th C | 8 | 5 | 63 | 7 | 88 | 2 | 25 | 2 | 25 | 1 | 13 | | | | | 2 | 25 | | | 1 | 13 | 1 | 13 |
| 4 | 16th C | 17 | 12 | 71 | 15 | 88 | 9 | 53 | 8 | 47 | | | | | | | 3 | 18 | | | 1 | 6 | 2 | 12 |
| 3b | late 14th – early 16th C | 9 | 8 | 89 | 9 | 100 | 6 | 67 | 5 | 56 | | | | | 2 | 22 | 2 | 22 | 1 | 11 | | | | |
| 3a | late 12th – late 13th C | 17 | 9 | 53 | 14 | 82 | 5 | 29 | 6 | 67 | 2 | 12 | 1 | 6 | 1 | 6 | 1 | 6 | 1 | 6 | | | | |
| 2 | first half of 12th C | 38 | 28 | 74 | 33 | 87 | 12 | 32 | 3 | 8 | | | 1 | 3 | 2 | 5 | | | 2 | 5 | | | | |
| 1 | pre-conquest | 9 | 4 | 44 | 7 | 78 | 3 | 33 | | | | | | | | | | | | | | | | |

CONTEXTS CONTAINING IDENTIFIED ANIMAL BONE:

PHASE 6: 1, 11, 12, 42, 45

PHASE 5: 3, 37, 41, 43, 47, 78, 80, 103

PHASE 4: 8, 9, 14, 15, 18, 20, 23, 27, 28, 29, 48, 49, 53, 64, 72, 75, 79

PHASE 3b: 10, 17, 21, 33, 35, 54/55, 58, 63, 89

PHASE 3a: 24, 25, 30, 32, 38, 69, 74, 87, 94, 104, 106, 108, 113, 116, 137, 145, 148

PHASE 2: 7, 16, 26, 36, 67, 70, 71, 81, 82, 86, 88, 92, 93, 97, 98, 100, 101, 102, 107, 111, 112, 126, 128, 129, 130, 131, 134, 135, 138, 140, 143, 146, 150, 153, 154, 156, 161

PHASE 1: 96, 115, 118, 119, 121, 123, 125, 127, 147

TABLE 7: DISTRIBUTION OF ANIMAL BONE FRAGMENTS IN SELECTED CONTEXTS FROM PHASES 3, 4 AND 5.

| PHASE | SHEEP/ GOAT | S/G SIZED | CATTLE | CATTLE SIZED | CALF | CALF SIZED | PIG | PIG SIZED | FALLOW DEER | RABBIT | CAT | HORSE | TOTAL |
|---|---|---|---|---|---|---|---|---|---|---|---|---|---|
| | N | N | N | N | N | N | N | N | N | N | N | N | N |
| **5** | **122** | **75** | **24** | **75** | **13** | **8** | **6** | **11** | **1** | **5** | **3** | | **343** |
| very young | 1 | | | | 13 | 8 | 1 | | | | | | 23 |
| cut | 44 | 43 | 10 | 34 | 5 | 3 | 2 | 7 | | | | | 148 |
| chewed | 10 | 2 | 4 | | 2 | | 1 | | | | | | 19 |
| **4** | **134** | **126** | **36** | **138** | **77** | **17** | **10** | **10** | **3** | **4** | | | **555** |
| very young | 4 | 4 | | | 77 | 17 | 4 | 3 | | | | | 109 |
| cut | 47 | 47 | 28 | 51 | 15 | 2 | 3 | 4 | | | | | 197 |
| chewed | 15 | | 1 | 1 | 4 | | | | | | | | 21 |
| **3** | **98** | **27** | **75** | **85** | **2** | | **18** | **5** | **1** | | | **2** | **313** |
| very young | 10 | 8 | 6 | 1 | 2 | | 1 | 1 | | | | | 5 |
| cut | 14 | 1 | 10 | 20 | 1 | | 1 | | | | | | 47 |
| chewed | | | | 5 | | | | | | | | | 31 |

KEY:    **PHASE 5**: context 78
           **PHASE 4**: contexts 8 & 9
           **PHASE 3**: contexts 58, 54/55, 35, 74

TABLE 8: SUMMARY STATISTICS FOR SHEEP/GOAT MEASUREMENTS
Measurements have been taken in accordance with A. von den Driesch, 'A Guide to the Measurement of Animal Bones from Archaeological Sites', *Peabody Museum Bulletin*, i (1976).
All measurements are in millimetres.

| SCAPULA | GLP | SLC | NECK HEIGHT | |
|---|---|---|---|---|
| Number | 17 | 22 | 21 | |
| MEAN | 32.0 | 18.8 | 19.5 | |
| SD | 2.55 | 4.15 | 1.87 | |
| Minimum | 28.6 | 16.2 | 16.1 | |
| Maximum | 39.3 | 23.8 | 23.6 | |
| HUMERUS | SD | BT | hght T | GLC |
| Number | 16 | 49 | 50 | 1 |
| MEAN | 14.6 | 27.7 | 18.0 | 145 |
| SD | 1.13 | 1.37 | 1.09 | |
| Minimum | 12.0 | 24.5 | 15.1 | |
| Maximum | 16.4 | 31.8 | 20.6 | |
| RADIUS | Bp | SD | Bd | GL |
| Number | 35 | 53 | 10 | 4 |
| MEAN | 30.2 | 17.4 | 27.9 | 141 |
| SD | 1.37 | 1.12 | 0.78 | 4.74 |
| Minimum | 26.8 | 15.4 | 27.1 | 135 |
| Maximum | 32.6 | 21.8 | 29.4 | 147 |
| TIBIA | SD | Bd | Dd | |
| Number | 24 | 37 | 36 | |
| MEAN | 14.0 | 25.2 | 19.3 | |
| SD | 3.15 | 4.55 | 3.53 | |
| Minimum | 11.7 | 22.9 | 17.6 | |
| Maximum | 17.2 | 30.1 | 23.2 | |

(Phase 3b). The presence of the goat horncores is particularly interesting since none of the postcranial bones from the site could be positively identified as definitely deriving from goats, whereas many of them could be identified as sheep.[52]

Throughout the phases, some of the sheep/goat and cattle bones conform to the slender-boned types common throughout Holocene Britain until the post-medieval period. However, there are also some massive cattle bones, and some wide sheep/goat bones in the later phases. Massive cattle bones were noted from L8 and L9 (Phase 4, 16th century), and L3 and F78 (Phase 5, 17th century). Large sheep/goat bones were also noted from L3 and F78. It is significant that none of the earlier phases produced any of these larger bones, which probably derive from early forms of 'improved' breeds. The newly re-founded college may have had access to these (then) comparatively new forms. Evidence of this kind is still comparatively uncommon on British sites, but there is a growing interest in this topic (see, especially, the work of P.L. Armitage). Standardised measurements using von den Driesch[53] were taken on the sheep/goat bones and the few cattle bones for which they were feasible. The detailed measurements and summary statistics for each phase are

[52] Identifications were aided by the use of W. Prummel and H-J. Frisch, 'A Guide for the Distinction of Species, Sex, and Body Size in Bones of Sheep and Goat', *Jnl. Archaeological Science*, xiii (1986), 567–77, and J. Boessneck, 'Osteological Differences between Sheep (*Ovis aries* Linne) and Goat (*Capra hircus* Linne)', in D. Brothwell and E. Higgs (ed.), *Science and Archaeology* (1969), 331–58.

[53] A. von den Driesch, 'A Guide to the Measurement of Animal Bones from Archaeological Sites', *Peabody Museum Bulletin*, i (1976).

given in tables kept with the site archive and will be made available upon request to the Oxford Archaeological Unit. Table 8 gives summarised data for the commonest sheep/goat measurements.

The ages of the animals tend to cluster around adolescence and young adulthood, when they would have been in prime condition for meat. Very few jaws or teeth were recovered, so estimates of age are based mainly on epiphyseal fusion states. The majority of the sheep/goat radii have their proximal epiphysis fused and their distal epiphysis unfused, indicating an age (in modern sheep) of between one and three years.[54] There is no indication of any pathology due to any disease, trauma nor ageing process on any of the bones in the total assemblage. Many of the pig bones come from very young animals (perinatal or just a few weeks old). The few pig jaws and teeth that were recovered indicate that the animals were young males (whether they were wild or domesticated cannot be ascertained). Similarly, a few of the sheep/goat bones come from neonatal lambs or kids, and most of the pelves that could be sexed appear to come from entire or castrated males. Calf bones were recovered from several contexts of Phases 4, 5 and 6. L8 and L9 (Phase 4) produced fragments from several jaws and skulls of calves, as well as a large number of post-cranial calf bones (many of which have butchery marks). The jaws come from calves that had been weaned (the teeth have light wear indicating that the animals had been eating vegetation rather than just suckling milk), but the wear is so slight and the eruption of the first and second molars is at such an early stage that it is unlikely that the calves were more than two or three to six months old when they died.[55]

In summary, the majority of the animal bones from the excavation almost certainly represent refuse from prime meat sources, mainly mutton and beef, with a little pork and chicken and occasional wild game. The graves of the earliest phase (Phase 1) appear to have cut through earlier refuse deposits and, in Phases 2 and 3, some manufacturing activity may be hinted at by the presence of sheep and goat horncores. However, the material from Phase 3 onwards indicates that, from the late 12th century until modern times, the people eating the beasts whose bones were deposited in the excavated area enjoyed a very high standard of meat consumption. Quantities cannot be guessed at, but the quality was certainly excellent. Succulent young animals (calves, piglets and lambs/kids) sometimes formed quite a considerable proportion of the diet represented. The presence of large bones from 'improved' breeds as early as the 16th century is yet another indicator of the privileged position held by these people. It is important to note that this evidence is for earlier improvement than is suggested in documentary sources, though the latter do not become informative until *after* the earliest late medieval breed improvements had taken place. The analysis has thus been able to show that the changes in types of livestock occurred nearly a century earlier than is usually assumed from written evidence, and (as shown by Armitage's work) is supported by material from sites in London.

## DISCUSSION AND INTERPRETATION

### *Phase 1: Pre-Conquest*

Sequences of up to four superimposed graves were excavated in the N.E. area of the site. Their density and regular layout, and the quantity of charnel from these and later contexts, suggests that the excavated area had been part of a more extensive cemetery in use for a considerable time. Burials found in Tom Quad in 1972 are presumably of the same cemetery.[56]

The activity of Phases 2 and 3 (below) dates the end of formal burial on the site to the mid 12th century, but no archaeological horizon was excavated which might provide a *terminus post quem* for the earliest graves, and so some indication of when the cemetery came into use. The only such evidence came from the Tom Quad burials, charcoal from one of which gave a radiocarbon date centering on the 9th century.[57] Bone samples from four stratigraphically-related inhumations (F96, F119, F123, F127), two of which (F96,

---

[54] Figures taken from I.A. Silver, 'The Ageing of Domestic Animals', in Brothwell and Higgs, op. cit. note 52, 250–68.

[55] Ibid.

[56] T.G. Hassall, 'Excavations in Oxford 1972: fifth interim report', *Oxoniensia*, xxxviii (1973), 270–2.

[57] Ibid.

TABLE 9: RADIOCARBON DATES FROM BURIALS AT CHRIST CHURCH

| Site | Context | HAR-Ref. | ¹⁴C Age | Calibrated Age(s) | | Calibrated Ranges | |
|---|---|---|---|---|---|---|---|
| | | | | | | one σ | one σ |
| OXCCL 1985 | F96 | 6817 | 1160±40bp | AD 886 | BP 1064 | AD 808–941 | AD 775–976 |
| OXCCL 1985 | F119 | 6818 | 1150±40bp | AD 889 | BP 1061 | AD 827–954 | AD 779–982 |
| OXCCL 1985 | F123 | 6819 | 1110±40bp | AD 900<br>AD 902<br>AD 953 | BP 1050<br>BP 1048<br>BP 997 | AD 888–980 | AD 827–1009 |
| Mean of HAR 6817–9 | | | 1140±25bp | AD 891 | BP 1059 | AD 884–940 | AD 820–972 |
| OXCCL 1985 | F127 | 6820 | 1250±40bp | AD 772 | BP 1178 | AD 685–790 | AD 668–884 |
| TOM QUAD 1972 | | none | 1110±100bp | AD 900<br>AD 902<br>AD 953 | BP 1050<br>BP 1048<br>BP 997 | AD 790–1020 | AD 680–1157 |

NOTE: The alternative calibrated ranges for OXCCL F123 and Tom Quad 1972 are generated by the radiocarbon calibration curve.

F123) bracketed the same stratigraphic sequence (Fig. 10), were therefore submitted to the low-level measurements laboratory at A.E.R.E. Harwell for radiocarbon dating. The results, and that from the Tom Quad grave, were calibrated by R.J. Otlet, using the University of Washington Quaternary Isotope Laboratory radiocarbon calibration programme 1987, and are presented in Table 9.[58] Three of the results, from F96, F119 and F123, accord with the observed stratigraphic relationships and are statistically indistinguishable, their weighted mean giving calibrated date-ranges for the sequence of burials of A.D. 884–940 at one σ and A.D. 820–972 at two σ. The fourth, however, from F127, gave a significantly earlier date which, at one σ, reverses the stratigraphic relationship between F127 and F96. There are no grounds for querying the observed stratigraphy, and so, although this result can be reconciled with the other calibrated ranges at two σ, the contradiction must otherwise remain unresolved.

Although from a small and fragmentary sample, these results confirm a pre-Conquest date for the cemetery, which was in use during the 9th, or, at latest, by the 10th century. F123, stratigraphically the latest burial to be radiocarbon dated, is unlikely to post-date the early 11th century at latest, and may be considerably earlier. This might suggest a hiatus in burial of up to 150 or 200 years before re-use in the first half of the 12th century, when there is unequivocal stratigraphic evidence for formal inhumation on the site (Phase 2, below). However, this may apply only to a small area. Equally, it is possible that other excavated graves are later than F123 and represent continuous burial until the final abandonment of burial on the site: the median radiocarbon determination for F123 is the same as that from the 1972 Tom Quad grave, also a charcoal burial, which is cut by later graves.[59]

The importance of the cemetery is twofold: it demonstrates the existence of a 9th- or 10th-century community, and it may imply the existence of a contemporary religious foundation. The later graves, if it is accepted that burial was continuous through the 11th century and into the 12th, must almost certainly have been associated with the pre-Conquest minster. In view of the tradition that a monastery was founded here for, or by, St. Frideswide in the later 7th century (below, p.225), it is disappointing that the radiocarbon date for F127 must be treated with caution.

F147 is unlikely to be earlier than the mid 11th century (above, p. 33), and although assigned to Phase 1 on stratigraphic grounds it could equally be attributed to Phase 2. The residual Romano-British and possibly early Saxon material is too sparse for any assessment of activity on the site before its use as a cemetery, although it should be noted that some of the Phase 1 burials appear to have been cut through earlier deposits containing domestic refuse (above, p. 56).

*Phase 2: First Half of the 12th Century* (Fig. 30)

Only 20 sherds were recovered from the backfill of F149/170, insufficient, in themselves, to date it securely. However, some 200 sherds were retrieved from the contexts which had accumulated, or been dumped, immediately over the backfill in gully F140, enough for chronological conclusions to be drawn with confidence from a sherd count by fabric type. 68 per cent of the sherds from these contexts were of local fabrics AC and Y, which

[58] M. Stuiver and G.W. Pearson, 'High-Precision Calibration of the Radiocarbon Timescale, A.D. 1500–500 B.C.', *Radiocarbon*, xxviii (1986), 805–38.

[59] Hassall, op. cit. note 56.

constitute respectively 48 per cent and 20 per cent of the assemblage. The relative proportion of these fabrics is chronologically significant.[60] Fabrics AC and Y constituted *c.* 60 per cent and *c.* 30 per cent respectively of the pottery from St. Aldates Phase 6b, dated to the first half of the 12th century,[61] but in assemblages from contexts dated to the second half of the century, such as St. Aldates Phase 7 and The Hamel Phase D2, fabric Y has replaced AC as the largest single group.[62] This suggests that the contexts immediately overlying the backfill of F149/170 accumulated during the first half of the 12th century, and the predominance of fabric AC suggests that the gully had been filled by the middle years of the century. F149/170 appears to have been open for only a short time before backfilling, and so a date in the first half of the 12th century also seems likely for its excavation; the small pottery assemblage from the backfill is consistent with this. The function of F149/170 is unclear. Two possibilities suggest themselves: that it was a gravel pit; or the excavation for the undercroft of a S. cloister range which was never built. Such a project might be attributed to the 1130s, being abandoned when royal permission allowed building further S. on the line of the city defences, but with any subsequent work being suspended as Oxford's defensive requirements became paramount during the civil war between Stephen and Matilda.[63] This theory is attractive, but it has to be stressed both that the full dimensions of the feature and its orientation are unknown, and that this alternative does not explain similar but slightly later adjacent substantial excavations, such as F145 (Phase 3, below), which are consequently interpreted as gravel pits. However, an excavation of this size is most plausibly associated with major building work in the immediate vicinity, and, given its apparent date, this seems most likely to have been rebuilding of the church, or construction of conventual buildings, after the site of the minster was confirmed to the Augustinian canons in *c.* 1122 (above, pp. 227–8).

Of the four graves overlying F149/170, which represent the final episode of formal burial on the site, only F88 can be closely dated: it is stratified within the fill of gully F140 and so must be assigned to the second quarter or middle years of the 12th century. It seems unlikely that the three cist burials (F7, F16, F122) are much later than F88; indeed, if the partial infilling and consolidation of gully F140 (L97–100, L101, L86) was to extend the area available for burial, this might imply that F88 is the latest of the four. In either case, abandonment of this area of the cemetery shortly after the mid 12th century at latest is argued. Supporting the head of the corpse with a stone at either side, as in F88, is a common feature of 10th- and 11th-century burial practice,[64] but is less common at this later date. Inhumation in mortared cists, however, can be paralleled at the 12th-century graveyard of All Saints church, Oxford.[65] Charnel from later medieval pits cut into the backfill of F149/170 suggests that they destroyed other graves of this phase, and some of the burials at the N.E. of the site, in particular the possible cist burial F144, may also be this late.

Very little is known about the earliest Priory buildings, which were damaged by fire in 1190 (below, pp. 134–5, 240–2). However, it is clear that neither the cloister, nor any

[60] M. Mellor, 'Pottery', in Palmer, op. cit. note 10.

[61] Durham, op. cit. note 9, Fig. 14.

[62] Ibid., Palmer, op. cit. note 10, Figs. 7 & 8.

[63] I am grateful to Brian Durham for this suggestion. See T.G. Hassall, 'City Walls, Gates and Posterns', *V.C.H. Oxon.* iv, 301.

[64] W. Rodwell, *The Archaeology of the English Church* (1981), 158; W. Rodwell and K. Rodwell, 'St. Peter's Church, Barton-upon-Humber: Excavation and Structural Study, 1978–81', *Antiquaries Jnl.* lxii (1982), 301–2.

[65] Durham, op. cit. note 8. [And see below, p. 89, for another cist-burial at St. Frideswide's cut by the late 12th-century choir.]

Fig. 30.   Excavated 12th-century features along the E. side of the cloister. The deep feature in the centre is
the partially-excavated F149/170.

associated buildings S. of the church, including the chapter-house, could have been built on their present site while the pit F149/170, or the subsequent gully F140, remained open. While there is no conclusive archaeological reason why the backfilling of gully F140 and the subsequent burials should not be dated nearer to 1125 than 1150, the evidence for several episodes of activity post-dating the presumed *terminus post quem* of 1122, including, apparently, an attempt to consolidate the edges of the gully, argues that none of the claustral buildings was begun much before the middle of the century at the earliest; and, given that the surviving W. wall and doorway of the original chapter-house are of the 1140s or 1150s (below, p. 116–21, 160–7), and that there is archaeological evidence to suggest that the cloister itself was not completed until well into the second half of the century (Phase 3, below), a later rather than earlier date seems likely.[66] In the interim, a claustral layout elsewhere belonging to the minster church may have remained in use.

It seems to have been the building work, rather than the conversion to an Augustinian priory, which forced the eventual abandonment of this part of the minster cemetery, which elsewhere presumably continued to serve the parish of St. Frideswide through the 12th and 13th centuries.[67] The quarrying of the minster cemetery is difficult to explain, and may strengthen the suggestion that this part of the cemetery was temporarily disused. The prompt backfilling suggests the undesirability of an open quarry here; however, the gully which remained was left open and used for refuse disposal before it was partially consolidated and used for burial. The layers of gravelly loam which sealed the fill of F88 (L71, L67), are interpreted as deliberate infilling to level the site, perhaps preparatory to building, with which pits F70 and F92 may have been associated.

### Phase 3: Second Half of the 12th Century – Early 16th Century

This encompasses the time when the excavated area was part of the Priory cloister garth. Most features of this phase fall into two distinct periods. However, others cannot be closely dated (see above) and may be associated with any, or none, of the episodes attributed to sub-phases 3A and 3B.

### Sub-Phase 3A: Second Half of the 12th Century – Mid 13th Century

The four shallow pits containing redeposited human skeletal remains (F113–4, F116, F141), in one of which (F116) was the possible infant burial F95, formed a distinct horizon cut into the upper fills of the latest graves at the N.E. of the site, but were not cut by subsequent graves, arguing that they post-date abandonment of formal burial on the site. They were cut by pit F74, dated to the first half or middle of the 13th century. F145, a substantial feature excavated and backfilled towards the end of the 12th century, is interpreted as a gravel pit. This also seems a plausible explanation for F32, dated to

---

[66] This may seem a long delay, but it is not unparalleled. For instance, at another Augustinian house, Haughmond Abbey in Shropshire, the cloister was not attended to until some thirty years after a general rebuilding began *c.* 1170. See W.J. Blair, P. Lankester and J. West. 'A Transitional Cloister Arcade at Haughmond Abbey, Shropshire', *Med. Arch.* xxiv (1980), 210–11. John Blair has also pointed out to me that the present cloister at Christ Church seems to be contained within a southward extension of the town defences created for this purpose, and that the settled years after 1154 provide a plausible context for the deflection of a town wall in the interests of a religious house (see below, pp. 236–7).

[67] *V.C.H. Oxon.* iv, 381.

the late 12th or 13th century, and F74, both cut into the natural gravel and, like F145, containing less material than might be expected if they had been dug for refuse disposal.

Gravel digging at this time was presumably prompted by the extensive rebuilding which followed the fire of 1190.[68] Work on the church had begun by 1194,[69] and the chapter-house was rebuilt in the first half of the 13th century;[70] and it seems likely that such an extensive reconstruction also involved work on the cloister. The lower layers overlying F32 (L24–5, L30) contain pottery of the mid 13th century, and were perhaps dumped to raise or level the garth after the completion of building work.

F145 is very close to the cloister arcade, and almost certainly extends beneath it. This suggests either that the cloister had not been completed by the time of its excavation, or that for some other reason – severe damage, or demolition before rebuilding, for instance – it was no obstacle to gravel extraction here. It is interesting that there are no deep features at the N.E. of the site; presumably gravel digging here would have posed too great a threat to the standing remains of the church and chapter-house, and to any completed, or surviving, sections of the cloister.

*Sub-Phase 3B: Late 14th Century – Early 16th Century*

The later medieval pits were all cut into the fills of earlier features, and were all in the centre of the garth, presumably so as not to undermine the buildings of the cloister. Their purpose is obscure: they *may* have been refuse pits, although this seems inappropriate to the garth, but they contained relatively little pottery and bone; the lower fills of F35, the only one to be substantially excavated, which was bottomed at over 2 m. below the modern ground level, were virtually sterile. It is possible that some were abortive attempts to dig gravel, undertaken without knowledge of the extent of previous quarrying. The latest features contained pottery of the late 15th or early 16th century, and so a context for such activity might be sought in building work of the late 15th century, when a Prior's lodging was added to the S. of the dorter-range and the cloister rebuilt.[71] The latter had been completed by 1499.[72] The layer of gravelly loam (L10, L58) which seals the fill of earlier features was presumably dumped to raise or level the garth after rebuilding of the cloister had been completed. Its level, relative to the surviving surface of the natural gravel, suggests that subsidence due to the settling of pit fills may have been a problem, and perhaps underlay the need to rebuild the cloister.

It is difficult to account for inhumation F89. Residual pottery gives it a *terminus post quem* in the late 13th century at the earliest, but lace-ends from the fill, which are otherwise known only from contexts contemporary with or later than L58, indicate a date in the late 15th or early 16th century. There is no other indication that the garth may have been used for regular burial at this date.

---

[68] Ibid., 364–5.
[69] Ibid. cf. below, p. 134.
[70] *R.C.H.M. Oxford*, 29, 46.
[71] Ibid., 29, 46–7. cf. below, pp. 188–91.
[72] Ibid., 46; M.E.C. Walcott, 'The Bishops of Chichester from Stigand to Sherborne', *Sussex Archaeological Collections*, xxix (1879) 25, and cf. below, pp. 97–8.

*Phase 4: 16th Century (Fig. 31)*

The foundation was of rough mortar-and rubble masonry. Its depth, where established, varied from as little as *c.* 0.3 m. where it was bedded directly on undisturbed natural gravel to *c.* 1.7 m. where it cut into the medieval pit fills.[73] It was nowhere wider than *c.* 1 m. at the highest level to which it survived, and sloped inwards below this. This tapering, and the nature of the construction trench, which where detected was discernible only as a shallow and usually narrow disturbance, indicates that the foundation was trench-built. It was *c.* 13 m. across the buttresses, which protruded 2.5–3.0 m. beyond the line of the walls. The N.–S. walls were slightly closer together than the E.–W., forming a rectangular interior *c.* 5.7 by 4.5 m.

Fig. 31. The 16th-century stone footing revealed in Trenches One and Two.

[73] Where the northern E.–W. wall of the foundation ran under the paved area of the garth the natural gravel was very close to the modern ground surface, and the foundation was little more than a shallow spread of mortar on the surface of the gravel.

There is no known record of either the erection or the demolition of the building to which this foundation belonged. It cannot have been constructed before the late 15th century, as mouldings of this date were re-used in its fabric. These probably came from demolished Priory buildings: the foundation is aligned on the E. range of Tom Quad rather than the Priory cloister, and so almost certainly post-dates 1525, when the W. end of the Priory church and the W. cloister range were demolished, and work began on the buildings of Wolsey's college.[74] Fragments of Rhenish stoneware from the internal floor levels confirm that these accumulated after *c.* 1500; construction in the second quarter of the 16th century therefore seems likely. The post-holes and shallow features sealed by the internal floor levels (L48–50, F28, F171) were most probably associated with erecting the superstructure. This was presumably dismantled before the interior was filled in, but the condition of the internal surfaces suggested little or no time-lapse between the two events, indicating that demolition and backfilling should be treated as a single episode. Pottery and small-finds from the dump layer are compatible with deposition in the middle years or second half of the 16th century, but a demolition date after 1577 seems unlikely as no reference to this has been identified in the disbursement books, which survive for 1548 and in an unbroken sequence for the years 1577–1617.[75] The fragments from St. Frideswide's shrine give a *terminus post quem* for the backfilling of 1538, the traditional date of its destruction,[76] but whether this can also be considered a *terminus ad quem* for demolition and infilling is another matter. The decorated floor tile and other masonry almost certainly comes from the Priory church, but the presence of 16th-century green- and yellow-glazed domestic floor tiles may argue against the backfill deriving from any single episode of demolition or building; the shrine fragments may therefore have come from a builder's dump which also included material from subsequent work. It is argued below that the most plausible *recorded* context for demolition of the building is refurbishment of the church in 1545–6, when the See of Oxford was transferred from Oseney to St. Frideswide's.

The foundation is too flimsy and irregular for a stone building. It is certainly not the base of a stone bell-tower, and is most unlikely to be part of the original plan for Wolsey's college: the foundations of Wolsey's work in Tom Quad, where investigated by Sturdy, are at least 3 m. deep and *c.* 3 m. wide. Most probably it was the footing of a timber-framed building, supporting sill-beams above the level to which it had been reduced. The superstructure must have been substantial. The length of the buttresses implies heavy external bracing of the corner posts and considerable height, and the depth of the footing is also surprising even in relatively unstable pit fills: 16th-century house footings cut into similar material at 79–80 St. Aldates, although of similar width, were no more than 0.7 m. deep.[77]

The function of such a substantial timber-framed building is unclear, and its location in the garth puzzling. Perhaps it is most plausibly interpreted as a timber belfry, the sunken interior being the floor of the ringing chamber. The basic structural elements suggested by the footing are very similar to those of the 15th- and 16th-century timber belfries of Essex and Worcestershire churches. At their simplest these are turrets which appear integral with the church roof when viewed from the outside, but which in fact stand on corner posts, joined with tie-beams, braces and framing, which are visible inside the building. Where set up outside the church, abutting the W. wall of the nave,

[74] *R.C.H.M. Oxford*, 29; *V.C.H. Oxon.* iii, 228–30.
[75] W.G. Hiscock, *A Christ Church Miscellany* (1946), x–xi.
[76] *V.C.H. Oxon.* iii, 235.
[77] Durham, op. cit. note 9, 92, 99.

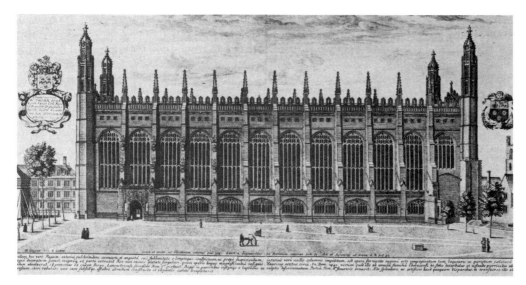

Fig. 32. David Loggan's 1690 engraving of King's College Chapel, Cambridge, showing (extreme left) the timber belfry.

the belfry in effect forms a W. tower, but is in fact free-standing.[78] In many such cases, as at the churches of St. Lawrence, Blackmore,[79] St. Margaret, Margaretting,[80] St. Thomas, Navestock,[81] and All Saints, Stock,[82] all in Essex, and at St. Peter's, Pirton, Worcestershire,[83] the belfry is surrounded by lower aisles or an ambulatory, the framing of which supports and buttresses the main structure. At Christ Church the evidence suggests external buttressing, and there is no trace of aisles or ambulatory, but these are superficial differences: these lower stages are in effect simply framing external to the main structure which has been roofed and walled. There is a great similarity between the plan of the Christ Church footing and the sill-beams of the Blackmore belfry, which also appear to rest on rough stone foundations. The main structure at Blackmore (dated to the late 15th century), which is supported on four substantially-braced corner-posts with a single less substantial intermediate post on the N. and S. sides,[84] gives an idea of how a belfry erected on the Christ Church footing might have been framed. However, still more striking is comparison with the 15th-century timber belfry which survived at King's College, Cambridge, until the 18th century.[85] This is shown on the extreme left

[78] *R.C.H.M. Essex* iv (1924), xxxiv; N. Pevsner, *The Buildings of England: Essex* (1954), 28; C.A. Hewett, 'The Timber Belfries of Essex: their Significance for the Development of English Carpentry', *Archaeological Jnl.* cxix (1962), 225–44.

[79] *R.C.H.M. Essex* ii (1920), 11–15; Pevsner, op. cit. note 78, 76–7, Pl. 23; Hewett, op. cit. note 78, 233.

[80] *R.C.H.M. Essex* ii, 183–5; Pevsner, op. cit. note 78, 268–9; Hewett, op. cit. note 78, 232–3.

[81] *R.C.H.M. Essex* ii, 190–1; Pevsner, op. cit. note 78, 276; Hewett, op. cit. note 78, 227–9.

[82] *R.C.H.M. Essex* iv, 155–6; Pevsner, op. cit. note 78, 372–3; Hewett, op. cit. note 78, 230–2.

[83] N. Pevsner, *The Buildings of England: Worcestershire* (1968), 244; *V.C.H. Worcs.* iv (1924), 182–4.

[84] *R.C.H.M. Essex,* ii, 11–15; Hewett, op. cit. note 78, 233–5, Pl. 34.

[85] R. Willis and J.W. Clark, *The Architectural History of the University of Cambridge* i (1886); J.W. Clark, 'History of the Peal of Bells belonging to the King's College, Cambridge', *Cambridge Antiquarian Society Communications,* iv (1878–9), 233–44; J. Saltmarsh, 'King's College', *V.C.H. Cambs.* iii (1959), 388 n. 56.

of Loggan's 1690 engraving of King's College chapel from the S. (Fig. 32),[86] and also appears on three 16th-century maps of Cambridge – by Richard Lyne (1574), George Braun (1575) and John Hamond (1592)[87] – which clearly show a two-stage building with a pyramidal roof and, at the first stage, heavy external bracing of the corner-posts pitched at about 45 degrees. The foundation, plotted as a parch-mark in the lawn in 1955,[88] is very similar in plan and dimensions to the footing at Christ Church. The main difference is the presence at King's of a third buttress foundation midway along each wall, but these appear to be late 16th-century additions to the structure: they are shown on Hamond's map of 1592, but not on those by Lyne or Braun. Loggan's engraving shows further alterations: the middle buttresses have been removed and a second post, pitched at a steeper angle, has been added at each corner, bracing the upper stage; also, a stage of louvred walling just below the roof has replaced the window-like openings shown in earlier depictions. Loggan's engraving suggests that the King's belfry was c. 45 ft. high. The similarity in ground-plan dimensions may suggest a very similar height for the Christ Church belfry, although it may have been taller if it was intended that the bell should be heard far over the surrounding buildings. The conjectural reconstruction offered in Fig. 33 is based on these sources.

The building accounts of Wolsey's College contain references to work which might help to explain this structure (and see Martin Biddle's discussion below, pp. 205–10). Four enigmatic entries in the accounts for 1528–9 record payments 'for carriage of earth and rubbell from the fayre gate and the newe stepull', 'for makinge scaffolds for the takinge downe of the old stepull', 'for two crowes for the carpenters to take downe the bells with', and, to William Hobbs and Richard Cooper, 'for bringinge in of the bell frame in their drinkinge time'.[89] Unfortunately these accounts were incomplete, and are now lost, so neither the exact nature of the work nor the sequence of events referred to is known. The 'old stepull', however, is almost certainly that of the Priory church: taken together, the payments suggest that the bells of St. Frideswide's were being taken down, or that it was intended that they should be taken down, prior to re-housing in the projected 'new stepull' of Wolsey's College.[90] But on Wolsey's attainder and death in the autumn of 1529 the College, with all its revenues and effects, reverted to the King and building work stopped.[91] Henry VIII may at one stage have intended to demolish Wolsey's buildings, but the College continued to function, and was formally re-founded by the King in 1532.[92] In 1545, upon translation of the See of Oxford from Oseney to St. Frideswide's, the College was again surrendered to the King, to be re-established as the Cathedral and Academic College of Christ Church by Letters Patent of 4 November 1546.[93] The Oseney bells, including Great Tom, were transferred to St. Frideswide's in

[86] D. Loggan, ed. J.W. Clark, *Cantabrigia Illustrata* (1905), Pl. 10.

[87] J.W. Clark and A. Gray, *Old Plans of Cambridge, 1574–1798* (1921); G.R. Versey, 'Some early Maps of the City and of the County of Cambridge', *Bulletin of the Society of University Cartographers*, vi(i) (1971), 12–16.

[88] *R.C.H.M. City of Cambridge*, i (1959), plan opp. 102.

[89] J. Gutch, *Collectanea Curiosa* (1789), 205–6.

[90] That the footing in the garth was the foundation of the 'new stepull', as suggested in *R.C.H.M. Oxford*, 29, and by *V.C.H. Oxon.* iii, 231, now seems unlikely. The coupling of the 'fayre gate' with the 'new stepull' in the account may suggest that both were on the same site, and that Wolsey intended a bell tower to rise above the main entrance to his college: *cf.* the contemporary detached bell tower at Evesham Abbey, *V.C.H. Worcs.* ii, 390–1; Pevsner, op. cit. note 83, 145, Pl. 39. However, Martin Biddle argues forcefully that Wolsey's 'new stepull' was either the tower E. of the hall, or was to be built on another site now unknown (below, p. 207).

[91] J. Ingram, *Memorials of Oxford*, i (1837), 43; *V.C.H. Oxon.* iii, 231.

[92] *V.C.H. Oxon.* iii, 232.

[93] Ibid.

Fig. 33. Conjectural reconstruction of the timber belfry from the W.

1545,[94] and surviving accounts indicate that considerable work was required in the bell-loft of St. Frideswide's before they could be hung.[95] This suggests that the bell-loft had been wholly or partially dismantled in 1528–9, but it is also possible that this work was necessary in order to accommodate the Oseney ring alongside some or all of the original bells. As Martin Biddle points out (below, p. 209), there is no direct evidence that any of the original bells were actually taken down from the steeple of the Priory church in 1528–9; the fate of the original St. Frideswide's bells is obscure. The Oseney ring was famous for its quality,[96] and this presumably prompted the decision to transfer it to the new Cathedral.

[94] Ibid., Hiscock, op. cit. note 75, 143–51; J. Cooper, 'Oseney Abbey', *V.C.H. Oxon.* iv, 365.
[95] W.H. Turner (ed.), *Selections from the Records of the City of Oxford*, ii (1880), 182–4.
[96] Wood, *City*, ii (1890), 220–1.

These events suggest a possible explanation for a timber belfry: that it was erected in 1528–9 to house the St. Frideswide's bells pending their installation in the new steeple. It *may* never have housed the bells; if it did, it is plausible that it remained in use as a *campanile* for the College after work on Wolsey's buildings stopped: it may in fact be the bell-tower referred to in an account book of 1530, which records payments to one William Bassett, bellringer, for work apparently of installation, and repair or unkeep, of bells.[97] Similar circumstances explain the belfry at King's College, Cambridge, which was intended to house the bells presented by Henry VI until they could be hung in the great bell-tower originally envisaged but never built.[98] In much the same way the more modest timber bell-house at St. Mary's church, East Bergholt, Suffolk, was built when the projected stone tower of the church was left unfinished *c.* 1525.[99] It seems unlikely that the similarity between the belfry at King's and that suggested by the footing at Christ Church is coincidental. Their occurrence in such similar contexts is also suggestive. There must be a strong possibility that the belfry at King's served as a model for that at Christ Church.[100]

A temporary belfry would have been redundant after installation of the Oseney ring, and so work in and around the new Cathedral in 1545–6 would provide a plausible context for its demolition and infilling.[101] Unfortunately, the archaeological evidence is not sufficiently sensitive to confirm this date decisively and it is possible, though perhaps unlikely, that the campanile remained standing into the third quarter of the 16th century. However, it had almost certainly been demolished by 1577; there is no mention of it in the Disbursement Books for this or any subsequent year, and it does not appear on Agas's 1578 map of Oxford.[102]

*Phase 5: 17th Century*

Pit F78 was filled with builder's debris. Pottery indicates deposition in the second quarter of the 17th century, when a considerable amount of rebuilding work was undertaken in or near the cloister. Brian Duppa (Dean 1629–38) initiated a remodelling of the Cathedral interior which involved demolition of several funerary monuments to make way for new stalls in the choir, replacement of much of the medieval glass, and re-paving of the nave, choir and aisles.[103] Samuel Fell, as Treasurer (1611–38) and Dean (1638–48), completed Duppa's work in the Cathedral and built the vaulted roof of the great staircase.[104]

[97] J.S. Brewer (ed.), *Letters and Papers, Foreign and Domestic, of the Reign of Henry VIII*, iv(iii) (1876), 3064.

[98] Willis and Clark, op. cit. note 85; Clark, op. cit. note 85; Saltmarsh, op. cit. note 85.

[99] T.H. Bryant, *County Churches: Suffolk*, ii (1912), 183–5; N. Pevsner, *The Buildings of England: Suffolk* (2nd edn. 1974), 195–6; H.M. Cautley, *Suffolk Churches and their Treasures* (4th edn. 1975), 58, 224.

[100] There is also an intriguing connection between Christ Church and Blackmore. The parish church of St. Lawrence was originally the church of Blackmore Priory, during which time the belfry was erected. The priory was suppressed by Wolsey in 1525, and its land and revenues granted to his college at Oxford the following year. See R.C. Fowler, 'Priory of Blackmore', *V.C.H. Essex*, ii (1907), 146–8.

[101] The surviving accounts for this work record a payment to 'John Wesburne, carpenter, and his iij servants', for 'vj daies abowt the clok howse' separate from his work of installing the bell-frame and bells in 'Friswides steple'. The 1530 payments to William Bassett for work about the bell tower included 20*d* 'pro capistro magnae campanae et horologii', and it is tempting to conclude that the bell tower mentioned in the 1530 accounts and the 'clok howse' mentioned in those of 1546 are the same structure. See Turner, op. cit. note 95, 183; Brewer, loc. cit. note 97.

[102] *Old Plans of Oxford* (O.H.S. xxxviii, 1884), sheet 4.

[103] A. Wood, ed. J. Gutch, *The History and Antiquities of the Colleges and Halls in the University of Oxford*, iii (1786), 462–3; *R.C.H.M. Oxford*, 37; J. Cooper, 'Christ Church Cathedral', *V.C.H. Oxon.* iv, 369–70.

[104] *R.C.H.M. Oxford*, 29; *V.C.H. Oxon.* iii, 232; below, pp. 215–17.

Only a little pottery was recovered from L47 but it included, in addition to sherds of the 16th century and earlier, material which could not have been deposited before *c.* 1650, including the clay pipe bowl of *c.* 1650–90, indicating that the 16th-century surface of the garth, and consequently the footing, remained exposed into the second half of the 17th century. Pottery from the mortar spread L43 shows that it was deposited after the middle of the century, perhaps during repair work in the cloister *c.* 1660.[105] Pit F57 contained no dating evidence.

At some time during the second half of the 17th century the surface of the garth was raised with a layer of gravelly loam (L3, L41) which originally buried the footing but which now survives only to the level to which it was reduced in 1871. The few fragments of later ceramics from this layer may be considered intrusive, deriving either from Gilbert Scott's work or from subsequent disturbances.

An engraving in Ingram's *Memorials of Oxford* records the N.E. quadrant of the cloister as it remained until 1871.[106] It shows, in addition to the high level of the garth, a path laid to give direct access from the hall to the chapter-house *via* a door inserted in the eastern arcade, from which the window tracery has been removed. Thompson attributed this arrangement to Brian Duppa,[107] but it is now clear that the garth was raised many years after his time as Dean, most probably under John Fell (Dean 1660–86) or one of his successors. However, Duppa does appear to have instituted some work in the cloister alley,[108] and, as it is impossible to determine archaeologically the date at which the tracery was removed and the door constructed, it remains possible, in principle, that he was responsible for one or both of these alterations.

ACKNOWLEDGEMENTS

The excavation was carried out under the auspices of the Oxford Archaeological Unit. Excavation and post-excavation were funded by Christ Church, and the governing body's generosity is gratefully acknowledged; especial thanks are also due to the Treasurer, Mr. J.K. Batey, and the Clerk of Works, Mr. R. Branch, for their whole-hearted and sympathetic co-operation during excavation. In addition to specialist contributors to the report, many individuals have been generous with advice and discussion; my thanks to them all, especially Dr. C. Currie, for advice on timber belfries, and Mrs. Mavis Batey, whose freely-shared knowledge and enthusiastic support have been invaluable. Thanks also to Mrs. E. Beard, who prepared plans, sections and drawings for publication, and last, but by no means least, to Judith Affleck, Bob Bailey, Hugh Cameron, Niall Donald, Sally Jones and Gerry Wait, who were as capable and enthusiastic a team of excavators as one could hope for.

---

[105] W.D. Caroe, *Wren and Tom Tower* (1923), 5, 7.

[106] Ingram, op. cit. note 91.

[107] Thompson, op. cit. note 1, 239–40.

[108] Wood, op. cit. note 103, 369, records that the cloister was 'new paved' at about the same time as the cathedral, and this almost certainly refers to re-paving of the alley rather than work in the garth: it is hard to accept that any of the 'monumental stones' removed as part of the old pavement could have come from the garth, which by this time had been greatly disturbed, and which had not been used for regular burial since the 12th century; burial in the cloister alley, on the other hand, was common monastic practice.

# Excavations in the Latin Chapel and outside the east end of Oxford Cathedral, 1962/3

by DAVID STURDY

With a contribution by NIALL DONALD

SUMMARY

*Excavations in and outside the N.E. chapels of the Cathedral revealed stages in the development of this part of the building. No evidence was found for Anglo-Saxon structures. A few graves (mainly with stone linings) were cut by the late 12th-century footings. The N. and E. walls of the late 12th-century 'pre-Latin' Chapel, and the N. wall of the early 13th-century Lady Chapel, were located. These and subsequent developments of the N.E. chapels, including the existing mid 14th-century Latin Chapel, were probably associated with St. Frideswide's shrine. The excavation also defined later phases in the development of the Latin Chapel, including the lowering of the floor and installation of wall-benches. Some time later the floor was raised again. Many decorated tiles from successive medieval floors were found, enough from the floor of c.1500 remaining in situ to permit a partial reconstruction of its pattern.*

INTRODUCTION

In 1963 the old floor of the Latin Chapel (Fig. 34), of red tiles and bricks set in mortar with some stone and marble slabs, was replaced by a stone floor laid on concrete. The new floor was designed by Mr. S.E. Dykes Bower as adviser for a larger scheme, initiated by the then Dean, the Very Revd. C.A. Simpson, to 'clean up' the Cathedral. Unable to avert the destruction of the old floor, in fact a much-altered and badly-worn medieval tile floor unrecognised by any previous scholar, we recorded it in detail and then excavated beneath it. Unfortunately the medieval stalls were not studied or recorded during removal. Generally presumed to have been the main choir-stalls, ejected to the Latin Chapel in the early 17th century, they were replaced after over-restoration. Volunteers from the Ashmole Club, the Oxford University Archaeological Society and elsewhere excavated Cuttings 1–3 within the chapel throughout the winter of 1963.[1] The Department of Antiquities, Ashmolean Museum, lent tools and equipment, and the writer paid all expenses of the work.

Stained glass fragments found in the Latin Chapel are reported on below by Niall Donald (pp. 100–2), and floor-tiles by Julia Green (pp. 103–14); the worked stone is described together with the material found in the cloister (above, pp. 48–52). The pottery and small-finds are stored in the Ashmolean Museum; no report on them is included. A report by Mary Harman on the skeletal remains (which were re-buried in the Cathedral Garden in 1989) is deposited, with the site records, at the County Museum, Woodstock.

---

[1] *Oxoniensia*, xxviii (1963), 91.

Fig. 34.    Latin Chapel, looking S.W. towards Nowers monument, before removal of tile floor.

## FLOOR-LEVELS, DEPTHS, LAYERS AND STRUCTURES

The general floor-level of the transepts and nave of the cathedral has remained, to judge from the column-bases, unchanged since the 12th century, during several relayings of the floor-slabs and many minor alterations. All depths noted below are from this level, which formerly extended across the E. aisle of the N. transept. The present floor of the Latin Chapel, like its predecessor, the late-medieval tiled floor destroyed in 1963, lies 15 cm. *below* this general level. An earlier floor of hard mortar, dating from about the mid 14th century, was found over much of the chapel 52–55 cm. below the general level. The laying of this floor involved the removal of over 50 tons of well-built rubble-foundation and other material. A similar, but less drastic, lowering of levels has also affected the three eastern bays of the Lady Chapel and N. choir aisle. The bases indicate that the floors here were about 23 cm. higher than at present before the 15th, or perhaps the 17th, century. There was probably a similar step-up of 23 cm. between the W. bay of the small two-bay precursor of the Latin Chapel, which was also part of the transept aisle, and its E. bay. The bases here were largely renewed in the 19th century, and cannot be entirely relied on to confirm this. If this step-up was indeed present in the 12th-century form of the chapel, the original floor of the second bay from the W. was 38 cm. higher than today. In the mid 14th-century lowering of the chapel floor, the level was brought down to 70 cm. below the 12th-century floor.

A widespread lowering of levels is in fact well-attested elsewhere in the area: in the S. choir aisle; in the cloisters and probably within the chapter-house (below, pp. 240–2); in

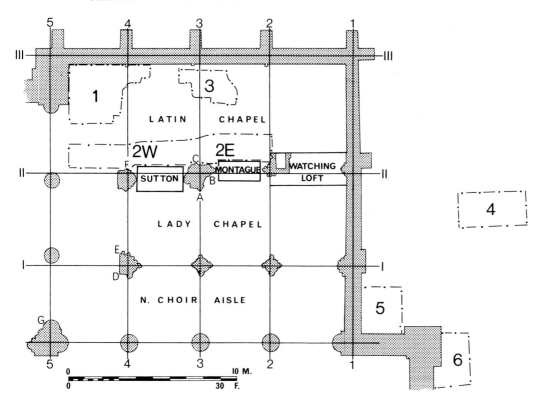

Fig. 35. The N.E. chapels, showing the locations of the 1962–3 trenches and the pier numbering system used in this and other papers.

Tom Quad to the W. of the cathedral, lowered by almost a metre in the 1660s[2] with the removal of well over 500 tons of soil and debris; in the gateway of Tom Tower, where the Tudor gates themselves have extra sections spliced on at the bottom; and even in the roadway of St. Aldate's outside, as can be seen from the plinth- and footing-lines of Wolsey's Almshouses, now the Master's Lodgings of Pembroke College. In this southern fringe of the town, large quantities of soil and rubble could readily be shovelled up, carted off and dumped on nearby meadowland. Indeed, the meadows' vulnerability to flood may sometimes have encouraged such dumping.

Layers and soil-deposits are numbered, structural features lettered. The excavation was measured in feet and inches, here converted into metric. The different cuttings are expressed in bold type (e.g. **6**), the various structures as A to K and layers as 1 to 12. Piers are referred to by the numbering system shown on Fig. 35.

[2] Wood, *City*, ii, 174; *Colleges and Halls*, 448.

EXCAVATIONS INSIDE THE LATIN CHAPEL (Figs. 34–41)

## Structures and Layers in Cutting 1

This cutting, 4.70 m. E. to W. by 3.65 m., occupied the N.W. corner of the Latin Chapel. On the S. it was limited by the need to allow access to the rest of the chapel and by the brick burial-vault of Edward Venables Vernon (1841–86).

A.  The stone base for the late-medieval stalls moved to the Latin Chapel in the 16th or 17th century. This base remained to be recorded only on the E. of the cutting.

1.  Stone step and stone-and-brick floor in soft brown mortar bedding, all at the general level of the church. The floor ran above Structures D and E.

2.  Loose filling of brown loam and off-white mortar (7–10 cm. thick) with jetton.

3.  The main tiled floor of the chapel with off-white mortar bedding, in all 6 cm. thick (see pp. 97–100). The mortar-bedding abutted on the wall-benches C and E. A section of 52 tiles, about 18 cm. square and all badly worn, remained in position, while the mortar-bedding just to the E. of the cutting preserved the impressions of ten more. All the tiles in this sector of the floor presumably lay square.

4.  Loose rubble and mortar with tips of brown gravelly loam (together 23 cm. thick) with broken floor-tiles (pp. 103–4) and 14th- to 15th-century pottery.

B.  Rough stone packing around a scaffold-pole hole dug through Layer 5.

C.  Plastered rubble wall-bench (34–37 cm. wide) along N. wall of chapel, abutting on wall-bench E.

D.  Rubble footing (40–43 cm. wide) in line with the W. wall of the chapel, blocking access from the W. into the chapel. This footing may be presumed to have carried a wooden screen.

E.  Plastered rubble wall-bench (38–43 cm. wide) along W. wall, just in front of footing D.

5.  Hard off-white mortar floor (10–14 cm. thick and 46–47 cm. below the general level). The footing D, the wall-bench E and this floor appeared to be contemporary.

F.  The coursed-rubble N. wall of the Latin Chapel, dated on architectural grounds to the 1340s or 1350s, abutting the 12th-century N.E. buttress of the N. transept. The base of the wall's foundation may lie at a depth of 2.20 m. or more, but space and safety alike prohibited any deep sounding in the narrow gap between this and the 12th-century footing G. The foundations are trench-built; they have no pronounced offset, but there is a slight bulging-out from a depth of 70 cm. to 1.30 m., the lowest point reached. Above 70 cm., the foundations are face-built, again with no offset, and merge into the wall-face. The shaft-bases indicate that the chapel was designed to be floored at the general level, but no sign of a floor could be seen at that level and the chapel may have been *lowered* to Layer 5 during construction. Fragments of red roof-tiles and ridge-tiles with greeny-brown glaze are built into the foundations.

G.  The rubble foundations of a small, two-bay, chapel of the 12th century, 1.50 m. wide, thickening to 2.30 m. for the transept buttress (Fig. 39) and to 1.95 m. for the central buttress of the N. wall. On its S. face, the footing is 2.30 m. deep, trench-built below 85–115 cm. Against the transept buttress it could be seen to have been face-built with an offset of 7–8 cm. at a depth of 45 cm., while on the N. face there was a wider offset of 15–19 cm. which showed that the alignment of this part of the church had been corrected by about five degrees anti-clockwise when the walls were set out.

H.  Stone-lined burial dug through Layers 7–9 and perhaps through Layer 6; perhaps earlier than the 12th-century footings.

6.  Hard-packed yellow-brown gravel and loam (22–24 cm. thick).

7.  Dark-brown gravelly loam (23–27 cm. thick).

8.  Hard-packed pale-yellow gravel (15–27 cm. thick).

9.  Dark-brown gravelly loam (90–115 cm. thick). Natural gravel was found at a depth of 2.10 m. at the S. end of the cutting and 2.20 m. in the centre, where the 12th-century footing G had been dug a further 10 cm. down into the gravel. This slope might continue to give a depth of 2.40–2.50 m. at the N. There was no trace of the natural red-brown loamy topsoil, and this part of the church was built in the filling of a considerable earlier ditch or hollow.

## Structures and Layers in Cutting 2W

A zone along the S. side of the Latin Chapel, roughly 1.20–1.50 m. wide and 11 m. long, had not been disturbed for the massive brick burial-vaults, some of them roomy enough for up to a dozen coffins, of Georgian and early-Victorian canons which filled the centre of the chapel and had destroyed all earlier deposits and burials over more than half its area. The high chantry chapel or 'watching chamber' stands in this

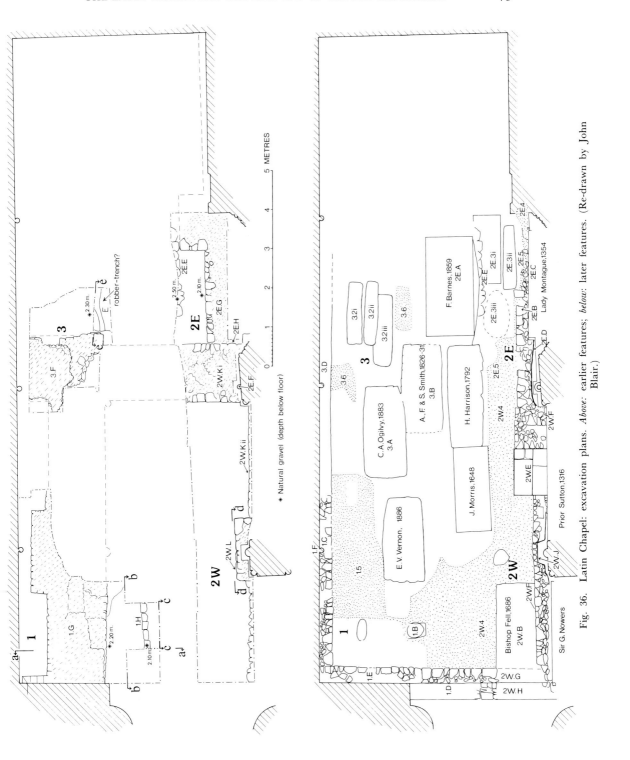

Fig. 36. Latin Chapel: excavation plans. *Above*: earlier features; *below*: later features. (Re-drawn by John Blair.)

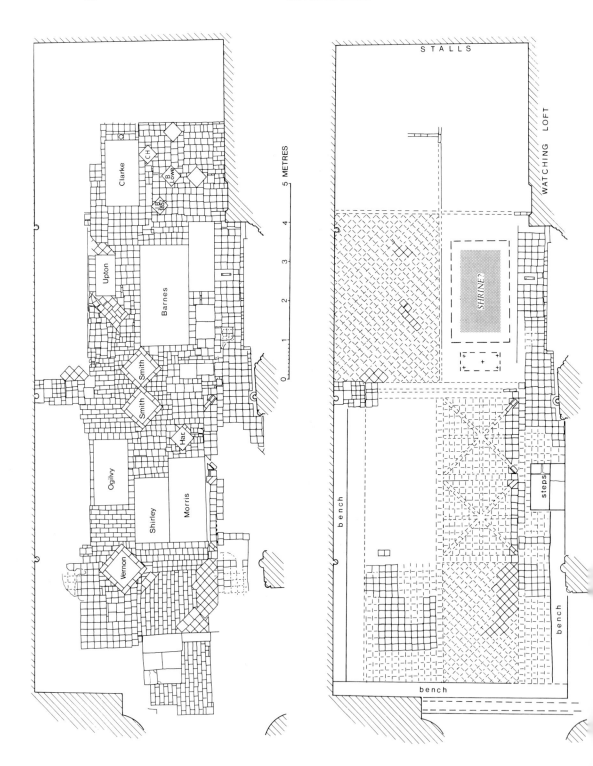

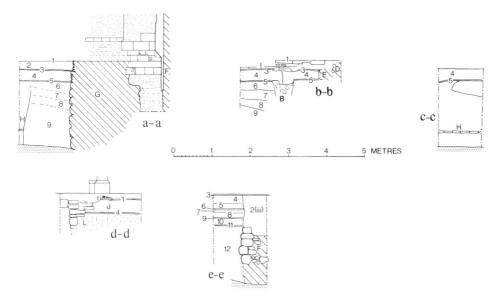

Fig. 38. Latin Chapel: sections. Letters correspond with section lines on Fig. 36, upper. (Re-drawn by John Blair.)

zone in the E. bay of the chapel. In the next bay, alongside the Montague monument, it was designated Cutting **2E** (below). In the third bay from the E., alongside the Sutton monument, the excavation was called Cutting **2W**; Dr. Fell's vault (which was not investigated) took up almost all the zone in the W. bay adjoining the N. transept, also reported on here. The 12th-century floor of the third bay was perhaps 38 cm. *above* the present floor (above, p. 76), so that no ground- or floor-levels relating to the standing architecture could be expected to survive.

A.      Square stone supporting-blocks inserted, presumably by Scott in the 1870s, below the bases of the wall-shafts.

B.      Barrel-vaulted brick burial-vault (1.07 m. wide, 2.50 m. long, its top at a depth of 80 cm.) constructed 10–12 July 1686 for the burial of Dr. John Fell, Dean 1660–1686,[3] the barrel-vault no doubt being completed within a day or two of the funeral at 4 p.m. on Tuesday 13 July. The tile floor, Layer 1, had not been relaid over the vault, which lies beneath two blocks of the late-medieval stalls.

C.      The stone base for the stalls, remaining to be recorded only in part.

1.      The main tiled floor of the chapel with mortar bedding. About 130 of the tiles remained in position, most of them badly worn (below, p. 98); careful work with a soft brush recovered the impressions of another 20 in the mortar bedding left exposed where the stalls had stood. East of the stone steps E, the floor covered the wall-bench F, but to the W. it abutted against the wall-bench F, which must have been raised when this floor was laid.

2.      Loose gravelly loam and mortar with broken floor-tiles and 14th- to 15th-century pottery and glass.

E.      Two stone steps (1.15 cm. wide) with a plaster-faced rubble blocking (60 cm. wide) on the E. side of the steps, which led down into the chapel to the floor at Layer 3 (Fig. 40). The lower step had no doubt been covered by the main tiled floor 1, which must have abutted on the upper step. Enthusiastic undergraduate diggers unfortunately removed the tiles or bedding here before the late-medieval date of the floor was appreciated. This entrance into the chapel succeeded an earlier one through the western bay (see J below).

F.      Plastered rubble wall-bench (41 cm. wide on either side of the western, 12th-century wall-shaft, where it curved out sinuously, but 65 cm. wide further E.) with an opening 1.80 m. wide later filled by the steps and blocking E. Though structurally later, the steps E were perhaps the same date as

---

[3] *Wood's Life and Times*, ed. A. Clark, iii (O.H.S. xxvi, 1894), 192.

Fig. 39.   Cutting 1, looking westwards along footing of N. wall of 'pre-Latin' chapel (**1**.G) towards E. face of
original buttress at N.E. corner of N. transept.

Fig. 40.   Steps down from Lady Chapel into Latin Chapel (**2W**.E), looking S.

the wall-bench F, the distinction marking a change of plan during construction. Dr. Fell's vault B lies immediately N. of the W. stretch of this bench, but did not impinge on it.

G.    Plastered rubble wall-bench across the W. end of the chapel, abutted on by the S. bench F and dug through for Fell's vault B, leaving only a stump of two stones in the extreme S.W. corner of the chapel.

H.    Footing of rubble and re-used ashlar for screen across the W. end of the chapel.

3.    A few small sections of mortar-bedding abutting on the plaster facing H, no doubt largely removed, with all the tiles that the bedding had held, when the south bench F was constructed.

J.    An almost vertical plaster facing at a depth of 23 to 50 cm. covered the footings exposed when the level was lowered for floor 4 (Fig. 41). This facing was stepped-out with canted sides round the base of the western, 12th-century, wall-shaft (II.4.F). The facing, which did not run far to the W. of this shaft, seemed to be the same date as a broad opening into the chapel beneath the Nowers monument. Further E. it had been cut through when the steps E were built and then turned sharply northward to curve round the 12th-century corner shaft and 13th-century wall-shaft of the central pier of the chapel's S. side (II.3.D and C). The upper finish of the facing had all been knocked away, by the workmen who fitted-in the stalls and their bases C in the 17th century or by the Victorian restorers who put in the supporting blocks A.

4.    Hard off-white mortar floor, the same date as the footing H, at depth of 50 cm. Layers 3 and 4 and structures G, H and J might all be of the mid 14th century.

K(i)  The mortared-rubble foundations of the E. wall of the much smaller 12th-century precursor of the Latin Chapel (1.52 m. wide; depth not found, but presumably about 2.10 m. or more). A shaft at the S.E. corner of this chapel (II.3.D) still stands to full height, but without its capital; it is not supported by the foundation but overhangs, no doubt because of a re-alignment when the walls were set out. The E. face of this foundation is recorded under Cutting 2E, H.

K(ii) Rough rubble footing underlying the Sutton monument, interpreted here as the S. wall of the 12th-century chapel.

L.    Rubble corner of a foundation (Fig. 41), exposed to a depth of five courses or 65 cm. below the floor 4, projecting 38 cm. N. of the footing K(ii) which abuts on it. The trench-built N. face of the footing remained for a length of 1.5 m. westwards from this corner. Exposed for a further 2.6 m. westwards was a rough footing of small rubble, interpreted here as the same structure but with its facing robbed away at some date before the construction of the wall-bench F, which ran above it. If K(ii) was indeed late 12th-century, L may be identified as the corner of the N.E. transeptal chapel of an earlier 12th-century church.

5.    Brown gravelly loam, not dug out to bottom.

No attempt was made to find natural gravel.

Fig. 41.  S. face of cutting **2W**, showing base of shaft II.4.F above plastered face (**2W**.J) and corner of early footing (**2W**.L).

## Structures and Layers in Cutting **2E**

1.  Granite slab, with brass to Dr. Francis Barnes (1770–1859), set into main floor, Layer 2.

A.  Brick burial-vault of the Barnes family, with capping-slabs at a depth of 68 cm.

2.  Main tiled floor with soft mortar-beddings of various dates. About 60 worn tiles remained in position, all square-set, in three rows at the centre of the cutting and seven-and-a-half at the W. end. Most of them were part of the belt of tiles along the S. side of the chapel. This belt was interrupted by a row of narrow border-tiles running N.–S. (below, p. 98), which may help to indicate where St. Frideswide's shrine stood from about 1350 until the 1530s (below, pp. 95–6). The floor lay over the wall-bench B in this cutting and in part of Cutting **2W**, right up to the Montague monument C.

3.  Two late- or post-medieval burials lay side-by-side at a depth of 1.05 m. (i) beneath an uninscribed or worn slab 1.78 m. long and (ii), between it and the Montague monument, beneath tiling (perhaps relaid) and a Purbeck slab with a recess or indent for a fixing or brass inscription, the slab being 51 cm. wide. This burial showed traces of a wooden coffin. There was also (iii) a large charnel deposit W. of (i), of very many disturbed bones including nine skulls, from 80 to 140 cm. down. Two stone slabs, roughly 50 cm. square, and relaid tiles were over these bones. They may have been Tudor or Stuart burials dug out and reburied when the Barnes vault was made, presumably in the 1840s or 1850s, or medieval burials disturbed in the 16th or 17th centuries. The stratigraphy, all in deposits of soft brown gravelly loam, absolutely dry for centuries, was not clear. If medieval, the bones may have been from graves just outside the small 12th-century chapel, which was extended across this area late in the 13th century (below, p. 95). Since the shrine may have stood just to the N. (below, p. 96), these bones could possibly include the intermixed remains of Frideswide and Katherine Martyr (below, p. 254).

B.  Plastered rubble wall-bench against the monument C, continued from **2W**.D, just to the W. Although chopped back for the later burial 3ii, the small-rubble core of the bench continued along the Montague monument to within 48 cm. of its E. end, where the earlier, 14th-century, floor stepped up. The bench had been constructed over this floor and later flattened for the main tiled floor 2.

C.  Lady Montague's monument, probably not *in situ*, stands on (but is slightly shorter at the W. end than) a sub-base of two courses of ashlar, which have a thin plaster facing. This sub-base had been cut into the plaster facing D, and its plaster facing made up to match that. Both these facings were abutted and concealed by the wall-bench B. The sub-base may have been constructed for an altar-tomb for Thomas de Blewbury, who was buried next to the feretory in 1293 (below, p. 251). This monument must have been dismantled before 1633, when Lady Montague's monument was moved here from further S.

D.  An almost vertical plaster facing covered the foundations exposed or dug into when the chapel floor was lowered (above, p. 76) for the floors 4 and 5. The facing curved out round the base of the early 13th-century shaft F (=II.3.C). It had been cut into and at once patched-over for the foundation-courses of the monument C.

4.  Fragments of a tiled floor and its mortar bedding remained in places under the wall-bench B and laid against the monument C and the facing D. The floor lay at a depth of 48–50 cm. as far E. as the end of the wall-bench B, where it stepped up to 30–34 cm. No stone of the step itself remained, but the end step against the monument C was probably 25 cm. wide, if the gap between the last stone of the badly-damaged bench and the closest stretch of mortar-bedding gave a true indication. The workmen who built the bench had lifted almost all the tiles along its length. One remained in position at the higher level, between the monument and the 'watching chamber', and altogether about 12 at the lower level. Later, when the level was raised and the floor 2 laid, all the tiles N. of the bench were also lifted.

5.  Hard off-white mortar floor at a depth of 49–51 cm., presumably a working-level during the completion of the chapel before the tiled floor 4 just above it was laid. This floor continued at the same level beneath the step-up noted above.

E.  Two roughly-laid courses of very large rubble stones project about 15 cm. to the S. below the base of Dr. Barnes's burial-vault, Structure A. They may form a structure 2.30 m. or more long N.–S., whose width might be about 1.85 m. to judge from Cutting **3**. At the time of excavation these stones, at a depth of 1.95–2.35 m. below the present floor, were taken to be the base of Dr. Barnes's burial-vault, Structure A. The likelihood that they are part of the foundations of Frideswide's shrine is discussed below (p. 95).

6.  Brown gravelly loam and many disturbed human bones at a depth of 1.20–1.95 m. may represent burials disturbed during the construction of structures E or G.

F.  The 13th-century wall-shaft or vaulting-shaft (=II.3.C) at the centre of the S. side of the chapel should be included here, although its stratigraphy was destroyed by the lowering of the general floor-level for layer 5. It is structurally later than the later 12th- and early 13th-century footings, H and G, and earlier than the present chapel and its concomitant works, Structures C and D and Layers 4 and 5. The walling on either side of this shaft, and in bond with it, is out of line both with the largely-destroyed 12th-century work and with the present chapel by some six degrees north-of-east.

G.      A coursed-rubble foundation, clearly of the N. wall of the present Lady Chapel, abuts on the 12th-century E. wall of the smaller, two-bay, precursor of the Latin Chapel and runs 2.30 m. eastward to a buttress some 60 cm. deep, which may have been reduced to build the crude rubble footing, Structure E. The Montague monument, Structure C, stands above the S. face of this foundation and the 'watching chamber', rather too close above the E. face of the buttress to permit safe investigation, so that the widths of the wall and of the buttress could not be found. The 'buttress' might alternatively be the E. wall of an early 13th-century eastward extension to the chapel.

H.      The lower footings of the E. wall of the earlier chapel below the Latin Chapel were exposed (also as Structure K(i) of Cutting **2W**). Cautious horizontal tunnelling beneath the N.W. corner of the Montague monument, Structure C, located this chapel's S.E. corner buttress.

7.      Brown gravelly loam.

Natural gravel was exposed at a depth of 2.10–2.50 m.


## Structures and Layers in Cutting **3**

This cutting was laid out to expose the N.E. corner buttress of the small 12th-century chapel, whose N. and E. walls had already been revealed in Cuttings **1** and **2**.

1.      Two diamond-set marble slabs to Anne Smith (1782–1826) and Francis (1826–7) and Samuel Smith (1801–31), set in brick surrounds surrounded by small square red tiles, and the granite slab with brass to Charles Arthur Ogilvy (1793-1883), surrounded by square red tiles and bricks.

A.      The Ogilvy vault, of brick, capped with slabs at a depth of 86 cm., with its base at 2.10 m., had entirely destroyed much of the core and S. face of the N. foundation of the 12th-century chapel (F) for about 2.30 m. to the W.

B.      The Smith vault, presumably constructed in 1826 or 1827, of brick, capped with slabs at a depth of 90 cm., with its base at 2.75 m., had entirely destroyed the inner N.E. angle and the N. half of the E. wall of the 12th-century chapel (F).

C.      The 17th-century stone bases to the reset late-medieval stalls stood on the main tile floor, Layer 3, but had already been removed and could not be recorded in detail.

2.      Three burials of the 16th or 17th century lay in *échelon* across the NE. part of the cutting: (i), furthest to the E., at a depth of 1.45 m., its head cut deeply into the E. face of the 12th-century buttress; (ii), at 1.15 m., with its head and shoulders cut into the top of the buttress-footing; and (iii), to the S.W., at 1.20 m., had its whole head and trunk hacked down into the buttress-footing, leaving a single corner-stone at a depth of 1 m., within 3 cm. of Layer 11. These graves were all back-filled with loose brown gravelly loam with rubble, mortar and medieval pottery. The two northerly burials lay beneath the stalls; the tiles of the floor 3 had not been relaid over them, or had been removed. Over Burial (iii), which seems to be that of William Phillips, scholar of Christ Church (d.1647),[4] the tiles had been poorly relaid square-on, though originally laid diagonally here to judge from nearby undisturbed tiles.

3.      The main tiled floor of the chapel with its mortar bedding (2–5 cm. thick) had about 39 tiles still in position above this cutting (see p. 99). Along the N. side was a miscellaneous assemblage of square-set tiles, some small and 14th-century and others very large. Perhaps this most out-of-the-way part of the chapel was finished off with a belt of old tiles. They stretched over the wall-bench E right to the N. wall.

4.      Loose brown gravelly loam with stones and mortar (19 cm. thick), with tile-fragments.

5.      Rubble and mortar (15 cm. thick) with medieval pottery and broken tiles. Layers 3 to 5 all seem to date from about 1500.

D.      A plastered rubble wall-bench (33 cm. wide) along the N. wall. This bench was not removed, which left unresolved the relationship of the mortar floor 6 with the N. wall of the chapel and the character of the foundations of this wall.

E.      Along the S. edge of the cutting, the fairly narrow surviving tongue of deposits that provided the

---

[4] Wood, *City*, ii, 550 and plan opposite.

main exposure of Layers 6–11 had been cut through, perhaps for a burial, but perhaps by the robber-trench of a wall. The presence of Layer 6 this far S. demonstrates that the shrine could not have stood in the centre of the chapel here, but must have been somewhat to the S.

6.    Hard off-white mortar floor, at depth of 52 cm., remaining in two patches, at the N.E. of the cutting and along the E. part of its S. face (3–4 cm. thick).

7.    Loose dark-brown loam with small rubble (7.5 cm. thick). Layers 6 and 7 are probably both mid 14th-century.

8.    Brown gravelly loam (12 cm. thick).

9.    Yellow-brown gravel (2.5 cm. thick).

10.   Hard-packed brown gravelly loam (19 cm. thick) with 12th-century pottery.

11.   Stone-slate fragments, stone-chippings and mortar (4 cm. thick), clearly the construction-level of the chapel standing above the foundation F.

F.    The mortared-rubble foundation of the N.E. corner buttress of the 12th-century chapel. The foundation had been badly cut about at various times noted above. It was trench-built for the whole of its surviving depth, from 1 m. to 2.30 m.

12.   Brown gravelly loam (1.45 m. thick).

Natural gravel was found at a depth of 2.30 m.


## EXCAVATIONS AT THE EAST END OF OXFORD CATHEDRAL (Figs. 42–3)


### *Introduction*

After the excavations within the Latin Chapel described above, some areas outside the Cathedral were investigated during the following summer. They lay in the close-packed medieval burial-ground, N. and E. of St. Frideswide's Priory church, which was used as a canon's garden[5] from soon after the founding of Christ Church in 1546 until 1959. By 1961 it was sadly decayed and overgrown; the Friends of Oxford Cathedral, with the writer as Secretary of its Garden Committee, undertook to reclaim the jungle and replant it as a Cathedral Garden.

In March 1963 the Oxford University Archaeological Society, helped by stalwarts from the College Boat Club, dug Cutting **4** a little to the E. of the Lady Chapel. Between late June and early August, student-volunteers, maintained by a grant of £120 from Christ Church and housed in the Cathedral Choir School by kind permission of the Revd. D.R. Dendy, Headmaster, excavated three more areas: Cutting **5** against the N. choir aisle; Cutting **6** against the choir; and Cutting **7**, not reported on here, on the medieval roadway and earlier occupation-deposits beneath it just outside the burial-ground, in the N.E. corner of the garden, whose N. boundary wall marked the frontage line on the N. side of the road. The University Chest administered the joint finances of these operations.


### *Layers in Cutting* **4**

This cutting, 4.50 m. E. to W. by 1.80 m., and sited 5.90 m. E. of the Lady Chapel, was excavated under the supervision of J.R. Maddicott. No structures were encountered (apart from an old gas-pipe), and the following layers were found:

1.   Dark-brown loamy topsoil (50–60 cm. thick) with much 17th-century pottery.

2.   Mortar (at the W. end of the Cutting, 4–6 cm. thick).

---

[5] Bodl. MS Wood F28, f.207, and N. Denholm-Young, *Cartulary of the Medieval Archives of Christ Church* (O.H.S. xcii, 1931), 197, Lease MM 54.

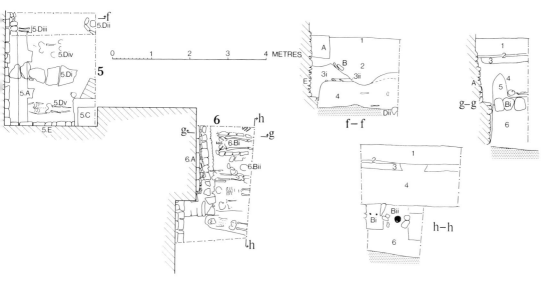

Fig. 42.    Trenches outside E. end of Cathedral: plan and sections. (Re-drawn by John Blair.)

3.    Brown gravelly loam (up to 95 cm. thick) with medieval pottery including abraded 12th-century sherds.
4.    Dark-brown gravelly loam (1.30–1.40 m. thick) with burials, very large numbers of disarticulated human bones and some medieval pottery.

Natural gravel was encountered at a fairly uniform depth of 2.75 m.

## Discussion of Cutting 4

The natural loamy topsoil and the top of the gravel had been entirely dug away for burials and charnel-pits to a depth of a metre or more between the 12th and the early 16th centuries. All earlier surfaces and features had been completely removed, as was to be expected here from the findings of the 1961 section[6] on the N. side of the medieval burial-ground. Despite this we can be fairly confident that there was no deep earlier ditch, like those found in Cutting 6 and in Cuttings 1–3, in the area of this cutting. The final late-medieval surface of the burial-ground, Layer 4, seemed to be at a depth of 1.35–1.45 m., though there was another turf-line 30 cm. higher at the E. end of the cutting. Layer 3 was probably dumping from some nearby part of the college during 16th-century foundation-digging, Layer 2 the debris of a minor work such as the 17th-century rebuilding of the old precinct wall a little to the E. Loggan's view of the college in 1673 showing this as a very orchard-like garden,[7] and Williams's engraved plan of 1733[8] with a stiffly formal layout here, confirm the clear evidence of Layer 1 of more than four centuries of garden use.

## Structures and Layers in Cutting 5

This cutting, 2.40 m. E. to W. by 2.90 m., in the angle between the E. wall of the N. choir aisle and the N. wall of the choir's projecting bay, was limited by the drains (Structure C) installed at one of the Victorian restorations. It was sited above the southern, and least unconvincing, of three supposed apses revealed by J.P. Harrison in 1887.[9] The aisle wall, palpably of 12th-century date, has a later builders' opening cut through it, as

[6] D. Sturdy, .'Recent Excavations in Christ Church and Nearby', *Oxoniensia*, xxvi-xxvii (1961–2), 30 and Fig. 8.

[7] David Loggan, *Oxonia Illustrata* (1675), Pl. xxvii.

[8] William Williams, *Oxonia Depicta* (1733), [unpaginated] plan of Christ Church.

[9] Harrison's excavations, and his debate with J. Parker, are reported in *Proc. Oxford Archit. and Hist. Soc.* n.s. v (1886–93), 89–108; J.P. Harrison, 'Recent Discoveries in Oxford Cathedral', *Archaeol. Jnl.* xlv (1888), 271–83.

does the 13th-century Lady Chapel wall just to the N. Harrison asserted that these were Anglo-Saxon arches and that another, larger, one lurked behind the 12th-century corner-buttress of the aisle between them.

The structures found were:

A.       A shallow brick retaining-wall 34 cm. E. of the aisle wall.

B.       Two stones of the outer face of Harrison's alleged apse, stratigraphically part of the late 19th-century Layer 2.

C.       Part of a brick-bedded drain and two drainage-points, at the S.E. and N.W. corners of the cutting.

Di.      A stone-capped burial (1.20 m. N. of the choir wall) containing a 14th-century sherd, dug into the modified natural topsoil (Layer 4).

Dii.     The head end of a stone-lined burial dug into the top of the natural gravel (2.45 m. N. of the choir wall).

Diii.    A burial, all but its legs cut away by the choir aisle footing.

Div and   Two burials; their stratigraphical relationship with the church could not be defined.
Dv.

E.       The foundations of the aisle and choir walls, very well bonded together and clearly contemporary. The upper footings had a similar slight batter and their alignments had been slightly changed during construction by the same amount, about 5 degrees clockwise. At the N. end of the cutting the aisle wall is bedded on natural gravel at a depth of 1.70 m., the lowest 25 cm. being offset by 25 cm. The much taller choir wall has a bad internal crack above the S. end of the cutting and we left its lower footings quite undisturbed.

The layers found were:

1.       Dark-brown loamy topsoil (about 23 cm. thick, but much confused with Layer 2) with medieval to 19th-century pottery.

2.       Dark-brown gravelly loam with stones, with a layer of small stones at 60 cm. and of dark-yellow gravel at 80 cm. (60–100 cm. thick). The excavations of 1887 and 1936 could not be clearly defined.

3i.      Light-brown very gravelly loam and stones, cut into by the lower part of Layer 2 and filling the construction-trench of the aisle wall.

3ii.     Stone chips and pieces in light red-brown loam (up to 10 cm. thick).

4.       Red-brown gravelly loam (65–73 cm. thick) with some bone-fragments and a smudge of mortar.

Natural gravel was revealed at a depth of 1.70–1.75 m.

## Discussion of Cutting 5

The natural loamy topsoil in the cutting was actually present (layer 4). It was also revealed in the 1961 excavation[10] and in Cutting 7, both 40 m. to the N., but had been removed in the other cuttings reported on here. The topsoil was much thicker in these three exposures than usual on central Oxford sites. In this cutting it had been considerably disturbed, perhaps in prehistoric times, but no early pits or postholes were found here. No apse or any other part of an Anglo-Saxon church had been built within the cutting. The natural topsoil had been cut through by the foundation-trench for the somewhat broader offset foundation of the aisle wall. The same must be true of the choir wall, which was plainly constructed at the same time as the aisle wall as the first substantial building here, since their upper foundations, plinths, walls and stringcourses match and bond. The construction-level of these walls could be recognised as Layer 3ii, with its stone-fragments. As construction of the upper walls proceeded, the foundation-trench was backfilled and the general level raised by 40 cm. or more with Layer 3i, which was simply the disturbed natural topsoil from foundation-digging nearby, left lying about in spoilheaps and then shovelled back against the newly-built church walls. Layer 2 represented five or six conflated deposits which could not be separated: the late-medieval churchyard surface, the Tudor to Victorian garden topsoil, the drainage-laying of the 1850s or 1870s, Harrison's dig of 1887, the digging-out along the aisle wall to install the retaining-wall, and an inconclusive excavation here in 1936.[11] Part of Harrison's best 'apse' was however still to be found (Fig. 42, section f-f). It was simply a couple of stones packed together, clearly within this late and much-disturbed Layer 2. The kindest solution is to conclude that Harrison's labourers, knowing that he wanted to discover some parts of a Saxon church such as, possibly, apses, determined to provide them for him, to please him and thus to get a more satisfactory reward for their labours. The stone-capped burial, Structure Di, looked as though it had been met with twice, in the centre by Harrison's men and at the head by the later Victorian or Edwardian builders of the retaining-wall, but left largely undisturbed.

[10] Loc. cit. note 6.
[11] R.C.H.M. Oxford, 35.

## Structures and Layers in Cutting 6

This cutting, only 1.40 m. E. to W. at the N. end by 2.80 m., was laid out to investigate the E. end of the cathedral with minimal disturbance, in view of the long cracks above the lower N. and S. windows of the projecting E. bay of the choir, which show that the E. wall of the choir is inclining outwards. The structures found were:

A.    The foundations of the choir E. wall and N.E. buttress, standing in a large ditch or depression and based probably at a depth of 2.75–2.85 m., trench-built below 1.30 m. and face-built above, with one offset at that point and another at 75 cm. As in Cutting **5**, the foundations lie at a slight angle to the walls above, the alignment having been corrected or adjusted during construction and at the offsets by about 5 degrees, clockwise. Just below the present surface, the buttress has a second chamfered plinth 10 cm. wide (omitted for its southernmost 20 cm.) on the short return and on the E. wall itself.

Bi.    The hips and thighs of a burial in a stone-lined grave, lying on very dark-brown loam or charcoal with a little gravel, cut through at the waist by the buttress-foundations (Fig. 43). Its lower legs remain E. of the cutting. The bones are those of an adult woman with no signs of extreme age (ex inf. Mary Harman).

Bii.    The head of a burial in a stone-lined grave, just below Bi and sealed by it. The rest of the skeleton remains E. of the cutting.

The layers found were:

1.    Brown loamy topsoil (40–45 cm. thick).

2.    Mortar (up to 6 cm. thick).

3.    Hard-packed yellow gravel (15–20 cm. thick) with 19th-century pottery.

4.    Dark-brown gravelly loam (90 cm. thick) with medieval pottery, glass and tile. Four burials in this layer post-dated the buttress footing, and had their heads laid over or up against it.

5.    Light-brown gravelly loam (60 cm. thick) cut by the buttress foundation-trench and by burials of Layer 4.

6.    Light yellow-brown gravel with some bone fragments (excavated to a thickness of 70 cm., probed to a further 45 cm.).

Natural gravel was found at a depth of 2.75–2.85 m.

Fig. 43.   Cutting 6, showing stone-lined burial (**6**.B.i) truncated by N.E. corner buttress of choir.

*Discussion of Cutting* **6**

The E. wall of the choir stands above a hollow dug nearly 2 m. into the natural topsoil and gravel, and filled with less compact material. This explains the very evident cracks above the windows either side of the high altar. The hollow may be a prehistoric ditch running, at this point, N.–S. (as the cracks are opposite each other), perhaps part of a Neolithic causewayed camp. The filling of the ditch, Layer 6, was gravel without much extra material. Layer 5 represented a redeposited loam, bringing the area up, perhaps still in prehistoric times, to a fairly even level, being very similar to Layer 4 in Cutting **5**, which had not, however, been removed and brought back, as this must have been. The main medieval churchyard-deposit, Layer 4, was very like its continuation, as Layer 4, in Cutting **4**. A Regency or early-Victorian carriage-drive, Layer 3, was covered with mortar, Layer 2, doubtless of George Gilbert Scott's works while reconstructing the E. windows of the choir above, while the late-Victorian and modern flower-bed topsoil, Layer 1, has brought the ground-level up to cover the lower plinth of the buttress, always, for some reason, left incomplete.

CONCLUSIONS

*Geology*

The natural red-brown loamy topsoil, familiar from many exposures throughout central and north Oxford, was found, very much thicker than usual, in one area (**5**.4). It had been found in 1961 only 20 m. to the N.[12] and a large area of it was exposed in 1963 in Cutting **7**, not reported on here, 25 m. to the N.E. A similar red-brown soil, redeposited or reformed, was found a short distance to the S.E. (**6**.5) over what is almost certainly a prehistoric ditch. The usual bright-yellow natural gravel was found wherever excavations were carried down far enough to reach it.

*Prehistory*

Large cracks on either side of the high altar of the cathedral are best explained by the E. wall having been built in an old N.–S. ditch. A deep cutting against the E. wall revealed deposits (**6**.6) which could well be the filling of a prehistoric ditch, a Neolithic causewayed camp or perhaps a river-fort of the Iron Age. Alternatively, they could represent a gravel-pit similar to that found in the cloister (above, pp. 62–5).

*The Anglo-Saxons*

Natural gravel did not turn up at the expected depth beneath the Latin Chapel. Here, as under the E. end of the choir (above, *Prehistory*) there seems to have been a deep ditch, not as old, since natural topsoil, or something very like it (above, *Geology*), had *not* been redeposited above the filling of this ditch. This deposit or filling (**1**.6–9; **2W**.5; **2E**.7; **3**.12), of brown or dark-brown gravelly loam, contained no finds, and is stratigraphically earlier than the mid 12th century. One stone-lined burial (**1**.H) had been dug into it (below, *Burials*). The large ditch implied by these widely-spread findings must have run E.–W. and is best interpreted as the S. defences of Saxon Oxford, perhaps laid out at the end of the 9th century, despite the violence this view does to the long-accepted tradition

---

[12] Loc. cit. note 6.

that St. Frideswide founded a nunnery here in the 8th century. Such a nunnery or a remaining church is not likely to have been left just outside the defences.

No material remains of an early nunnery or of an Anglo-Saxon church, in the sense of walls, sculpture, pits, pottery, metalwork or postholes, have ever been found at the cathedral. In 1869 G.G. Scott dismissed notions that part of the cathedral was Saxon with some vigour: 'I need hardly say there is not a shadow of foundation for such a supposition'.[13] This absence of good evidence, coupled with the prospect that the site lies outside the Saxon defences, requires us to consider other locations for the church that housed Frideswide's relics in about the year 1000 (below, p. 226). Material evidence suggests as possible both the present parish church of St. Aldate's (below, pp. 233–5) and the former St. Martin's at Carfax.[14]

*Burials*

Five relatively early burials capped or lined with stones were found in the excavations. Others, W. of the cathedral, have been dated to the 9th century,[15] while others from the cloister have become 'Middle Saxons' with 'high precision' dates of around the 9th century (above, pp. 60–2; below, p. 233). The burials reported on here do not demand such dramatically early dates. One found within the Latin Chapel (**1**.H) had been dug into the filling of a possible town- or fortress-ditch (above, *Anglo-Saxons*) and could thus be of the late 11th or early 12th century. Another (**6**.Bi) had been chopped through by the choir E. wall of the 1160s or thereabouts. A third (**6**.Bii), close beside this, seemed to be a little earlier. Not far off a fourth (**5**.Diii) was cut by the E. wall of the N. choir aisle; a stone-lined burial to its E. (**5**.D.ii) lacked clear evidence of date. These burials could all be later than 1100. The writer believes that the other burials in the cloister and west of the Cathedral are probably also of this early 12th-century date, much later than that assigned to them from the scientific results. He has always thought it rash to accept such results as historical and unwise to base elaborate chronologies on 'dates' that are no more than probabilities resulting from the mathematical working-out of complex scientific processes.

*Early-Norman Church*

The chapter-house range, with its doorway of about 1130–50 (below, pp. 160–7), must have been planned and built with or up against a church earlier than the present cathedral. The central triforium opening on the W. side of the S. transept has, all re-used, two monolithic window-heads and three shafts, whose base-mouldings are best paralleled in churches of 1070–1120. The opposite triforium opening has, re-used as a sill, a slab decorated with diagonal rows of dots, which must be of much the same date. The excavations revealed what may be part of a smaller and older church (**2W**.L): the E. corner of its N. transept, or rather of its N. transeptal chapel, exactly matching the point where the S. transept (rebuilt in the late 12th century) and its chapel (rebuilt again in the 14th century) meet the slype. This evidence suggests that the S. transept, of two

---

[13] G.G. Scott, *Report . . . on the Cathedral Church of Christ Church* (1869).

[14] For finds from the latter see E.M. Jope, 'Late Saxon Pits under Oxford Castle Mound', *Oxoniensia*, xvii–xviii (1952–3), 108, No. 6 in index of sites.

[15] T.G. Hassall, 'Excavations at Oxford, 1972', *Oxoniensia*, xxxviii (1973), 270–4.

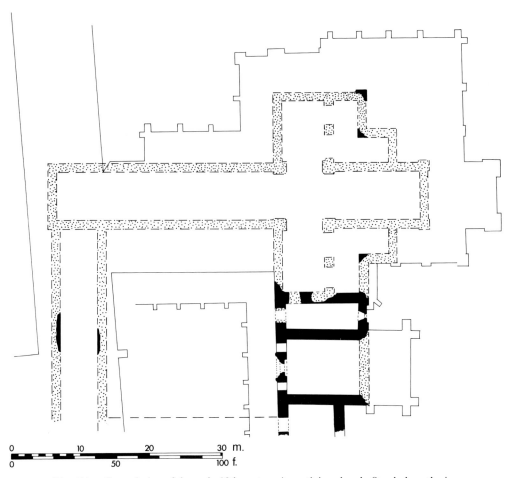

Fig. 43A.   Ground-plan of the early 12th-century Augustinian church: Sturdy hypothesis.

bays at ground-level, was once balanced by a two-bay N. transept. Each had an outer chapel of one bay and probably, to judge by other Augustinian monastic houses such as Lilleshall, an inner two-bay chapel giving a 'stepped' plan (Fig. 43A). After the N. transept was rebuilt, perhaps in the 1170s (p. 94), with three bays and chapels or aisles on both sides, the S. transept was, in about the 1190s, rebuilt in its turn. A third bay was contrived, at upper levels only, above the slype; the W. aisle, which could not be built because it would have impinged on the cloister alley, had to remain as an illusion marked by a blind arcade. In the restoration of the 1870s, it was at first assumed that the W. aisle of the S. transept had once existed, but had been demolished in the 15th century when the present cloister was built. Consequently Gilbert Scott proposed pulling down that corner of the cloister and rebuilding the now missing aisle, but eventually realised, as we can see from his notes,[16] that it had never existed. J.C. Buckler

[16] G.G. Scott notebook, 1869–70 (Christ Church archives D.P.vii.a.8), f.18ᵛ. [However, cf. the opposite conclusion reached by Halsey, pp. 149–52 below.]

tried to persuade himself,[17] in an exercise that combined wonderful powers of observation and recording with the most determined stupidity in interpretation, that the slype had been inserted into an originally open third bay of the transept.

The first Romanesque church may have been a cell of Abingdon Abbey (cf. below, p. 226), a parochial or collegiate foundation of Bishop Roger of Salisbury, or an Augustinian colony that had not yet acquired Frideswide's relics. The plan of the central tower, wider from N. to S., may be one of the elements remaining from this earlier church as a 'fossil', although no part of its present fabric seems to be earlier than the 1170s-90s. If so, it could hint that Roger of Salisbury established the church, since St. Mary's, Devizes, generally viewed as his work, has this uncommon feature. J.P. Harrison's assertion of the 1890s that much of the choir is Saxon[18] is a fantasy of the same nature as his 'Saxon apses' (above, p. 88) or James Ingram's claim in the 1830s[19] that the tower is Saxon.

### Late-Norman Church, East End

The earliest major part of the present church is probably its E. end, begun perhaps in the 1150s or 1160s. There were already burials (**6**.Bi and Bii) in the area and the E. wall of the main body was, no doubt quite accidentally, laid out above a deep ancient ditch (**6**.6) long ago filled in and covered by a loam (**6**.5) almost indistinguishable from natural. The side walls of the aisles and their E. walls were built with the projecting bay of the main body. From the start all these outer walls were planned to be pretty well as they are today, and there is no indication that any apses were ever intended, inside or out.

Before analysing the foundations, we can briefly consider the function or intended function of the building-works. There must already have been a choir (above, *Early-Norman Church*), perhaps half the length of the present one. The present E. end may well have been begun neither as a rebuilding nor as an extension. Rather, we should see it as a grand annexe, either as a Lady Chapel or as a shrine-chapel, or perhaps both at once. The internal elevations of the projecting bay are a bad match for the main elevations of the present choir, their string-courses and arch-heights clashing discordantly (Fig. 56). A most elegant solution to this is provided by assuming that the projecting bay was planned for an entirely different interior arcade and elevation, which was changed in execution. The reason for this change may have been a decision to rebuild the choir while completing an annexe to it. The very richly-carved capitals half-way along the present choir suggest that the high altar was at first located here against a screen, with a separate eastern chapel approached from the aisles. This arrangement might have remained until the 13th or 14th centuries. The foundations, of local corallian rubble with cream to brown mortar, are firmly bedded on the natural gravel, the lower parts from 45 to 75 cm. below the original ground-surface being trench-built in foundation-trenches up to about 40 cm. wider than the wall on the outer face. There is an offset up to 23 cm. wide at the top of the trench-built lower footings, where the overall layout must have been checked and corrected. The alignment of the whole E. end was here corrected by about five degrees clockwise, probably to line up with an existing earlier

[17] B.L. MS Add. 27765 E, ff.54–78.

[18] [J.P. Harrison], *Archaeologia Oxoniensis* (1892–5), 286–7.

[19] J. Ingram, *Memorials of Oxford*, i (1837), Christ Church section, 11–12 and 17.

choir (above, *Early Norman Church*). Above this correction-level, the upper footings are face-built with a slight batter for 130–165 cm. up to the plinths. The upper footings and lower walls of the E. wall of the N. choir aisle and the N. wall of the choir (**6**.4) bond and match in every detail, as do those of the E. wall of the choir and its N.E. buttress (**5**.E), all of them being clearly part of the same few seasons' work. The eastern bay or two of the S. choir aisle must also have been built at this time, but the foundations were not investigated by these excavations.

The choir E. wall seems to be 2 m. thick, with corner-buttresses 2.45 m. E. to W. by 2.60 m. The side walls are 1.65–1.70 m. thick, the E. walls of the aisles only 1.0–1.05 m. thick with corner-buttresses 1.37 m. each way.

## Late-Norman Church, North Wing

The N. transept with aisles on both sides, a remarkable feature for such a small church, and an extra chapel E. of the N. bay, was built perhaps in the 1170s. On various grounds (above, *Early-Norman Church*) the earlier church can be assumed to have had two-bay transepts and no W. aisle. The new outer W. and N. walls were probably constructed to a good height before any demolition of the old took place. Unlike the E. wing of the church, which seems to have been built in stages with a final appearance very different from the first intentions, the transept simply followed the internal elevation of the E. wing, as it was finally worked out. Nothing remained of the old transept, except perhaps the core of the tower-piers and possibly the E. wall of the central bay, which might have been apsed.

The small extra chapel is best explained as a new shrine-house, removing pilgrims from beyond the high altar, and the large transept itself as circulation-space for large numbers of pilgrims, flocking to venerate or seek the help of Frideswide (below, pp. 248–9). The relics themselves may have been kept in a niche in the S. wall of the projecting chapel, where Prior Sutton's monument now stands (between piers II.4 and II.3). The secondary place of veneration in the late 12th century, the supposed 'grave' (below, p. 247), may have been in the centre or on the N. side of the present choir, close to the former high altar, or perhaps in a chapel or apse of the earlier N. transept.

The N. bay and projecting chapel of the new transept were built into the filling of a possible ditch (above, *Anglo-Saxons*), which the earlier two-bay transept may largely have avoided. The foundations here were unlike those of the E. end, in that they lacked a broad off-set base. The E. wall of the chapel (**3**.F) was trench-built; its upper part had been robbed in Cutting 3 and no evidence remained of alignment-correction. The N. wall-footings were trench-built below 85 to 115 cm. There are (p. 78) slight offsets, at 45 cm. below the original floor, of barely 7 cm. on the inner face and up to 19 cm. on the outside, where enough remained of the upper footings above the offset to show that the layout was corrected at this level by about five degrees anticlockwise. Above the plinth, the chapel walls were probably 1.37 m. wide.

## The North-East Chapels, 1200–1340

Early in the 13th century, perhaps about 1220, the N. wall of the N. choir aisle was pierced with three new arches and the present Lady Chapel was added, its three bays continuing the central aisle bay on the E. of the transept. Only one bay of the vault now remains, the other two having been rebuilt in the mid 14th century. The E. wall still stands largely intact; the foundations of the N. wall **2E**.G were partly found in the excavation.

This fairly small addition may have been built as a Lady Chapel, the high altar being moved E. from the centre of the present choir at that time. Or perhaps it was planned to serve as an extra link between the small transept-chapel, if this held the shrine and relics, and the centre or N. side of the present choir, perhaps still viewed as the 'grave' of the saint.

Late in the 13th century, probably in the 1280s, a two-bay extension was built where the two eastern bays of the Latin Chapel now stand. All that now remains is two shafts (II.2 and II.1), one, concealed within the 'watching chamber' at the S.E. corner of the Latin Chapel, the other (**2E**.F) half-way along the S. side. All the rest of this chapel was rebuilt in the mid 14th century. The walling on either side of the mid-way shaft II.3.C slants markedly N. of E. Through an oversight we did not locate the N. wall of the late 13th-century chapel: presumably it either lies beneath the E. half of the existing N. wall, or is represented by the possible robber-trench **3**.E (above, pp. 85–6), which would give a chapel considerably narrower than the present one. The purpose of this lost chapel may well have been to provide a home for the fine shrine-base associated with the translation of 1289 (below, p. 251).

*The Shrine, 1289–1537*

The supposed remains of St. Frideswide, probably housed from 1180 in the projecting small N.E. chapel whose foundations were found beneath the third bay from the E. of the Latin Chapel, were no doubt moved eastward in 1289, into the two-bay late 13th-century extension. In the E. bay of the extension, 9 m. from the old chapel, the shrine could have been sited on the centre-line, but if it was in the W. bay, 4.50 m. from the old chapel, it must have been S. of the centre to be on the line of sight for pilgrims coming from the W., since the new chapel was some 2.30 m. wider than the old. Although there is no evidence for either location at this period, the W. bay, now the second from the E. of the present Latin Chapel, is to be preferred in that it reduces the number of Frideswide's moves and simplifies the sequence.

There is slight and inconclusive material evidence, a few degrees better than pure fantasy, that the shrine stood, from about the 14th century until its destruction in the 1530s, in the second bay of the Latin Chapel, just S. of the centre-line. It can thus be argued that the shrine was put up in this position in 1289 and that it remained standing, boxed-in for safety and the actual reliquary moved elsewhere, when the chapel was rebuilt around it in about the 1330s. The evidence, such as it is, consists of:

(i) The proximity of Lady Montague's tomb, in or near the adjoining bay of the Lady Chapel (below, pp. 251–2).

(ii) Two very rough courses of large limestone rubble, **2E**.E, protruding over a length of 2.30 m. from beneath the bottom of the brickwork of Dr. Barnes's vault at a depth of 2.10 m. to 2.50 m., the deepest point reached inside the church by the excavations. No dating evidence was found, and this stonework might be anything from a defensive bastion built out in the 11th century across the large ditch here to a base for the mid-Victorian vault.

(iii) The very precise layout of the late-medieval tiled floor (below, pp. 97–100) strongly suggests that, in about 1500, the centre-line of the chapel was not obstructed by any large obstacle, like the shrine, when the floor was set out. The cumulative error of alignment was less than 3 cm. in over 13 m., or less than a quarter of one per cent, even after so much digging up and relaying that no original tiles, or perhaps only two, remained in position on the centre-line, which had nonetheless been followed by four 19th-century masons laying grave-slabs. The early-Tudor tiler must have stretched a cord right down the centre of the chapel, perhaps sighting it along the N. side of a plinth or step on which the shrine-base stood.

(iv) In Cutting **3** we cleared the mid 14th-century mortar working-floor 6 back to a disturbance, trench or grave-edge, **3**.E, 37 cm. N. of the central line. The presence of this floor here alone makes it clear that the shrine could not have been sited in the centre of this bay, since no room for it remained.

This evidence admits of two versions of the shrine's precise position: (a) as far W. as possible, directly over the recorded length of rough foundation, and (b) up to 70 cm. further E., allowing room for a stone altar to stand against the W. end of the shrine above the W. end of the foundation. The westerly position (a) leaves the sub-base on which Lady Montague's tomb now stands more level with the shrine, while the easterly position (b) fits more satisfactorily between the two residual N.–S. bands of narrow border-tiles in the tiled floor of about 1500 which was presumably laid around the standing shrine.

Evidence which might resolve this question of the shrine's precise location, and confirm its position in the Latin Chapel, lies under many tons of loose mortar-flashing and other debris in the roof-space over the vaulting above the likely site of the shrine. It is now, even at the ridge, well over 5 cm. deep in this debris, which is piled against and over the timbers wherever, as with the wall-plates, they come low enough. Investigation here should benefit the roof-timbers, by removing a certain source of damp and decay, and might also reveal the backs of iron hooks for pulleys to hoist the shrine-canopy on specially sacred occasions.

### *The Present Latin Chapel*

In the 1340s or 1350s, the odd-looking mixture, mentioned above, of a narrow old chapel with short bays and a later extension with longer bays was torn down and replaced by the present chapel. The master-mason ingeniously spaced out the bays of the new construction, so that each is longer than the one to its W., although he, or perhaps a more ham-fisted successor, did not manage the vaulting at all well. Perhaps even before the chapel was finished, the floor was lowered to well below the designed level and a hard mortar working-floor laid down, recognised (**1**.5; **2W**.4; **2E**.5; **3**.6) in all the excavated areas. A screen-wall (**1**.D) and wall-bench (**1**.E) were built at the same time across the W. end of the chapel. For the next two or three centuries access was from the S., first through the third and later through the fourth bay from the E. As soon as the working floor was down, the various exposed footings along the S. side were plastered over (**2W**.J; **2E**.D) in a rather casual way which may betray the hand of the 'ham-fisted' mason.

This plastering was cut through, probably fairly soon after it was completed, to insert a footing of ashlar blocks for a sepulchral monument, now the sub-base of Lady Montague's tomb. A number of screens must have separated the chapels and chantries, but no fixing marks have yet been identified on any of the piers or columns.

The new chapel was finished off with a tile floor (**2E**.4) laid a few cm. above the working floor (**2E**.5), which stepped up by the foot of the Montague monument. The characteristic hard-fired tiles of the mid 14th-century floor are published and discussed below (pp. 103–14).

*The Chapel, 1360–1490*

There were various minor alterations to the chapel during the following century and more. Wall-benches were installed along the N. wall, (**1**.C; **3**.D) as far as the central shaft, and along the S. wall (**2W**.F; **2E**.B) with an opening 1.80 m. wide for access-steps under the third arch from the E. These changes cannot be closely dated. Later, the opening was reduced to 1.15 m. wide, with two steps (**2W**.E) coming forward between the sections of wall-bench. Around 1500, the 'watching-loft' and its accompanying tomb were inserted between piers II.2 and II.1, and the floor destroyed in 1963 was laid.

To summarise, the excavations produced no evidence for a Saxon church, apart from a fake 'apse' concocted by Victorian labourers in 1887. We can suggest, from this and other data, anything up to eight successive settings for Frideswide's relics:

1. From the 10th century to the 1150s, in another church somewhere else.
2. From the 1150s to the 1160s, above or beside the high altar of a shorter choir on the cathedral site.
3. From the 1160s to 1180, halfway along the present choir, in roughly the same place as (2), but now backing against a screen for the high altar.
4. From 1180 to 1289 in the small N.E. chapel, excavated in 1963 beneath the third bay of the Latin Chapel, perhaps in a niche in the S. wall (but cf. below, pp. 139–46, 242, for an alternative interpretation of this chapel). For some time (3) continued to be venerated as the 'grave' of the saint.
5. From 1289 until the 1340s in the W. bay of a new shrine-house added to the E. of the older N.E.chapel. The shrine stood S. of the centre-line on the splendid shrine-base whose pieces were discovered in 1875 and 1985.
6. From the 1340s to about 1500 in the same place and on the same shrine-base, both chapels, noted in 4 and 5, having been rebuilt as what is now called the Latin Chapel, with the shrine in its second bay. At a late stage in the works, the floor was lowered and laid with tiles at a level 50 cm. below the intended floor (planned at first to be at the same level as that of the nave and transepts). A wall-bench was built to the W.
7. At two occasions in the late 14th or 15th centuries minor alterations were made to the shrine's immediate surroundings. First, wall-benches were constructed along the N. and S. walls as far as, or some way along, the shrine. Second, the wide entrance from the S. was narrowed and steps moved S.
8. From about 1500 until the shrine's destruction in the 1530s, it remained in the same place and on the same base. The floor-level was raised to 15 cm. below the nave and transepts and new tiles were laid, some over the eastern lengths of the benches.

When the shrine was torn down, its site must have been patched over with tiles more-or-less uniform with the latest floor, which remained worn, but substantially complete, well into the 19th century. It was recognised as ancient only during its destruction in 1963.

THE LATE MEDIEVAL TILED FLOOR (Fig. 37)

In about 1500, no doubt following the repaving of the major part of St. Frideswide's priory church during the 1490s by Robert Shirburn, Dean of Chichester,[20] who also

---

[20] M.E.C. Walcott, 'Bishops of Chichester . . . to Sherborne', *Sussex Archaeol. Colls.* xxix (1879), 25.

rebuilt the cloister (above, p. 66 and below, pp. 188–91) and refectory,[21] the floor of the Latin Chapel was relaid in tiles. The tiles of an older, 14th-century, floor which lay 42–43 cm. below the general level of the church floor (above, p. 76) were lifted, none of them being found in position, apart from a few (p. 84), which had been buried long before beneath the S. wall-bench of the chapel. Some late 13th- and 14th-century tiles were evidently used in the new floor (below, p. 109). To bring the new floor-level up to only 15 cm. below the general level, gravelly loam, mortar and rubble were brought in, perhaps from a simultaneous *lowering* of the floor-levels of the present Lady Chapel just to the S. The new floor was laid over this dumped material, which also contained broken tiles from the old floor and some casualties smashed during delivery. In 1963 well over 300 tiles still remained in position, or survived as impressions in the mortar-bedding. The new floor must have comprised more than 2000 tiles, so that enough remained to make a fairly certain reconstruction of the original design (Fig. 37), discussed section by section below.

In the first days of the excavation, we dug through two areas of flooring without recording the existing tiles and without noticing the mortar-bedding, which accounts for the gaps over Cuttings **1** and **2W**. But the sharp eyes of two 10-year-old helpers, set to sweep up the dust and mess from beneath the old stalls, soon put us to shame, as they found and pointed out the mortar-impressions and made us realise that the floor was not a Georgian or early-Victorian brick one with odd patches of re-set tiling round the edges, but a medieval tiled floor with a network of patches across the centre, including several of fairly recent brickwork.

When this floor was laid, the W. wall-bench of the mid 14th century, and the western 4.40 m. length of the rather later S. bench, were left in position and no doubt raised to suit the new level. The N. wall-bench, also later, was probably raised for a length of 6.90 m. between the W. end and the centre wall-shaft. The E. sections of the N. and S. benches were levelled and the floor extended over them. The remaining S. bench was shorter because access to the chapel from the S. remained through the third bay from the E. Here what is now the Lady Chapel was divided, its second bay from the E. being the Montague chantry, the two W. queuing-space for pilgrims, if large numbers still flocked to be cured by Frideswide's relics. The reduction of the extent of wall-benches could reflect a reduction in pilgrim-numbers, a change in arrangement of the area round the shrine, or an attempt by the canons to extract more cash from visitors, by putting in an extra barrier to go through.

The design of the floor fitted into the bays of the chapel, although its complex structural history meant that they were all of different lengths, the longest to the E., while the widths were fairly irregular. Along parts of either side were rows of square-set tiles, three tiles wide on the N. and from four to seven on the S. Right down the centre of at least the eastern half of the chapel, as a base-line for the whole design, there seems to have been a line of narrow border-tiles, possibly once glazed black or very dark greeny-brown; two remained in position against the altar-steps at the E. end. The exact line continued westward as the S. edge of the slab to Dr. Clarke (d. 1877), the N. edge of Dr. Barnes's slab of 1859 and the centre-line of the diamond-laid slabs of 1826 and 1827–31 to members of the Smith family. All this suggests that the main outlines of the design survived far into the 19th century; such an analysis depends on a survey accurate to the nearest twenty-fifth of one per cent.

---

[21] D. Sturdy et al., 'The Painted Roof of the Old Library, Christ Church', *Oxoniensia*, xxvi-xxvii (1961–2), 215–17.

The S. half of the W. bay was of diamond-set tiles. Of about 200, many cut to fit around the edges, some 40 were still in position, three of them, close under the stalls on the S. side, with visible patterns. Two more tiles of this section and seven more of the adjacent square-set belt still retained their patterns (Figs. 46–7), protected as they were in the 17th century by the stalls. The designs are discussed further below (p. 109). The N. half of this bay had square-set tiles, 52 of which were in position and 18 possibly in position, with the impressions of another 8 recovered from their mortar bedding. Originally there were about 200 tiles in this section, and eight of those in position ran precisely one row N. of the presumed centre-line mentioned above. This bay of the floor had received the most wear and had a large brick patch by the entrance. But it was least disturbed by burials in the 16th to 19th centuries and consequently retained the highest proportion of tiles in position. We can therefore be most confident in restoring the original design here.

The next bay, the third from the E., was effectively the centre of the chapel, into which pilgrims stepped down from the entrance (above, p. 81) on the S. side. The floor pattern in this bay was separated from the bay to its W. by a single row of square tiles, only one of which remained, and from the bay to its E. by a triple row of square, narrow and square tiles, ten of which remained. The S. half of the bay was divided into two squares; each of these squares had a 'Union Jack' pattern formed by a straight and a diagonal cross of narrow border-tiles, the remainder of the field being filled with square tiles laid square. Although only 40 of these tiles remained, in a narrow strip along the S. edge, they were enough to permit a reliable reconstruction of this spectacular feature. The design of the northern half of this bay is less certain, but two square-set tiles remaining in its N.E. corner suggest that the 'Union Jack' pattern was not repeated here. The large slab to Dr. Ogilvy (d.1883) took up most of the space and a careful study of old photographs might reveal something more of the original design here.

In the next bay, the second from the E., the N. half was laid with diamond-set tiles, like the S. half of the W. bay and probably also of the E. bay, as we shall see. Only seven tiles remained in position out of more than 250, but two patches, one at each end of Dorothea Upton's slab of 1654, show that the reconstruction is valid, even if they have been relaid. To judge from a single tile, the N. belt of square-set tiles stopped just past the central wall-shaft and the diamond-set tiles ran up to the N. wall.

The S. part of the bay had square-set tiles. Most of these were re-laid, but a belt four tiles wide on the N. side of Lady Montague's tomb, incorporating a small stone bearing the indent of a brass inscription, could have been *in situ* if the graves below it (**2E**.3 i-ii) were in fact pre-Reformation. Slightly W. of the centre of the bay, the S. belt of tiles was interrupted by a line of three narrow border-tiles running N.–S. This line, if it extended northwards, might mark the position of a shrine-altar or the W. side of steps leading up to the shrine. The shrine itself (above, p. 95) could well have stood S. of the centre-line, in the middle of this half-bay, to be seen better from the N. transept. On this interpretation, the two 'Union Jack' squares in the bay to the W. would have emphasised the liturgically important space in front of the shrine.

In the E. bay of the chapel all the tiles were, in 1963, square-set. However, in its S. half there were six diamond-set marble slabs of 1636 to 1857, indicating that the tiles here were originally diamond-set also. As already noted (above, p. 98), the S. edge of the slab to Dr. Clarke (d.1877) marks a very satisfactory central design-line that is perpetuated along the full length of the chapel, although without a single original tile in position except for two here by the altar steps. The slab and all the tiles near it were square-set and presumably the tiles always had been. While almost every tile in this bay appeared to have been relaid at one time or another, a line of five narrow border-tiles ran

Fig. 44.   Stalls against E. end wall of Latin Chapel, photographed c.1865 (enlargement of Fig. 76).

N.–S. just below the foot of the slab, exactly at the centre of the bay. They may have been in position or relaid to follow an old division-line that was later lost elsewhere.

It is unclear from the remaining architecture and fittings quite how the easternmost bay, which would have been behind the shrine and its altar, was used liturgically. Presumably the canons kept this bay screened off, perhaps housing cope-chests and safe-boxes for valuable items used in worship at the shrine, possibly also a cash-box for instant safekeeping of offerings at the shrine. A lithograph of about 1850 (Fig. 101), imaginative in that it portrays a cavalier and his family but exact in architectural detail, shows the E. end of the Latin Chapel with a row of late-medieval stalls against it. The view is towards the E., to include a good deal of the 'watching chamber', and only six out of perhaps ten stalls appear. They appear again in a photograph of the 1860s (Figs. 44, 76), now cut down to eight in number and converted into a makeshift reredos by the removal of their arm-rests and seats and the addition of an oversize cresting and over-tall end-posts by some enthusiastic gothiciser. These stalls may have been in that place in the chapel from about 1500, and must have been discarded during an ill-documented restoration in 1890. The canons perhaps used them for resting during long services at the shrine.

MEDIEVAL WINDOW GLASS FROM THE LATIN CHAPEL (Fig. 45). By NIALL DONALD

Three of the four windows in the N. wall of the Latin Chapel contain original glass from the 14th century. The main lights are largely intact, although not necessarily in their

Fig. 45.   Latin Chapel: excavated glass fragments. *Scale 1:2.*

original positions; but the tracery, the borders and the trellises of white grisaille have mostly been restored. It has proved possible to match up much of the glass recovered during the 1963 excavations with the original and restored designs. This is especially the case with the grisaille. From the E., the three windows will be referred to as the St. Frideswide, the archbishop saint and the Virgin and Child windows, after the figures depicted in the central lights. For the glass which cannot be attributed to these windows, the original source can only be surmised. It may well come from either or both of the other windows in the chapel. One possibility that can be discounted is that it comes from earlier glazing, since all the glass in the assemblage is 14th-century in character.

In total 40 fragments of window glass were recovered from the 1963 excavations. Of these, 31 were painted. One complete clear and unpainted rectangular glass quarry was recovered.

Fig. 45 Nos. 1–11 depict the glass from the grisaille trellises of the three windows. Nos. 5–6 can be attributed to the archbishop saint window and 1–2 to the Virgin and Child window. Nos. 3–4 can also be attributed to the last, but with less certainty. However, the slight variations in patterning may only be apparent due to the restoration work. Each quarry in the trellis of each window has a narrow border of yellow stain delineated on the inner side by two parallel painted lines, one thick and one thin. The St. Frideswide window has trails of roses, the archbishop saint trails of daisies and the Virgin and Child oak-leaves and acorns as the grisaille design.

Fig. 45 Nos. 12–13 show fragments of bird wings, which probably originated in the border to the main lights of the archbishop window with its array of grotesque beasts, monkeys and birds.

The remaining 12 fragments cannot be attributed to any of the three surviving windows. No. 14 is a fragment of drapery, or possibly of background. Nos. 15–17 are fragments of architectural designs painted on clear glass. Nos. 18–20 are background designs: 18 is picked out of a matt wash on yellow. Nos. 21–25 are border pieces with either simple geometric designs (23–25) or something more complex (21–22).

The recovery of this glass suggests that the chapel was the original location of the windows. Alternatively, the lack of any figural fragments or drapery in the assemblage may suggest that the fragments result from the refitting of the old windows into a new position. If the glass was cut to a new shape, a concentration of waste border and grisaille fragments might be expected if the work was carried out in the chapel.

Provenances:
*Cutting 1*: Fig. 45 Nos. 1, 5–7, 10–14, 19–21, 23–5.
*Cutting 2*: Fig. 45 Nos. 2–4, 8–9, 15–18, 22.
*Cutting 3*: one fragment, not illustrated.

# Medieval Floor-Tiles from St. Frideswide's Priory

By Julia Green

Incorporating previous research by David Ganz, Margaret Mullett, Brian Prescott-Decie and Michael Trend

SUMMARY

*Tiles (now in the Ashmolean Museum) from the Latin Chapel, Cathedral Gardens, 'watching chamber' and Meadows Building site are analysed and discussed, and previously unpublished designs are illustrated. The Latin Chapel tiles are mostly of 'Stabbed Wessex' (c.1280–1320) and 'printed' (c.1330–80) types, with a few printed tiles of c.1500. It is suggested that they may represent three floors: (a) associated with the 1289 shrine; (b) associated with the rebuilding of the Latin Chapel c.1330–50; and (c) the late medieval floor of which fragments remained* in situ.

The excavations in the Latin Chapel produced over 400 floor-tile fragments, and those in the Cathedral Gardens 35 fragments. In addition, the floor-tiles from the 'watching chamber' and those found on the site of the Meadows Building in 1862–4 have been included in this report. A draft report was prepared in 1971 by Michael Trend, David Ganz, Margaret Mullet and Brian Prescott-Decie which, with the accompanying card-index and notes, has proved useful in the preparation of this account. Unfortunately some tile fragments appear to have been mislaid since the draft report was written, and only the tiles now in the Ashmolean Museum are included here. The tiles have been re-examined to record details of their fabrics; I am grateful to Maureen Mellor who kindly arranged a loan of the Oxford Archaeological Unit's tile fabric series to ensure compatibility with their reports.

## LATIN CHAPEL AND CATHEDRAL GARDENS

The tiles from these two excavations have been dealt with together as they are very closely related as groups. The majority of the tiles from the Cathedral Gardens, which were found in unstratified deposits, may have originally been laid in the Latin Chapel and removed from there during 19th-century restoration work.

*The general character of the tiled pavements*

As described above by David Sturdy, the Latin Chapel excavations revealed the existence of at least two successive tile pavements, the later 25 cm. higher than the earlier. The first ('Stabbed Wessex') pavement had been destroyed by the laying of the

Fig. 46.   Latin Chapel: *in situ* fragment of tile pavement, looking S.W.

later pavement, and its design thus lost. Table 1 gives the occurrence of particular designs. Nearly fifty different tiles of 'Stabbed Wessex' type are represented, so the overall design must have been complex.

Sturdy discusses the design of the later pavement (above, pp. 97–100). Unfortunately, there is very little stratigraphical evidence for most of the tiles from this later floor, so an accurate reconstruction of the design is impossible in most cases. The exception is the fragment of pavement illustrated by Emden and republished here (Figs. 46–7).[1] It is the junction between two sections of floor, one square-set and one diamond-set (cf. Fig. 37). The *in situ* tiles consist of Haberly designs CXXI and CXXII (arms of Archbishop Chichele), a variant of CXXIII (LC18, arms of Burghersh) and a new design (LC15, illustrated Fig. 49 No. 15).[2] Enough of the tiles retain their locational information for it to be possible to reconstruct a small section of this floor.

Over twenty designs were present in the later pavement as a whole (see Table 1). Table 2 gives the numbers and percentages of two-colour decorated tiles, mosaic tiles and plain floor-tiles. As the main purpose of this table is to demonstrate the small number of mosaic and plain tiles in relation to two-colour decorated tiles, a division between 'inlaid' and 'printed' tiles has not been made.[3] The one relief tile from the Cathedral Gardens (Fig. 48) has been omitted from the table, as it does not fit in with the rest of the group and may be a stray from a different part of the Priory.

[1] A.B. Emden, 'Some Patterned Paving-Tiles in the Latin Chapel', *The Christ Church Cathedral Record* (1964), 13–16.

[2] L. Haberly, *Medieval English Paving Tiles* (1937).

[3] The term 'printed' is used here to define the technical development from the method of inlaying solid clay, following Haberly. The precise method of manufacture requires extensive further study. Mrs. Eames decided to abandon the distinction and refer to both types as two-colour decorated but I feel that the development is important. (Cf. E. Eames, *Catalogue of Medieval Lead-Glazed Earthenware Tiles in the Department of Medieval and Later Antiquities, British Museum*, i (1980), 45–8).

TABLE 1 DISTRIBUTION OF DECORATED FLOOR TILES

Cutting 1

| Type | No. | Type | No. |
|---|---|---|---|
| XXII | 1 | LIV | 6 |
| XXIII | 1 | LVI | 1 |
| XXIV/V | 2 | LIX | 1 |
| XXV | 1 | LXI | 2 |
| XXVIII | 1 | LXX | 1 |
| XXXI | 1 | LC3 | 6 |
| XXXII | 2 | LC4 | 2 |
| XXXVIII | 3 | LC7 | 1 |
| XL | 1 | LC8 | 1 |
| XLIV | 1 | LC11 | 4 |
| XLIV/V/VI | 4 | LC12 | 1 |
| LVI | 1 | LC13 | 1 |
| LC3 | 1 | Unid. | 5 |
| LC10 | 1 | *Inlaid* | *104* |
| LC11 | 2 | LXXX | 1 |
| LC14 | 1 | CXIV | 1 |
| HOHLER W9 | 1 | CXXI | 5 |
| HOHLER W35 | 1 | CXXII | 2 |
| Unid. | 5 | CXXIII | 4 |
| *Inlaid* | *31* | CCXLVI | 1 |
| CXXI | 2 | LC15 | 3 |
| LC18 | 2 | LC17 | 1 |
| Unid. | 1 | LC18 | 7 |
| *Printed* | *5* | LC21 | 2 |
| *Total* | *36* | LC22 | 3 |
| | | Unid. | 9 |
| | | *Printed* | *39* |
| | | *Total* | *143* |

Cutting 2

| Type | No. |
|---|---|
| IX | 1 |
| X | 1 |
| XI | 1 |
| XXII | 6 |
| XXIII | 4 |
| XXIV/V | 9 |
| XXV | 3 |
| XXV/VI | 1 |
| XXVII | 2 |
| XXVIII | 2 |
| XXXI | 6 |
| XXXII | 2 |
| XXXIII/IV | 1 |
| XXXV | 6 |
| XXXVI | 1 |
| XXXVII | 3 |
| XXXVIII | 1 |
| XL | 1 |
| XLIV | 8 |
| XLIV/V/VI | 7 |
| XLV | 1 |
| XLVI | 1 |
| L | 1 |
| LIII | 3 |

Cutting 3

| Type | No. |
|---|---|
| I | 1 |
| III | 1 |
| XXII | 1 |
| XXIII | 1 |
| XXIV/V | 1 |
| XXVII | 1 |
| XXIX | 1 |
| XXXI | 2 |
| XXXII | 1 |
| XXXV | 1 |
| LIII | 1 |
| LIV | 1 |
| LCI | 1 |
| LC3 | 1 |
| LC8 | 1 |
| Unid. | 1 |
| *Inlaid* | *17* |
| CXXI | 1 |
| Unid. | 2 |
| *Printed* | *3* |
| *Total* | *20* |

Cutting 4

| Type | No. |
| --- | --- |
| XLIV | 1 |
| LC4 | 1 |
| *Inlaid* | *2* |
| *Total* | *2* |

Cutting unspecified

| Type | No. |
| --- | --- |
| I | 5 |
| III | 1 |
| XXII | 9 |
| XXIII | 3 |
| XXIV | 2 |
| XXIV/V | 12 |
| XXVI | 1 |
| XXVII | 3 |
| XXVIII | 5 |
| XXXI | 3 |
| XXXII | 1 |
| XXXVIII | 2 |
| XL/I | 1 |
| XLI | 1 |
| XLIV | 1 |
| XLIV/V/VI | 4 |
| XLV | 1 |
| XLVI | 1 |
| LIII | 1 |
| LIV | 2 |
| LVI | 2 |
| LXI | 1 |
| LXVII | 1 |
| LXIX | 2 |
| LXX | 1 |
| LXXIII | 1 |
| LC2 | 1 |
| LC5 | 1 |
| LC6 | 1 |
| LC9 | 1 |
| LC11 | 3 |
| HOHLER W9 | 3 |
| Unid. | 9 |
| *Inlaid* | *86* |
| LXXIX | 2 |
| IC | 1 |
| CXXI | 4 |
| CXXII | 2 |
| CXXIII | 8 |
| CLXVIII | 3 |
| CLXX | 3 |
| CCXXXVI | 1 |
| CCXLIII | 1 |
| CCLIX | 3 |
| LC15 | 1 |
| LC16 | 1 |

| Type | No. |
| --- | --- |
| LC17 | 2 |
| LC18 | 7 |
| LC19 | 1 |
| LC20 | 9 |
| LC21 | 2 |
| LC22 | 10 |
| Unid. | 11 |
| *Printed* | *72* |
| *Total* | *158* |

Cathedral Gardens

| Type | No. |
| --- | --- |
| XXIV | 1 |
| XXIV/V | 2 |
| XXVI | 1 |
| XXVIII | 1 |
| XXIX | 1 |
| XXXI | 1 |
| XXXII | 2 |
| XXXV | 1 |
| XXXVI/VII | 1 |
| XXXVII | 1 |
| XL | 1 |
| XLII | 1 |
| XLIV | 1 |
| XLVI | 2 |
| LIV | 2 |
| LVI | 1 |
| LC1 | 1 |
| LC10 | 1 |
| LC11 | 1 |
| Unid. | 8 |
| *Inlaid* | *31* |
| LXXX | 1 |
| C | 1 |
| Unid. | 1 |
| *Printed* | *3* |
| CG23 | 1 |
| *Relief* | *1* |
| *Total* | *35* |

Watching Chamber

| Type | No. |
| --- | --- |
| XXVII | 1 |
| XXVIII | 1 |
| XXXI | 2 |
| XXXII | 3 |
| XL | 1 |
| XLI | 1 |
| XLII | 1 |
| LXI | 1 |
| LC11 | 1 |
| WC24 | 1 |

| Type | No. | Type | No. |
|------|-----|------|-----|
| WC25 | 1 | XXXVIII | 1 |
| WC26 | 1 | LIV | 1 |
| HOHLER W39 | 3 | MB29 | 1 |
| Unid. | 1 | MB30 | 1 |
| *Inlaid* | *19* | MB31 | 2 |
| CXXI/II | 1 | MB32 | 1 |
| LC18 | 2 | MB33 | 1 |
| WC27 | 1 | Unid. | 1 |
| WC28 | 1 | *Inlaid* | *12* |
| Unid. | 2 | MB35 | 1 |
| *Printed* | *7* | *Relief (early medieval)* | *1* |
| *Total* | *26* | *Total* | *13* |

Meadows Building

| Type | No. |
|------|-----|
| XXIV/V | 1 |
| XXVI | 1 |
| XXXI | 1 |

Roman Numerals = Haberly types
Hohler = C. Hohler's types from Bucks.
LC = Latin Chapel types (illustrated Figs. 49–50)
CG = Cathedral Garden type (illustrated Fig. 48)
WC = Watching Chamber types (illustrated Fig. 50)
MB = Meadows Building types (illustrated Fig. 50)
Unid. = Unidentified fragments

TABLE 2 Proportion of two-colour, mosaic and plain floor tile fragments

| | Two-colour | | Mosaic | | Plain | | Total |
|------|-----|-----|-----|-----|-----|-----|-----|
| | No. | % | No. | % | No. | % | |
| Cutting 1 | 36 | 68 | 12 | 23 | 5 | 9 | 53 |
| Cutting 2 | 143 | 85 | 16 | 10 | 9 | 5 | 168 |
| Cutting 3 | 20 | 83 | 3 | 13 | 1 | 4 | 24 |
| Cutting 4 | 2 | 50 | 0 | – | 2 | 50 | 4 |
| Cutting unspecified | 158 | 90 | 9 | 5 | 8 | 5 | 175 |
| Cathedral Gardens | 34 | 89 | 1 | 3 | 3 | 8 | 38 |

*Two-colour decorated tiles*

Table 1 shows that no one design or group of designs dominated either of the tile pavements, and that many designs are represented by only very few fragments. As Sturdy (above, p. 98) estimates that the later pavement alone would have consisted of more than 2000 tiles, and only *c*.425 were recovered during excavation from sections of both pavements, it is impossible to say whether this represents a true picture of the design.

Almost all the tiles illustrated in Figs. 49–50 are designs not previously published from the area, or variants of ones which have been published.

*Relief tiles*

The one relief tile from the Cathedral Gardens (CG23, Fig. 48) resembles Haberly CCXLIII, but this was published as a 'printed' tile.

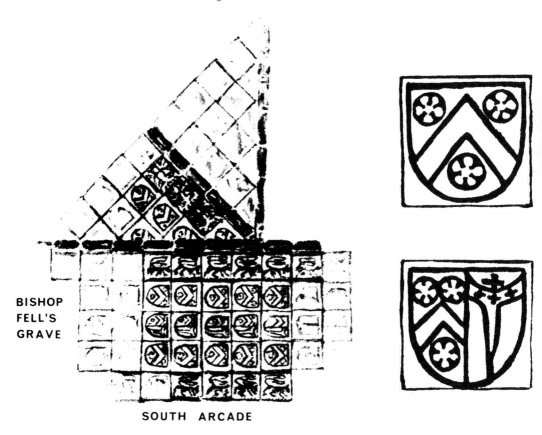

Fig. 47.   Latin Chapel: A.B. Emden's drawing of the fragment of pavement shown in Fig. 46, reproduced from
*Christ Church Cathedral Record* 1964.

Fig. 48.   Relief tile from Cathedral Gardens (tile No. 23). *Scale 1:2.* (Drawing by Sarah Blair.)

*Mosaic tiles*

About 40 fragments of mosaic tiles were found, of which three are rectangular ?border tiles. The rest are small square and triangular shapes, all but three of which are in Fabric IIIB which equates with the earlier pavement of 'Stabbed Wessex' type tiles. The small square tiles are either *c.*67 mm. or *c.*77 mm. square, and the triangular tiles were made from diagonally scoring and breaking the squares. Most of the mosaic tiles are worn, but where evidence of glaze colour remains, yellow, brown and dark green are represented in roughly equal proportions. No record of how these tiles were laid remains.

*Plain tiles*

Of the 28 plain tile fragments recovered, 12 are in Fabric IIIB and may be parts of mosaic tiles, but the fragments are too small to determine this. The other plain tile fragments are equally divided between Fabrics IVb and IVc. These fabrics belong to the later pavement of 'printed' tiles. Only seven of the fragments retain any trace of glaze, and of these six have green glaze and the other has yellow-brown glaze.

*The dates of the Latin Chapel pavements*

The earlier pavement seems to have been made up exclusively from 'Stabbed Wessex' tiles, which are usually assigned to the date-range *c.*1280–1320. The tiles relate well to those from St. Peter's-in-the-East, dated by Emden to *c.*1330,[4] and if the Decorated rebuilding of the Latin Chapel can be assigned to the 1330s (rather than the '40s or '50s), it seems possible that they represent its original floor. However, this stretches the dating somewhat, and the floor might more convincingly be associated with the installation of the new shrine in 1289.

The 'printed' tiles of the second floor include several Penn-type designs, datable to *c.*1330–80. The presence among these of tiles with the arms of Burghersh (LC18) suggests a connection with Bishop Burghersh's chantry, founded in 1338 (below, p. 245). On the other hand, the *in situ* section (Figs. 46–7) included tiles with the arms of Archbishop Chichele (Haberly CXXI and CXXII) also used in All Souls College chapel,[5] and a minority of the *ex situ* tiles are of *c.*1500. Probably the best explanation is that a complete floor of Penn-type tiles was laid after the rebuilding of the Latin Chapel in the 1330s or 1340s, and that a high proportion of these were re-used in the new floor of *c.*1500.

THE 'WATCHING CHAMBER'

The Ashmolean Museum contains a collection of 26 two-colour decorated tiles and four plain tiles found in the filling of the tomb-chest under the 'watching chamber' in 1889. Many of the designs reflect those in the Latin Chapel and it is possible that they were

---

[4] A.B. Emden, 'Medieval Floor Tiles in the Church of St. Peter in the East, Oxford', *Oxoniensia*, xxxiv (1969), 32; cf. Eames op. cit. note 3.

[5] Emden op. cit. note 1.

either laid at the same time or that they are wrongly labelled and in fact are part of the Latin Chapel pavements. Three new designs of 'Stabbed Wessex' type tiles and two of 'printed' tiles are illustrated in Fig. 50. Table 1 gives the occurrence of particular designs.

MEADOWS BUILDING

This collection of 13 tiles in the Ashmolean Museum was found during the digging of foundations for 'New Buildings' (i.e. Meadows Building), Christ Church in March 1863 (see below, p. 229). All except one are 'Stabbed Wessex' types and five new designs are represented (see Fig. 50). The other, an important late Anglo-Saxon relief tile, is discussed below (pp. 259–63) by Martin Biddle and Birthe Kjølbye-Biddle. Table 1 gives the occurrence of particular designs. The fact that only one design is represented by more than one tile suggests that recovery was selective. The discovery of decorated floor-tiles at this site implies that buildings other than the church in St. Frideswide's Priory were laid with tile pavements, and this would parallel the findings at the Dominican Priory, Oxford.[6]

## CATALOGUE OF ILLUSTRATED TILES

The two-colour tiles in Figs. 49–50 are designs not previously published from Oxfordshire, variants of known designs, or more complete examples of designs known only fragmentarily. Two of the Latin Chapel tile designs (LC1 and 10) have been illustrated by combining fragments from the Latin Chapel with fragments from Cathedral Gardens where this enabled a more complete design to be recorded.

The following abbreviations have been used:

| | |
|---|---|
| Ash: | Ashmolean Museum Accession number |
| Eames: | E. Eames, *Catalogue of Medieval Lead-Glazed Earthenware Tiles in the Department of Medieval and Later Antiquities, British Museum* (two vols., 1980). |
| Haberly: | L. Haberly, *Medieval English Paving Tiles* (1937). |
| Hinton: | D.A. Hinton, 'A New Tile Design from Abingdon', *Oxoniensia*, xxxiv (1969), 106–7. |
| Hohler: | C. Hohler, 'Medieval Pavingtiles in Buckinghamshire', *Records of Bucks*. xiv (1942), |
| Lambrick and Mellor: | G. Lambrick and M. Mellor, 'The Tiles', in G. Lambrick, 'Further excavations of the Dominican Priory, Oxford', *Oxoniensia* l (1985), 179–86. |

LATIN CHAPEL (Figs. 49–50)

*Inlaid 'Stabbed Wessex' tiles*

1. Three fragments (composite illustration). Two fishes depicted head to tail, apparently joined by a line, and within a square frame. Similar to a tile from Abingdon (Hinton). Stabbed keys. Fabric IIIB. (Cutting **3**, Ash. 1985.185 (two fragments); CG 1961, Ash.1985.188.)
2. Seven fragments which join to form *c.*70% of one tile. A five-petalled flower and a group of ?oak-leaves with the same design reversed above. Similar to Lambrick and Mellor No. 12. Stabbed keys. Fabric IIIB. (Ash. 1976.475.)
3. Eight fragments (composite illustration of three). Hunting scene showing a huntsman blowing a horn and a dog chasing a stag. Hohler W2 from Notley Abbey; these fragments give additional detail of the design. Stabbed keys. Fabric IIIB. (Cutting **2**, Ash. 1985.185.)

[6] G. Lambrick and M. Mellor, 'The Tiles', in G. Lambrick, 'Further excavations of the Dominican Priory, Oxford', *Oxoniensia*, 1 (1985), 179–86.

Fig. 49.   Two-colour tiles. *Scale 1:4.* (Drawing by Sarah Blair.)

Fig. 50. Two-colour tiles. *Scale 1:4.* (Drawing by Sarah Blair.)

4. Three fragments (illustration is of two which join). Variant of Haberly XI/XII with the inner corner blank. Stabbed keys. Fabric IIIB. (Cutting **4**, Ash.1976.203; Cutting **2W**, Ash.1976.203.)

5. Virtually complete tile in five pieces. Variant of Haberly XXIV which has piercing in the main band and a circle in the corner, here replaced with part of another ring. Stabbed keys. Fabric IIIB. (Ash.1976.228.)

6. One fragment. Variant of Haberly XXIV/XXV with larger lobed foliage in the inner corner. Similar to Hohler W39. Stabbed keys. Fabric IIIB. (Ash.1976.230.)

7. One fragment. Probably a variant of Haberly XXIX with the base of the foliage altered. Stabbed keys. Fabric IIIB. (Ash.1976.278.)

8. Two fragments. Variant of Haberly XXXII which has a quatrefoil piercing the fleur-de-lys. Stabbed keys. Fabric IIIB. (Cutting **3**, Ash.1976.302.)

9. One fragment. Variant of Haberly XXXIII which has triangular piercings in the band around the central flower. Stabbed keys. Fabric IIIB. (Ash.1976.303.)

10. Two fragments (composite illustration). A griffon. A reversed version of Haberly XXXVI. Stabbed keys. Fabric IIIB. (Cutting **1**, Ash.1976.315; CG I, Ash.1976.312.)

11. Ten fragments (composite illustration). Variant of Haberly XLVIII where the flowers in the centre of each side are formed of inlay, not outlined by it. Stabbed keys. Fabric IIIB. (Cutting **2**, Ash.1976.366–7.)

12. One fragment. Variant of Haberly L which has a piercing in each lobe of the quatrefoil. Stabbed keys. Fabric IIIB. (Cutting **2W**, Ash.1976.369.)

13. One fragment. Border tile. The design has been stamped off-centre. Stabbed keys. Fabric IIIB. (Cutting **2**, Ash.1985.185.)

14. One fragment. Letter I placed diagonally. The edges are scored and broken on two sides, indicating that these small letter-tiles were made in groups on larger tiles and then divided for use. Stabbed keys. Fabric IIIB. (Cutting **1**, Ash.1985.185.)

## 'Printed' tiles

15. Four fragments (composite illustration of one complete tile and one fragment). Lion mask with protruding tongue. The complete tile is very worn, with only traces of the design remaining. Unkeyed. Fabric IVa. (*In situ* tile 9, Cutting **2W**, Ash.1985.187; Cutting **2**, Ash.1985.188.)

16. Complete tile, very worn. An eagle displayed with a block of slip on either side of tail. Scored diagonally. Unkeyed. ?Fabric IVb. (Ash.1985.187.)

17. Three fragments (composite illustration of one complete tile and one fragment). A ?dragon with leafy tail in a cusped quadrant. The complete tile is very worn with only traces of the design remaining. Similar to Hohler P119–24 and Eames 1398–9. Unkeyed. Fabric: moderate amounts of subrounded quartz, sorted, 1 mm. (Cutting **2E**, Ash.1985.185; Ash.1985.185.)

18. Sixteen fragments (composite illustration of three). Variant of Haberly CXXIII which has wavy-edge borders and no circles. Unkeyed. Fabric IVb. (Ash.1976.440; Cutting **1**, Ash.1976.439; *in situ* tile 1, Cutting **2W**, Ash.1985.188.)

19. Complete tile. Worn. Variant of Haberly LXVII (arms of See of Exeter), which has fleur-de-lys in the two lower corners and a slightly different positioning of the sword. Unkeyed. Fabric IVa. (Ash.1985.187.)

20. Nine complete or near-complete tiles. Variant of Haberly CCXXVIII, which has a five-pointed star between two five-lobed leaves with two similar leaves below. Five of the tiles have been diagonally scored. Unkeyed. Fabric IVc. (Ash.1985.184–5, 188.)

21. Four fragments (composite illustration of three). Border tile. Unkeyed. ?Fabrics IVa and IVb. (All Ash.1985.186.)

22. Thirteen fragments (composite illustration of two which join). Border tile. Unkeyed. Fabric IVb. (Both Cutting **2**, Ash.1985.188.)

CATHEDRAL GARDENS (Fig. 48)

## Relief tile

23. One fragment. Squirrel, possibly holding a nut. Good green glaze. Similar to Haberly CCXLIII. Unkeyed. ?Fabric IVb. (Ash.1985.188.)

WATCHING CHAMBER (Fig. 50)

### Inlaid 'Stabbed Wessex' tiles

24. Complete tile. Variant of Haberly II, which has three-part foliage in the centre of each side instead of the five-part foliage on this tile. Worn. Keying obscured by mortar. Fabric IIIB. (Ash.1970.554.)
25. One fragment. Stabbed keys. Fabric IIIB. (Ash.1970.569.)
26. One fragment. Uncertain design. Unkeyed. Fabric IIIB. (Ash.1970.575.)

### 'Printed' tiles

27. One fragment. Variant of Haberly CLXXIX, which has quatrefoils in the corners instead of fleur-de-lys. The design is badly executed, the slip having smeared and obliterated part of the design. Unkeyed. Fabric IVb. (Ash.1970.576.).
28. One fragment. Variant of Haberly CXVIII, which has a trefoil design within the quadrant. The back of the tile has sheared off and so no evidence of keying remains. Fabric IVc. (Ash.1970.571.)

MEADOWS BUILDING (Fig. 50)

### Inlaid 'Stabbed Wessex' tiles

29. Complete tile broken into three pieces. Part of a four-tile design of animals (?griffons) set within a quatrefoil. Trifoliate cross in outer corner, and stylised ear of corn enclosed by the intersection of the foils. Stabbed keys. Fabric IIIb. (Ash.1970.543, 547.)
30. One fragment. An eagle displayed. Half-tile with scored and broken edge. Stabbed keys. Fabric IIIB. (Ash.1970.544.)
31. Two fragments of scored half-tiles (composite illustration). Foliate spray in outer angle with floral or foliate motif beneath. Stabbed keys. Fabric IIIB. (Ash.1970.545–6.)
32. One fragment. Scored half-tile. Variant of Hohler W18, which has circular piercings in the centre motif and all the stars pierced. Stabbed keys. Fabric IIIB. (Ash.1970.550.)
33. One fragment. Similar to Eames 2084–8. Stabbed keys. Fabric IIIB. (Ash.1970.551.)

# The 12th-Century Church of St. Frideswide's Priory

By Richard Halsey

## SUMMARY

*No documentary or direct chronicle evidence exists for the 12th-century church of St. Frideswide's Priory. Although regular Augustinian canons were established on the site of the old minster associated with St. Frideswide by 1122, none of the present church can be dated on stylistic evidence to much before c.1160. However, remaining parts of the cloister are clearly earlier, the chapter-house doorway sculpture being attributable to an Oxfordshire Romanesque workshop of c.1140–50. The chancel was built prior to the translation of St. Frideswide in 1180, the transepts and nave following quite quickly, but on an enhanced scale to the original conception. The plan of the church c.1200 can be reconstructed with aisled transepts and a seven-bay nave, with a N.E. chapel presumably associated with the cult of St. Frideswide. Analysis of architectural details, especially the capital sculpture, demonstrates an awareness of architectural work well beyond the Thames Valley. The use of a 'giant order' elevation of some sophistication suggests that this form of elevation could have once been more common than is realised, perhaps associated earlier in the 12th century with the royal patronage of Henry I and his court.*

## ACKNOWLEDGEMENTS

Much of this article is taken from my incomplete Ph.D thesis, the research having been undertaken in the early 1970s. For great freedom of access to the Cathedral in that period I have to thank the then Dean, the Rev. Prof. Henry Chadwick; the verger, Mr. Holloway; and the Clerk of Works, Mr. Major. At that time, I received discreet guidance from my supervisor at the Courtauld Institute, Dr Peter Kidson, and stimulus and support from Eric Fernie, Sandy Heslop, Prof. Peter Lasko, Veronica Sekules, Malcolm Thurlby, Christopher Wilson and Prof. George Zarnecki (among many) then working at the Courtauld Institue. Great practical help came from Jill Kerr and especially my wife, Alison Halsey. It is Dr. John Blair who has persuaded me to dust down my thesis and contribute to this issue of *Oxoniensia*, and organised access to the Cathedral with the kind help of Edward Evans, now the verger. Finally, but by no means least of all, I thank my typists Mrs. Jackson & Mrs. Corben for persevering through so many revisions.

## INTRODUCTION

Perhaps because of its small scale, perhaps due to its seclusion behind Tom Quad, or perhaps simply because it is so difficult to categorise, Christ Church Cathedral, Oxford,

Fig. 51.   The chapter-house front. (R.C.H.M.: Crown copyright reserved.)

has not received as much attention from architectural historians as most other English cathedrals. This is all the more odd because it is a remarkably rich mine for those interested in that much-studied period, the Transitional style in England, when the insular (but highly developed) late Anglo-Norman Romanesque architectural style became infused with northern French, early Gothic ideas and motifs.[1]

Two of the most recent authoritative architectural accounts have suggested that the church of St. Frideswide's Priory was built after 1190. Pevsner, in the absence of documentary dates, reaches this conclusion from an analysis of the capital types;[2] the *V.C.H.* relies on the entry in the Oseney Chronicle recording for the year 1190: 'Combusta est ecclesia Sanctae Frideswidae cum maxime parte civitate Oxenfordi'.[3] Both presume an earlier rebuilding sometime after the establishment of the Augustinian

[1] Jean Bony, 'French Influences on the Origins of English Gothic Architecture', *Jnl. of the Courtauld & Warburg Institutes*, xii (1949), 1–15, established the basic principles, perhaps over-emphasising the role of the Cistercian Order at the expense of other patrons, whose buildings have not survived in such numbers. Typically Oxford Cathedral is not mentioned!

[2] J. Sherwood and N. Pevsner, *The Buildings of England: Oxfordshire* (1974), 113–18.

[3] *V.C.H. Oxon.* iv (1979) 364, 369; The Oseney Chronicle in *Annales Monastici* iv, ed. H.R. Luard (Rolls Ser. xxxvi, 1869), 43.

canons (confirmed by Henry I *c.*1122, cf. below, p. 227), and believe that the triforium-level window in the W. wall of the S. transept comes from that church.

Both authors also believe that the 12th-century church was built quickly, endorsing the 1939 R.C.H.M. statement that it 'must have been completed within twenty years after this date'.[4] But the date the R.C.H.M. refers to is that of the translation of St. Frideswide (mistakenly given as 1181) and the start of building is given as 'after the middle of the 12th century . . . . the E. part of the church probably completed . . . . in 1181'. Alfred Clapham was then the Secretary to the Commission, and he had written of the cathedral that 'the character of its mouldings and decoration insist upon a period not earlier than 1170–80'.[5] Finally, Peter Kidson, in describing the Romanesque work as being the 'ultimate sophistication' of the Anglo-Norman style, suggests *c.*1160.[6] It is one of the aims of this paper to re-establish the pre-1180 date for the chancel.

Despite the attempts of some antiquaries to locate visual evidence for either Frideswide's 8th-century nunnery or Æthelred's church of 1004, there is nothing visible on the site today that can be stylistically dated earlier than *c.*1120; indeed, very little material clearly earlier than the mid 12th century is associated with the Priory. Given the usual pattern in England, a re-building of the secular canons' minster can be expected in the first few decades after the Conquest, and certainly in connection with the establishment of a regular Augustinian house *c.*1111–1122.[7] William of Malmesbury's comments of *c.*1125 (written after visiting the church) give Roger, bishop of Salisbury, the credit for establishing the Augustinian priory and appointing Prior Wimund, but make no mention of buildings; this is possibly of some significance in view of Malmesbury's praise elsewhere for Roger's architectural patronage.[8] The lack of any mention of new buildings in documentary sources cannot of course be taken as evidence that there was no building activity. But the lack of both documentary and material evidence, combined with the certainty that this not-very-wealthy house rebuilt its church *c.*1160–1200 (a long period for a fairly modest priory church), does suggest that the new canons made do with the existing buildings (presumably built in stone by Æthelred after the burning of the minster in 1002), possibly remodelling the E. end for their own liturgy.[9]

There is some evidence for a stone church existing before the present structure and roughly on the same site. Most obvious is the existence of the chapter-house doorway and slype, the former (Fig. 51) decorated with motifs paralleled elsewhere in mid 12th-century Oxford, Oxfordshire and Berkshire Romanesque work, probably derived from Reading Abbey founded in 1123 (see Appendix). During Scott's 1871 restoration work a 'muniment room' which had been built within the 15th-century N. cloister walk was removed, involving an almost complete rebuilding of the S. nave aisle wall. J.C. Buckler was constantly in attendance, and recorded that a 'large amount of ornamental work of the meanly reduced cloister [his term for the 15th-century work] . . . was executed upon the handsomer and more highly wrought capitals of Early Norman

---

[4] *R.C.H.M. Oxford*, 35.

[5] A.W. Clapham, *English Romanesque Architecture*, ii (1934), 97.

[6] P. Kidson, P. Murray and P. Thompson, *A History of English Architecture* (2nd edn., 1979), 37.

[7] The exact foundation date is not known; see below, p. 227 note 45, for a discussion of the problems.

[8] William of Malmesbury, *De Gestis Pontificum Anglorum*, ed. N.E.S.A. Hamilton (Rolls Ser. lii, 1870), 213, 315. For Roger of Salisbury see R.A. Stalley, 'A 12th-century Patron of Architecture; a Study of the Buildings Erected by Roger, Bishop of Salisbury.' *J.B.A.A.*, 3rd ser. xxxiv (1971), 62–83.

[9] David Sturdy might have found part of this putative early 12th-century church in his excavations; see above, pp. 91–2.

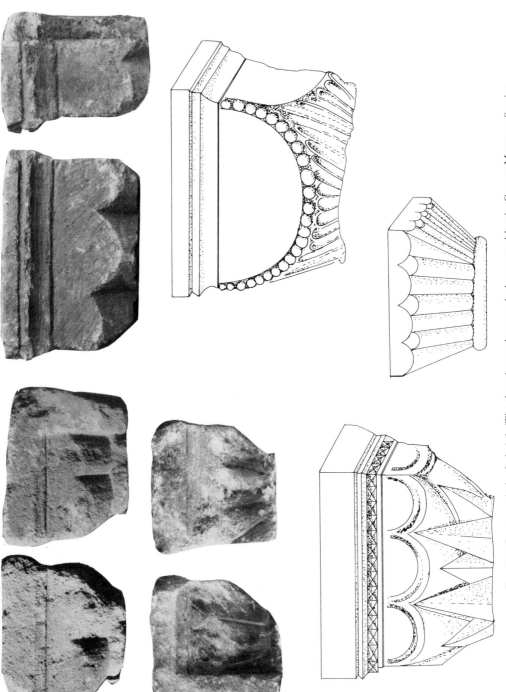

Fig. 52. *Ex situ* capitals. *Scale 1:6.* (The three items photographed are stored by the County Museums Service; the other three, now lost, are re-drawn from Buckler's sketches in B.L. MS Add. 27765E, enlarged to scale according to Buckler's dimensions. Phh. John Blair.)

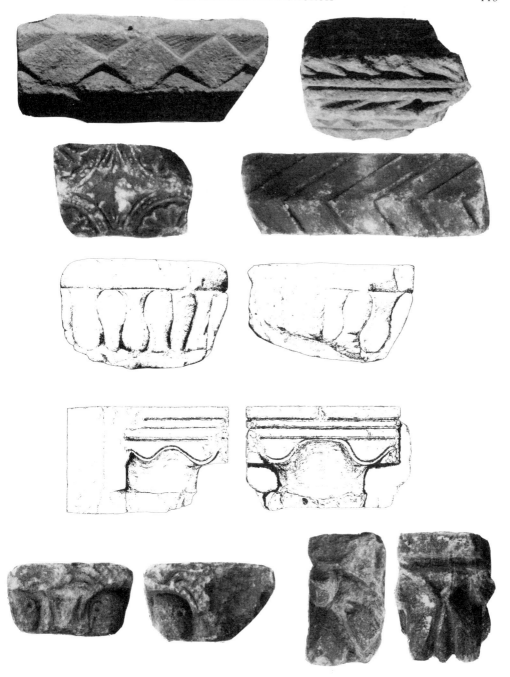

Fig. 53. *Ex situ* string-course fragments, capitals and corbel. *Scale 1:6.* (Stored by the County Museums Service. Phh. John Blair, drawings by Sarah Blair.)

date'.[10] The more elaborate of these capitals cannot now be located, and as there are few pieces of old stone within Scott's work they have presumably been lost, but luckily Buckler drew three of them. The known examples (Fig. 52) show the full range of the 12th-century English scallop capital designs, from the simple decorated cubic shape to the multi-fluted scallop only otherwise seen on the internal lantern passage arcade of the central tower. Later in his account, Buckler notes: 'Other fragments of anglo-norman workmanship were countless, but of a structural character – not sufficiently instructive to be copied. The former cloister is without the slightest recognisable representation among the numerous discoveries which have been made.'[11] It is most unfortunate that the 'structural character' of the 'countless' fragments was not described or drawn in more detail. Buckler presumably means pieces of shaft, plain ashlar blocks and perhaps string-course fragments and arch sections (as found in the E. wall of the chancel, Fig. 53, upper).

Some pieces which he does depict can be identified with stones among the collection from Christ Church now stored by the Oxfordshire County Museums Service. One such piece 'found in the cloister walls' is a springing stone from blind arcading (Fig. 54, left), with a raised zig-zag and with a base width of about a foot (30 cm.); it could therefore fit onto one of the capitals that Buckler illustrates. On the same page of drawings is a 'fragment of a small arch [i.e. a voussoir] . . . from the walls of the cloister' with this same zig-zag and accompanied by the note 'This pattern is profuse'.

From the existing chapter-house doorway, the location of this re-used work, the size of the capitals and the other material, it is reasonable to suggest that a cloister was being erected around the middle of the century. It is doubtful, in fact, that the Priory could have expanded or funded any expansion until the mid 12th century. From charters made shortly before his death, it seems that Bishop Roger had retained control of many of the choicer endowments of St. Frideswide's, presumably from the foundation of the Priory (cf. below, p. 227).[12] The rapid rise of Oseney Priory (founded 1129), a remarkably adjacent 'alternative' Augustinian house heavily patronised by local families (especially the castellan d'Oilly family), would also suggest that St. Frideswide's was not popular.[13] Comparison of royal and papal confirmations does indicate that after a slow start, patronage increased substantially after the middle of the century and, more obviously, after the translation of the relics in 1180.

As argued below by John Blair (pp. 236–7), it seems likely that the S. range of the cloister lies across the line of the original S. city wall. Charters of the 1120s confirm that there was a road near the wall touching the canons' land, and that the canons were permitted to restrict access to a gate and to have access to their garden beyond the wall.[14] Given the *Gesta Stephani* description of Oxford as being 'very securely defended' when Queen Matilda was being besieged by King Stephen in 1142,[15] it is highly unlikely that the walls were breached much before the later 1140s. With the stylistic evidence, then, it can be confidently suggested that a new cloister was added to an existing church

---

[10] British Library MS. Add.27765 E, f.98.

[11] Ibid. f. 86.

[12] *Cart. Frid.* i, 17, No. 13; *The Cartulary of Oseney Abbey*, ed. H.E. Salter, ii (O.H.S. xc, 1929), ii, 233–4, Nos. 793–4.

[13] Oseney was founded in 1129, its first prior Ralph being a canon of St. Frideswide's. It was elevated to abbatical status in 1154, having absorbed the rich secular college of St. George-within-the-Castle in 1149: *V.C.H. Oxon.* ii, 90, and *V.C.H. Oxon.* iv, 365.

[14] *Cart. Frid.* i, Nos. 6, 12 and 514.

[15] *Gesta Stephani*, ed. and trans. K.R. Potter (1935); 90–1; an interpretation of the attack can be found in *V.C.H. Oxon.* i, 437.

Fig. 54. *Ex situ* voussoirs and springer. The item illustrated bottom-right comes from the E. wall, above the E. window. *Scale 1:6* (Stored by the County Museums Service. Phh. John Blair.)

from the late 1140s, the walled area of the city being extended to take it (cf. Figs. 92–5). This follows the appointment in the late 1130s of Robert of Cricklade (known as Canutus) as prior.[16] If St. Frideswide's was ever associated with the establishment of a scholastic community in Oxford it must have been now, and a cloister would surely have been essential to this learned and devout man.[17]

Two further aspects of the existing church might suggest that the present building replaces an earlier structure on the same site: the S. transept and the eastern arm.

## THE S. TRANSEPT

Although both N. and S. arms of the transept are of three bays, and have a similar length at clearstorey level of 14.325 m. (47 ft.), the S. transept has only two complete bays at ground level as the southernmost leaps across the slype. Measuring between the centres of the main arcade upper capitals, this bay has a colossal 5.283 m. (17 ft. 4 ins.) width. The remaining space between the slype and the crossing piers had to be divided evenly into two bays, only 3.96 m. (13 ft.) in width (column centres), narrower than either the chancel bays with an average width of 4.23 m. (13 ft. 10½ ins.) or the nave bays with a width of 4.388 m. (14 ft. 4¾ ins). As the horizontal levels obviously had to be maintained, the upper main arcade of the southernmost bay describes a very flat segmental arch, luckily only seen from the top of the S. transept gallery.

---

[16] For a consolidated list of references to Robert see Blair, 'St F.', 80, notes 8 and 9.

[17] Soon after his arrival, Robert gave a mill to the priory; could this have been his donation? *Collectanea*, ii, ed. M. Burrows (O.H.S. xvi, 1890), 161.

Fig. 55.   S. transept, W. wall, glazed triforium in middle bay. (Ph. John Blair.)

References to a tower in the miracles associated with St. Frideswide's relics eight years before the translation of 1180 have been taken by a number of authors (reasonably enough) as evidence for Æthelred's church of 1002–4 having a tower, probably over the crossing.[18] As the great majority of Romanesque cloisters have their E. range aligned with the transept of a cruciform church, the likelihood of the existing chapter-house and slype being aligned (as now) with the southern arm (or *porticus*) of the 1002–4 (or post-1111) church lends some support for the existence of at least a cruciform church by the later 1140s.

A number of authors have suggested that the 'glazed triforium' in the middle bay of the W. wall of the S. transept (Fig. 55) is part of an earlier church (of either 1002–4 or *c*.1120), usually in an effort to explain the giant order elevation.[19] (An externally similar window, without internal arches, exists in the southernmost bay, lighting the room above the slype; it is now all Scott's work.) The single-scallop capitals can be dated to the first half of the 12th century; their closest parallels exist in the chapter-house, within

[18] Though Canon Bright, *Handbook to the Eastern Cathedrals* (1862), 5–6, interpreted this entry as evidence for the present tower having been completed in 1172.

[19] J. Park Harrison in various articles, but especially *Proc. O.A. & H.S.* n.s. v (1886–93), 88–108, was keen to establish this window as the clearstorey of the 1004 church. His *c*.1888–91 protagonist, J. Parker, thought it part of the early 12th-century church, faced-up later in the century to create the 'Giant Order' elevation. Pevsner (op. cit. note 2, 117) considers the features *retardataire* work and belonging 'to the building of 1122'. The *R.C.H.M.* (op. cit. note 4, 35, 40) believes these features to be re-used material, but without discussing when or where from.

the partly-revealed side wall arcading. Other examples of this common type of capital can be seen amongst the *ex situ* material in store (Fig. 52). The central capital is not decorated on the side facing the glass, where it has a hacked surface. The shafts have been cut as though for the insertion of glazing, though these grooves do not align with each other in the present positioning of the shafts. Parts of this two-bay arcade are irregularly reddened, presumably by fire, but not in their present position, and there have been substantial piecing-in repairs (presumably by Scott). The bases have no parallels in the rest of the buildings and the variety of their bulbous mouldings and their upright form suggest a date in the first decade or so of the 12th century.

Externally, the walling is faced in coarse rubble, of markedly poorer quality than the clearstorey walling above. Recent restoration has accentuated this difference in the wall-face and created a better defined stone frame for the glazing; previously the windows were of a thinner section. The only comparable windows are those in the lower tower walls flanking the flashings of the former steep roofs. Internally, the capitals and bases are not coursed into the surrounding fabric, as in other triforium openings.

The fabric evidence, then, indicates that the internal twin arches of the middle bay re-use stonework from elsewhere, and that the two windows are pierced through a wall which was not intended to be exposed to the elements. Such work could have taken place at two dates in the medieval period: *c.*1180 or *c.*1490.[20] If it were the earlier date, then this could be seen as further evidence to support the argument that the creation of both transept aisles was a late 12th-century afterthought to the original concept. However, it is highly unlikely that these ordinary and poorly finished capitals and bases would have been used late in the 12th century, and quite improbable that the small area of wall enclosed by the upper arch of the giant order would have been considered worth retaining.

The later date of *c.*1490 is more plausible, especially as the rebuilding of the cloister about that time would have made available a lot of 12th-century material (and Buckler documented much re-use of Romanesque material in the cloister walls). Whether the building of the new cloister removed a single-bay western 'aisle' from the S. transept or not (see below, pp. 149–52), its lower floor level and flatter roof revealed enough wall at triforium level to permit the creation of a window. The internal elevation was retained either out of respect for the unity of the interior or, more likely, because of the structural difficulties in making a larger contemporary window. Quite why the late 12th-century two-bay arcade could not have been voided behind the arches is unclear; perhaps it was simply too inconvenient for the site masons.

## THE EASTERN ARM

There are many differences between the details of the eastern arm and those of the nave and transepts, indicating two separate campaigns, though since the basic elevation design remains constant it is likely that the campaigns overlap to some extent. Careful measurement of the five chancel bays suggest an E. to W. build. The bays next to the eastern crossing-piers have a width of only 2.74 m. (9 ft.) between the bases, whereas the

---

[20] Loggan's view *c.*1675, in *Oxonia Illustrata*, only shows a domestic-style two-light casement window to the southernmost bay (by that time converted to a house). Given the usual accuracy of these views, it must be considered possible that the middle-bay window was created in the post-medieval period. J. Storer's view in *History and Antiquities of the Cathedrals and Churches of Great Britain* (1817), iii, pl. I shows both round-headed windows in the walling, but both are blocked. The date of the glazing is not recorded; it is unlikely to be Scott's work (or Park Harrison would have known).

other chancel pier bases are a uniform 2.845 m. (9 ft. 4 ins.) apart and the bases of the western responds are less than semi-circles; this suggests that building of the E. arm proceeded westwards, the crossing-piers having a fixed position in line with the chapter-house doorway. The E. wall of the chancel was presumably built as close as possible to the city wall while allowing for an intra-mural roadway.

Mr. Sturdy has shown (above, pp. 89–90) that the sanctuary bay was built over a deep excavation into the natural gravel, so explaining its apparent instability in the past. However, as the foundations themselves are intact the re-facing of the upper side walls of the sanctuary bay can be attributed to the number of major fabric alterations in this area: the insertion of a big E. window *c*.1300; the vaulting of the whole chancel *c*.1480; and Scott's restoration work in 1870.[21] Whilst Scott renewed most of the internal details, the capitals on the N. window might be original. They are more similar to the lower capital of the E. respond of the N. chancel arcade and the adjacent capital below the diagonal rib of the aisle vault, both of which are medieval, than to Scott's fancier E. wall capitals. The continuation eastwards of the abacus mouldings of the eastern responds of the main arcade and westwards of the westernmost capitals of these windows (Fig. 56), whilst awkward, is explicable in the context of this church. The abaci of the transept clearstorey capitals continue to the edge of the vault, and externally the abaci of the clearstorey window capitals continue to the pilaster buttresses. The thin mouldings of the latter (where still visible on the N. chancel clearstorey) also explain the thinness of the sanctuary bay abaci, inside and out. So, although the fabric might initially suggest that these windows are later additions, their details can be paralleled elsewhere in the chancel and the broken coursing attributable to restorations. But the existence of the keeled shafts at the lowest level of the E. buttresses is puzzling, as keeled sections otherwise only appear W. of the eastern crossing-piers.

There is a clear diagonal break in the stonework through the eastern crossing-piers, most clearly seen from the chancel aisles. Both piers were heavily rebuilt on the sides facing into the main area after the removal of Dean Duppa's high panelled stalls in 1856, so the lowest courses, at least up to the height of the lowest main arcade capital, cannot be used as medieval evidence. At triforium level, though, the coursing is consistent from the transepts, across the transept arch responds and along the crossing-piers to the 15th-century half-shaft below the western arch of the chancel vault. However, the capital sizes of the N. transept E. arcade S. respond and the W. respond of the N. chancel arcade differ, and the motifs on the crossing-pier capitals and frieze have their best parallels in the transepts and not the chancel.

I believe that the chancel and the immediately adjacent parts of the eastern crossing-piers were built together at least up to the clearstorey string-course. The vaults over the western chancel aisle bays could not be erected until the first column of each transept E. arcade was built, but their ribs were cut in readiness and the springing stones set with the same profile as the rest of the chancel aisle vaults. A temporary wall could then be made on the W. side of the first chancel columns E. of the crossing, leaving the new chancel free from building work. Access to the chancel from the cloister would then be via the slype and a small round-headed doorway, now only visible on the exterior of the S. chancel aisle wall, directly below the 'Bishop King' window (which doorway otherwise has no known purpose). This entrance could have been used for

---

[21] The engravings published by J. Britton, *Cathedral Antiquities of Great Britain*, ii (1821), Pls. II, X show the side windows of the sanctuary bay blocked-up and the internal mouldings removed for the erection of the high panelling inserted by Dean Duppa *c*.1630, though externally the roll-moulded round arch and shafts are visible.

Fig. 56.   Chancel N. side, to show awkward junction between abacus mouldings of arcade and window. (Ph. John Blair.)

anything up to ten years, depending on the speed of the campaign, but certainly long enough to merit its single order and hood-mould. Once the S. transept was built and normal access to the church obtained, this door was filled up; but the opening was only made good on the inside, the exterior work not, presumably, being worth the trouble of complete removal.

The principal differences between the eastern arm and the rest of the church can be summarised under five headings:

### 1.   *The middle storey (triforium)*

This is the most obvious design change, the wall behind the small columns being voided in the chancel, but solid elsewhere. In the nave, moreover, this two-bay arcade seems to be taller; the main dimensions are the same, but this optical effect of greater height is evidently produced by thinner shafts with narrower capitals and reduced bases (Fig. 57). I use the term 'triforium' for convenience, although neither the open nor closed versions strictly fulfil the medieval use of the term (a wall-passage fronted by an open arcade). In the chancel this 'triforium' is really a very reduced pseudo-tribune, as can be seen in the giant order elevations at Romsey and Jedburgh. In the blocked version the middle storey should strictly be termed a 'blind arcade' or perhaps 'pseudo-triforium'; it resembles the middle storey of Burgundian/Cluniac churches. None of the versions at St. Frideswide's

Fig. 57.   Elevation of one bay on S. side of nave, illustrating the giant order system.

have passages or any sort of connection between them; indeed, there is no access to the aisle roof-spaces they front, except through the triforium arches where they exist.[22]

The net result is a three-storey elevation, thus associating St. Frideswide's with the great abbeys and cathedrals rather than with the humble, two-storeyed parish church. After all, although not a rich foundation, the Priory was the largest and oldest religious centre in the city of Oxford and its church contained relics of some antiquity. If the giant order system had not been used, the triforium arches would have risen through the whole height of the middle storey, resulting in an elevation like New Shoreham (Sussex) or Worksop (Radford) Priory (Notts.).

## 2. *Columnar piers*

The piers of the nave alternate between round and octagonal forms. Arcades of octagonal piers became quite common in Gothic architecture, but in the 12th century octagonal forms are rarely used, and are then confined to a 'minor pier' position:[23] that is, the arcade has supports of alternating forms with the larger 'major' pier corresponding to important supporting positions, especially crossing-piers and responds. If the octagon was considered a 'minor' form at Oxford, this may explain why octagonal piers were not used in the three-bay transepts (Fig. 61): the northernmost respond would have taken the minor form. The nave most probably had seven bays, which again would have entailed a minor W. respond form. But if western towers were planned, then the penultimate piers would probably have been larger than a single drum and so could include semi-circular W. responds to the arcades.

More likely, though, the transepts were under construction before the decision to use alternation had been taken. The adoption of an alternating system can be directly attributed to the influence of the new choir at Canterbury Cathedral, begun in 1175. This derivation is confirmed by the design of the main arcade capitals on the octagonal pier immediately W. of the N.W. crossing-pier (Fig. 58), which are clearly modelled on capitals placed in position at Canterbury in the 1179 campaign (according to Gervase of Canterbury's account).[24] Generally speaking this distinctive, fleshy-leaved acanthus capital-type was not much copied beyond Kent and is certainly not present elsewhere in Oxford. Therefore, the transept arcades, which do not employ alternation or any Canterbury-type capitals, are unlikely to be later than the early 1180s. The use of alternation at Oxford was perhaps the result of a visit to Canterbury by the patron or master-mason of St. Frideswide's. It would not be unreasonable to suggest that Prior Philip made a pilgrimage to St. Thomas's shrine, and wished to emulate that setting for his own church around the shrine of St. Frideswide.

The influence of Canterbury could also explain the appearance of pointed-arch windows in the nave clearstorey. However, as so few original 12th-century windows survive, it is perhaps unwise to be too confident that the use of pointed arches only

---

[22] It must be presumed that access to the roof-spaces was originally via external traps or dormers in the roofs, accessible from the parapet gutters.

[23] Although the architect of Peterborough Cathedral choir had experimented with alternating round and octagonal columnar piers after 1118 (probably inspired by the post-1096 choir at Canterbury), the concept had not apparently been taken up with much enthusiasm in the Midlands. The cloister arcades of Reading Abbey had both round and octagonal shafts, presumably alternating, and individual octagonal shafts are known throughout the 12th century, used particularly on doorways e.g. Iffley.

[24] Gervase of Canterbury, *Historical Works*, ed., W. Stubbs (Rolls Ser. lxxiii; vol. i. 1879–80), 21–2.

Fig. 58.   Canterbury-derived capital in nave N. arcade. (Ph. John Blair.)

began in the nave. Nevertheless, the W. wall of the S. transept has round-headed clearstorey windows and in terms of stylistic chronology the S. transept seems to follow directly on from the chancel.

### 3.   *Vaults*

It is clear from the evidence remaining in both transept arms that 12th-century quadripartite rib vaults existed over their main spaces, as well as over the aisles. It is virtually certain from this evidence that the chancel was also vaulted, but the physical evidence is not so conclusive for the nave. The 'shadow' of the S. transept vault is still quite clearly visible on the upper clearstorey walling and the *tas-de-charge* remain (partially restored) above the vault capitals. The N. transept walls have been better repaired after the removal of the vaults (probably by Wolsey, *c*.1525–9),[25] and the

---

[25] A loose voussoir that might have come from the main vault survives. As there is now little physical evidence for a stone vault over the nave comparable to that existing in the transepts, it is possible that it did not receive a stone vault in the 12th century. This would certainly be consistent with the poor-quality sculptural details. However, the upper walls might have been cleaned-up either when the nave roof was first erected *c*.1500 (and the vault shafts given new capitals in the manner of the chancel) or when it was 'renewed' in 1816.

There is no documentary evidence for the removal of the 12th-century transept vaults. *R.C.H.M. Oxford*, 39, suggests that the N. vault was removed for the erection of vaults 'similar to that in the presbytery' and dates

northernmost bay, refaced under the terms of the will of James Zouch (d. 1503)[26] retains the profile of a late 12th-century vault (and possibly some of the masonry still exists at high level above the 16th-century stonework).

As the upper parts of the chancel vault shafts and the internal clearstorey walls[27] were rebuilt for the present late 15th-century vault, no comparison can be made with the evidence to be seen in the S. transept.[28] However, all aisle rib-vaults survive more or less in their original form (the N. nave aisle ribs are of plaster or Roman cement but some apparently original springing stones exist). The rib profiles (Fig. 59) demonstrate a refinement between the chancel and the rest of the church, and this can also be seen in the manner in which the vaults spring from their supports. In the chancel aisles, the single aisle wall-shaft supports the transverse arch and the diagonal ribs spring from corbels attached to the half-shaft capital. Elsewhere, corbels are omitted and both diagonal ribs also spring from the half-shaft capital.

The use of corbels (as was common in the experimental vaults of the first half of the 12th century) and the generally clumsy appearance of the chancel aisle vaults suggest an inexperience or unfamiliarity with vaulting on the part of the mason. Columnar piers, especially within a giant order elevation system, are not easy to integrate with rib vaults (as the even clumsier solutions adopted at Romsey and Jedburgh Abbeys demonstrate). In the transept aisles there is a more rational approach to rib-vaulting, and even though the main vaults do not survive, the slight widening of the main spaces of the nave and transepts (in comparison to the chancel) and the addition of an extra shaft to the crossing-pier clusters in the nave and transepts to accommodate the main vault suggest that lessons had been learnt from the experience of the chancel.

---

the existing wooden roof to c.1510 (p. 41). Both the S. transept and nave roofs are dated to c.1500. The removal of vaults is an expensive and disruptive process, and although the canons may have been embarking on a concerted re-roofing campaign (beginning with the chancel in the late 15th-century), the transept roofs are very simple structures, given the frequent richness of timberwork c.1500/10, and the making good of the walls is shoddy. Why remove stone vaults to erect such plain roofs? Wolsey is known to have been preparing to demolish the Priory church as his new chapel rose on the N. side of the new college quad: the chancel remained in use as a temporary chapel but the steeple was scaffolded and payment made for the bells to be dismantled (see J.G. Milne and J.H. Harvey, 'The Building of Cardinal College, Oxford', *Oxoniensia*, viii/ix, (1943–4), 148; see also above, pp. 67–72, and below, pp. 205–10, 220). I suggest that it was Wolsey who demolished the old roofs and vaults of the transepts after 1525, and that after his fall in 1529, Henry VIII, or rather one of his Deans, had the present roofs erected. However, there are apparently no records for such work and it might be expected that the roofs would contain some visual reference to Henry's patronage. If the nave roof is not work of Wolsey's time – and he did demolish much of the nave – then it must be seen as early 16th-century work by the Priory, attempting to enhance the nave to 'match' the chancel. It is of course, much less ambitious (the clearstorey was not re-modelled, for instance) and as a stone vault would be so expensive and disruptive to dismantle, I think it more than likely that c.1200 the nave only received a wooden ceiling, not a vault.

[26] The will of James Zouch, a local notary, proved 1504, requests burial in a tomb to be erected in the midst of the window 'which he had caused to be built' in the N. transept, and for permission to do so he bequeaths £30 'to the convent for the vaulting or adorning of that part of the church' and 40s. to the Prior (for the grave itself), and to the Convent and the University to say prayers for his soul. He was, in short, attempting to create a large chantry chapel for himself. £30 would hardly go far towards a new vault, so the end bay of the N. transept, forming a setting for his tomb under the N. window, was 'adorned' by being re-faced with tracery: *Trans. Mon. Brass Soc.* ix (1962), 509–11 (and see below, p. 256).

[27] Externally, though, the 12th-century pilaster-buttresses and much of the masonry around them still exists. Clearly all the ostentation was reserved for the interior.

[28] The cones at the base of these shafts are longer in the chancel than elsewhere, with a band of raised decoration marking the top of the cone and a grotesque head at the bottom of the shaft. The band is omitted in both the nave and the transepts and the heads (if used) are much smaller; the N. transept shafts sometimes terminate in sprigs of foliage.

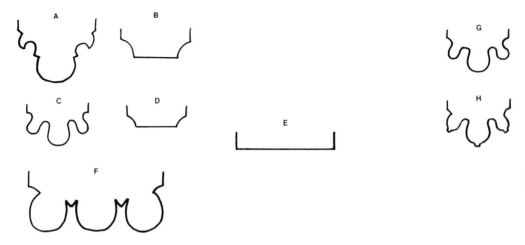

Fig. 59.   Rib profiles (not to scale): A: chancel aisle, diagonal. B: chancel aisle, transverse. C: N. transept
aisles, diagonal. D: N. transept W. aisle, transverse. E: N. transept E. aisle, transverse. F: S. transept main
vault, tas-de-charge. G: N. nave aisle and E. bay of S. nave aisle, all ribs. H: S. nave aisle (except E. bay) and
Lady Chapel, all ribs.

### 4.  *Mouldings and features*

Generally speaking, the mouldings used in the nave and transepts are more refined in
profile and scale than those in the chancel. Scope for radical change was of course limited,
as the giant order elevation system was continued. Throughout the nave and transepts the
roll-mouldings of the upper arches of the main arcades and the clearstorey string course
are keeled, whereas their equivalents in the chancel are not.[29] Throughout the church,
though, the plain, square-section lower arches of the main arcade have a normal roll
hood-mould above them as their only decoration. All the crossing arches have round
profile roll-mouldings too, except the hood-moulds of the (pointed) N. and S. arches
which have a keeled section. As the capitals of the crossing-piers have their closest
parallels in the transepts (in particular the use of a row of upright five-lobe leaves) it seems
that the crossing arches, though obviously planned with the chancel, were built at about
the same time as the transepts. That the eastern arch into the chancel was the earliest to
be cut or erected is shown by its individual intrados moulding, which has a hollow chamfer
(and broach stop) to the edges like the transverse arches of the chancel aisles (which also
run N.–S.). The western arch intrados has round-profile roll-mouldings, but both N. and
S. arches have plain square-section profiles.
     The lower arches of the main arcade are visually the least important in the
elevation, and their lack of decoration compared to the upper arches (which do not even
span an open space) does not focus any undue attention on them. The square section
does nevertheless seem rather heavy for *c.*1170 work. Similar arches can be found in a
number of contemporary churches throughout the country of similar scale and
architectural pretension, e.g. Minster-in-Thanet (Kent), St. German's Priory (Corn-

---

[29] Exceptionally, the lowest of the three rows of arcading on the external clasping-buttresses of the E.
chancel wall contain keeled shafts (supporting intersecting round arches). The equivalent shafts on the
clasping buttresses of the N. transept are, however, not keeled.

wall), Wisbech (Cambs.); churches with otherwise very decorated arcades sometimes
have plain unmoulded crossing arches, e.g. St. David's Cathedral, Winchester St. Cross.
More locally, the arch leading into the choir of Dorchester Abbey has such a profile and,
further afield, the intrados of the main arcades of the two western bays of Worcester
Cathedral (c.1175) has a thick-square profile beneath keeled roll-mouldings.[30] However,
the use of a square profile to the lower arch seems to be common to all the known
English giant order elevations (except Romsey Abbey, where a thick soffit roll-moulding
is added to the arch); it is also used at Notre-Dame, Etampes, c.1130–40.

The greater refinement of mouldings is best demonstrated at the junction of the
chancel and transept responds to the E. of each of the eastern crossing-piers. In the
chancel the abaci and capitals are deeper than those of both nave and transepts. As the
upper part of the abacus of the higher main arcade capitals is continued between
capitals as the string course below the triforium, it follows that this string is shallower in
the nave and transepts. Much of the deeper chancel abacus is taken up by an unmoulded
block, or 'lower abacus', between the abacus/string and the capital sculpture. This
feature is much reduced in the nave and transepts, but the area available for capital
sculpture is not increased. The profile of the abacus remains the same throughout the
church for all capital sizes (although the upper part of the large chancel capitals has a
deeper moulding), except for the W. responds of the chancel upper arcades and the S.W.
respond of the lower chancel arcade, which all have a deep abacus with an unusually
complex profile.

Many of the bases and plinths, especially on the main arcades, were restored when
the box pews were removed in 1856 and in 1870 and cannot be relied upon as dating
evidence. As a general rule, the large bases of the chancel arcade are more upright in
shape and less undercut than those of the nave and transept arcades, but both are
tending to the water-holding type. There is a significant difference between the minor
bases, though. The bases of the shafts at the E. end of the N. chancel aisle sit
comfortably on their plinth, but the equivalent bases at the N. end of the N. transept W.
aisle overhang the plinth on two sides. Some of the chancel triforium bases have little
spurs, and the lower bases of the E. chancel windows have flat corner-leaf spurs too, but
there are none present in the nave or transepts. The plinths of the chancel arcades are
between 10 and 20 cm. (4–8 ins.) deeper than those further W. in the building. It would
also seem from the chamfers present on the plinth (at a constant height from the top)
that the chancel floor was about one step, say 15 cm. (6 in.), higher than the uniform
transept and nave floor levels.

## 5.  *Capital Sculpture*

The very diverse capital sculpture of St. Frideswide's requires a full study in itself.[31] As
Pevsner says, the capitals are 'of great variety and few are run-of-the-mill'. But because

---

[30] This combination of square arches and keels in a late Romanesque context could provide a source for the
use of keeled profiles at St. Frideswide's, especially as Dr. Christopher Wilson has identified a number of
parallels in the capital sculpture of Worcester and St. Frideswide's: 'The Sources of the late 12th Century
Work at Worcester Cathedral', in *Medieval Art and Architecture at Worcester Cathedral* (Trans. of BAA Conference
1975, 1978), 84–5. Keels are not used at Canterbury, so did not accompany the concept of alternation. Dr.
Wilson suggests a c.1170 starting date for St. Frideswide's.

[31] There are very few recognisable 12th-century capitals remaining on the exterior. The replacements of
c.1974 on the N. transept and N. nave clearstorey were inspired by internal capitals; the originals were very
much simpler (like the capitals still surviving (1988) on the S. nave clearstorey).

he believed the frequency of 'crocket' capitals to be a late 12th-century phenomenon, Pevsner dated the whole building to 1190–1210.[32] A detailed examination, though, shows that the chancel capitals have volutes in the classical manner, i.e. leaves curled in a spiral, and that crockets, i.e. leaves collected together in a looser configuration, are mainly used in the main capitals of the nave (with a few visible amongst the smaller upper capitals of the transepts). As Francis Bond pointed out, the basis of these forms can be found in classical capitals;[33] and as at Canterbury Cathedral (1175–9)[34] the breaking-down of classicizing foliate capitals to new capital types, using individual leaf forms, is readily discernible at Oxford.

There are enough small details in common between some of the capitals at Oxford and at Canterbury to suggest either a common prototype or at least a common background for the sculptors. That source will almost certainly be found in the Ile-de-France, as it was there that masons had been so assiduously dismembering the Corinthian capital from the 1130s.[35] In France, the process created a simple, almost spiky design also called the 'crocket' capital. In England, the 'stiff-leaf' capital emerges, usually quite animated and with much detail in the lobed leaf form. There are also many regional variations, dependent on the locally dominant workshop.

The process by which these stiff-leaf capitals emerge is harder to see in England because so few buildings of the 1140–1180 period survive. St. Frideswide's, although clearly not in the top class of architectural endeavour, is nevertheless a nearly complete building from those years: some elements of its capital sculpture can be paralleled in the known English recipients of French Early Gothic stylistic influences, like the Temple in London, St. Cross Hospital church in Winchester (both *c*.1160), and of course Canterbury Cathedral choir (1175–79).

However, there are also some capitals (in the chancel only) that show the Anglo-Norman interlace capital in its final form. The leaf forms are sparse and more like frilled lobes than anything natural. The interlace itself has become very tubular; with the degree of undercutting and occasional use of clips to group the tubes together, these capitals have a metallic quality to them. But they retain the bell-rim derived from the Corinthian capital and incorporate masks (and on one capital heads below the volutes), demonstrating their author's background in stone carving. These capitals have little to offer in the creation of the nave and transept capital types, and although of high quality they are not seen outside the chancel.

A smaller third group, again with a classical starting-point, also begins to be seen in the chancel, but is more influential on the development of the capitals of the nave and transepts. In this group, a 'coronet' of large upright leaves of roughly equal size rings the capital, with volutes (and in the transepts crockets) shooting out from behind the coronet to the underside of the abacus at each corner. The leaves in the chancel are derived from the anthemion, but in the nave and transepts the small 5-lobe leaf and the large, ribbed, plantain leaf are used. Sometimes, in the smaller chancel triforium capitals, two coronets are used with the leaves alternating or superimposed.

Pevsner's account also draws attention to the rarity of waterleaf. As the most obvious waterleaf capitals can be seen in the N. transept and as Pevsner believes

[32] Sherwood and Pevsner, op. cit. note 2.

[33] Francis Bond, *Gothic Architecture in England* (1905), 420–9.

[34] J. Newman, *The Buildings of England: NE and E Kent* (1976), 180–1. See L. Stone, *Sculpture in Britain: The Middle Ages*, Pelican History of Art (1955), 102–3 for a comparison of Oxford and Canterbury capitals.

[35] Dr. Wilson (op. cit. note 30, footnote 38) suggests that some capitals in the chancel aisles 'might almost be the work of a French carver'.

waterleaf 'was popular to about 1190', he concludes that the capitals of the N. transept are the earliest. Consideration of the N. transept W. aisle vaults forces him to reject that conclusion (and ought also have raised doubts about the stylistic dating concepts on which it was based). The earliest waterleaf capital to be seen (if indeed it is medieval) is that on the exterior of the N. window of the sanctuary bay. Given the loss of all the other external capitals of the chancel at aisle and clearstorey level and the simplicity of external capital sculpture in comparison to the interior (still visible in the nave and transepts), there may well have been more waterleaf types originally. But there are few internally: the most obvious are in the N. transept, where two large capitals use waterleaf decoration, though the most numerically are found in the upper levels of the nave where the capital decoration becomes almost rudimentary in its simplicity.

The ubiquitous English multi-scallop capital is hardly seen in the church: most of the capitals to the passageway around the lantern (above the crossing arches) are of this form, and two-scallop capitals exist at clearstorey level in the S. transept. It seems then that this capital design was not welcomed.

In general, the quality of capital design declines in the clearstorey of the transept arms and W. of the first nave bay. Indeed, some of the nave clearstorey-level capitals are barely carved at all, and the westernmost medieval main arcade capitals (thankfully disguised by the organ casing) are extremely poorly carved. The best-quality work is found in the classicizing work of the chancel, and the wreathed head corbel in the N. chancel aisle (visible on Fig. 62) must be considered a first-class piece of medieval sculpture.

DATING EVIDENCE

The internal development of the capital sculpture suggests a building sequence of: chancel, crossing arches and lower levels of N. and S. transepts; upper transept levels, lantern, lower levels of eastern nave bay; rest of nave and clearstorey of first nave bay. Whilst difficult to date accurately, a starting date of c.1165–70, with the eastern nave bay being erected c.1180–5 (after an imput of ideas directly from Canterbury),[36] would be acceptable on comparative stylistic grounds. The progressive refinement of the mould-ings and the sequence of vault-rib profiles also support such date brackets, though keeling on its own is found as early as c.1160 in English Cistercian architecture (and uniquely, as early as 1133 in the Durham chapter-house). With so few of the local Benedictine monasteries (such as Abingdon and Reading) surviving, and with little known of the houses of the reformed orders like Cistercian Thame (f.c.1140) and Bruern (f.1147), or Augustinian Cirencester (f.1131), Dorchester (f.c.1140), Missenden (f.1133), Notley (f. by 1162) and Oseney (f. 1129 and created an abbey in 1154), it is difficult to determine accurately a context for the stylistic details at St. Frideswide's. The reformed houses in particular might be expected to show northern French influences in their architecture, though by c.1170 the larger Benedictine patrons would have been adopting French stylistic fashions.

Whilst St. Frideswide's was probably not right in the forefront of architectural fashion, the experimental and eclectic nature of the capital sculpture does suggest some adventure and sense of fashion, presumably on the part of the patrons. If those patrons

[36] See above and note 24. Although pilgrimages to Becket's place of martyrdom became increasingly popular in the later 1170s (and Prior Robert of Cricklade was one of the first to write of the miracles at the tomb, see note 16), the incomplete choir was first used by the monks on 19 April 1180 (according to Gervase, op. cit. note 24) and presumably only generally visible after then.

were successive priors, Robert of Cricklade and Philip, both learned and well-travelled men, it is reasonable to suppose that, despite the use of the giant order elevation system, St. Frideswide's church was built quite quickly in the decades on either side of the translation of the saint's relics in 1180.

This stylistic dating clashes with the only clear documentary reference to the fabric of the church, the Oseney Chronicle passage quoted at the beginning of this article. If the church really was burnt in 1190, the absence of fire-reddened stones inside the church (except the re-used material in the glazed triforium of the S. transept) would imply a later date for the whole fabric. Although this view has recently been accepted by the *V.C.H.* and Pevsner, it makes the building exceptionally *retardataire*, and this seems unlikely in the second half of the 12th century when fashions moved very quickly and when the translation of relics usually marked the successful completion of a building campaign. It is curious that the only fire-reddened feature *in situ*, the chapter-house doorway, was thought worthy of retention when the present splendid chapter-house was built some thirty years later.[37] If a Romanesque church suitable for so grand a translation in 1180 had been similarly affected but totally rebuilt, surely this not-very-special piece of Romanesque decoration would have been replaced too?

Two other documentary references to the condition of the church in the 1190s can perhaps throw further light on the Oseney Chronicle statement.[38] H.E. Salter prints in full a sermon preached by Alexander Neckam on Ascension Day:[39] 'How dreadful is this place of the church of St. Frideswide at this moment and horrible because of the ruin of its walls . . . . . for the holy church is without a roof and open to the assaults of the air and wind'. Salter suggests Ascension Day 1191 or 1192, following the fire of 1190; but nowhere in the sermon is a fire specifically mentioned as the cause of this sad state of affairs. In the St. Frideswide's Cartulary is a bull of Pope Celestine III, dated 2 June 1194, requesting alms from the faithful to enable the Prior and canons to rebuild their church, 'domos et officinalia . . . vehementis ignis incendio combusta'.[40]

Clearly some intensive fund-raising was underway. The papal bull will obviously state the facts as reported by the beneficiaries, and will almost certainly exaggerate. It is unfortunate that none of the original external S. walls of the church exist, nor any part of the Romanesque cloister other than the chapter-house. Almost certainly, the cloister walks would then have been roofed in wood, and as the reddening is darkest at the putative original floor-level, the remaining fabric does demonstrate that there was a serious fire in the Romanesque cloister that could have taken place in 1190. It did not destroy the Romanesque chapter-house as the canons did not apparently rebuild it until after 1220; the stonework on the rear of the doorway is not reddened either.

The Oseney Chronicle entry was perhaps inaccurate in recording the damage to St. Frideswide's, as indeed it exaggerates the damage to the city: there is little other

---

[37] The date of the building of the chapter-house is, surprisingly, not recorded. Stylistically it can be dated to *c*.1220–40; it is of very good quality, with fine sculpture to the corbels beneath the vault shafts and on the vault bosses. Given its quality, it is indeed remarkable that the opportunity was not taken to create an equally splendid entrance. Perhaps this was going to be part of a re-building of the E. walk of the cloister – which did not in fact occur until 1489?

[38] The editor of the Oseney Chronicle (op. cit. note 3) used the British Library MS. Cotton Tib. A.9, which is written in one hand to 1233 and after that date in different hands.

[39] H.E. Salter, *Mediaeval Oxford* (O.H.S. c, 1936), 37.

[40] *Cart. Frid.* No. 39. The editor notes that this charter is not included in the most reliable copy of the cartulary of *c*.1415–50, but is included in the earlier copy of *c*.1310–20.

evidence to suggest that a greater part of the city was also destroyed.[41] Whilst clambering over the roofs in late 1975, I did notice that another fainter roof-line 'shadows' the obvious mortar line of the 12th-century roof flashing. At the base of the N.E. tower 'turret' the ashlar around this fainter line was fire-stained. Although this faint line was outside the stronger mortar line on the E. face of the tower, it was inside the flashing on the other faces and no firemarks could be seen (although the ashlar of the other turrets may have been more thoroughly restored). Is it possible that the chancel roof (and any other roofs existing in 1190) was burnt off, but that the stone vault saved the new chancel? Neckam was accurately bewailing the 'roofless church' but he was referring especially to the unfinished nave and damaged chancel and/or transepts, using his oratory to loosen the purses of his audience!

However, the most convincing evidence against substantial fire-damage to the church is the total lack of references to the relics of St. Frideswide, so recently (and expensively?) translated with great pomp. Prior Philip, who recorded her miracles, was certainly alive in 1191,[42] and a prior so concerned to promote the cult would surely have taken energetic steps to remedy any loss. As none of the documents mentions damage to the shrine, total destruction of the church in 1190 must be dismissed as an exaggeration of a cloister fire or a serious roof fire.

There can be little doubt that the monastery needed money. By c.1190, the excitement and income generated by the translation and Prior Philip's writings had probably evaporated and the canons were building a church of greater pretension than their funds warranted. Any further expense through fire-damage was no doubt most unwelcome after years of fund-raising. It is very evident from the surviving four nave bays that the high standards of the c.1170 chancel were gone: the work is of poor quality, and without that sense of experimentation visible in the eastern parts. It is also possible that the canons themselves had lost interest in building a nave that could hardly have been of much use to the community. Perhaps it was once intended to make it parochial (as in many other Augustinian houses founded in ancient minsters or colleges),[43] and the arrangements had foundered.

Nothing is known of the three nave bays demolished by Cardinal Wolsey, but the speed of his work would suggest that no substantial W. towers were destroyed. The existing central tower and spire are of modest scale for a cathedral, but the latter (Fig. 74) is of especial interest as one of the earliest stone spires remaining in England.[44] Once again, it is likely to be based ultimately on a French model, as many more stone spires had apparently been built in northern France than in England during the second half of the 12th century. This type of faceted spire (using tall corner pinnacles to effect the visual transition between the octagon and square and with gabled lucarnes to the base of each cardinal face) can be seen in Normandy during the later decades of the 12th century, for instance on the W. towers of St. Etienne at Caen.[45] There were probably

---

[41] H.E. Salter (op. cit. note 39) suggests on rather flimsy evidence that St. Mary's church was also burnt, but quotes no other documentary evidence to support the Oseney claim. The 1846 edition of Dugdale's *Monasticon Anglicanum*, vi, 139, also notes that the event is not recorded 'in any other of our ancient chronicles, so that the fact is probably to be discredited'.

[42] He witnesses a charter dated 4 July 1191 in the Oseney Cartulary (op. cit. note 12, iv, 89).

[43] See J.C. Dickinson, *The Origins of the Austin Canons and their Introduction into England* (1950), 233. The parish altar of St. Frideswide's was suppressed in 1298 (below, p. 256).

[44] Most authoritative accounts suggest a late 12th- or early 13th-century date for the spire: e.g. E.S. Prior, *A History of Gothic Art in England* (1900), 370, although he mistakenly states it to have been 'rebuilt by Sir G.G. Scott'. For a section and a plan of the spire, see *The Builder*, cxxvii (11 July 1924), 41.

[45] For other examples see E. Lefevre-Pontalis, 'Clochers de Calvados', *Cong. Arch.* lxxv, (1908), ii, 652–84.

more stone spires in England c.1200 than now exist, so it is equally likely that the spire of St. Frideswide's is based on a lost model. The parish churches of Witney and Bampton have 13th-century central steeples (and Shipton-under-Wychwood a W. tower) based on St. Frideswide's, suggesting either that the putative lost model was also in the Oxford area (at Oseney, perhaps?), or that St. Frideswide's had itself introduced the feature to the locality from further afield, even directly from France.

THE 12TH-CENTURY PLAN (Fig. 60; cf. Figs. 95, 97)

Before discussing the plan of St. Frideswide's, its state c.1200 state has to be established. This involves close study of three areas;
1. the W. end of the nave, demolished by Wolsey 1524–5;
2. the N.E. corner between the chancel and the N. transept, rebuilt in the 13th and early 14th centuries (discussed by Richard Morris below, pp. 169–82);
3. the S. transept, substantially altered when the cloister was rebuilt 1489–99, and during Scott's restoration, 1870–6.

Because most of the external walls have been rebuilt at various periods, the only accessible 12th-century walls remaining at ground level are the E. walls of the chancel aisles. The thickness of the 12th-century S. nave aisle wall cannot be determined as the cloister was built onto it in 1489–99 and again in 1870–6. Before he rebuilt the S. chancel aisle wall, Scott noted the thickness as 3 ft. 7 ins.[46] I have measured the nave and N. transept wall thicknesses at clearstorey level, finding a similar figure varying between 3 ft. 5½ ins. and 3 ft. 7½ ins. When Parker and Harrison were disputing the date and function of the little arches in the E. walls of the Lady Chapel and N. chancel aisle[47] these walls were carefully measured, and the published drawings give a thickness of 3 ft. 6 ins. for the aisle wall. Therefore, when restoring the exterior walls, I have given them a thickness of 3 ft. 6 ins. (1.067 m.). This figure is very close to the thickness of the round and octagonal piers of the main arcades, which average 3 ft. 5 ins. Published plans also give similar wall-thicknesses, excepting the three walls of the unaisled eastern sanctuary bay which are given a thickness of c.5 ft. 0 ins. by both the R.C.H.M. and the *Builder* plans.[48] The bases and abaci of the chancel arcades are c.4 ft. 10 ins. (1.27 m.) thick and the N. and S. walls of this bay appear to continue on the same plane as the interior.

1. *The W. end*

The Priory was suppressed in April 1524, and the foundation-stone of Cardinal College laid on 15 July 1525. By early 1526 the E. range 'be upon the outer side erect unto the old church door and in the inner side nigh as far as is required'.[49] Access to the cathedral church from 1526 to 1876 was via the cloister, through the door still existing in the S. nave aisle wall. The earliest plan I have located, of the early 18th century,[50] shows a

---

[46] In his sketchbook, now in Christ Church Library MS D.P. vii, a.8.

[47] *Proc. O.H.S.* n.s. v (1885), 88–108.

[48] *R.C.H.M. Oxford*, 35, and *The Builder* lxii (4 June 1892), drawn by Roland Paul. I have found the latter to be the most consistently accurate.

[49] L.F. Salzman, *Building in England down to 1540* (1967), 411. The reference to 'all this Christmas' suggests the letter was written early in the year.

[50] In the Red Portfolio for Oxfordshire in the Society of Antiquaries library dedicated to 'William Bradshaw, Bishop of Bristol' (1724–32)' and reproduced in Browne Willis, *Survey of the Cathedrals of England* (1730), iii.

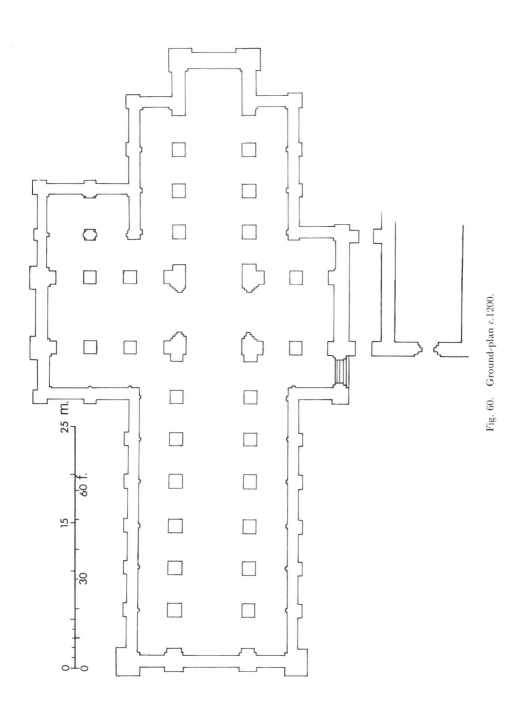

Fig. 60. Ground-plan c.1200.

large W. nave window but no W. door (as the E. range of Tom Quad was not pierced with the present double opening until 1872). Therefore the door mentioned in 1526 is that from the cloister and Wolsey's men had already demolished the medieval W. front. It can safely be assumed, from the shortness of the period, that there were no W. towers of any size and a reference to scaffolding the steeple must be to the existing central tower.[51]

Perhaps because four nave bays remained after Wolsey's activities (his new W. wall being built between the fourth pair of piers W. of the crossing),[52] and perhaps because of the alternating pier system, some writers have thought that four bays were demolished. But most scholars have reckoned that only three bays disappeared, and there are substantial arguments to support this view.[53]

Up to August 1871 two large foundation walls six feet wide and eighteen feet apart existed under the E. range of Tom Quad, which Buckler considered to be the remains of the W. range of the 12th-century cloister. 'This stubborn piece of Norman builders work was left wherever its room was not wanted. A length of eleven feet is still to be seen with the springers of the stone arch on the sides; the wall at its height is barely six feet.'[54] He goes on to regret that by August 1871, much old work in the basements of the E. range and under the Great Hall had been removed. The R.C.H.M. plan published in 1939 shows two pieces of foundation work which exactly correspond to Buckler's reported eleven feet of stonework.[55] New floors have been laid since but Mr. Major (Clerk of Works until 1975) assured me that all work had previously been levelled and nothing could be deduced from the remains.

If the W. foundation line marked on the R.C.H.M. plan is extended northwards, then the W. wall of the church can be determined and the nave completed with three bays. This presumes, of course, that the W. wall of the W. range was in line with the W. wall of the church. But the E. foundation wall is not so easily accounted for. If it is presumed to be the W. wall of the W. cloister walk (as the R.C.H.M. suggests), then the cloister was rectangular and the W. range barely 18 ft. in width. If it is the foundation of the arcade or the E. side of the W. cloister walk, then the cloister could be reconstructed as a square, but the other (westernmost) foundation must represent the eastern wall of the W. range, giving an overlarge W. cloister walk in comparison to the existing work and a W. range that lay completely beyond the W. wall of the church (in itself not without parallel). These walls cannot, therefore, be taken as unequivocal evidence for the site of the W. end of the 12th-century church. Indeed, Buckler himself was able to consider an eight-bay nave on the evidence of these walls and also to suggest a trapezoidal 15th-century cloister.

Further evidence (again not in itself complete proof) for a seven-bay nave comes from the paced dimensions of William Worcestre. In August 1480, this early architectu-

---

[51] For this subject see above, pp. 70, 128–9 note 25, and below, pp. 205–7.

[52] The top part of the W. wall and window can be seen in Loggan's *c.*1675 view, and the gap between the cathedral and the E. range of Tom Quad is visible in Agas's *c.*1580 view of Christ Church. The account in *The Ecclesiologist*, vii (1847), 47, says of the W. window 'it seems to have been built up again at the destruction of the west front, as well as a Romanesque string below it'.

[53] Browne Willis shows four bays in his plan (1730), and Scott promoted four bays in his 1869 privately-printed report. John Britton (1817) thought three bays had gone, and this view is the one most commonly held. Canon Bright (O.H.S. n.s. v, 1888, 109), thought two bays had gone and J.H. Harvey, editing *William Worcestre's Itinerary* (1969), 275, also suggests the nave may have had only six bays originally.

[54] B.L. MS Add.27765 E. ff 167–8.

[55] Dr. John Blair has told me (ex inf. Julian Munby) that part of a barrel-vault corresponding with the line of these walls still survives on the W. side of the cloister, where the visitors' toilets were created *c.*1980.

ral metrologist visited Oxford and paced-out a number of buildings. For St. Frideswide's he states 'Its length is 106 paces and its width 30 paces' (53 ft.).[56] The most recent editor of the Itinerary, John Harvey, deduces a length of 187 ft. 3½ ins. (57.086 m.) 'in proportion to the width' and so suggests a six-bay nave, with an even alternation system. He then points out the foundation evidence and suggests Worcestre paced from the E. end of the S. chancel aisle and not the E. wall of the E. end. It is clear that Worcestre usually measured the area beyond the chancel as a separate entity (as it was often a Lady Chapel, as at Oseney Abbey). The width paced was most likely the nave (possibly the transept) as there would be too many obstructions like screens or stalls in the chancel. The nave width averages 53 ft. (16.154 m.), making Worcester's pace 1 ft. 9¼ ins. (0.538 m.) and the 106 pace length, therefore, 187 ft. 3½ ins. (57.075 m.).

The length of the S. chancel aisle and crossing to the W. respond of the W. pier is 82 ft. 5 ins. (25.121 m.). The nave paced by Worcestre would therefore be 104 ft. 10 ins. (31.957 m.) long, and if of seven bays each bay would be 14 ft. 11¾ ins. (4.565 m.) wide. The present nave bays average a width of 14 ft. 4¾ ins. (4.387 m.), a discrepancy over seven bays of over 4 ft. (1.22 m.), which is really too great. However, the N. nave aisle wall is late 15th-century work, most likely associated with the Zouch work begun in 1503, after Worcestre's visit. At its base this wall is now thinner than any surviving 12th-century wall, and this, combined with the fact that Scott rebuilt most of the S. aisle wall, suggests that Worcestre's 30-pace width ought to be based on an average of the chancel and transept widths, 51 ft. 9 ins. (15.773 m.), where more 12th-century walling survives. This dimension then gives a pace of 1 ft. 8¾ ins. (0.527 m.), a nave length of 100 ft. 5 ins. (30.610 m.) and an average bay width (assuming seven bays) of 14 ft. 4 ins. (4.369 m.), almost identical to the four bays that still exist.[57]

## 2. *The N.E. Corner*

No documentary evidence is available for the development of the area between the N. transept and the N. chancel aisle (Fig. 61), but much structural evidence exists, amplified by the evidence of Sturdy's excavations. The following discussion uses the pier numbering system shown on Fig. 35 (p. 77), and should be read in conjunction with Figs. 36, 60 and 98–100.

The exterior buttress at the N.E. corner of the N. chancel aisle is identical in all respects to that now existing on the S.E. corner of the S. chancel aisle (from Buckler's drawing of c.1850, it is clear that Scott only rebuilt the upper portions of this aisle). It can therefore be identified as a corner buttress, not a flat pilaster buttress as it now appears. Within the church, enough 12th-century shafts and arches exist to give at least two single-bay chapels off the E. side of the N. transept. The very large and awkward central pier (II.3) of the arcade between the Lady and Latin Chapels indicates a substantially earlier, 12th-century core, which could be consistent with the existence here of an external pilaster buttress and internal respond. As the builders in both the 13th- and 14th-century campaigns went to such lengths to keep or re-use old work (rather than replace it), the lack of any 12th-century work in the easternmost pier of this arcade (II.2) strongly indicates that no work of that date ever existed here. David

---

[56] Op. cit. note 53. The 53 ft. measurement is presumably taken by Dr. Harvey from the *R.C.H.M.* plan.

[57] Worcester's pace is obviously a variable measure. Harvey op. cit., note 53 reckons that in 1480 the average was just under 1 ft. 8½ ins. (0.52 m.), which is the smallest average for three years 1478–80, 'a sign of old age?' (p.xviii).

Fig. 61.   The N.E. chapels, looking S.E. from the N. transept through its E. aisle. (Painting of 1889: R.C.H.M. Crown copyright reserved.)

Sturdy's excavations in the Latin Chapel and Richard Morris's study of the visible 13th- and 14th-century work (above, p. 94, below pp. 169–75), both reach the same conclusion.[58]

As the 14th-century N. wall of the Latin Chapel has replaced all previous work, the northern extent of the 12th-century chapel is not apparent above ground, but Sturdy's excavations (Fig. 36) have uncovered an earlier foundation that indicates an E.–W. wall continuing the line of the end wall of the N. transept and another foundation running northwards from pier II.3. There is a shaft apparently of late 12th-century date on the N.W. corner of this pier, without a capital and with a 13th-century base. Its position might indicate that it is a nook-shaft, equivalent to that on the W. face of pier II.4. But it stands N.E. of a straight line between piers II.5 and II.4 and its apparently 12th-century stones are larger in diameter than the II.4 nook-shaft. More probably it was a corner shaft to receive the diagonal of a rib-vault (like the shaft existing to the N. of the N. chancel arcade E. respond at the E. end of the N. chancel aisle).

Generally speaking, the N. transept (and noticeably the E. arcade) runs at a N.W. angle to the chancel arcade. It seems from Sturdy's foundations (Fig. 36) and the existing fabric of piers II.4, II.3 and I.4 that the N.E. chapels and the N. chancel aisle were laid out with the chancel in the first phase of work, as they are parallel with the N. chancel arcade and not at right-angles to the E. arcade of the N. transept. However, the style of the capitals and friezes of piers II.4 and I.4 belongs with the second-phase work of the transept.

---

[58] It seems that these later campaigns were on a small scale, building the new outer walls first, then demolishing such internal walls as was necessary, using small 'barrow-holes' in the E. wall of the neighbouring chapel/aisle to dispose of the rubble. The outlines of these access points were, because of their crudity, mis-identified as Saxon fabric, especially by J. Park Harrison, op. cit. note. 19.

Whilst this slight discrepancy can be attributed to difficulties in laying out the new work while the old fabric still existed (as suggested above, there was probably a transept and 'crossing' tower between the new eastern arm and the 1140s cloister), the great discrepancies in alignment between the piers of the N. transept E. arcade and the E.–W. walls of the N. chancel aisle and chapels must result either from a major error or from a change of plan. The root cause would appear to be the introduction of a S. respond to the E. arcade on the northern face of the N.E. crossing pier. Whilst the vaults are arranged better in the three bays behind the other crossing piers, all involve extending a diagonal rib and/or swinging a transverse arch out of its true arc (at right angles to its springing points).

As the building is generally laid out well it must be assumed that these discrepancies arise from a change of plan, and the most likely alteration is the introduction of an eastern arcade to the transept arms. If the two northern chapels were planned to be two bays deep, running directly E. from an earlier N. transept wall on the line of the existing arcade, then they would be analogous to the transept chapels seen in many mid/late 12th-century monastic houses.[59] However, the great majority of these chapels are just one bay deep (like the Lucy Chapel off the S. transept) and there is some evidence to suggest that the N. chapels formed one square chapel of four bays around a central pier, II.4. (cf. below, pp. 143–5).

The similarity of the remaining Romanesque work in the N. and S. chancel aisles suggests that they were identical when first built and that the N. wall of the N. chancel aisle was solid throughout its length, i.e. from pier I.4 to I.1. As there is no evidence for a chapel earlier than the existing 13th-century work N. of the two eastern bays of the N. aisle, these bays were presumably only voided by windows, just like their counterparts in the S. aisle. The identical construction of the Romanesque half-shafts surviving on piers I.2 – I.4 strongly suggests that they were all bonded into a wall and none formed part of any sort of ashlar pier. Both aisles use corbels, throughout their length, to receive the diagonal ribs of the 12th-century vault, whereas shafts might be expected (at least on pier I.4 if it had always been a pier). The 13th-century masons seem to have treated all three N. aisle bays in an identical fashion and if there had been any Romanesque piers here (especially at I.4), those masons would surely have created more graceful and accomplished structures than the messy work that exists today.[60]

[59] A Cistercian example is Fountains Abbey, where two single-bay chapels with solid walls flank a slightly longer inner chapel that connected to the chancel through a doorway; it was not an aisle as existed at St. Frideswide's. Augustinian houses tended not to have aisled chancels, but if aisles existed then there were fewer chapels. Some Benedictine houses founded in the mid to late 12th century reflected the reformed orders in adopting square-ended forms. Ewenny Priory (Monmouth), built and dedicated during the episcopate of Urban, Bishop of Llandaff (1107–34), has two eastern chapels to each transept arm but no chancel aisle: see H. Brakspear, *Arch. J.* lxviii (1921), 392–3. A closer parallel for St. Frideswide's is the plan of the Benedictine nuns' church at Carrow, Norwich. The S. transept appears to have had two eastern chapels, and the chancel was flanked by a four-bay aisle that terminated in a square end, leaving an aisleless eastern sanctuary (probably of two bays). The abbey was founded in 1146 and the excavated remains suggest the E. end was built soon after: see E. Fernie in *Arch. J.* cxxxvii (1980), 290–1. Once again, the lack of information about the more local houses hampers discussion.

[60] I suggest that the 13th-century masons propped the N. chancel aisle vault, possibly with a solid 'wall' immediately to the S. of the original solid wall, and then demolished the fabric between the pilaster buttresses behind I.1 and I.2, including any corbel-table and parapet, rather than build an arch in the thickness of the wall below the vault or above any aisle window. Such a temporary wall could explain the over-deep N.–S. measurement of the Romanesque half-shafts. The area around pier I.4 and the creation of the western entrance arch to the new chapel was probably tackled last, given the more complex shoring needed and the different mouldings. These extra difficulties might explain why so great an error was made when placing the capitals on the E. side of pier I.4.

Fig. 62. Top of pier I.4 from the W., showing the thick transverse rib of the transept aisle vault, and the frieze of five-lobe leaves cut on the left by the 13th-century Lady Chapel work and on the right by the Goodwin monument. To the top-right is the undisturbed late 12th-century masonry of the S.W. corner of the pier. (Ph. John Blair.)

The W. end of the wall, now pier I.4 (Fig. 62), was presumably like its counterpart existing between the S. chancel aisle and the Lucy Chapel: a plain unchamfered mass of masonry (literally the W. end of the S. wall of the S. chancel aisle), with a length of decorated frieze beneath the springing of the transverse arch. Unfortunately, the rebuilding and repair which pier I.4 has undergone over the centuries (not least the insertion of the monument to William Goodwin, d.1620), has rendered detailed analysis of its stonework an almost impossible task. However, it would seem that the stonework to its upper S.W. corner (rising above the monument), between the transverse arch and the diagonal rib of the vault behind the N.E. crossing-pier (D on Fig. 36), is the original 12th-century work. The frieze of upright five-lobe leaves (virtually identical to those used in the equivalent position in the S. transept aisle) did not run all the way to the S.W. corner. The existing break to the left of the monument is so neat because the frieze was formed on two stones, as on the adjacent pier II.4 (where the leaves are slightly different in form on each stone and quite different to the leaf forms of I.4). It can therefore be presumed that there were no corner nook-shafts such as exist on pier II.4.

By analogy with its S. aisle equivalent, and as the end of a solid wall, the W. face of what is now pier I.4 should have been about 3 ft. 8 ins. (1.12 m.) wide. Its present width is nearly 5 ft. (1.51 m.), including an added 13th-century corner-shaft (E on Fig. 36) that supports the 12th-century diagonal rib of the middle aisle bay and part of the remaining 12th-century frieze. Although this diagonal rib has been extended by the 13th-century mason (in almost vertical stones) to more neatly meet the new corner shaft,[61] it replaces

[61] This diagonal rib has the same profile as the diagonal ribs of the vaults in the N. transept W. aisle, N. nave aisle (where the stone springers survive on the piers) and the eastern bay of the S. nave aisle.

the northern edge of the unmoulded transverse arch that has clearly been shaved away. This arch once sprang directly from the original plain ashlar N.W. corner, as can be seen in the equivalent position in the S. transept. The diagonal rib originally died away behind the arch, like the other 12th-century diagonals.

Therefore, the W. face of what is now pier I.4 must have had a width of at least 5 ft. (1.52 m.), which is surely too great a thickness for the solid wall proposed between the N. chancel aisle and the N. transept chapel, i.e. between piers I.3 and I.4. It is likely, then, that this part of the fabric was built unsymmetrical and with an awkward shape.

When creating his Lady Chapel, the 13th-century mason had numerous problems to solve at this point. His new capitals were at a lower level than the Romanesque; his chapel width was constrained by Romanesque work in piers I.4, II.3 and II.4; and his re-fashioning of the piers and walls was further constrained by the obvious need to support the existing vaults of the N. chancel aisle, N. transept E. aisle and, presumably, the pre-Latin Chapel. By setting the Lady Chapel entrance arch from the N. transept aisle behind the aisle vault, the structural stability of the surrounding vaults was assured without compromising the new work. The supporting triple-shafts probably replaced Romanesque half-shafts like that still existing on the N. aisle of pier II.4 at (F). The visual integrity of the new work was further enhanced by using a vault rib profile not dissimilar to that existing in the N. transept aisle.

Morris suggests (below, p. 173) that in building the Lady Chapel, early 13th-century masons 'cut through the former wall to the pre-Latin Chapel'. But the crude stonework above the 13th-century arch between piers II.4 and II.3 might also be read as the remains of a 12th-century arch. In particular, the square-edged stones at the springing-points on the Latin Chapel side seem too crude to be associated with either the Lady or Latin Chapel works. The rather poor correlation of the 13th-century capitals and their supporting shafts on the W. face of pier II.3 and the survival of the 12th-century nook-shaft suggest that more was done than simply piercing a wall. There was of course a rib-vault to the pre-Latin Chapel, probably similar to those of the E. transept aisle.

The surviving 12th-century parts of pier II.4 (Fig. 63, left) suggest that this pier could have been free-standing. It differs from the western 'ends' of the chancel aisle outer walls by having corner nook-shafts, the northernmost 'supporting' the broad transept aisle transverse arch (with no sign now of where the diagonal rib of the end bay vault sprang from) and the southernmost supporting the diagonal rib of the centre aisle bay, which just clips the corner of the transverse arch. Between the shafts runs a length of foliage-decorated frieze.[62] On the N. face of pier II.4 is a 12th-century attached half-shaft complete with its capital (F), now supporting a 14th-century vault-rib in the Latin Chapel, but for which an exact parallel exists on the west aisle wall of the N. transept. On the S. face of the pier, a presumed matching shaft has been replaced by the triple shaft of the early 13th-century Lady Chapel. Yet the short length of plain ashlar east of this triple shaft appears to be 12th-century, ending in a chamfer at the S.E. corner. Thirteenth-century shafts are now attached to the E. face.

If there was a solid wall between the Lady and Latin Chapels (as between the N. chancel aisle and Lady Chapel), why were the nook-shafts used? If pier II.4 is reconstructed as a square pier with nook-shafts to each corner and larger attached half-shafts to the N. and S. faces, the arch between its E. face and a reconstructed E.

---

[62] At Fountains Abbey, similar nook-shafts disguise the lower level of the transverse arch springing-point compared to the adjacent main arcade. The Fountains piers would otherwise be a variant of the giant order column principle. Woburn Abbey was founded in 1145, directly from Fountains; might it have had a similar system?

Fig. 63.   *Left*: Pier II.4 from the N.W. *Right*: Islip, N. arcade pier. (Phh. John Blair)

respond on the W. face of pier II.3 (below the rough putative 12th-century arch) would span the same width as the arch between piers II.4 and II.5. Quite how the resulting double (or 4-bay?) chapel would work liturgically is difficult to conjecture. By *c.*1180 transept chapels are inter-connecting architecturally, even if sub-divided at ground level by substantial stone walls as at Ripon Minster.

The proposed reconstruction of II.4 is not a common pier-type for a major building, but excavations of the Augustinian Priory of St. Martin at Dover (founded by Archbishop William Corbeil in 1131 and reported as complete in 1139) also showed such a pier for the nave arcades.[63] The responds of the choir aisles at the point of entry to the transepts at St. Cross, Winchester (*c.*1150) and at St. Serge, Angers (*c.*1220) adopt a similar form, with nook-shafts linked by a length of frieze continuing the foliage of the nook-shaft capitals (i.e. just one half of the proposed Oxford pier). In parish churches, of course, this pier-type is more common, especially if the pier is the result of

[63] *Archaeologia Cantiana*, iv (1861), 1. The N. nave arcade of the Arrouasian Augustinian nuns' church at Harrold (Beds.) also has rectangular piers with corner nook-shafts. *V.C.H. Beds.* iii, 63, considers this arcade to be punched through an older wall.

an arcade 'punched through' an existing wall. There are examples local to Oxford at Little Missenden, Bucks. (c.1180) and Stanford Dingley, Berks. (c.1220).[64] Only seven miles from Oxford, at Islip church, a late 12th-century N. arcade includes an odd pier that may reflect that proposed at St. Frideswide's (Fig. 63, right).[65] It is a drum with four attached corner shafts; the E. and W. responds of the same N. nave arcade have flat faces with nook-shafts.

The thick, unmoulded semi-circular transverse arches of the two eastern aisles of both N. and S. transepts (Fig. 62) are identical to – if narrower than – the lower arches of the main arcades, and quite unlike the earlier transverse arches of the chancel aisles. Their uncompromising form demonstrates that the master-mason was still thinking in terms of building compartments to fill with vaults in the Romanesque manner, rather than considering all the major structural components of walls and vaults as integral parts of a single system. Yet in the chancel aisles, the N.–S. transverse arches are already of much thinner section with a hollow-chamfer edge. It can only be presumed (as with the crossing arches) that these square-edged, thick arches were considered appropriate to their E.–W. position, defining the principal compartments of the buildings.

Exactly when the decision was made to create aisled transepts is not clear, though it must have pre-dated the decision to use pier alternation in the nave. Such a date is certainly sustainable on stylistic grounds. The W. bay of each chancel aisle (that also forms the inner bay of the E. aisle of each transept arm) has the diagonal rib mouldings of the first-period chancel aisle vaults. The bay behind the N.E. crossing-pier is the most deformed, and this is directly attributable to the positioning of its N.W. springing-point, on the columnar pier I.5, much further N. (about 18 ins., 0.457 m.) than its N.E. springing-point, on pier I.4. So whereas the N.E.–S.W. arch describes the less-than semicircular shape common to all the chancel aisle diagonal ribs, the northern half of the S.E.–N.W. arch is much elongated to reach pier I.5. Something similar happens to the equivalent rib in the bay behind the S.E. crossing-pier, but it is less distorted because the S. transept E. arcade has narrower bay widths (13 ft. 3.96 m.) than the N. transept (14 ft. 4 ins., 4.388 m.).

From this evidence, it follows that the whole chancel arcade (including the W. responds) and the chancel aisle walls were far advanced before the change of plan was initiated. If the first-period campaign work was advancing W. onto an existing building, then it is likely that the external walls of the N.E. chapel were also well under way (although the discrepancy between piers II.5 and II.4 is much less obvious and as much attributable to the shift in axis between the N. transept and chancel as to the new arcade). The puzzling feature is the perverse use of these thick arches. They can hardly have been advanced much beyond the first springing stones on the eastern side of the aisle before the columnar arcade piers existed, given the significant inclination in their arc. The chapels and aisles might have been intended to have solid walls right up to the eastern wall of an aisleless transept arm (sited on the line of the present E. arcade). The thick transverse arches could then be the result of some demolition of solid walling. However, this seems improbable as surely the opportunity would have been taken to

[64] Little Missenden in V.C.H. Bucks. ii, 358–59; Stanford Dingley in V.C.H. Berks. iv, 112. Other examples near Oxford can be found at Wraysbury (V.C.H. Bucks. iii, 324–25), N. arcade c.1200; and at Turweston (V.C.H. Bucks. iv, 253), where there are compound piers of a similar type c.1190.

[65] A close parallel for the Islip pier can be seen in the undercroft of the E. range and in the chapter-house of Rievaulx Abbey (Yorks.), c.1150–60, which may indicate the possibility of a more local monastic source. Font supports also take a similar form, e.g. Iffley.

make a better job of pier I.4 and both it and the S. transept equivalent are apparently first-phase work.

I suggest that the original intention was to have arches exactly as those existing, but springing on the W. from decorated friezes inserted into either an existing E. transept wall or into square 'piers' similar to the western face of II.4. The western entrance arch to each chancel aisle would also spring from a length of frieze, or possibly a half-shaft (or two) attached to the rear of the crossing-pier.[66] The appearance of the transept elevation would then be like that still to be seen in many Cistercian or Augustinian houses, e.g. Fountains Abbey. Having decided on this formula, the columnar pier arcade was simply substituted for the original wall and frieze and the original idea of a 'transverse' arch retained. The vaults were subsequently erected within the spaces formed by these large arches.

Throughout the chancel aisles, the awkward springing-points on the main arcade piers and the extensive use of corbels indicates a greater familiarity with groin-vaults. The giant order system does not help, of course, but a tidier appearance could have been obtained (and was in the nave aisle vaults) by a master more experienced in rib-vaulting techniques. It is possible that groin-vaults were present in the prototype and envisaged at Oxford, the decision to use rib-vaults only being taken during construction. The solid walls of the transept and nave middle 'storey' disguise the higher apex of their aisle vaults, whereas in the chancel there is an odd sloping sill to the voided openings. As only one shaft rises up the main elevation, the high vault of the chancel may also have used corbels for the diagonal ribs, reflecting their use in the aisle vaults. The survival of the capitals in the S. transept shows that all the ribs of the high vault there sprang from one capital, reflecting the system of the nave and N. transept W. aisle.

The arcades of the transepts and nave have slightly larger average bay-widths than the chancel arcades. This alteration was probably made at the same time as the main space width between the arcades was increased to allow for the addition of a nook-shaft on each crossing-pier. But the additional shaft to the N.E. crossing-pier (marked G on Fig. 35) only exacerbated the difficulties in aligning column 1.5 of the second-phase N. transept E. arcade with the existing respond, the W. face of pier 1.4. In such a prominent position, the elevation of this bay could hardly be squashed-up without doing serious visual harm. The columnar pier 1.5 was therefore positioned to allow a uniform bay size, and all the re-alignments to match it to the existing first-phase work were made within the aisle bay. The result is a mis-shapen vault, messy springing-points, the very irregular pier 1.4 and an awkward junction between the half-column responds of the N. chancel and N. transept E. arcades (emphasized by the stylistic changes). Even without the nook-shaft, it is clear that no allowance had been made for a half-column respond (G) when the chancel was laid out, supporting the theory that the N. transept was not originally conceived with aisles.

The equivalent eastern chapel of the S. transept (St. Lucy Chapel) confirms the argument that the concept of an eastern arcade to the transepts was introduced when the first phase of work was nearing completion. The transverse arch between the first columnar pier S. of the crossing-pier and the end of the S. chancel aisle wall is skewed to the S.W. to rise more neatly from the latter. However, the bay sizes here are quite different (and smaller) than elsewhere, because of the existence of the slype and chapter-house, of late 1140s date.

---

[66] Twin attached shafts are used for the entrance arches to the chancel aisles of Gloucester Cathedral and Tewkesbury Abbey, the latter having a giant order and both using an elongated crossing-pier form. The square piers could have been further articulated to the W. with an attached half-shaft rising up the elevation (rather like the shafts on pier II.4).

3.  *The S. transept*

The planning of this part of the church was complicated by the existence of at least an E. range, if not a complete cloister, no more than forty years old at the time of the translation in 1180 (and some buildings were probably barely finished). Obviously it was not intended to destroy this new work and perhaps the original plan was to have just a two-bay, aisleless S. transept. If the chancel was begun E. of an older church (as argued above), then the equivalent of a two-bay S. 'transept' presumably already existed. Once the decision was taken to rebuild the whole transept with aisles, the slype (with its lower floor-level) had to be absorbed into the body of the church. As previously explained, although on a ground-plan the N. transept appears to be one bay larger than the S., both have three bays in elevation. The southernmost bay of the S. transept at both triforium and clearstorey levels is carried over the slype passage, allowing the southern gable wall to rise up from the N. wall of the late-1140s chapter-house. Measuring from the centre of the crossing-piers to the outer walls, both transept arms are about 47 ft. (14.325 m.) in length.

The present Early English style of the N. wall of the slype and its upper chamber is by G.G. Scott, who had no evidence for either the style, the two openings or even for creating an accessible gallery. Evidence existed for the stairway up from the church to a room over the slype and the door from the church down into the slype, the slype floor level being over 4 ft. (1.22 m.) below the church floor. Despite the indignation expressed by the *Ecclesiologist* in 1847,[67] it was only in 1871 that Scott demolished the verger's house that had filled the last bay of the S. transept from floor to ceiling. He may have just re-faced some of the lower parts of the wall facing into the church, but otherwise all disappeared down to the level of the slype barrel-vault crown (about 5 ft. 6 ins. (1.676 m.) above transept floor level). The cloister end of the slype had been re-modelled when the present cloister was built in 1489–99, so Scott restored the barrel-vault at this end and removed the partition that had divided the slype passage.[68] While Scott's works were under way, J.C. Buckler took it on himself to provide a detailed record of the 12th-century evidence discovered (and frequently destroyed), and his drawings are invaluable for reconstructing the original appearance of this area (Fig. 64).[69]

From Buckler's work, it is clear that Scott re-made the two 12th-century levels as he found them, and although the rib-vaulted room over the slype is a total re-build the original vault profiles etc. were followed. One or two original voussoirs are re-used, and an original typically early to mid 12th-century monster-head corbel was re-used and copied for the others. The door adjacent to the S. respond of the E. transept arcade was unblocked by Scott, and the staircase immediately behind (blocked when the verger's house was created and wooden staircases inserted) was re-opened to give access to the upper room. This seems to have been the only medieval entry. The steps from the room onto its roof, i.e. the gallery floor, are Scott's invention, and since there has never been any access to this gallery floor from the clearstorey passage it appears in the middle ages to have been a dead area, like the space over a chantry chapel.[70]

There may have been a door in the S. wall of the rib-vaulted upper room giving

---

[67] 'In so vast a college, the hire of a single room cannot be dispensed with, but the House of God must be defiled', referring to the verger's house rising to the roof of the S. transept, with a large chimney built out of the S. gable window: *The Ecclesiologist*, iii (1847), 48.

[68] See the plan of 1820 in Britton's *Cathedrals*, op. cit. note 21, for the pre-Scott arrangement.

[69] B.L. MS Add. 27765 E and F.

[70] Access to the S. transept clearstorey is still gained today by means of a wooden ladder (of some age!).

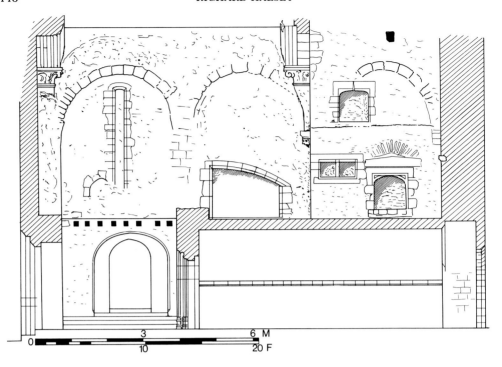

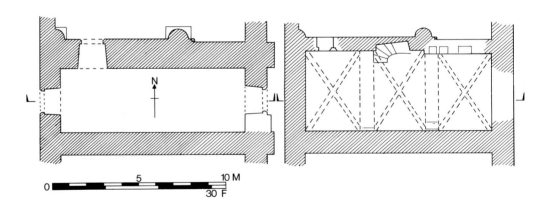

Fig. 64. The slype and vaulted chamber: section looking N. and ground-plans, by J.C. Buckler, 1870.
(Re-drawn from B.L. MS Add. 27765E ff. 56, 80ᵛ by John Blair.)

access to the upper floor of the E. range, which was presumably a dormitory. A night stair might then have existed through the upper room and down the present stairway to the church; there is certainly much wear to the plinth of the E. arcade respond adjacent to the door, indicating heavier traffic than the occasional sacristan, if, indeed, the upper room did function as a sacristy.[71] Such use, with its need for security, does not seem compatible with regular night-time access. Certainly there can have been no access across the W. end of the present chapter-house of *c*.1230.

Buckler concluded from the evidence in front of him that the S. transept was originally built complete up to the existing chapter-house wall, the slype passage and the room over it being built into the church 'shortly after its completion', i.e. very late in the 12th century.[72] Apart from the contorted arguments he uses to support this idea – for instance, he omits to mention the huge width of the southernmost bay, patently forced to be of this size by the pre-existence of the slype – there is the problem of levels. The slype today has a concrete floor that is 4 ft. 2½ ins. (1.28 m.) below the church floor level; the apex of its barrel-vault is about 9 ft. 10 ins. (2.99 m.) above the floor, or *c*.5 ft. 6 ins. (1.67 m.) above the transept floor-level. The floor above the vault (i.e. the floor of the upper room) is *c*. 7 ft. 3 ins. (2.21 m.) above church floor-level. As the present paving of the 1489 E. cloister walk is another 1 ft. 1¾ ins. (0.349 m.) below the slype floor, it follows that there is now a difference of 5 ft. 4 ins. (1.625 m.) between church and cloister levels. It is clearly nonsense to suggest that the slype has been hollowed-out of the church foundations. The chapter-house floor has, like the others, been re-laid and the 12th-century entrance arch jambs have been repaired at their bases, so the 12th-century floor levels are strictly speaking, unknown. It is likely (as Martin Biddle has suggested, see below pp. 241–2) that the chapter-house door-jambs were lowered after the 1190 fire, suggesting that the original cloister level was some 18 inches lower than the church floor-level.

From Buckler's drawings, it is certain that the upper room above the slype was added to the main piers of the post-1180 work; yet both the original corbel and the profile of the vault-ribs are unparalleled within the church and could easily be up to fifty years earlier in date. Perhaps the vault has been re-used from a demolished structure (it could even have been originally built *c*.1150 in a similar room above the slype). Although not a happy compromise, this is not a very important part of the church; and it is obvious from the contrast between the nave and the high-level work in both transepts that money became tight and the initial quality was not maintained. The essential point is that the present S. transept was built onto an existing chapter-house and slype, the 'upper room' being built (probably as a sacristy) above the barrel-vaulted slype, whose floor was considerably lower than the new church floor-level.

At St. Frideswide's this issue is made more complicated by the evidence for the existence of a W. aisle to the S. transept from the late 12th century to the building of the present cloister after 1489. Both Buckler and Scott were convinced that a western aisle was built and demolished to make way for the present N. cloister walk, after 1489. Both suggested that there was no 12th-century N. cloister walk (at least once the present church was built), but Buckler proposed a two-bay W. aisle, therefore enclosing the

---

[71] There are later 12th-century ground-floor vaulted rooms, most probably built as sacristies, at Ely (where the W. aisle of the S. transept was walled off), Peterborough (where a new building was added to the W. side of the S. transept), Hereford (where a sacristy was added to the E. side of the S. transept) and Old Sarum, though the large building at the N. end of the N. transept there is possibly more analogous to the Treasury Prior Wibert added to the N. side of the Canterbury Cathedral.

[72] B.L. MS Add. 27765E, ff. 63–78.

slype entrance within the church proper, a rather unlikely solution in view of the different levels and the usual open corridor function of a monastic slype.

Buckler's drawings make it clear that the engaged column at the corner of the S. transept and S. nave aisle was built as a free-standing column and was subsequently enclosed.[73] This was surmised by a number of 19th-century writers[74] but not by the R.C.H.M.: 'the engaged cylindrical column of the transept arcade has the half-capital of its sub-arch cut into the wall of the aisle, which seems to imply that this wall is of earlier date than the general design of the church.'[75] However, the Commission's plan indicates the whole of the S. aisle S. wall and the W. wall of the S. transept to be of one 12th-century date. The text does not discuss the possibility of there having been a W. aisle, or the problem of the 12th-century cloister access.

Although there is a straight-joint between the wall and the column masonry, the tooling either side looks very similar, probably because of the 19th-century cleaning.[76] Both the windows of the two eastern bays and most of the walls and windows of the other two bays are Scott's work, as is virtually all the cloister side of the wall. There is no evidence for the R.C.H.M.'s 'earlier wall' and neither Scott or Buckler claimed to have seen one, although the latter did note that the walling on demolition contained many worked 12th-century stones, likely to have come from the first cloister. Further evidence in favour of this aisle wall being of 15th-century date, at least in its lower courses between the late 12th-century responds, is the remains of an internal low bench in the two eastern bays, only otherwise found along the 15th-century N. nave wall.[77] Finally, if not conclusively, there is no parallel in original medieval work for such a corner 'engaged column' and particularly not at St. Frideswide's. On the N. side, although the N. nave aisle wall is a 15th-century rebuild, the corner with the W. aisle of the N. transept is original late 12th-century work, the vault of this shared bay being undisturbed and of stone, unlike the plaster vaults in the rest of the N. nave aisle. There is no attempt even to chamfer the corner: like the corners between the transepts and chancel aisles, it is square and undecorated.[78]

The conclusion to be drawn is surely that the S. nave aisle wall is abutting the column, its capital and base. The capital and its foliage decoration continue (as far as can be seen) on the obscured W. face, but the springing stones of the diagonal vault rib overlap it by a few inches. This cannot have been the original arrangement and once again, it seems that the rib has been extended and to a different curvature. It originally would have died into the angle formed above the capital between the transverse arch and the lower arch of the W. transept main elevation. As the S. nave aisle vaults seem on stylistic grounds to be the last to be erected, it is just possible (but in my view unlikely) that this change in curvature and the blocking-off of the S. transept W. aisle took place soon after the erection of the column, i.e. the aisle was intended in c.1180–90 when the S. transept was being built, but abandoned once the nave aisle came to be vaulted, c.1210–20.

[73] Ibid., ff. 54–5, 80v–81.

[74] See, for instance, John Britton's 1820 plan (op. cit. note 21) and Roland Paul's plan in *The Builder*, lxi (June 4, 1882).

[75] *R.C.H.M. Oxford*, plan 36, text 40–41.

[76] 'The interior stonework has been cleaned and made good' (*The Builder*, xxix, October 21, 1871). It is always possible, of course, that these are 12th-century ashlars re-used c.1489 and it is not known whether Scott revealed this junction in his restoration.

[77] A bench also exists on the S. chancel aisle wall, but this is apparently all Scott's work.

[78] Although all published plans (except the large College plan in *R.C.H.M. Oxford*) show an attached half-shaft to the nave wall, none exists – and presumably has not existed since the c.1500 rebuilding of the N. aisle wall.

If this W. aisle was built, then it is likely that there was just one bay S. of the nave aisle, its S. wall in line with the S. wall of the St. Lucy Chapel-cum-E. aisle. A door in this wall would then lead to a few steps descending to the E. cloister walk, finishing in front of the slype entrance (which was presumably an open archway). Although not symmetrical with the three-bay aisles of the N. transept, the S. transept arm with its two-bay aisles would at least have aisles that echoed each other. On the W. side of the S. transept, the existing infill wall (on which is mounted the 1683 wall monument to Edward Littleton, Lord Mounslowe) is set within an arch, with a hood-mould like all the other lower arches of the main elevation, which surrounds the abaci of the lower main arcade capitals. As neither the chancel or the transepts continue the giant order elevation on their gable walls, it is unlikely that such an arched feature would have been used here if a solid wall had been intended. Therefore, the column flanking the slype was presumably structurally identical to its equivalent on the E. side of the transept; that is, a quarter capital at the lower level, with an attached shaft to the aisle side and a complete upper capital.[79]

It is not common to have steps up from a cloister into a transept, rather than into a nave aisle. For instance, both the surviving Romanesque cathedrals with aisled transepts, Ely and Winchester, have doors leading directly into the nave.[80] It is most unlikely that any eastern nave door existed at St. Frideswide's, as the chapter-house entrance is in line with the W. arcade of the S. transept and not its W. wall. If any 12th-century door and staircase had existed in the nave aisle wall, then it can be expected to have been retained or re-modelled when the present cloister was created after 1489.[81] At that time, the slype was altered so that the S. transept could be reached from the E. cloister walk via its western end, and a flight of steps cut into the N. slype wall, an arrangement seen in pre-1870 plans. The ogee'd water-stoup carved out of the S. 'respond' of the W. arcade of the S. transept is adjacent to this door and consistent with a post-1489 date. It may replace a similar feature on the other side of this 'respond', now buried in the infill wall.[82]

If it is accepted that the pre-1489 access to the E. cloister walk was through the S. wall of the W. aisle of the S. transept, then the N. walk of the cloister either had an 'elbow' bend around the S. transept, or came to a stop against the transept W. wall. Neither of these suggestions has a parallel; perhaps it was thought preferrable to do away with the late-1140s N. cloister walk – if, of course, it had been built. A close parallel for such a cloister exists at Wells Cathedral (as both Buckler and Scott recognised), where both transepts have E. and W. aisles and the first Lady Chapel, sited E. of the E. walk, was aligned with the W. arcade of the S. transept, i.e. in the manner of the chapter-house at St. Frideswide's.[83] A doorway and a flight of five steps connects the

[79] The top of the upper capital abacus can still be seen, buried in the gallery floor: Buckler drew the battered remains of the decoration (B.L. MS Add. 27765E ff. 57–8).

[80] Ely also has a door leading into the S. transept W. aisle, but through the W. wall, and this aisle was made into a sacristy at about the same time as the door was built, c.1140.

[81] Neither Buckler nor Scott reported finding any E. doorway when the N. cloister walk was rebuilt by the latter. I presume that there was a W. cloister door in one of the bays that Wolsey demolished, the present doorway having been made c.1526 to compensate for the lack of either a W. or N. entrance for the public. This door is now Scott's work, and I have found no illustration of its previous appearance. Britton's plan (op. cit. note 21, pl.I), like others, shows a porch with straight sides like the doorway itself, perhaps incorporating parts of the cloister. The staircase shown by Britton leading down to the E. cloister walk from Keene's Muniment Room of 1772 is precisely the form of staircase I propose existed in the late 12th century.

[82] There may always, of course, have been a door between the slype and the 12th-century church, e.g. as at Roche Abbey (Yorks.), but such a door is never a principal entrance to the cloister.

[83] W. Rodwell, 'The Lady Chapel by the Cloister at Wells Cathedral and the site of the Anglo-Saxon Cathedral', in *Medieval Art and Architecture at Wells and Glastonbury* (Trans. of B.A.A. Conference 1978, 1981), 1–9.

W. aisle of the S. transept with the E. cloister walk and no N. walk was ever built. Wells was not monastic, but the secular canons needed a cloister for study and recreation and to reach the Lady Chapel. The Bishop also used the E. walk to reach his Palace. The Wells cloister was probably planned with the earliest phase of *c*.1180 and so may have been available as a prototype for St. Frideswide's (unless, of course, a destroyed church elsewhere also had such an arrangement). However, the actual doorway at Wells between the church and the E. walk has capitals closer in style to those of the nave than the transept, so was probably not built until *c*.1190.

Therefore, St. Frideswide's had a W. aisle of two bays to its S. transept and no N. cloister walk (or at least, none connected to the E. walk until after 1489). The eastern access to the cloister was through a door in the S. wall of the W. aisle. After 1489, access was obtained through the W. end of the slype, there were normal N. and E. walks to the cloister, as now, and the S. transept W. aisle was removed and the arcade blocked-up. To compensate for the loss of a lower-level window, the triforium of the middle bay of the W. side was pierced and glazed, reusing mid 12th-century material from the recently demolished cloisters. Access from the W. walk of the cloister was presumably through a door in one of the nave bays demolished by Wolsey: the existing door in the S. nave aisle wall was created *c*.1526.


MEASUREMENTS


It has long been known that medieval buildings were erected with the aid of geometry and the use of numerical ratios, but it is only since the last war that a more systematic study of the proportions used in English great churches has taken place. This has demonstrated that the $1:\sqrt{2}$ proportion is the most consistently used proportional system in early medieval architecture.[84] Geometrically it is simply generated, being the relationship of the side of a square to its diagonal. But arithmetical equivalents of this ratio had also been known since Antiquity, and these series of figures formed part of the mason's jealously-guarded craft secrets.[85]

The clearest uses of the $1:\sqrt{2}$ ratio at St. Frideswide's are seen in the smaller elements. For instance, the columnar piers have an average diameter of 3 ft. 5 ins. (1.04 m.) and their bases a square of 4 ft. 9 ins. (1.44 m.); the average width of the chancel aisles is 11 ft. 2 ins. (3.40 m.) which multiplied by $\sqrt{2}$ gives the internal width of the aisle and the arcade, 15 ft. 9 ins. (4.80 ins.).[86] On a larger scale, the internal length of the single eastern bay is in a $1:\sqrt{2}$ relationship with its width, i.e. 14 ft. : 19 ft. 10 ins. (4.26 m. : 6.05 m.).

The important levels in the elevation are also in a $\sqrt{2}$ sequence. The height of the abacus of the lower arch of the giant order is 14 ft. 7 ins. (4.45 m.) above floor level; when multiplied by $\sqrt{2}$, the height of the upper capital abacus is reached, 20 ft. 6 ins. (6.25 m.). When this measurement is multiplied by $\sqrt{2}$, the result is 28 ft. 11 ins. (8.81 m.) the height of the main vault springing point. Used again, the $\sqrt{2}$ calculation gives 41 ft.

[84] The basic groundwork was laid by Prof. Peter Kidson in his unpublished Ph.D Thesis, *Systems of Measurement and Proportion in Early Mediaeval Architecture*, University of London, 1956. Prof. Eric Fernie has measured a number of Romanesque buildings, but only his findings at Norwich and Ely have been published. 'The Ground Plan of Norwich Cathedral and the Square Root of Two', *J.B.A.A.* cxxix (1976), 77–86; and 'Observations on the Norman Plan of Ely Cathedral', *Medieval Art and Architecture at Ely Cathedral* (Trans. of B.A.A. Conference 1976, 1979), 1–7.

[85] L. Shelby, 'The Geometrical Knowledge of Mediaeval Master Masons', *Speculum*, xlvii (1972), 395–421.

[86] See Fernie, 'Norwich Cathedral', op. cit. note 84, 78–9 and (at Bury St Edmunds) 85.

(12.49 ins.) which is roughly the level of the crown of the vault.[87] Repeated once more, then the result 58 ft. (17.68 m.) could well be ridge level of the original steeply-pitched roof.

Of more interest is the apparent use of a basic unit of measurement equivalent to the diameter of the piers, 3 ft. 5 ins. (1.04 m.). The above elevation heights then become the sequence $4\frac{1}{4}$:6:$8\frac{1}{2}$:12:17. The latter, 12:17, is a well-used pair of numerical equivalents, an 'otherwise unlikely combination of numbers'.[88] Applied to the ground plan the length of the church (with a seven-bay nave) at c.196 ft. 3 ins. (59.82 m.) is virtually 58 units and its average internal width, 51 ft. 9 ins. (15.77 m.), 15 units. The crossing at 24 ft. (7.31 m.) square (column centres) is 7 units, and the E. cloister walk internal length of c.96 ft. (29.26 m.) 28 units.

Applying the 1: $\sqrt{2}$ ratio to the ground plan does not produce such a clear demonstration of its use. This is perhaps due to the changes in plan from the original conception c.1160–70 (or even c.1150?) to the end product c.1200. Taking the line between the chapter-house doorway to the western crossing-piers as the 'base-line' the total internal length of the new E. end is 98 ft. 2 ins. (29.92 m.), or nearly 29 units. This measure is in a $\sqrt{2}$ ratio to the internal length of the chancel measured from the W. responds to the E. wall of the single bay, 69 ft. 6 ins. (21.18m.) or $20\frac{1}{2}$ units.

This putative base-line also marks the half-way point in the total internal length, which is surely more than a coincidence. In addition, 98 ft. 2 ins. (29.92 m.) is not much less than the internal length of the transept floor as it now exists (from the N. slype wall to the N. wall of the N. transept) and it would be almost identical to the internal length measured to a putative Romanesque N. transept N. wall. The E. walk of the cloister, at c.96 ft. (29.26 m.), is also close to this figure. In a general way, the number of nave bays is in a $\sqrt{2}$ ratio to the chancel bays, 7:5, and when converted to units of 3 ft. 5 ins. (1.04 m.) the ratio becomes 29:21, another frequently-used numerical approximation.

There is not as neat a relationship between the elevation and plan and between the various parts of the plan as has been demonstrated in other Romanesque buildings, and these discrepancies can probably be explained by the major change in plan, the addition of aisled transepts c.1180.[89] But there is clear evidence of the use of the $\sqrt{2}$ ratios to create important levels and the dimensions of very many elements. There also seems to be the use of a basic unit equivalent to the diameter of the columnar piers, which may have some bearing on the derivation of the giant order elevation from Vitruvius. Until more buildings are accurately measured and their units and ratios established, little context can be given for either the use of the $\sqrt{2}$ ratio or the basic unit of 3 ft. 5ins. at St. Frideswide's.

CONTEXT

As has been said previously, our lack of knowledge of the greater churches near Oxford, most especially the really grand buildings of Reading and Abingdon Abbeys, seriously

[87] B. Singleton, 'Proportions in the Design of the Early Gothic Cathedral at Wells', in *Medieval Art and Architecture at Wells and Glastonbury* (Trans. of B.A.A. Conference 1978, 1981), 15.

[88] Ibid. 10. 29:41 is another of these approximations, these figures being the rounded measurements of the vault springing point: vault crown at St. Frideswide's. The same measures of 14 ft. 8 ins., 29 ft. and 41 ft. are used in the Wells elevation, ibid. 11.

[89] The slight changes in bay sizes and aisle widths between the chancel campaign and the nave transepts probably compound the 'inaccuracy' too.

hampers discussion of the context and source of the 12th-century architecture of St. Frideswide's Priory. Neither the scale of the building nor the revenue of the house suggest that any remarkable piece of architecture should be expected, though the craftmanship seen in the chancel and transepts is certainly of a good quality in a period when both the mason's craft and design capabilities are frequently of a high standard. There are, though, four elements that need to be discussed: the aisled transept plan, the use of a giant order elevation system, the use of rib-vaults and the capital sculpture.

Although the giant order might not have been quite so unusual *c*.1180 as the few survivals suggest, the use of aisled transepts is most extraordinary. Transepts with both an E. and W. 'aisle' – even if in practice used as chapels – were first adopted in England in the late 11th-century cathedrals at Winchester (1079), Ely (1081–93) and Old St. Paul's (1087). Aisles were added to cross spaces in Early Christian times and the Duomo at Pisa, 1063/1089, can be seen as a continuation of this idea. But it was in 11th-century France that aisled transepts became a regular feature in the plan-forms of the grandest Romanesque churches like Tours (St. Martin) and Reims (St. Remi), and it is presumably from such buildings that the idea was taken up in England. To our certain knowledge, only Roger of Salisbury's extension to Old Sarum Cathedral, built in the first quarter of the 12th century, continued the idea,[90] possibly because there was little need for a western aisle (even if its use could create more grandiose spatial effects at the crossings). Old Sarum was not a large cathedral and although Bishop Roger virtually doubled its length to about 270 ft. (82.3 m.), the transepts were not as deep N.–S. as St. Frideswide's, though broader E.–W. He was presumably enhancing his cathedral and demonstrating his munificence by using a plan-form only otherwise used by the very greatest churches.

None of the major English churches of *c*.1120–*c*.1170 are known to have used aisled transept plans,[91] whereas in northern France any church with any pretensions had aisled transepts, including of course the Early and High Gothic cathedrals. Then, about 1180, Wells Cathedral, St. Frideswide's Priory and the Cistercian Byland Abbey (N. Yorks.) all use aisled transepts[92] (followed in the next century by York and Beverley Minsters and Westminster Abbey). All three buildings owe something to the Early Gothic architecture of northern France, at Wells and possibly at Oxford filtered through the churches of the reformed monastic orders; the plan-form might therefore be from that source. The use of aisles around the chancel and transepts at Byland has been explained in terms of the necessity for extra altars,[93] which might also be the case at Wells.

Although there would not appear to be a need for extra chapels at Oxford, extra space might well have been needed in connection with the boosted cult of St. Frideswide's relics. The fabric does show that aisled transepts were not envisaged when the new chancel was begun in the 1160s, and the decision to enlarge the re-building campaign seems to have been taken *c*.1180 when the saint's cult was at a peak. If the sites of the shrine, the 1002–4 church and the parochial altar were exactly known, the adoption of the grander plan with aisled transepts might be more explicable. The

[90] *R.C.H.M. City of Salisbury*, i (1980), 15–24.

[91] The plan of Hyde Abbey, Winchester is not known and, given its location, the possibility that it had aisled transepts cannot be ruled out.

[92] For Wells see L.S. Colchester and J.H. Harvey, 'Wells Cathedral', *Archaeol. Jnl*. cxxxi (1974), 200–14; for Byland see P. Fergusson, 'The South Transept Elevation of Byland Abbey', *J.B.A.A.* 3rd ser. xxxviii (1975), 155–76.

[93] C.R. Peers, *Byland Abbey* (H.M.S.O., 2nd ed., 1952).

awkwardness created by adding a western aisle to the S. transept shows that aisled transepts were thought to be essential, and whether this was for practical spatial reasons or to enhance the status of the establishment can now only be conjectured.

Unless a more local source existed in a church belonging to the reformed orders (and neither of the largest local churches at the Benedictine abbeys of Abingdon and Reading had aisled transepts), Wells Cathedral seems to be the closest and most recent example for this unusual plan. If status was the driving force, then an association with the older cathedral churches of Winchester, Ely and London, all with important Anglo-Saxon shrines, can be tentatively suggested.[94] But their example is hardly more obvious *c.*1180 than that of the numerous examples to be seen in the contemporary Gothic churches of Northern France. However, the lack of any other direct French references at St. Frideswide's does tend to suggest that the source of the aisled transept plan should be sought in England. Similarly, other ideas might be expected to accompany knowledge of the Wells plan, but apart from the use of keeled roll-mouldings (which were becoming quite widely used in England *c.*1180) and the omission of a N. cloister walk, there is nothing to further the claim for Wells as the source-building for the adoption of aisled transepts *c.*1180 at St. Frideswide's.[95]

The choice of a giant order elevation system in the late 1160s is obviously a separate issue from the adoption of aisled transepts *c.*1180. In an earlier article on Tewkesbury Abbey (probably the first building to use a giant order in Romanesque England), I have outlined the likely existence of other 12th-century giant order elevations than those that exist now at Romsey (Hants.), Jedburgh (Roxburgh), and Oxford.[96] The fact that the dates of these four surviving buildings stretch over seventy years and that other buildings incorporate giant columnar elements within their elevations (like Dunstable Priory and Holy Trinity, Aldgate, London)[97] surely makes it probable that more giant order elevations existed. There is clear evidence for large-scale columnar piers being used in buildings throughout the S. and W. of England,[98] and circumstantial evidence for the existence of a giant order in the pre-Gothic churches of Glastonbury and Sherborne Abbeys.[99]

Of the greatest interest to St. Frideswide's are the columnar piers used at both Abingdon and Reading. The site of the former was so thoroughly robbed after the Dissolution that very little can ever be known of the fabric. But it is known that Abbot

[94] Canterbury Cathedral was clearly not the source, as there are no aisled transepts there.

[95] As the elevation was not changed, the use of triple-shafts or continuous and complex mouldings could not be attempted at Oxford. There is certainly no sign of the Wells capital and sculpture style either, and in fact the type of keel used at Wells is more ogee'd than that seen at Oxford.

[96] R. Halsey, 'Tewkesbury Abbey: some Recent Observations', in *Medieval Art and Architecture at Gloucester and Tewkesbury* (Trans. of B.A.A. Conference 1981, 1985), 27–9.

[97] Only the seven western bays of the nave survive at Dunstable and the form of the E. end is unknown: *V.C.H. Beds.* iii (1912), 356–66. John Carter included some drawings of Holy Trinity, Aldgate in *The Ancient Architecture of England* (1798), pl.xxi.

[98] Although large columnar piers are seen in the E. of England, e.g. at Ely, Bury St. Edmunds, Norwich and Peterborough, only St. Botolph's Priory at Colchester seems to have used them consistently and not just as occasional minor forms. There is, though, a columnar element in many East Anglian pier forms: see B. Cherry, 'Romanesque Architecture in Eastern England', *J.B.A.A.* cxxxi (1978), 1–29.

[99] The source of the interesting elevation at Glastonbury, which attempts to integrate a giant order and an articulated rib-vault, is hard to find. Is it possible that the monks there held the same conservationist sentiments about their Romanesque church, destroyed in the 1184 fire, as the monks at Canterbury felt for their church in similar circumstances a decade earlier? No evidence for the pier forms of Herlewin's church begun *c.*1120 has so far been reported from the numerous excavations. Sherborne Abbey has an essentially Romanesque core to many of its walls and arcades: if the chancel piers have a Romanesque core too, then a giant order could be hypothesied: *R.C.H.M. Dorset*, i, *West* (1952), xlvii–l, 200–6 and Supplement.

Faritius (1100–1117) built the nave, and William Worcestre said of the nave piers in 1480 that *columpne rotunditas in circuitu continet 5 virgas*,[100] roughly 5 ft. (1.52 m.) diameter.

Reading Abbey (founded 1121 and consecrated 1164)[101] was more fortunate, in that less robbing took place, though various public enterprises on or adjacent to the site have removed or buried most of the fabric.[102] However, two bases of the S. chancel columnar piers exist *in situ*, each with a diameter of 6 ft. 6 ins. (1.98 m.). Excavations in 1971–3 established a plan for the Romanesque choir, and this evidence (with that of J.C. Buckler) suggests that the Reading choir had a plan of similar form and dimensions to Tewkesbury.[103] The existence of large columnar piers does not of course mean a giant order elevation, but the Reading piers have an attached shaft to their aisle face that is less than a semi-circle on plan. An identical 'sunken' attached shaft can be seen on the aisle side of the nave piers of Evesham Abbey (built by Abbot Reginald of Gloucester, 1130–49), and the same type of shaft is added to the four cardinal points of the tribune piers of Gloucester choir.[104] By adding these shafts with their capitals, a visually neater junction can be achieved between the curving mass of the cylindrical pier and the arch or vault shaft springing from it (and there may have been some structural advantages too).[105]

The enhanced integration of a pier with the arches and vaults it supports becomes a pre-occupation of mature Romanesque architecture (especially once rib-vaults are used), and the use of large scale columnar piers – particularly in a giant order system – exacerbates the problems encountered. One ungainly experimental solution can be seen on the aisle side of the single columnar giant order pier at the E. end of the S. nave arcade at Romsey Abbey (*c.*1140), where no less than three shafts are added beneath the diagonal and transverse ribs of the aisle vault.[106] Reading Abbey evidently had rib-vaulted transept chapels, and given the royal patronage and the 1120s date, it is most likely that the aisles were rib-vaulted too, perhaps in the manner of the contemporary Gloucester nave aisles. However, the shaft added to the aisle face of the Reading columnar piers is less than a semi-circle and unlikely therefore to be a full structural member in the manner of normal attached shafts seen within compound piers (or those used at Romsey). I suggest that it was being used in conjunction with a Tewkesbury capital-cum-corbel within a giant order elevation, integrating the transverse arch of the aisle vault with the columnar pier and creating a larger area at capital level for the springing of the diagonal ribs. (St. Frideswide's piers drop the shaft, but create a larger capital-cum-corbel to the aisle to receive all the ribs.) Even if groin vaults were used at Reading (as at the contemporary church of St. Bartholomew, Smithfield, London), this shaft would still stand beneath a transverse arch and be something of an advance on the awkward arrangements seen at Tewkesbury.

[100] M. Biddle et al., 'The Early History of Abingdon, Berkshire and its Abbey', *Med. Archaeol.* xii (1968), 26–69; Harvey op.cit. note 53, 282.

[101] *V.C.H. Berks.* ii (1907), 62–3.

[102] A Civil War fortification buried the nave, a new prison was built over the easternmost area of the church and various municipal activities (including clearance work by the unemployed in 1857) have taken their toll: *V.C.H. Berks.* iv (1923), 339–42.

[103] C.F. Slade, 'Excavations at Reading, 1971–3', *Berks. Arch. Jnl.* lxviii (1975–6), 29–37. J.C. Buckler's notes of 1878 are in B.L. Add. MS. 36400 A and B. For a comparison of the measurements see Halsey, op. cit. note 96, fn. 86.

[104] For Evesham see *Vetusta Monumenta*, v (1835), pl. lxvii (plan) and pl. lxviii (piers). For Gloucester see C. Wilson, 'Abbot Serlo's Church at Gloucester (1089–1100): Its Place in Romanesque Architecture', in *Medieval Art and Architecture at Gloucester and Tewkesbury* (Trans. of B.A.A. Conference 1981, 1985), 52–83.

[105] See Cherry, op. cit. note 98, especially footnote 51.

[106] M.F. Hearn, 'Romsey Abbey, a Progenitor of the English National Tradition in Architecture', *Gesta*, xiv (i) (1975), 27–40.

If Reading and Abingdon did have giant order elevations, as well as huge columnar piers, then the 1160s chancel of St. Frideswide's can be seen as a local variant. The influence of Reading had already been felt in Oxford from the late 1140s, at least in the architectural sculpture, if not in the design, of the St. Frideswide's chapter-house (see below, pp. 160–7). Reading was only consecrated in 1164 (and surely the prior of St. Frideswide's would have attended such an occasion?), and although the details of the design conceived *c.*1121 may have seemed old-fashioned forty years later, a clear association with such a prestigious foundation could have been thought desirable.

Once it is accepted that Reading Abbey had a giant order system, then the apparently maverick use of such elevations at Romsey and Jedburgh becomes explicable in terms of prestige and status. Both abbeys had royal associations and Jedburgh in particular had reason to imitate Reading (the mausoleum of Henry I after his death in 1135) if the Anglophile King David of Scotland saw it as his own creation, as Henry created Reading.[107] However, Jedburgh was a re-foundation for Augustinian canons, and there is a discernible – if tenuous – interest in linked storeys at some larger Augustinian churches.

It is unfortunate that so little is known of the two most important early Augustinian foundations, at Holy Trinity, Aldgate (just inside the eastern boundary of the city of London), founded *c.* 1107–8, and Merton Priory (on the river Wandle S. of Wimbledon, S.W. London), founded by 1117.[108] Nothing is known of the internal elevations of Merton, but Carter's drawing of Holy Trinity suggests that a columnar element rose up from the ground, not as a giant order like St. Frideswide's, but like the piers at Dunstable Priory, another large Augustinian house.[109] The first prior at Dunstable, founded *c.*1125, was Bernard, brother of Norman, the founding prior of Holy Trinity, Aldgate, and an architectural link could be expected. Both houses had some links to the court too, but then so did St. Bartholomew's, Smithfield and St. Botolph's, Colchester, and although they both use columnar piers, neither have giant orders or linked storeys in their elevations.[110]

Master Robert of Cricklade, prior of St. Frideswide's in the 1160s, was a well-travelled and learned man.[111] If he was the patron who decided in favour of a giant order he may have been looking around locally for inspiration (at Reading?), or he may have looked to other Augustinian houses (and what did Oseney, raised to abbey status in 1154, look like?). The nave at Dunstable was still being built in the 1160s and the elevation that Carter drew at Holy Trinity, Aldgate is unlikely to have been much earlier than *c.*1140 (and so probably work done after the 1132 fire).[112] Not that these two options are exclusive: apart from Oseney, Notley Abbey (Bucks.), an Arrouasian Augustinian house, was begun about 1160[113] and Missenden Abbey (Bucks.), again Arrouasian, was founded in 1133.[114] Both are known (from fragmentary evidence) to be under construction around the middle of the 12th century, and indeed Notley uses

---

[107] There is no reason to suppose that David wished to be buried at Jedburgh, or create a dynastic mausoleum.

[108] Op. cit. note 97, and Dickinson, op. cit. note 43.

[109] Op. cit. note 97.

[110] Norman, prior of Holy Trinity, came from St. Botolph's, having learnt the Augustinian customs at Mont-St-Eloi, north-east France: *V.C.H. London*, i (1909), 465.

[111] Blair, 'St. F.', 80, notes 8 and 9; and cf. above, p. 121.

[112] *V.C.H.* op. cit. note 10, 466.

[113] *V.C.H. Bucks.* i (1905), 377–9, and W.A. Pantin, 'Notley Abbey', *Oxoniensia*, vi (1941) 22–43.

[114] *V.C.H. Bucks.* i (1905), 369–76. Excavations and demolition following a fire in the 18th-century house have revealed many fragments that will be published by the Aylesbury County Museum shortly.

columnar piers in its *c*.1200 nave (the chancel piers are unknown). Further afield, very little is known of Robert's previous house at Cirencester, beyond the 'skeleton ground plan of the foundations' of the 12th-century church, though it was begun in 1117 and the first canons came from Merton to reform the old minster.[115]

On the other hand, Robert might well have read Vitruvius's description of his basilica at Fanum, which had a giant order of colossal size.[116] The proportions of St. Frideswide's do not relate to those given by Vitruvius, and there is no use of pilasters or galleries as at Fanum. However, Prior Robert could have been attempting to commission a building to resemble the Roman basilica, as described by Vitruvius.

There is too little firm information to be sure even of the patron of St. Frideswide's, let alone his intentions. Despite its infelicities, the design of the elevation is surely not something that could have been conjured out of a none-too-clear classical text, and its generally sophisticated character equally suggests that the mason-architect was working to an established precedent. My belief is that the use of the giant order at St. Frideswide's follows its use at other 12th-century great churches, and the local abbeys at Reading and Abingdon are certainly known to have had columnar piers of large dimensions. Reading, in particular, seems to me to share enough features with the choir of Tewkesbury Abbey (which certainly did have a giant order elevation) to make such an elevation a probability.

Although the exact details are not certain, there can be little doubt that the main spaces of St. Frideswide's were originally rib-vaulted (with the probable exception of the nave),[117] and that the elevation was designed to receive the ribs on shafts terminating above the abaci of the upper capitals. The normal Anglo-Norman arrangement was to terminate vault shafts at the base of the triforium – as at Durham or Gloucester, for instance – and the resulting emphasis on creating horizontal layers (rather than vertical bays in the French Gothic manner) was to continue in English Gothic elevations. St. Frideswide's is something of a compromise, in that the vault shafts, whilst not descending to the floor, do reach down as far as the abaci of the main arcade, as, for instance, at Canterbury choir (1175). It might be argued that since the triforium has been compressed into the main arcade by the use of a giant order, these shafts are continuing the Anglo-Norman arrangement. Yet their solid form gives them a strong visual function in continuing the verticality of the columnar pier upwards (and once, presumably, vice versa, bringing the rib-vaults visually down to the ground).[118]

Few large-scale vaults of the middle decades of the 12th century survive in England, though they are known to have been erected, for instance by Bishop Alexander at Lincoln Cathedral. Numerous smaller-scale vaults exist in parish churches or subsidiary monastic buildings, and Oxford has two such examples in the chancels of St. Peter's-in-the-East (*c*.1150) and Iffley. Both use ribs decorated with chevron, but it seems highly unlikely that chevron was used in the vaults at St. Frideswide's. It is not

---

[115] P.D.C. Brown and Alan D. McWhirr, 'Cirencester 1965', *Antiq. Jnl.* xlvi (1966), 240–54.

[116] Vitruvius, *De Architectura*, Bk. V. Peter Kidson gives an interpretation of the text and its possible application at Tewkesbury in 'The Abbey Church of St. Mary at Tewkesbury in the 11th and 12th Centuries', in *Medieval Art and Architecture at Gloucester and Tewkesbury* (Trans. of B.A.A. Conference 1981, 1985), 13–15. See also my comments in the same volume, 24.

[117] The areas between the nave clearstorey windows are less messy than those of the transepts, and no clear indication (or 'shadow') of a vault can be seen. See note 25.

[118] The Dunstable piers are the result of imposing vault shafts onto a giant order, though it seems unlikely that the Dunstable main spaces were vaulted. Carlisle Cathedral nave elevation *c*.1160 includes a shaft that rises from the top of the abacus of the main arcade capital, but it does not rise through the tribune stage as built.

used elsewhere in the church, and the chancel aisle ribs have a simple profile, though one that is difficult to parallel (see Fig. 59).[119]

Once again, lost local monastic churches might have provided a context for the vaults. But on presently existing evidence, St. Frideswide's seems to demonstrate that the use of large-scale rib-vaults over main spaces was not unusual in England in the middle decades of the 12th century, and that there may well have been an English development of the rib-vault, evolving almost independently (or in parallel) to that in northern France. Whilst the reformed orders and French-inspired work like Canterbury Cathedral choir undoubtedly introduced new decorative structural forms (such as the sexpartite vault) to England, English Romanesque architecture was perhaps not as starved of rib-vaults as might be thought from the lack of survivors.

The same problems in tracing the local context bedevils any discussion of the capital sculpture, though again, the possibility arises that St. Frideswide's is demonstrating the existence of a more complex English mid 12th-century architecture than can be deduced from the surviving monuments. On present evidence, it seems that a small band of sculptors came to St. Frideswide's, bringing with them a wide variety of designs for capital sculpture, mainly using leaf forms culled from the debased form of Corinthian capital prevalent in Paris and the Oise Valley c.1135–50. The other (minority) designs (such as the interlacing tubular forms in the chancel) can be traced to the highly-developed, local late Romanesque style. From this base develops – as elsewhere – the Early English stiff-leaf capital, though earlier leaf-forms are not easily displaced and the waterleaf capital makes a strong appearance in the N. transept. An odd design, modelled on a capital erected in Canterbury in 1179, appears in the nave (Fig. 58), imported alongside the concept of alternating piers.

The most difficult question to answer, though, is where did the original workshop come from? St. Frideswide's was not a rich priory and cannot be thought a 'plum' job that attracted the best craftsmen from far and wide. But it was probably prestigious enough to attract a least a good-quality workshop from the surrounding region. Oxford is very centrally placed, of course, and good parallels can be drawn with capitals in places as far apart as Worcester Cathedral (N. transept), Winchfield (near Basingstoke, Hampshire), the church of the Hospital of St. Cross, Winchester and the Temple Church in London.

But equally, there are individual capitals in a number of northern French Early Gothic buildings that also look very similar to individual capitals in Oxford.[120] The lack of chevron decoration (or any other rich, later Romanesque decoration, beyond a few capitals) and the generally crisp and straightforward use of mouldings (again, without the superabundance of indigenous late Romanesque work) also point to a knowledge of the characteristics of French Early Gothic. The plan form (at least as originally conceived) and the use of rib-vaults throughout could also be thought sympathetic to contemporary French ideas, most especially in the architecture of the reformed orders. Once again, our lack of knowledge of the local Cistercian and Augustinian houses frustrates further discussion.

However, the most dominant and decisive architectural element at St. Frideswide's is the giant order elevation, which is much more difficult to place in contemporary France. The only surviving examples are of a previous generation (like Etampes, c.1125)

---

[119] The sharply undercut 'rolls' flanking the broad central rib are very distinctive. Something similar can be seen in the rib profiles of the Temple Church, London: R.W. Billings, *Illustrations & Account of the Temple Church* (1838), pl.vii, no. 9.

[120] See notes 30 and 35.

or even earlier (like St. Germain, Auxerre, c.1070).[121] Some interest was being shown in linking storeys within the elevation of some contemporary French buildings (e.g. St. Remi, Rheims), but the columnar pier of the giant order was not in favour – except on a spectacular scale at Bourges Cathedral, c.1185.

If I am correct in saying that the giant order at St. Frideswide's was selected for its association with local great houses of the previous generation, then the 'cloaking' of this established formula with modern French Gothic-inspired dress is contradictory, even confusing, in the sort of message the architecture is attempting to put across. Perhaps it was seen as a successful mix of new and old; perhaps it appeared as idiosyncratic then as it does now. An easy explanation would lie in hypothesising a building that had already combined these disparate elements; but that is stretching credulity. In my view, St. Frideswide's must be seen as a last attempt to re-vamp a trusted idea, the giant order, with new detail ultimately coming from N. France, perhaps through the buildings of the reformed orders. That the general disposition was acceptable is demonstrated in the continuance of the design throughout the extended campaigns that enlarged the transepts and rebuilt the nave. However, there appear to be no followers of St. Frideswide's either: Glastonbury Abbey, begun in 1184, is later in date, but there can scarcely be any direct link to St. Frideswide's.

CONCLUSION

The priory church of St. Frideswide's, built from E. to W. from c.1165 to c.1200, is a truly 'transitional' building, in that it uses architectural ideas developed in the previous Romanesque period, but with detailing that looks forward to the period now known as Early English Gothic. It was clearly conceived as a building of some pretension (appropriate to its function in housing the relics of a revered Anglo-Saxon royal saint) and the unknown patron(s) seem to have turned to a number of grander buildings for inspiration. It is frequently held that the lesser monasteries and grander parish churches looked to their local abbey and cathedral churches for an artistic and architectural lead. This is most probably true for St. Frideswide's, but the irony lies in the fact that only St. Frideswide's has survived – a little truncated – to give some idea of the appearance of the great churches of this area. Whatever the original patrons were attempting to say architecturally, it would seem that St. Frideswide's had no imitators; it is the last of a long line of giant order elevations in Romanesque England. Its architecture has a grace and impact of its own, but it failed to inspire further development – the first of Oxford's fabled 'lost causes'?

APPENDIX: THE CHAPTER-HOUSE DOORWAY AND THE MID 12TH-CENTURY ARCHITECTURAL FRAGMENTS IN THEIR LOCAL CONTEXT

There are three main sources of evidence for the date and form of the Romanesque work at St. Frideswide's carried out before the existing church was begun c.1165:
1.  The extant chapter-house doorway with its flanking openings.
2.  J.C. Buckler's drawings of carved work discovered in Scott's restoration, 1869–71, now in B.L. MS Add. 27765, especially volume E.

---

[121] See Halsey op. cit. note 96, 25–7, and Kidson op. cit. note 116, 12.

Fig. 65. *Above*: St. Frideswide's chapter-house front, N. side of doorway. *Below*: Iffley, W. front, N. side of doorway. (Phh. John Blair.)

3.   Stones stored formerly at Christ Church, now in the Oxfordshire County Museums
     Service store at Botley.

The doorway (Figs. 51, 65 upper) is apparently complete in that there has been
little replacement of stone, though it is possible that a further inner order once existed,
though not a tympanum. However, the two inner orders of continuous overlapping
chevron and the two outer orders of detached shafts have been extended downwards to
the present, lowered, cloister floor by unreddened coursed stones, including simple
bases of late 12th-century date (Fig. 96). As much of the stonework of the doorway has
been stained pink by heat, it is most probable that this facade suffered from the 1190 fire
reported in the Oseney Chronicle.[122] However, the existing chapter-house must be
dated at least thirty years later: was the Romanesque chapter-house undamaged, or
patched up?

The two-light round-headed openings flanking the doorway are apparently contemporary (sharing similar capital designs and having common stone courses), but are more
heavily restored. In 1847, they were described as 'elliptical'[123] but were by 1887 restored
to their present shape, which is likely to be the original size.[124] The N. jamb of the N.
opening must be original, since it bears a 12th-century wall-painting of a pointing male
figure (below, pp. 268–70).

The two capitals of the left-hand jamb of the doorway allow a close derivation to be
suggested for the sculptor, and therefore perhaps for the whole doorway. The use of an
essentially cubic shape, with cats-heads to the corners and interlacing strapwork, links
them to a group of capitals likely to come from the cloister at Reading Abbey. Indeed,
Professor Stone goes as far as to suggest that the link was owed 'most probably to a
transfer of a group of Reading masons to St. Frideswide's'.[125] Other elements of the
Oxford work seen at Reading include the superimposed rows of chevron,[126] the use of
lobed foils or semi-circles,[127] beakhead and similar scalloped capitals (Fig. 66, lower).

It was George Zarnecki who first documented the influence of Reading Abbey on
the Romanesque sculpture of the surrounding counties.[128] The sculpture was then
thought to be of c.1120–40 date on stylistic grounds, but more recently, Professor
Zarnecki has confirmed a c.1125 date for those capitals and other carved fragments
thought to come from the cloister.[129] Henry I laid the foundation of the new abbey on 23

---

[122] For the fire reference see note 3. *V.C.H. Oxon.* iv (1979), 24, does also refer to other medieval fires.

[123] *The Ecclesiologist*, vii (1847), 47, states: 'In the west wall of the chapter-house is a splendid Romanesque
doorway commonly said to have been removed from the west front of the church. There are certainly marks
which seem to show that it is not at present in its original place; yet two elliptical Romanesque windows, one
on each side, point the other way, and they can hardly have been removed.' The 'marks' referred to are
presumably the c.1190 lower stones and the pre-restoration cloister roof which cut-off the top foot or more of
the arch. J.C. Buckler thought the side windows 'originally circular, elongated at an early period and
afterwards clumsily restored to their shape'; in 1870, then, they were still circular (B.L. Add. MS 27765 E, ff
130, 193).

[124] Their restoration is attributed to Bodley and Garner in 1881 by P. Metcalfe and N. Pevsner, *The Cathedrals
of England (Southern)* (1985), 218. Although Scott had renewed the roof of the E. cloister walk by 1871, the
chapter-house itself only underwent restoration in 1880–1, by Bodley and Garner.

[125] L. Stone, *Sculpture in Britain: The Middle Ages* (Pelican History of Art, 2nd ed. 1972), 242, ch. 5, note 8. A
good example of this Reading capital group is illustrated in the exhibition catalogue, *English Romanesque Art
1066–1200* (1984), 168, illus. 127b.

[126] Ibid., 170, illus. 127n.

[127] Ibid., 174, illus. 129. The lobed foils of the Oxford chapter-house doorway hood are very similar to those
runnng along the top of the Reading beakheads (Fig. 66 lower). A relic of St. Frideswide is listed among the
Reading relics at the Dissolution: *V.C.H. Berks.* ii (1907), 70.

[128] G. Zarnecki, *English Romanesque Sculpture, 1066–1140* (1951). See also Stone op. cit. note 125, 59–61.

[129] Zarnecki in catalogue op. cit. note 125, 167.

Fig. 66.   *Above left*: Barford St. Michael, N. door, E. side. *Above right*: Iffley, S. door, E. side. *Below*: Beakheads
          with lobed foil decoration from Reading Abbey (now at Reading Museum).

June 1121, and in a charter of 1125 stated that he had built the monastery.[130] Even allowing for royal patronage, it would be safer to allow a date bracket of *c*.1120–1140 for the wide variety and great quantity of work surviving from a cloister no less than 145 ft. (44.2 m.) square. The chancel was at least complete by 1135 when Henry I was buried before the altar there, and it would be reasonable to think that the principal claustral buildings were well under way by then. The monastic church was finally consecrated by Archbishop Thomas Becket in 19 April 1164.[131]

The Reading chapter-house was huge, 42 ft. (12.8 m.) by 79 ft. (24.01 m.), barrel-vaulted and approached through 'three semi-circular arches with a window over each'.[132] No ashlar, let alone decorated stonework, survives *in situ* today, and it is not known from where in the Abbey the surviving decorated stones come. The common motifs between Reading and St. Frideswide's could indicate that the latter's chapter-house doorway is a reflection of one of the Reading doorways, at least in its use of parallel orders of continuous chevron and lobed foils to the hood-mould. The Reading doorways had three orders and apparently were without tympana.

A distinctive sculpture workshop can be identified, working *c*.1140–70 in Oxford itself and a few parish churches nearby. Their primary works in the city are the chapter-house doorway at St. Frideswide's (and judging from the few fragments (Fig. 54) and Buckler's drawings, at least a blind arcade too); the church of St. Peter's-in-the-East; and St. Ebbe's W. doorway (now much renewed and re-set). Beyond the city are the churches at Barford St. Michael (Fig. 66 top-left) and Iffley (Fig. 65 lower, 66 top-right).[133] The simplicity of the decoration of St. Frideswide's suggests that this was an early work, the complexity of Iffley conversely suggesting a later, more mature expression. It was possibly the St. Frideswide's cloister project that attracted the workshop (perhaps just one mason?) from Reading and the other commissions followed (as well, no doubt, as others for which no physical evidence survives).

Unfortunately none of the buildings is securely dated; the following table summarises the published opinions.[134]

|  | R.C.H.M. | Zarnecki I | Stone | Pevsner | Zarnecki II |
|---|---|---|---|---|---|
| St. Frideswide's (chapter-house doorway) | mid-late C12th | – | (*c*.1150) | 'Norman' | – |
| St. Peter's-in-the-East | *c*.1140–50 | – | – | crypt *c*.1130–40; church *c*.1160 | – |
| St. Ebbe's (W. door) | mid-C12th | *c*.1150 | (late 1140s) | *c*.1170 | – |
| Barford St. Michael | – | 1140–50 | – | *c*.1150 | – |
| Iffley | 1175–82 | 1175–82 | *c*.1175–82 | *c*.1175–80 | *c*.1175 |

A voussoir-shaped stone at Christ Church (Fig. 68 bottom-left), carved on three sides, could be a section of vault-rib. It is stained pink, like the stones of the chapter-house doorway, and could be a casualty of the same fire. It closely resembles the

[130] *V.C.H. Berks*. ii (1907), 62.

[131] Ibid., 63.

[132] Sir Henry Englefield, 'Observations on Reading Abbey', *Archaeologia*, vi (1779), 62.

[133] The Iffley sculpture has been linked to that of Reading Abbey by G. Zarnecki, *Later English Romanesque Sculpture, 1140–1210* (1953).

[134] *R.C.H.M. Oxford*; Zarnecki I (note 133); Stone (note 125); Pevsner (note 2); Zarnecki II (in catalogue note 125). The Stone dates in brackets are dates construed from the text, rather than categorically stated.

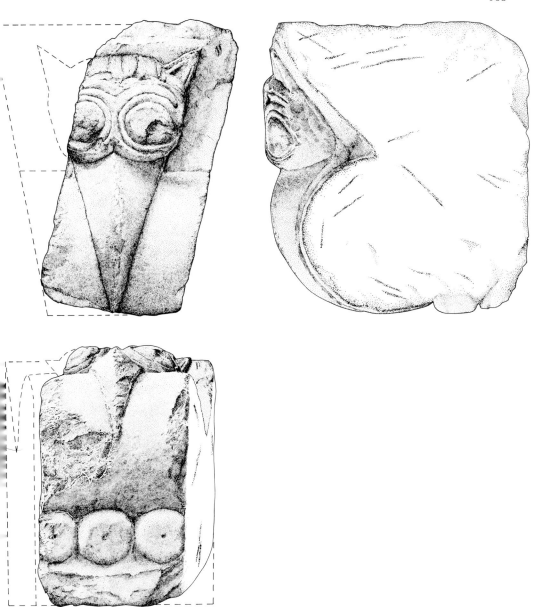

Fig. 67.  Beakhead from St. Frideswide's. *Scale 1:3.* (Stored by the County Museums Service. Drawing by Sarah Blair.)

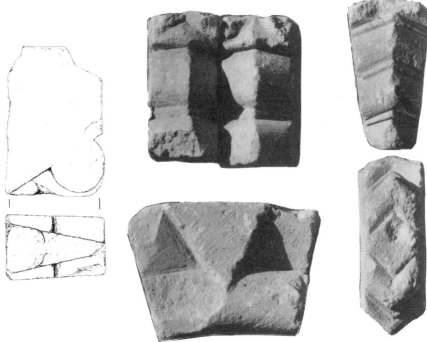

Fig. 68. *Left*: Beakhead and voussoirs from St. Frideswide's. *Scale 1:6*. (Stored by the County Museums Service. Phh. John Blair, drawing by Sarah Blair.) *Right*: Iffley, internal N.E. corner of chancel, showing window and rib voussoirs resembling the examples from St. Frideswide's. (Ph. John Blair.)

design of the Iffley chancel vault-rib (Fig. 68 right), with a lozenge on the intrados, flanked by two parallel rows of chevron. Another similarly fire-stained stone could also be part of a vault-rib, but of a profile closer to the transverse arch design at St. Peter's-in-the-East and certainly different to the Iffley section. Could these stones be from a rib-vaulted chapter-house?

Two carved beakheads at Christ Church (Figs. 67, 68 top-left), of different sizes and from unknown arches, presumably within the St. Frideswide's site, have their closest parallels at St. Peter's and St. Ebbe's. Other pieces with uncarved triangles breaking into a roll-moulding can be paralleled on Iffley's S. door and chancel windows (Fig. 68 middle-left and right). The 'chevron set on several planes'[135] is common to the door of St. Frideswide's chapter-house, the W. door of Iffley and the chancel windows of St. Peter's, although both the latter examples seem to be of a slightly better quality, with extra little ridges and beading between the rows of chevron. In this respect, they are close to the chevron work amongst the Reading Abbey fragments.

The scalloped capitals on the right jamb of the chapter-house entrance at St. Frideswide's (Fig. 51) are also distinctive, with strictly local parallels. The inner capital of the two, a cushion shape with spear-tips rising from the necking at each corner, has an exact parallel at Iffley in the capital on the right-hand marble shaft of the western tower arch. The outer capital, the restored capitals of the flanking openings (Fig. 65 upper) and two of the capitals found in the cloister walls (Fig. 52 bottom-left) have a two-scallop design to each face, with extra ridged wedges at the base of their cones, which can only be seen in Oxford at St. Peter's, in the crypt and on the chancel transverse arch capital.[136]

Another capital that Buckler illustrates (Fig. 52 centre-right, now lost) has a decorated cushion form with a beaded row defining the shape and thin flutes rising from the necking to the edge of the cushion. The only direct parallel for this design in Oxfordshire is on the N. door of Barford St. Michael parish church, near Banbury. But a similar attitude towards capital design can be seen in the figurated capitals on the S. door at Iffley, and on the left jamb-capitals of the St. Frideswide chapter-house, where the cubic shape is retained within the decoration. It is these capitals that in their form and detail most resemble capitals from the Reading Abbey site.

[135] Alan Borg, 'The Development of Chevron Ornament', *J.B.A.A.* 3rd ser. xxx (1967), 122–40.
[136] The extra wedge at the base of the scallop is quite commonly used elsewhere, particularly in the W. of England, but there is rarely an extra point between the wedges themselves.

# The Gothic Mouldings of the Latin and Lady Chapels

By RICHARD K. MORRIS (University of Warwick)

SUMMARY

*The study of the mouldings provides evidence for three main phases in the architectural development of the N.E. chapels of Oxford Cathedral in the Gothic period. The Lady Chapel was added c.1230 and is the work of masons employed previously on the choir of Pershore Abbey, as well as including stylistic features from the Winchester/Salisbury workshops. More work occurred in the late 13th century, of which there are partial remains between the Lady and Latin Chapels. The rebuilding of the Latin Chapel in its present form is shown to belong to c.1330–40 and constitutes a rare example of Decorated architecture in Oxfordshire with a firm date. Some of its more distinctive mouldings show close affinities with later Decorated works in the Bristol area, but the most coherent stylistic connexions seem to be with Master Henry Wy's work at St. Albans Abbey (after 1323), and he is suggested as the master-mason of the Latin Chapel.*

The N.E. chapels of Oxford Cathedral constitute one of the most interesting corners in any church in England for studying the development of Gothic mouldings and their value in documenting the history of the building. After the completion of the 12th-century church, the mouldings allow us to distinguish three main phases. First, about 1230, the Lady Chapel was constructed, communicating through new arcades with the N. choir aisle, the E. aisle of the N. transept, and the 'pre-Latin Chapel'. Second, it appears that in about 1290 arcades were opened up in the N. wall of the Lady Chapel (Figs. 35 and 98, bays II.1–2 and 2–3), and presumably the 'pre-Latin Chapel' was extended E. at this time to the same length as the Lady Chapel. This work appears to have been unsatisfactory because, in a final phase in the later Decorated period, about 1338, the outer walls were entirely rebuilt to create the Latin Chapel as we see it today, with a new vault and associated arches and window tracery. These phases can be dated reasonably accurately by comparison with other works, and two of the phases are closely connected with specific workshops.

The following discussion uses the pier numbering system shown on Fig. 35 (p. 77), and should be read in conjunction with Figs. 98–100.

## THE LADY CHAPEL

The mouldings of the Early English Lady Chapel exhibit such convincing parallels with the choir of Pershore Abbey, Worcestershire (*c.*1220–39),[1] that the master-mason of the

---

[1] R. Stalley and M. Thurlby, 'A Note on the Architecture of Pershore Abbey', *J.B.A.A.* 3rd ser. xxxvii (1974), 113–18.

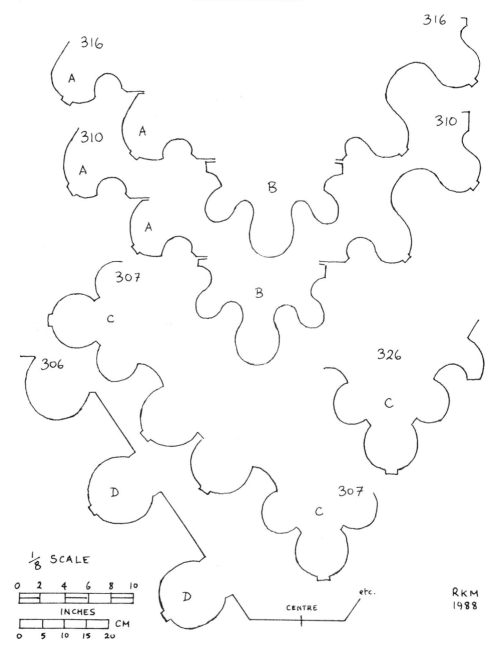

Fig. 69. Lady Chapel profiles, arches and piers: 306, S. arcade, E. respond (demi-section); 307, S. arcade, pier (quarter section); 310, S. arcade, arch; 316, N. arcade, W. bay, arch; 326, vault respond, N. side, pier II.3.A.

Chapel must have worked there previously. All the arches of the S. arcade and of the N. arch into the former 'pre-Latin Chapel' make repetitive use of undercut roll and fillet mouldings, canted downwards (Fig. 69, 310.A and 316.A), a characteristic of the choir arcades at Pershore, illustrated by Andrews.[2] The idea appears to be a feature of the west midlands and south-west in this period, a similar usage occurring on the E. crossing arches of Worcester Cathedral (*c*.1230),[3] but the specific link with Pershore extends also to the piers and responds. The E. respond of the S. arcade consists of a series of large filleted shafts, each projecting from the flat chamfer plane of the respond on a short strip of necking (Fig. 69, 306.D): shafts of the same design and very similar size are used in a comparable way in some of the piers at Pershore (Archive PER.256).[4] The angles of all the Pershore piers terminate in a triplet of shafts, a characteristic of Brakspear's 'West Country School of Masons',[5] but unlike earlier examples at Glastonbury and Wells Cathedral, the triplet design at Pershore has a prominent fillet on the axial shaft and thus constitutes an exact parallel for the type employed for all the piers in the Lady Chapel (Fig. 69, 307.C and 326.C).[6]

The profiles of the main types of bases and foliage capitals used for the lateral arcade arches[7] and all the vault responds except the capital of pier II.3.A may also be explained by reference to Pershore choir. None of the forms is especially distinctive, but Pershore makes use of both the typical Early English 'water-holding' base, a rather crude version of which is prevalent at Oxford (Fig. 70, 313), and of the torus-derived base found also at Oxford (Fig. 70, e.g. 312, 325).[8] In particular, the chamfered sub-base is exactly the same size at both churches (Fig. 70, 312, 313, 324.C: and Archive PER.257). For the foliage capitals, the general form is similar, with the fillet of the abacus moulding canted downwards and frequent use made of a blunt profile for the necking (Fig. 70, 311).[9] In addition, all the capitals and bases in the Lady Chapel and in Pershore choir are carved in freestone; no use is made of marble components or of detached shafts.[10]

Other profiles present in the Lady Chapel suggest the presence of a mason with experience of early Gothic work in the Winchester/Salisbury area. An instance of this is the undulating design of the soffit mouldings in the arcade arches, and of the rib profile (Fig. 69, 310.B, 316.B; and Fig. 71, 328), a motif not encountered at Pershore but quite frequently seen in the south of England especially from the 1220s. It is common for rib profiles, as at Winchester retrochoir, Salisbury and the Temple Church in London,[11] but it is less usual for the soffit of an arch, in the way it is used at Oxford. In this respect, a rare parallel is provided by the profile of the entrance arch into the eastern chapels of

[2] F.B. Andrews, *The Benedictine Abbey of SS. Mary, Peter and Paul, at Pershore, Worcestershire* (1901), page of 'Details of Mouldings', centre.

[3] Other examples in the west include Glastonbury, galilee; Lichfield N. transept, W. clearstorey; and Gloucester, 'reliquary' in N. transept: Warwick Archive drawing numbers GLA.665 etc., and GLO.575 etc.

[4] References in this style refer to the drawing number in the Warwick Mouldings Archive, c/o Dr. R.K. Morris, History of Art Department, University of Warwick, Coventry.

[5] H. Brakspear, 'A West Country School of Masons', *Archaeologia*, lxxxi (1931), 1–18.

[6] See Andrews op. cit. note 2, 'Details of Mouldings', centre; and Archive PER.254.

[7] And probably for the N. arcade bay II.3–4; traces remaining on pier II.3 suggest bases of the water-holding type.

[8] See Andrews op.cit. note 2, 'Details of Mouldings', bottom left; and Archive PER.257 and 154.

[9] Andrews op.cit. note 2, 'Details of Mouldings', top left, 'Choir Arcade'; and Archive PER.160.

[10] The use of marble at Pershore is restricted to the Lady Chapel area, which is a different phase of the work; see further Stalley and Thurlby op.cit. note 1.

[11] There are also examples in the west, at Gloucester (passage to infirmary cloister) and Tewkesbury (N.-E. chapel of N. transept); Archive GLO.832 and TEW.420.

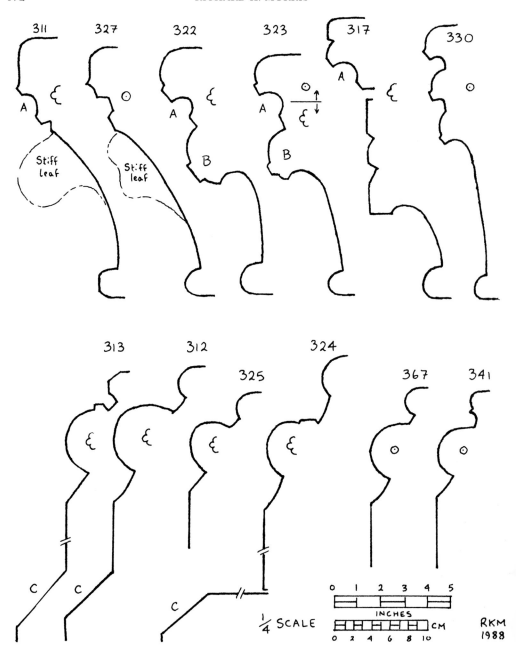

Fig. 70.  Lady Chapel profiles, capitals and bases: 311/312, S. arcade and vault responds; 313, S. arcade, E. respond; 317, N. arcade, W. bay; 322/325, arch to transept, S. respond; 323/324, arch to transept, N. respond; 327, vault respond, N. side, pier II.3.A; 330, blind arcade, pier II.3.B; 341, E. window, rere-arch; 367, base *ex situ* in Latin Chapel, pier II.3.C.

the retrochoir of Winchester Cathedral (*c*.1200–20),[12] where the only significant difference to the design of the Oxford arcades is that the axial roll is filleted (Archive WIN.141). Another characteristic of the Winchester retrochoir which recurs at Oxford is the use of two fillet mouldings separated by a semi-circular hollow as the basis for abaci and stringcourses (Fig. 70, 311.A, 322.A, 323.A, 317.A; Fig. 71, 332: Archive WIN.105, 112 (Purbeck), 302). The evidence suggests that this idea may have originated at Winchester, perhaps initially as a design for Purbeck marble components; other examples, apart from Oxford, span the period *c*.1220–50, e.g. Romsey nave W. bays, Chichester nave S. chapels, Gloucester 'reliquary' in N. transept (Archive ROM.624, 635, etc.; CHI.663 (Purbeck); GLO.594).

The entrance arch which leads into the Lady Chapel from the E. aisle of the N. transept is somewhat different in character from the lateral arcades, as also are its capitals. The distinctive feature of the arch is the symmetrical undercut roll and fillet moulding used for the soffit (Fig. 71, 321.A), which is not frequently encountered in this position on arches, but which is found in a relatively similar formation at Salisbury Cathedral, in the arches between the choir aisles and the retrochoir, dating from the early 1220s (Archive SAL.144). The only difference is that it employs keel mouldings for the lateral mouldings instead of the undercut roll and fillet mouldings used at Oxford (Fig. 71, 321.B). The symmetrical undercut roll and fillet occurs most frequently in ribs, occasionally as early as the late 12th century, e.g. Chichester Cathedral retrochoir (Archive CHI.116), but is most common in the 1220s and 1230s and later, e.g. St. Albans W. porches, Portsmouth Garrison Church, Ely choir (arcade arch, 1234sqq.), Chichester nave aisles, Romsey E. clearstory (Archive POG.113, ELY.250, CHI.614, ROM.205). On this evidence the Oxford arch is unlikely to date before *c*.1230, and this is corroborated by the style of the capitals. The latter introduce into the Lady Chapel the three-unit moulded capital (Fig. 70, 322, 323), which was beginning to appear in both the south and the west towards 1230, as in the Castle Hall at Winchester (1222–36), the clearstorey of Worcester Cathedral (Archive WOR.270 etc.) and the passage to the Infirmary cloister at Gloucester (Archive GLO.830). Either area could have inspired the general design of the Lady Chapel examples, but the specific detail of an undercut roll and fillet moulding is more typical of the west, e.g. Wenlock Priory nave, Gloucester 'reliquary' (Archive WEN.614, GLO.591, 592). Thus the Lady Chapel entrance arch demonstrates a synthesis of ideas from the west midlands and from the Wessex area which is compatible with the stylistic analysis above of the sources of the main arcades.

With regard to the relationship of the work with Pershore, it seems more likely that it postdates the choir there. First, it has been shown that a number of features in the Lady Chapel are likely to date from around 1230 and thus later than the generally accepted date for the Pershore choir. Second, the complete combination of mouldings in the Lady Chapel makes it more credible that the influence came from Pershore rather than vice-versa. For example, though a type of undercut roll and fillet is used earlier in the Wessex area in the Winchester retrochoir (e.g. Archive WIN.141), the form taken by this moulding in the Lady Chapel looks to be much more of a direct derivation from Pershore rather than having evolved from earlier examples like Winchester.

The mouldings of the Lady Chapel are reasonably uniform, except on the S. side of the former 'pre-Latin Chapel' site, where their variety suggests some hesitation and inconsistency in the building process. Here (between II.3 and II.4), where an arch was cut through the former wall to the 'pre-Latin Chapel' or inserted to replace a

---

[12] P. Draper, 'The Retrochoir of Winchester Cathedral', *Archit. Hist.* xxi (1978), 6–7.

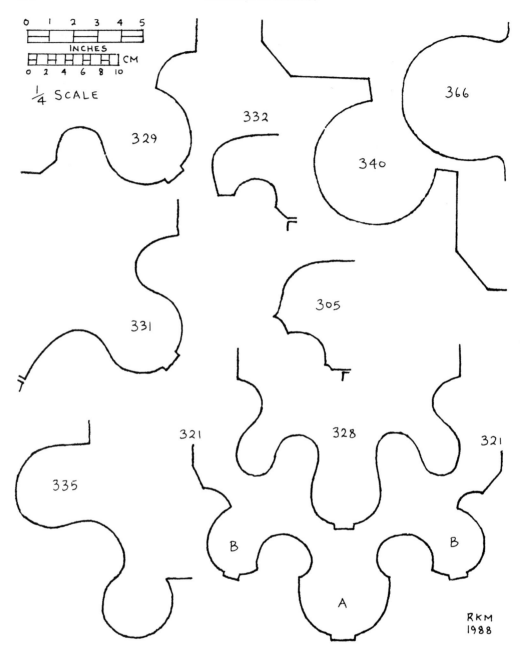

Fig. 71. Lady Chapel profiles, miscellaneous: 305, E. wall, interior stringcourse (renewed); 321, arch to transept; 328, vault, main rib; 329, vault, wall-rib; 331, vault, wall-rib (N. side, variant); 332, stringcourse used as arch, pier II.3, S.-E. face; 335, piscina, arch/jamb; 340, E. window, rere-arch, jamb; 366, shaft (probably *ex situ*) in Latin Chapel, pier II.3.C.

Romanesque arch, other hands appear, as implied by the rather crude and somewhat old-fashioned design for the arcade capitals (Fig. 70, 317). Was this perhaps one of the first works carried out in the Lady Chapel campaign? Also, at the former S.-E. angle of the 'pre-Latin Chapel', the capital for the Lady Chapel vault springing is different from any of the others (Fig. 70, 327; pier II.3.A). Furthermore, the adaptation of this angle, to accommodate the greater width of the Lady Chapel in the two bays E. of the 'pre-Latin Chapel', created a blind arch across the splay supported at its N. end by a capital unique in design to the Lady Chapel (II.3.B). It is a four-unit moulded capital, the top three elements of which consist of partial roll and fillet mouldings (Fig. 70, 330), and therefore presumably it belongs with the introduction of moulded capitals with comparable features in the entrance arch from the N. transept (Fig. 70, 322, 323). Like them, the thinking behind its design is probably western and a general parallel for it may be seen in the nave arcade capitals at Wenlock Priory (Archive WEN.614).

## THE NORTH ARCADE OF THE LADY CHAPEL

On first impression, it appears that the N. arcade in the two E. bays of the Lady Chapel (bays II.1–2 and 2–3) belongs with the general rebuilding of the Latin Chapel, as both works are in the Decorated style. However, closer examination suggests the possibility that the bases, piers and capitals of the arcade could date from the later 13th century, whereas the arcade arch above them and all the other main features of the Latin Chapel are clearly well into the 14th century, as will be shown later.

The profile of the arcade responds (Fig. 73, 360) and the centre pier is unconvincing as a mature Decorated design and lacks the stylishness of the arcade arches above. The use of a triplet of shafts at each of the axial points reflects loosely the earlier piers of the Lady Chapel, but the profile is actually extremely close to the responds of the tower arches at St. Mary Redcliffe, Bristol, usually dated shortly after 1294 (Archive BRR.704). In particular the prominence given to the circular core of the Lady Chapel pier is less likely in a 14th-century design, and this feature may be compared with the ambulatory piers executed at Hailes Abbey (Glos., 1270–77).[13] The base used on the responds and pier (Fig. 73, 365)[14] is of a double-roll type most common in the second half of the 13th century and found locally, for example, at Merton College chapel, 1289–94; though in the east of England it continued in use into the 14th century.[15] More distinctive is the sub-base (Fig. 73, 365.E), which appears to be a local design found again at Merton and also at the base of the tomb-chest of the military effigy in Dorchester Abbey (?c.1280–90).[16] Further afield, but still in the south of England, versions of this profile may be seen on sub-bases in the chapter-house undercroft of Wells Cathedral (?c.1250) and in the arcades of St. Thomas', Winchelsea, c.1290–1300 (Archive WEL.824, 85; and WIA.203).

The profile of the arcade capitals (Fig. 73, 363) is of the 'three-unit scroll' variety

[13] Illustrated in H. Brakspear, 'The Architecture of Hayles Abbey', *Bristol and Glouc. Arch. Soc. Trans.* xxiv (1901), 132; and Archive TED.700.

[14] And also the base cut into the earlier 13th-century shaft of the blind arch on pier II.3 at B, so that this arch also looks to be from the Decorated period at first sight; but is actually Early English, and goes with the wall-rib (Fig. 71, 331) abutting the later Decorated arcade arch in bays II, 1–2 and 2–3.

[15] See further R.K. Morris, 'The Development of Later Gothic Mouldings in England, *c.*1250–1400, Part II', *Archit. Hist.* xxii (1979), 26.

[16] P.J. Lankester, 'A Military Effigy in Dorchester Abbey, Oxon.', *Oxoniensia*, lii (1987), 145–72 and Fig. 9.

Fig. 72.   East respond of arcade between Latin and Lady Chapels (pier II.1), seen from inside watching-loft.
(Ph. John Blair.)

which was standard in the Decorated period,[17] and thus less helpful for dating purposes.
The Oxford examples are made slightly less conventional by having a keel moulding for
the bell (Fig. 73, 363.B), but even this variant of the 'three-scroll' enjoys quite a long
period of usage in the south of England: from the main arcade of Exeter Cathedral and
the dado of Wells chapter-house, both around 1290, to the ambulatory of Tewkesbury
Abbey and the S. bays of the nave at St. Albans in the 1320s and later (Archive EXE.201
(Purbeck), WEL.874, TEW.110, 116).[18]

However, two small details hint that the capitals may belong with the piers rather
than with the later Decorated work. First, the fillet from the axial moulding of the pier is
carried up as far as the bell of the capital (Fig. 73, 363.D; Fig. 72), which is a common
trait in Early English work, but usually encountered in the 14th century only in
conservative circumstances where an attempt has been made to blend in with earlier
work, as in the rebuilt nave bays at St. Albans (after 1323) or in the nave of Beverley
Minster. Second, there are slight differences of profile between these capitals and those
of the vault springers on the N. wall of the Latin Chapel, observable in the fillet beneath
the bead moulding of the abacus (Fig. 73, cf. 363.A and 370.A) and in the fillet beneath
the keel moulding (Fig. 73, cf. 363.C and 370.C). In these details, the capitals of the
vault responds on the S. side of the Latin Chapel, at piers II.1 and II.2, are exactly the

---

[17] Morris op. cit. note 15, 20sqq.

[18] For St. Albans, see J. Neale, *The Abbey Church of St. Alban, Hertfordshire* (1877), e.g. Pl. 18, 'Cap to Nave
Piers': the bell is more of a pear moulding than a keel.

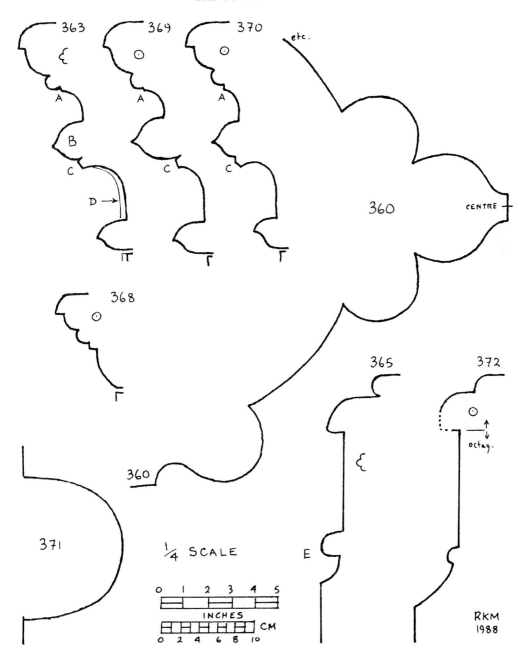

Fig. 73. Latin Chapel profiles, S. arcade and vault responds: 360, arcade respond (partial); 363/365, arcade capital and base; 368, vault respond capital, S. side, pier II.3.C only; 369, standard vault respond capital, S. side; 370/372, vault respond, N. side, capital and base; 371, vault respond, N. side.

same profile as those of the S. arcade (Fig. 73, cf. 363 and 369). Thus, the differences between the 'three-scroll' capitals on the N. and S. sides of the Latin Chapel might indicate two building periods, with the N. capitals representing a 14th-century attempt at replication. Moreover, this distinction between the vault responds applies more clearly to their bases, which also show slight differences in profile, and in particular the sub-bases of those on the N. wall are part-octagonal rather than curved (Fig. 73, cf. 365 and 372).

At this point it may be appropriate to comment on one anomalous area of masonry on the S. side of the Latin Chapel, at pier II.3.C. An early 13th-century base is visible here (Fig. 70, 367), supporting what must also be a wall-shaft of the same date, as its size and profile are closer to those of the Early English work in the Lady Chapel than to the 14th-century respond shafts on the N. wall of the Latin Chapel (cf. Fig. 71, 366 and 340; and Fig. 73, 371). Sturdy's excavations make it difficult to believe that the Early English base is *in situ* (above, pp. 79, 84), and therefore the base and shaft must have been moved to this position during a remodelling which involved the demolition of the old E. wall of the 'pre-Latin Chapel'. As the profile of the base is the same design as others still surviving in the eastern parts of the Lady Chapel (Fig. 70, 312), the most likely moment for this re-use is when the N. wall of the two eastern bays was replaced by the arcade and spare Early English components became available. Later, the shaft at II.3.C received its Decorated capital (Fig. 73, 368) when the Latin Chapel was vaulted in its present form, *c.*1338.

### THE LATER DECORATED WORK IN THE LATIN CHAPEL

There can be no doubt that the final remodelling of the Latin Chapel (Figs. 74–6) took place in the later Decorated period. The flowing tracery of the N. windows (Fig. 74) is reminiscent of the curvilinear patterns of north-east England and, more locally, of windows in Oxfordshire churches such as Witney and Chipping Norton, all dictating a date in the second quarter of the 14th century. It will be argued here that the other profiles which belong with the mouldings of the windows are the ground course mouldings (Fig. 75, 350, 351), the ribs of the vault, including the unusual wall-rib added in the two W. bays on the S. side (Fig. 75, 362), and the arcade arches in the two E. bays.

The mouldings are sufficiently distinctive to provide useful parallels, and though it will be seen that they connect with more than one region, the prevalent source of influence appears to be the south-west. The profile of the diagonal and transverse ribs of the vault (Fig. 75, 373) is exactly the same design as the wall-ribs of the main vault at Bristol Cathedral, *c.*1320–30 (Archive BRI.213), and related rib designs are characteristic of that area, e.g. Bristol St. Mary Redcliffe, N. porch, and Wells retrochoir.[19] In support of the Bristol connexion is the fact that the ridge-ribs of the Latin Chapel vault consist of a small profile (hollow-chamfer) decorated with square fleurons (visible on Fig. 76), both of which features are found in the aisle vaults at Bristol: the small profile in the ridge ribs (plain chamfer); and the fleurons decorating the 'bridges' beneath them. Moreover, the use of foliage looking rather like an arum lily to decorate one of the main bosses in the Chapel vault seems to relate to a similar motif used occasionally in the S. choir aisle and Berkeley Chapel at Bristol.[20]

[19] Morris op.cit. note 15, 16–18, 'Western, Third Variety'.

[20] See further R.K. Morris, 'Ballflower Work in Gloucester and its Vicinity', in *Medieval Art and Architecture at Gloucester and Tewkesbury* (Trans. of B.A.A. Conference 1981, publ. 1985), 104.

Fig. 74. The Cathedral from the N.E., showing the Latin Chapel and spire: engraving from J. Britton, *Cathedral Church of Oxford* (1821), Pl. II.

Parallels in the west can also be found for other features. The only usage known to the author of the main wall-rib design (Fig. 75, 375) is in the choir clearstorey at Tewkesbury (Archive TEW.214), and exactly the same design for the interior rere-arch of the windows also occurs in the same location (Fig. 75, 357; Archive TEW.206). The clearstorey zone is well dated to *c.*1330–40 and therefore constitutes a useful indicator as to the likely date of the Latin Chapel. The form of the other wall-rib/arcade arch moulding (Fig. 75, 362), used only in the W. bays abutting the earlier arcade arches (bays II.3–4 and II.4–5), recalls features in the retrochoir area of Wells Cathedral, but specifically resembles the recess arch of Sir Robert Stapledon's tomb at Exeter, *c.*1320 (Archive EXE.935). The steeply angled chamfer mouldings, as found in the N. window mullions (Fig. 75, 354), became increasingly popular during the 14th century, particularly in the west. Examples which are very close in size to either the interior or exterior profiles (Fig. 75, 354, 'INT', 'EXT') include the W. clearstorey window of Exeter Lady Chapel (same template as INT), the S. porch of Bristol St. Mary Redcliffe, and the great hall of Berkeley Castle (Archive EXE.307, BRR.650, BER.821). More locally, an early example of this type which is firmly dateable is the mullion profile of the sacristy at Merton

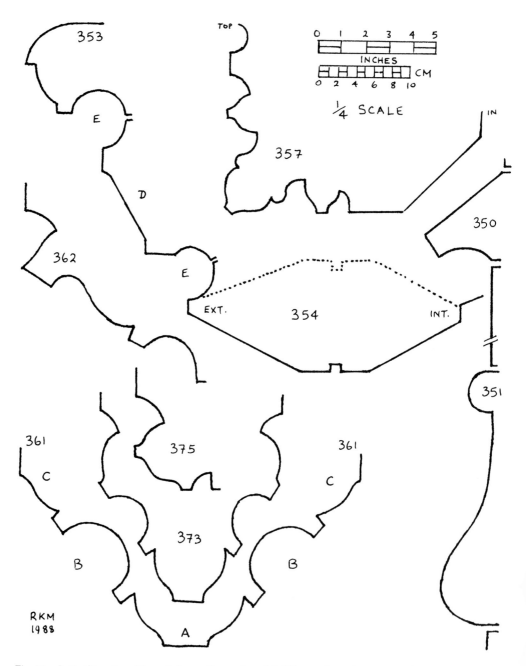

Fig. 75. Latin Chapel profiles, windows, ribs, arches: 350/351, exterior stringcourse and ground-course; 353, N. windows, exterior rere-arch; 354, N. windows, mullion; 357, N. windows, interior rere-arch; 361, S. arcade, E. bays, arch; 362, vault, wall-rib, S. side (W. bays only); 373, vault, diagonal and transverse rib; 375, vault, standard wall-rib.

College chapel, 1309–11 (Archive OME.404), which combines the exterior dimensions and interior geometry of the Latin Chapel mullion.

Turning to consider the arch design employed for the S. arcade in the two E. bays of the Latin Chapel, this is the most stylish element of the Decorated work but hard to appreciate fully because of the interference from the later 'watching-chamber'. Comparison with the main rib profile suggests a strong affinity in design between them (Fig. 75, cf.361 and 373), and we have seen that the rib has a western pedigree. Therefore it is not surprising to find several parallels in that area for its main characteristic, the axial moulding of the arch treated as a broad roll and fillet, flanked on each side by a semi-circular hollow with paired canted fillets (Fig. 75, 361.A and B). The best parallels are the main arches of the pulpitum at Exeter, 1317–25, a work of Master Thomas of Witney, and the S. arcade arches of the nave at St. Mary Redcliffe, Bristol, perhaps c.1340 (Archive EXE.907, BRR.615). However, the most exact comparison for the whole arch formation, with the demi-roll and fillet moulding returned at the top on each side (Fig. 75, 361.C), is the soffit of the N. arcade arches in the three W. bays of the E. arm at Ely, 1321–37 (Archive, ELY.202); and this leads one to consider other possible links with East Anglian workshops.

For example, another feature of the Latin Chapel which has always suggested Ely to the author is the use of fleurons to decorate the ridge-ribs of the vault, as found in the choir aisle vaults at Ely: though also employed at Bristol Cathedral, as we have seen. In addition, the design of the exterior frame of the N. windows (Fig. 75, 353) is of a type favoured in the E. of England in the later Decorated period. The characteristic feature is the sunk chamfer moulding in the centre of the formation, undercut at each end by deep three-quarter hollows (Fig. 75, 353.D and E). Numerous examples may be seen at Ely and Snettisham (Norfolk), and other Decorated churches in East Anglia use the three-quarter hollow moulding and the sunk chamfer, though not in combination, e.g. Trumpington (Cambs.), Ingham (Norfolk).[21] However, the feature was also in use in the south and nearer to the Oxfordshire area by the time the Latin Chapel was being built. An early example of the design is in one of the S. aisle tomb-recesses at St. Thomas's, Winchelsea (after 1322; Archive, WIA.901), and the design is also found in the upper parts of the S. nave bays at St. Albans, after 1323.[22] It is also relevant to note that Merton College chapel, Oxford, had consistently used comparable moulding formations for arches since 1289/90, through the sacristy of 1309–11 to the entrance arches for the proposed nave aisles (?1330). The formation shared with the Latin Chapel the use of a prominent scroll hoodmould and a series of three-quarter hollows with fillets; the hollow-chamfer was never used, but in the nave aisle arches a wave moulding is worked in a similar fashion on the chamfer plane between two of the hollows (Archive OME.752).

Considering all this information together, the case is still strongest for the west of England as the main source of the Latin Chapel's architectural style. In particular, there is evidence for the presence of a mason with experience of a major workshop at Bristol, and for links with the north Cotswolds area around Tewkesbury. In addition, one must take account of the inevitable presence of more local influence, as demonstrated in the connexions with the Merton College works, and also in this context the similarities with the Decorated bays in the nave at St. Albans must be given full consideration. Despite the one striking parallel with Ely, the overall weight of the evidence suggests that there

[21] See further Morris op.cit. note 15, 'Part I', Vol. xxi (1978), 29–31.
[22] Neale op.cit. note 18, Pl. 20.

is no direct link with the workshop there, but it could well be that St. Albans is the intermediary between them, as it shares features with both. For example, apart from the undercut sunk chamfer mentioned above, its arches and ribs make extensive use of the lower part of the Latin Chapel arcade arch design (Fig. 75, 361); and its decorative repertoire includes square fleurons.[23] Other parallels specifically with the Latin Chapel include the frequent use of bead mouldings and deep hollows to flank a roll and fillet, as in the Chapel window rere-arch, and also of a 'three-unit scroll' capital with a pear moulding for the bell, comparable to the capital type on the N. wall of the Latin Chapel, as noted above. Furthermore, we know from Neale that one of the nave aisle windows at St. Albans used plain sunk chamfer mouldings for its frame,[24] and this finds a parallel in the rere-arch of the E. window of the N. choir aisle at Oxford, which must belong with the Latin Chapel windows because their exterior mouldings are identical (as Fig. 75, 353).

In fact, a case can be made that the master mason of the Latin Chapel could have been Henry Wy, the master to whom the nave bays at St. Albans are attributed.[25] If so, it would appear possible that at some stage in his career he had gained experience in one of the western workshops, and that his might be an important name to consider in assessing the stylistic connexions between architecture in the home counties and the south-west in the early 14th century. Unfortunately, for the purposes of comparison with other buildings, we can glean little from St. Albans of Henry Wy's preferences in tracery design, partly because of later damage and restorations but mainly because most of the apertures in the new work consist of single lancets to blend in with the Early English bays. However, the surviving tracery of the Latin Chapel may now help to fill this gap and make further research possible.

## SUMMARY OF THE LATIN CHAPEL WORK AND ITS DATES

For the arcade in the two E. bays linking the Latin and Lady Chapels, the evidence of the bases and piers will allow a date anywhere in the last quarter of the 13th century, and thus might be connected with the translation of St. Frideswide's relics in 1289. If the capitals are considered to be part of the same work, then a date much before c.1290 is precluded.

If the hypothesis is correct that the lower parts of these arcades predate the rest of the work in the Latin Chapel, then it is unclear why the Chapel required rebuilding within fifty years. One explanation might be that the initial extension of the 'pre-Latin Chapel' was piecemeal and unsatisfactory in its narrow proportions: another might be that it was never finished. As for the date of the final remodelling, the parallels cited above give a clear indication that the work cannot be earlier than the 1320s, and most probably belongs to the decade c.1330–40. This tallies with the date towards the mid-century usually given for the glass in the N. windows, and may well be related to the establishment of the Burghersh chantry at St. Frideswide's altar in 1338 (below, p. 245). If so, it would provide a rare example of later Decorated architecture in Oxfordshire with a relatively firm date.

[23] Ibid. Pls. 18–22, for illustrations of these and what follows.
[24] Ibid. Pl. 22.
[25] J.H. Harvey, *English Mediaeval Architects: a Biographical Dictionary down to 1550* (revised ed. 1984), 351.

Fig. 76.   Latin Chapel: interior looking E. *c.*1865. (Taunt photograph: Local History Collection, Oxford City Library.)

# Christ Church, Priory House: Discoveries in St. Frideswide's Dormitory

By Julian Munby

SUMMARY

*In the construction of a new staircase in Priory House the Norman door to the cloister was uncovered together with the steps leading up to the dormitory, which was raised some 2 m. above the present level of the cloister, on a stone vault. Fragments of a similar vault survive at the S. end of the dormitory. The interior of the door showed signs of burning. No features of the post-fire dormitory or any 13th-century work was observed, though some re-used rafters in the upper floors may indicate a roofing in the 13th century, and a possible roof-line was observed. In the 15th century, probably when the cloister was rebuilt by Robert Sherborne c.1489, the present front door to Priory House was made, with a dog-leg stair leading up to the dormitory, having a tiled landing and covered with a small area of vaulting. At the same time an aperture to the cloister was made, with a small window or ventilator. After the Dissolution, the dormitory was converted into a canon's lodging and the present choir practice room was made, apparently by William Tresham in the years before 1560. Traces of wall-paintings indicate that the dog-leg stair was filled in (the rubble included a fragment of St. Frideswide's shrine), whilst another stair was made to the room over the E. cloister walk. These rooms, which have fireplaces, were later used as the muniment room, and from below the floorboards came a 13th-century charter and an account roll of Oseney Abbey.*

The E. range of the cloister next to the chapter-house, known as Priory House and now the lodging of the Canon of the second stall, is the site of the monastic dormitory (and perhaps the Prior's house). In 1986/7 the attics over the chapter-house were detached from the remainder of Priory House and converted to Cathedral offices, for which purpose a new stair was built to give access to them from a lobby behind the front door of Priory House in the cloister. The stair rises through the dormitory undercroft, the choir practice room (the room S. of the chapter-house, which has now been truncated), and two small rooms on the upper floors. The insertion of the new stair in December 1986 necessitated the removal of panelling and flooring from the W. end of the choir practice room and the upper rooms. A number of discoveries were made which throw light on the entrance to the medieval dormitory of the Augustinian Priory of St. Frideswide's; some of the features that were revealed have been left open for inspection in the completed staircase.[1]

[1] The recording work was undertaken independently by the author, with the encouragement of the architect, Mr. David Scroggie of Peter Bosanquet and John Perryman Associates, whose surveys have been used for some of the figures. The assistance of the contractors, the Oxford Archaeological Unit and Oxfordshire Museum Services is gratefully acknowledged.

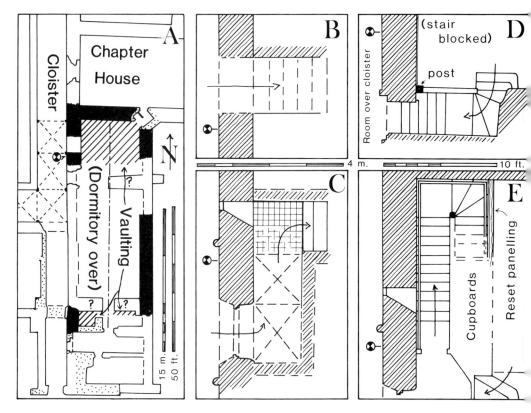

Fig. 77. Priory House (cloister E. range): A: Plan at ground level showing Romanesque walls and vaulting (note the position of the symbol shown in the same place on plans B to E.). B: 12th-century door and stair to dormitory. C: 15th-century door and stair. D: 16th-century stair to rooms over cloister. E: New stair to Cathedral offices.

THE NORMAN DORMITORY (Fig. 77)

Beneath the panelling on the W. wall of the choir practice room a round-headed arch was immediately visible (Fig. 79), with plain ashlar voussoirs set below an outer arch of rubble blocks set on end. These last, and the rest of the wall above and to the N., were all set in a brown mortar, and must have been original Norman walling; the N. wall of the room was of a different character, and perhaps belonged to the 13th-century rebuilding of the chapter-house.

A chamfer stop below the springing of the arch on the N. side continued as a plain chamfer down the door-jamb and ended in a plaster cast of a stop, the stone behind it having been removed. This plaster continued down to a level 2.98 m. below the soffit of the arch, where a single flat stone marked the level of the threshold (either as the actual step, or the base on which the step lay). This level was some 0.9 m. below the floor level of the room (i.e. below the crown of the stone vault), and some 1.1 m. above the present level of the E. cloister walk (Fig. 80).

The plastered reveal of the doorway also continued eastwards into the room as an ashlar wall (0.37 m. wide), extending as far as the excavations uncovered it (about 2 m.;

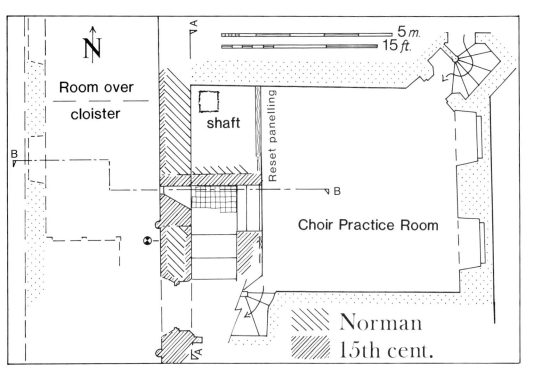

Fig. 78. Priory House: plan of features in choir practice room and section lines of Fig. 80.

Figs. 77B and 78). This wall presumably formed the N. side of the stair as it rose from the cloister up over the springing of the vault (the dormitory undercroft, aligned N.–S. along the range). Nothing else remained of Norman work here, and although the threshold level continued southwards for a short distance as a layer of brown gravel over the rubble footings and beneath later rubble blocking, the S. jamb of the door was removed by later works.

The arch itself was burnt red, like the exterior of the chapter-house door, but where the southern voussoir was cut back the colour did not penetrate very deep into the stone. This was no doubt a relic of the burning of the Priory in 1190, and the door must therefore pre-date that event. This entrance must have been the day stair (perhaps the only access) to the canons' dormitory.

In the N.W. corner of the room a stone-lined shaft descended between the cloister wall and the vault (Figs. 78 and 80). It was perhaps connected with a drain, and may have been a latrine, or a well used by the builders.[2]

At second-floor level a short sloping line of mortar on the chapter-house wall may have represented the original line of the dormitory roof on the W. side, whilst some of the floor joists at this level had mortices for notch-lap joints, indicating their former use as rafters. Samples from two of these were taken for dating by dendrochronology, one of them giving a tentative date about the middle of the 13th century.[3]

---

[2] The details of this feature were kindly supplied by David Scroggie.
[3] See more fully in 'The Roof Carpentry of Oxford Cathedral', below p. 199.

The vault below the choir practice room at the N. end of Priory House is only the northern extremity of a vault that must have extended for the full length of the dormitory (Figs. 77A and 80). The middle section has been removed for the entrance hall and stair to Priory House, and further to the S. the 'Priory Room' is ceiled with timber joists, perhaps of 16th-century date. However, at the S.W. end of the Priory room is a small cupboard which contains a portion of vaulting, and in the cross wall of the bathroom opposite is the curved outline of its continuation to the east (Fig. 77A). The dated R.C.H.M. plan shows the thick cross-wall immediately to the N. of this vault as being 13th century, but on what evidence is not clear.[4] It may be that the vault marks the S. end of the dormitory range, judging by the quoins by the side of the later door in the passage wall outside. The relationship of the vault to the wall on either side of it does not indicate any clear sequence of construction. The known extent of the vault would make the dormitory cover the width of the S. cloister range (which was rebuilt in the 15th century), but it may have continued further to the S.

At the N. end, below the choir practice room, the vault is plastered and whitewashed, with traces of masonry lines in red paint, similar to the decoration in the chapter-house. The fragment at the S. end has recently been stripped of plaster.


LATE-MEDIEVAL ALTERATIONS

The cloisters were rebuilt at the very end of the 15th century with a stone vault, as a gift from Robert Sherborne, then Dean of St. Paul's and later Bishop of Chichester.[5] One of the wall-shafts of the new vault in the E. cloister walk blocks the southern side of the Norman door to the dormitory (Figs. 77C and 78), and it was probably shortly before the vault was installed that a new door was built a short distance to the S. (the present front door of Priory House). The door is square-headed, with a hood-mould enclosing a two-centred arch, with bold roll mouldings and $\frac{3}{4}$ hollows running round it. The corbels on the hood-mould have carved portrait heads on them.

Inside this door, the new arrangements made for access to the dormitory were revealed by the uncovering of the internal wallface, and the excavation of the new staircase (Fig. 79). The Norman door was blocked with ashlar, its southern jamb was removed, and a square opening was made in the wall, splayed inwards from a small quatrefoil aperture onto the cloister. Removal of its blocking uncovered whitewashed reveals, and it must have been a light or a ventilator for the stair. The Norman threshold was raised some 0.25 m. with rubble, and a tiled landing made for the new dog-leg stair (Fig. 77C).

The tiles are of standard 13th-century type, with patterns known from elsewhere in the Cathedral.[6] Their date suggests re-use (or the re-use of an earlier landing), and a partial covering of mortar implies that some other surface was laid over them.

A new wall was also built immediately S. of the Norman E.–W. wall, with ashlar facing (mostly removed) and a rubble fill (Fig. 78). The edge of this wall shows in section where it toothed into the ashlar blocking of the door (Fig. 79).

[4] *R.C.H.M. Oxford*, plan opp. p. 32.

[5] *Sussex Arch. Colls.* xxix (1879), 25; S.A. Warner, *Oxford Cathedral* (1924), 169–70; A.B. Emden, *A Biographical Register of the University of Oxford to A.D. 1500*, iii (1959), 1685–7. Cf. above, pp. 66, 97–8.

[6] L. Haberly, *Medieval English Pavingtiles* (1937), Nos. XLIV and XXII. The tile floor was recorded by Brian Durham of the Oxford Archaeological Unit and lifted by Oxfordshire Museum Services.

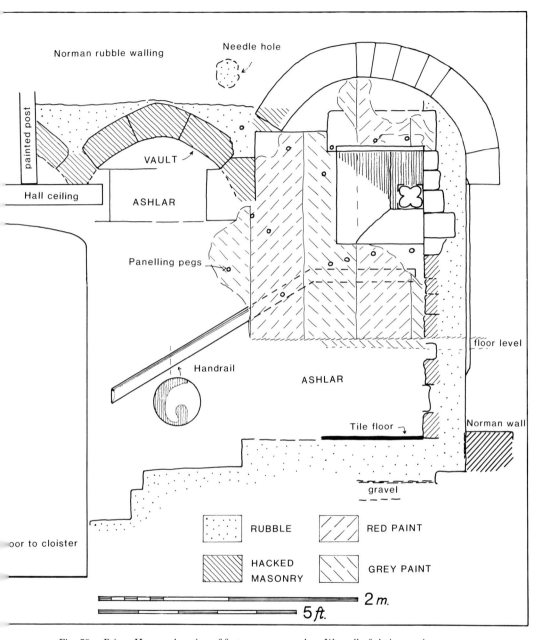

Norman rubble walling

Needle hole

painted post

VAULT

Hall ceiling

ASHLAR

Panelling pegs

Handrail

ASHLAR

floor level

Tile floor

Norman wall

gravel

oor to cloister

RUBBLE

RED PAINT

HACKED MASONRY

GREY PAINT

2 m.

5 ft.

Fig. 79.   Priory House: elevation of features uncovered on W. wall of choir practice room.

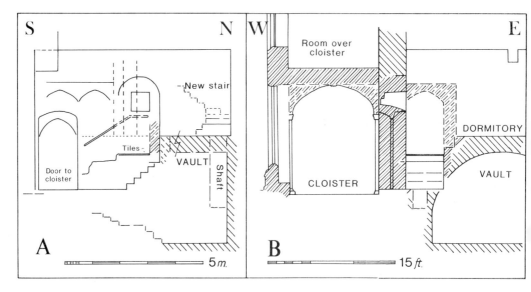

Fig. 80. Priory House: A: Sectional elevation of choir practice room, showing relationship of discoveries to floor-levels of dormitory, vault and cloister. B: section through cloister and choir practice room.

The stairs up from the new entrance did not survive (except for part of one at the bottom), but their general outline was given by the rising base of the ashlar blocking in the W. wall, and by the hollow handrail cut into the ashlar blocking of that wall (Fig. 79). On the return flight to the E., over the vaulting, the stairs themselves had been removed, but the stepped mortar surface on which they lay still survived. Parts of the L-shaped wall on the inner side of the staircase also survived, which gave the width of the stairs (Fig. 78).

A puzzling feature in the W. wall was the fragment of blind arcading immediately to the S. of the Norman arch, at about the level of the top of the splayed opening in the wall (Fig. 79). There was one arch of three voussoirs, resting on symmetrical responds, and the beginning of a second arch to the S. In the spandrels of the arches was a filling of rubble and white mortar, distinct from the Norman walling above (there was also a needle-hole in the wall over the N. respond, from the time of its construction). The surface of the arches and their responds had been hacked back (as had the end of the Norman arch), but the ashlar below them was smooth, and continuous with the ashlar blocking in the rest of the wall.

This feature was at first thought to be a blocked recess, but the character of the masonry suggested that this was unlikely, and that something more substantial had been removed. As John Ashdown observed, this was probably the side of a small two-bay vault covering the stair passage and entrance, with the vaulting later chopped back flush with the wall, and the rough spandrels representing the filling of the vault. The northernmost respond was opposite the corner of the inner wall of the stair, and the estimated position of the southernmost respond would be approximately over the southern jamb of the door to the cloister (Fig. 77C).

Assuming that all these features were contemporary (and the only evidence suggesting otherwise is the date of the tiles), the new entrance to the dormitory would have been made at the same time as the cloisters were rebuilt, and consisted of a new front door, a vaulted passage and stair turning on a tiled landing, with a small ventilator to the cloister (Figs. 77C and 80B).

POST-MEDIEVAL: THE PAINTED PLASTER

The plaster covering the Norman door (uncovered behind later panelling) was painted with broad painted stripes of red and grey (Fig. 79). This plaster covered all the features which were subsequently uncovered on the wall (the handrail had been filled in), and the paint ceased at the modern floor level, but did continue around the S. side of the room, red and grey stripes being visible on the timber framing next the stair. One post of this framing also had a painted decoration on two sides of it, representing a strapwork cartouche in imitation panelling (Fig. 81), a motif known from other Oxford buildings and perhaps dating to c.1600.[7] The painted timber was either *ex situ*, or was perhaps part of a decorative scheme on painted cloth (there are nail-holes on the back of the post). The stair behind the framing leads up to the room over the E. cloister walk, which contains two fireplaces and is probably of 16th-century date (Figs. 77D and 78). The 15th-century stair up from the cloisters was filled in at the time the room was decorated (if not before), and from the rubble fill came several pieces of moulded stonework, including another fragment from the shrine of St. Frideswide, painted with red and gold (Fig. 29 No. 19).

The ceiling of the room had plain chamfered joists, and a wallplate against the W. wall, integral with the framing in the S. wall. The ceiling of the first-floor room had re-used medieval rafters, mentioned above.

The broad painted stripes on the wall-plaster are similar to those in the much more elaborate scheme recently found in Trinity College, in a room below the Old Library, probably decorated for the first President's Lodgings in the reign of Queen Mary.[8] The

Fig. 81.   Priory House: 16th-century painted timber post from S.W. corner of choir practice room.

[7] Similar paintings have been found at 26 Cornmarket (Zacharias's) and 59–61 Cornmarket; see report on The New Inn', forthcoming.
[8] B. Ward-Perkins, 'Newly Discovered Wall-Paintings', *Trinity College Oxford, Report 1985–86*, Pls. 1–3.

Priory House scheme may date to the time of Canon William Tresham, who is reputed to have made this room.[9] Interestingly, Tresham was deprived of his canonry in 1560 for Catholic sympathies, and was the one who rebaptized the recast Great Tom as 'Mary'. He is better known as the maker of 'Tresham's Lane', now Blue Boar Street.[10]

## LATER ALTERATIONS

The Priory House was badly damaged by fire in 1669, and part was apparently blown up to prevent the fire spreading.[11] Perhaps this was the occasion for inserting panelling into the room, for at some date holes were made in the plaster and stone for the insertion of wooden pegs to secure panelling (Fig. 79). The panelling, prior to its removal, seemed to be made up to fit the room, possibly as late as the 19th century, though parts of it were much older. That some part of the room was not panelled is indicated by fragments of Gothick wallpaper found near the ceiling in the S.–W. corner by the stair.[12] In about 1880 the access from the newly-restored chapter-house was altered with the insertion of a spiral stair in the N.E. corner into the pre-existing passage; the room was used for chapter meetings before becoming the choir practice room.[13] The rooms above had partitions added to make passages, the framing of which was simply laid on the floor-joists and may be of 17th- or 18th-century date. That on the second floor will only have been needed when the attic space over the chapter-house was converted to rooms, perhaps about 1600 (the attics are shown on Sampson Strong's portrait of Wolsey, c.1610, Fig. 87).[14]

## THE ROOMS OVER THE CLOISTER

The stair in the S.W. corner of the choir practice room leads up to the rooms over the cloister walk (Fig. 78). A landing at the top of the stair has doors to the Allstree Library (above the S. cloister walk) and the long room over the E. walk (now used as the music and book store). This has a lean-to roof and plain windows to the cloister, perhaps of 16th-century date. There are two fireplaces in the E. wall, the southern one with a plain chamfered arch of four-centered profile, the northern with moulded jambs and spandrels. The latter has partly been obscured by the wooden vaulting inserted into the cloister by Scott to clear the chapter-house entrance, which raised the floor-level of the central part of the room. Although the room over the S. walk was built in 1612[15] that over the E. walk is probably older, certainly if the stairs leading to it were part of the mid 16th-century alterations to the choir practice room. It was used as part of the college Treasury, where Anthony Wood consulted the College deeds (the N. cloister range was converted in 1772 for a muniment room);[16] in lifting the old floorboards two strays from

[9] Warner op. cit. note 5, 170 & 175.

[10] A.B. Emden, *A Biographical Register of the University of Oxford A.D. 1501 to 1540* (1974), 1501–4; W.G. Hiscock, *A Christ Church Miscellany* (1946), 143.

[11] Wood, *Life and Times*, ii (O.H.S. xxi, 1892), 175 (1669).

[12] Cf. A. Wells-Cole, *Historic Paper Hangings from Temple Newsham and other English Houses* (1983), Nos. 39–40.

[13] Warner op. cit. note 5, 175; P. Dearmer, *The Cathedral Church of Oxford* (Bell's Cathedral Series, 1897), 41; the window on the spiral stair is shown on the Oxford Almanack for 1828.

[14] For works of 1600, see Hiscock op. cit. note 10, 212.

[15] Ibid., 215.

[16] Ibid; Wood, *Life and Times*, i (O.H.S. xix, 1891), 286 and ii (O.H.S. xxi, 1892), 112.

the muniments were discovered, preserved in the dry dust. One was an early 13th-century deed granting land in Iffley to Oseney Abbey, hitherto known only from a copy in the cartulary; the other a mid-14th century manorial flock account roll of Oseney.[17]


CONCLUSIONS

The discovery of medieval records and the fragment of St. Frideswide's shrine were unusual aspects of this minor exercise in building archaeology, which was initiated to investigate the roof of the chapter-house. The discovery of the Norman door was wholly unexpected, though finding painted decoration is commonplace on most building work in Oxford. The amount of information recovered from this small building operation at a key point in the fabric of the Priory is a reminder of the importance of watching and recording such works.

---

[17] *Cartulary of Oseney Abbey*, ed. H.E. Salter, iv (O.H.S. xcvii, 1934), 360 (320).

# The Roof Carpentry of Oxford Cathedral

By John Ashdown, Ian Fisher and Julian Munby

SUMMARY

*The medieval roofs of the Cathedral were all built for the Augustinian Priory of St. Frideswide, and are therefore to be seen in the context of monastic rather than cathedral carpentry. The oldest roof in the Cathedral is that over the chapter-house, belonging to the middle of the 13th century, and of standard rafter construction with no lengthways stiffening and employing notch-lapped joints. The Latin Chapel has its original roof of c.1320–40, interesting on account of its unusual form, being double-framed with side purlins and a ridge piece resting on a yoke (having affinities with cruck construction). The Lady Chapel has a late-medieval roof of unremarkable type, with butt-purlins and windbraces. The choir roof of c.1500 is a standard low-pitched king-post roof marking the change from high-pitched roofs to a low-pitch with leaded covering. Subsequently the transepts were given flat decorated ceilings, and the low-pitched nave roof of rather more elaborate type is probably also of early 16th-century date. The refectory of the Priory (the Old Library) was also built near the beginning of the 16th century, and its roof with the later painted ceiling has been described elsewhere.[1]*

INTRODUCTION

This description of the principal roofs of St. Frideswide's Priory has been undertaken to accompany the publication of the archaeological work in the church, and to provide for the first time a discussion of some of the earliest surviving carpentry in Oxford.[2] The roof carpentry of Oxford Cathedral has not been fully studied nor reported on before now, apart from passing mention in the standard works on the Cathedral.[3] The roofs were examined and photographed by Ian Fisher, now of R.C.A.H.M. (Scotland), in the 1960s, when the chapter-house roof was measured (and photographed when it had no water-tanks).[4] Cecil Hewett has described and illustrated the roofs of the nave and the Latin Chapel.[5]

---

[1] D. Sturdy, E. Clive Rouse and J.C. Cole, 'The Painted Roof of the Old Library, Christ Church', *Oxoniensia*, xxvi–vii (1961/2), 215–43.

[2] We are grateful to the Cathedral Verger, Edward Evans, and the Cathedral staff for their assistance in giving access to the roofs, and to David Scroggie of Peter Bosanquet and John Perryman Associates, for helping to uncover parts of the chapter-house roof, and encouraging the investigations there. The dendrochronology of the timbers has been kindly undertaken by David Haddon-Reece and Daniel Miles.

[3] J. Britton, *Oxford Cathedral* (1820) contains useful illustrations. G.G. Scott's *Report* (1869) does not mention the roofs in any detail. P. Dearmer, *Oxford* (Bell's Cathedral Series, 1897) is not without value, whilst S.A. Warner, *Oxford Cathedral* (1924) is very carefully researched. *R.C.H.M. Oxford* (1939), 43, only briefly describes the open roofs. The most recent general description and discussion of the cathedral is to be found in N. Pevsner and P. Metcalf, *The Cathedrals of England: Southern England* (1985).

[4] JM is most grateful to Ian Fisher for his generosity in placing these materials at his disposal in 1973.

[5] C. Hewett, *English Cathedral Carpentry* (1974) describes and illustrates the roof of the nave (pp. 34–5, Fig. 21), and that of the Latin Chapel (pp. 38–9, Fig. 25) though they are omitted from his second edition (see note 9 below).

Opportunities for a close re-examination of the roofs were provided by the cleaning of the roof of the nave in 1979, and the conversion of the chapter-house attics for Cathedral offices in 1986–7.[6] A survey of the Latin Chapel roof has also been undertaken, as this is a work of unusual form. The remaining roofs have not been surveyed, but are briefly described.

THE CHAPTER-HOUSE (Figs. 82–3)

The timber roof above the stone vault of the chapter-house is mostly obscured by the walls and ceiling of the attic rooms, now the Cathedral offices and formerly part of Priory House. The rooms, now approached up the new staircase in Priory House, are wholly within the roof-space, and the floor is level with the top of the side walls. There are three rooms, lit by windows in the end gables and the N. wall; the eastern two have corner fireplaces. A passage on the S. side of the rooms is lit by three dormer windows in the slope of the roof, and there are small rooms at each end of it, with windows in the gable wall. A chimney-stack in the W. wall rises from the fireplace in the room over the E. range of the cloister. The inaccessible roof-space over the chapter-house was perhaps converted to rooms in 1600, though work had been done on the roof covering in 1578;[7] windows and chimney-stacks are shown in Sampson Strong's portrait of Wolsey, c.1610 (Fig. 87), and Loggan's view of the College in 1675.

The rooms have a suspended ceiling below the lower collar-beam, and the roof above can be reached either from a door in the valley next the S. transept, or through a modern trap-door in the ceiling of the W. room. Since the roof was photographed in the 1960s some large water-tanks have been inserted at the W. end, slung on steel-work attached to the rafters. The roof has also been re-covered in recent years, with felting, some new timber firring pieces on the outside of the rafters, and Bradstone replica stone slates.

The roof consists of 29 individual rafter couples with no original lengthways stiffening, such support being provided only by the external covering. The trusses have two collar-beams, about 5 feet apart, and the lower collars had soulaces bracing them to the rafters. The rafters have a simple half-lapped joint at the apex, the collars and soulaces have open notch-laps (with what Hewett calls a refined entry profile). In addition to the usual face-pegs holding these joints, there are also pegs driven in at about 45 degrees from the lower foredge of the collar, through the lap-joint and into the rafter (Fig. 83, detail). These are an unusual feature, and were probably devised to draw the lapped end of the collar firmly back into the rafter; comparable double pegging has been noted in the 13th-century roof at Cogges Priory.[8] The soulaces have all been removed, but their lower mortices (now filled) can still be seen in the rafters which bisect the dormer windows in the passage.

Many of the collars are bowed upwards, as if from the applied load of the roof covering. The members are all substantial, being generally some 8 ins. (20 cm.) square, the upper collars being slightly smaller. Many waney edges are visible, suggesting that quarter-sawn trees were used. Two lower collars towards the E. end have each been

---

[6] For a description of the discoveries in 1986–7, see above, pp. 185–93.
[7] W.G. Hiscock, *A Christ Church Miscellany* (1946), 212.
[8] J. Blair and J.M. Steane, 'Investigations at Cogges, Oxfordshire, 1979–81: The Priory and Parish Church', *Oxoniensia*, xlvii (1982), 75 and 79.

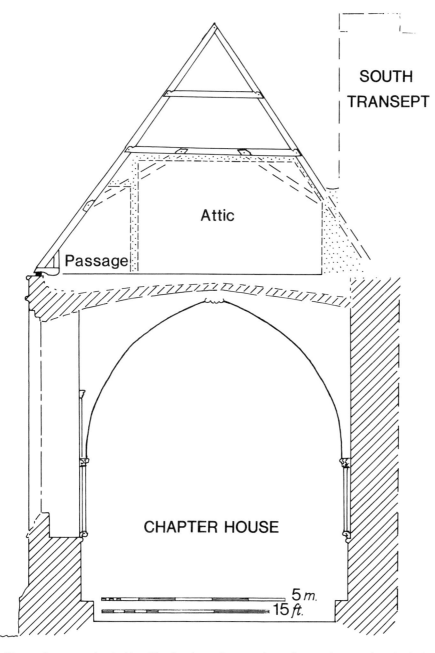

Fig. 82. Chapter-house: section looking W., showing attic rooms in roof-space above vault and relationship to S. transept.

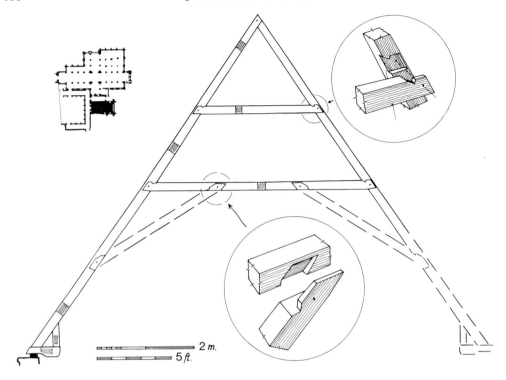

Fig. 83.   Chapter-house: 13th-century roof-truss, looking W.

replaced by two softwood planks, and one near the W. end has been cut for the trap-door. Secondary features of the roof include longitudinal diagonal bracing in softwood, probably of 19th-century date, and side-purlins laid along the end of the lower collars, probably of the same period.

The end walls are of plain rubble; the W. gable has the chimney-flue mentioned above, and the E. gable has two large ?putlog holes at about the level of the upper collar. The chimney-stack between the two rooms is not visible in the upper part of the roof.

The junction of roof and side walls was partly opened for inspection in the recent works. The N. side was seen only where the roof is adjacent to the transept, and the truncated rafters rested on modern posts embedded in brickwork. On the S. side the standard triangular base arrangement existed, with ashlar-pieces morticed into the rafters and into large sole-pieces carrying the rafter feet. No original tie-beams were observed, and do not seem to have been present. The sole-pieces were shallower on the outside where there had been a wall-plate (now replaced with bricks) resting on the stone table at the top of the wall; some of the inner ends of the sole-pieces stand on small stone piers that may rest on the vaulting, though this is obscured by rubbish. It is possible that there was an inner wall-plate standing on the inner face of the wall. The present floor is carried on large transverse joists, whose soffits are obscured by rubbish, and are presumably supported by the side walls. The crown of the vault was observed a short distance below the joist soffits near the centre of the room. The span between the walls in the chapter-house itself is 23 ft. 11 ins. (7.29 m.).

Comparable roofs are to be found in ecclesiastical contexts in the first half of the 13th century. At this time it was not the practice to include any lengthwise members, the outer covering of the roof and the gables being thought sufficient to prevent lengthways movement. Sideways movement was restricted by bracing with soulaces to the lower collars, and these employed notch-lapped (rather than mortice-and-tenon) joints, which became less frequent later in the 13th century. Some of the plainer roofs in the Cathedrals of Wells and Lincoln are of this type, though they have additional members between the two collars, and also tie-beams.[9]

It would be expected that the roof would be contemporary with the rebuilding of the Priory chapter-house in the second quarter of the 13th century. A loose notch-lap tenon, sampled for dendrochronology, was found to have a last ring dated to 1236 (without sapwood); although measured on the face of the timber rather than the cross-section, this sample matched very well with the Oxford dendrochronology mean curve.[10] Allowance must be made for missing heartwood and about 15–35 years of sapwood, giving a felling date probably no earlier than 1250. It is unlikely, given the nature of the roof and its jointing, that it can have been built long after 1250, so it must date from soon after the masonry of the chapter-house. Only further sampling can determine a closer date, but similar results have been obtained from samples taken from reused timbers in Priory House, which share the same detail of diagonal pegging on the notch-lap joints (see following).

THE DORMITORY (PRIORY HOUSE)[11]

The dormitory lay S. of the chapter-house, aligned N.–S. along the cloister, and its roof, if not removed in the post-Dissolution conversion to a canon's lodging, was probably damaged in the fire of 1669, after which the top floor was refashioned (small dormers are shown in the view of the College on the c.1610 portrait of Wolsey by Sampson Strong, Fig. 87, and the present ones in Loggan's view of 1675). In the recent construction work for the new staircase, a short length of an old roof-line was revealed at the W. end of the S. wall of the chapter-house, in about the right position for the dormitory roof. Two of the floor joists removed from the second floor to make way for the new stair were evidently reused, having mortices for notch-lap joints similar to those in the chapter-house roof. They are unlikely to come from the chapter-house itself, and may have been removed from the old dormitory roof in the 16th or 17th century. Two samples were taken for dating by dendrochronology, of which one (with 24 years of sapwood and the bark edge, i.e. complete) could not be dated, and the other (with incomplete sapwood) had a latest ring with a tentative date of 1241 and an estimated felling range of 1241–60. If indeed from the dormitory roof, this would have been about contemporary with the chapter-house roof.

---

[9] C.A. Hewett, *English Cathedral and Monastic Carpentry* (1985), 6 (Wells Nave, c.1200) and 16–17 (Lincoln Chapter House vestibule, c.1234). For the date of Lincoln, see N.D. Foot, C.D. Litton and W.G. Simpson, 'The High Roofs of the East End of Lincoln Cathedral', in *Medieval Art and Architecture at Lincoln Cathedral* (B.A.A. Conference Proceedings for 1982, 1986), 54.

[10] Oxford Mean Curve of dendrochronological samples from Oxfordshire buildings, by D. Haddon-Reece, D.W.H. Miles, J.T. Munby and the late J.M. Fletcher, publication forthcoming in *Oxoniensia*.

[11] For further description of Priory House see above, pp. 185–93.

THE LATIN CHAPEL (Fig. 84)

The Latin Chapel was built c.1320–40,[12] and the present roof is probably the original one. It is of four bays, like the vaulting of the chapel below, the trusses corresponding to the external buttresses. The W. bay has been partly removed, probably to give light to the clerestory window (which is late-medieval); half this bay for half its width has a flat lead roof, the resulting walls being of studwork, probably 19th-century, with a king-post and struts to the N. side. Against the W. wall is half an original truss, and there are four further trusses with the last inside the E. wall of the chapel. The tops of the side walls are mostly obscured by builders' rubbish from re-roofing, but there is at least one wall-plate on each side, in part ancient, with tie-beams resting on them and on short stone piers. The piers on the N. are flush with the inner edge of the wall and those on the S. side stand forward some 13 ins. (33 cm.). The distance between the walls is 19 ft. 6 ins. (5.95 m.). The trusses stand over the pockets of the vault, which are filled level with rubbish.

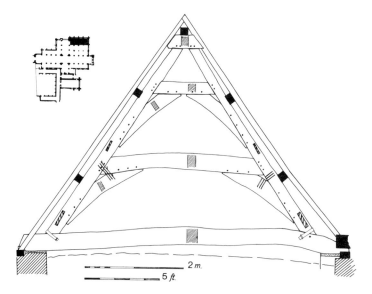

Fig. 84.   Latin Chapel: 14th-century roof-truss, looking E.

The roof is double-framed, with the principal trusses supporting four purlins and a ridge-piece, on which the common rafter couples rest. The principal rafters are joined together at the apex with a large yoke on which the ridge-piece is placed. There are two collars, each supported from below with curved braces. The side-purlins are supported by braces rising from the rafters, and are pegged to the principals, though not trenched into them. All the timbers are accurately cut and well pegged, though they are very waney and exceedingly irregular in outline, evidently being made from single branches and trunks.[13] The joints are all pegged mortice-and-tenons, and the purlins are scarfed

[12] A stylistic date of the 1320s to 1330s is proposed by Morris, above p. 182, while Blair suggests that Bishop Burwash's chantry, founded at St. Frideswide's altar in 1338, may indicate the actual date, below p. 245.
[13] Hewett, op. cit. in note 5, gives the roof too regular an appearance.

with simple splays and three pegs (the ridge has trait-de-Juppiter scarfs). Modern additions include a series of braces from the ties to the lower purlins, and collars beaked to the upper purlins, whilst many of the common rafters have been replaced. Iron rods have been inserted in the centre of the trusses. The roof has recently been recovered with Bradstone slates, and felted.

The roof is of interest because of the construction of the apex, which resembles a widespread form used for joining principals in cruck roofs (e.g. Swalcliffe Tithe Barn, of *c*.1400),[14] and is of striking appearance owing to its careful use of most irregular timber. These hidden features are somewhat at variance with the lavish decoration of stonework and glass in the Latin Chapel itself.

## THE LADY CHAPEL

The roof of the Lady Chapel, immediately S. of the Latin Chapel, is a later medieval replacement of the 13th-century original. Like the Latin Chapel roof, half the western bay has been removed and replaced with a flat roof. It has five bays, which do not match the disposition of the vault bays beneath (though the vault pockets are again filled with builders' rubbish and cannot be seen). The westernmost truss was moved inwards when the roof was shortened, and the sixth truss is next the E. wall of the chapel. The distance between the walls is *c*. 14 ft. 9 ins. (4.5 m.). There are single wall-plates carrying the tie-beams, the principal rafter couples have a single collar (slightly cambered), and two butt-purlins on each side, the lower ones supported by curved wind-braces of thin section. Between the upper purlins are a number of collars with beaked ends, probably a later addition. The purlins are joined to the principal rafters with tenons on their outer side, without haunches. The timbers are mostly regular, with few waney edges. Like the Latin Chapel, this roof has recently been felted and recovered.

The roof is of a standard late-medieval type, perhaps of *c*.1400, after which date the purlin joints would more likely have had diminished haunches (which were used at All Souls' College in the 1440s).

## THE CHOIR

The vaulting and reconstruction of the upper part of the choir was carried out *c*.1500, partly as a translation of timber hammer-beams roofs into stone. At this time the clerestory of the Norman choir was demolished, and the steeply-pitched Norman roof (the outlines of which can be seen on the central tower) was removed and replaced with a low-pitched roof covered with lead. This is carried on a series of heavy trusses with timbers of large section, having a tie-beam carrying a king-post and two raking side-struts from tie to rafter, with a deep ridge-piece. The tops of the king-posts are dovetailed to take the ends of the rafters, and thus act in tension rather than compression. Several king-posts and rafters have large chase-mortices and are reused. The eastern truss probably dates from the time of Scott's restoration in 1870–6.

Late-medieval low-pitched roofs gave little scope for variety. The principal features of this roof can also be seen in the upper part of the early 16th-century roof over the nave of Bath Abbey.[15] According to Francis Bond, a verger reported that in Dean Liddell's

---

[14] J.M. Steane, *South Midlands Archaeology*, 17 (1987), 50.
[15] Hewett, op. cit. in note 9, 62–3.

time the roof-space here was found to contain a considerable quantity of hay, thought to have survived from the time of the royalist occupation of Oxford.[16]

## THE TRANSEPTS

The intention to vault the transepts in the same manner as the choir can be seen at the end of the N. transept, where the first bay was altered, and contains the tomb of James Zouch (d.1503) who left money for new vaulting. This was not done, though the N. bay has shafts and wall panelling for it, and the present flat panelled ceiling was added some time later (see above, pp. 128–9), on a series of stone corbels high on the wall. It is of three bays, with moulded tie-beams, purlins and rafters. The S. transept roof is of similar style, divided into smaller panels, with the end bay a modern replacement.

## THE NAVE (Fig. 85)

The nave roof is based on polygonal-concave stone corbels, similar to those supporting the vaulting in the choir; thus the roof must be of the same date, or later, assuming that the choir corbels are contemporary with the vaulting. It would therefore be early 16th-century.

The roofs of the transepts and nave were cleaned from scaffolding in 1979, and the nave roof was examined and drawn in August 1979. It was found to be partly of softwood, probably the replacement of 1816 noted by Britton (though a view by Thomas Malton in 1802 shows that the original roof was of the same appearance).[17] It is of five bays, the westernmost largely of Scott's restoration (i.e. the western truss and probably the next). The next four bays and four trusses are contemporary, probably of 1816; the easternmost truss is hard against the tower.

The width of the nave between the walls is 22 ft. 5 ins. (6.83 m.), the full length from tower to W. wall 75 ft. 7 ins. (23.05 m.). Wall-posts with hollow chamfers are mounted on the corbels, with a plain butted scarf near their base. They support the tie-beams, which are braced by a semi-circular arch-brace (with an ogee moulding) rising from the corbels to the centre of the tie. It is in at least five sections, with free tenons joining the individual curved pieces (Fig. 85, detail), and presumably chase-tenons joining them to the tie. The spandrels between the brace and tie are filled with an open arcade of traceried lights, trefoiled in ogival heads. The wall-plates have a casement moulding and double ogee. The low-pitched principal rafters are supported by a king-post and two raking side-struts, all hollow-chamfered. The king-posts may have internal iron supports, having a peg on their W. side and a small wedge on the E. Above the tie the spandrels are also filled with open traceried panels. The ridge-piece is hollow-chamfered, and the purlins on the side-struts have in addition a roll and hollow. Where the ridge joins the later part of the roof there is a splayed and tabled scarf with under-squinted abutments, and two diagonal iron rods.

In the slope of the roof are numerous small rafters, with ogee mouldings, and battens supporting quatrefoil panels. There are 48 panels on each side in each bay, 24

---

[16] Francis Bond, undated letter to R.I.B.A. *Transactions*, *c*.1900; cf. F.J. Varley, *The Siege of Oxford* (1932), 105 (and *Supplement*, 15).

[17] Britton, *Oxford Cathedral* (1820), 18 & pl. v; T. Malton, *Oxford* (1802–10), un-numbered plate dated 30 June 1802.

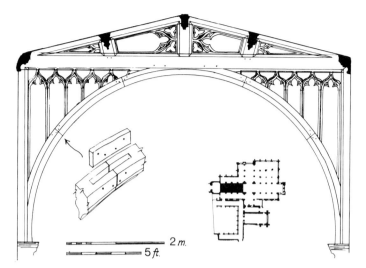

Fig. 85.   Cathedral nave: 15th/19th-century roof-truss looking E., with detail of scarf-joint.

above the purlin, and 24 below (in three rows of eight panels). At every intersection are applied plaques, decorated with faces, figures or foliage. These have a different patination from the rest of the roof, and may be original.

All the timber in the roof is cut very straight, with smooth surfaces, and would seem to be in part of softwood. It is all covered with a dark-brown varnish (Scott's bay is painted brown to match). The second bay from the E. is lighter, as if the varnish had been removed or was applied differently. Possibly it was more affected by the candles of the choir-stalls.

Apart from the plaques, the whole roof is of one date, and would seem largely to be work of 1816, judging from its even finish. As a low-pitched roof with arcaded spandrels it belongs to a group of late 15th-century roofs in Oxford (e.g. Duke Humfrey's Library and St. Mary the Virgin church). What is unusual in this one is the greater amount of decoration and (if original) the near semi-circular arcature of the spandrels.


OTHER ROOFS

The lean-to aisle roofs of the nave and choir are not accessible. The St. Lucy Chapel has a 19th-century open rafter-roof. The slype extends beyond the E. wall of the S. transept, and has a short length of pitched roof outside the transept, which is inaccessible. The post-medieval ceiling of the crossing was moved by Scott and replaced above the open lantern stage, though it is shown by Britton at a lower level; above this there is no ancient timberwork in the belfry or spire, though a plain 19th-century timber framing stands inside the lower part of the spire.


CONCLUSION

The roofs of St. Frideswide's Priory are unexceptional, but belong to a church of no great size or pretension. The chapter-house preserves what is probably the earliest roof in

Oxford, a fine mid 13th-century rafter roof of the first phase of Gothic carpentry, when no lengthwise support was provided for the rafter couples, and notch-lap joints were preferred to the mortice-and-tenon variety. Neither this nor the roof over the Latin Chapel was intended to be seen, but in the latter case the uneven appearance of the carpentry contrasts with the excellence of the 14th-century stonework over which it stands. By this period roofs were double-framed, with the trusses supporting purlins in a rigid framework on which rafters could be laid. The vernacular detailing of the Latin Chapel is in contrast with the more regular appearance of the Lady Chapel roof. In the last phase of Gothic carpentry, which saw the increasing use of lead-covering, the low-pitched king-post roof became the norm, and the examples surviving in the Cathedral provide an interesting contrast, that above the stone vault of the choir being plain and utilitarian, whilst the other open ones are decorated with panelling.

# Wolsey's Bell-Tower

By MARTIN BIDDLE

SUMMARY

*Wolsey made preparations to remove the bells of St. Frideswide's to a temporary bell-frame in the cloister and to demolish the steeple, but his fall in 1529 halted the works. The steeple was not demolished and there is no evidence that the bells were moved. The temporary (perhaps abortive) bell-frame was erected beside Wolsey's new and still incomplete tower at the E. end of the hall. Intended to be the great bell-tower of Cardinal College, as the Victorians always believed, the construction of this tower at the S.E angle of the quad would have brought all the principal elements of Wolsey's new college (except the kitchen) into a single integrated complex.*

The primary evidence for the progress of the works by which Wolsey undertook the construction of Cardinal College between 1525 and his fall in 1529 is contained in a series of building accounts now preserved in Oxford and London. In one form or another these accounts cover the whole period of building, from 16 January 1525 to 24 October 1529, with the exception of some part of 1528.[1] The accounts are supplemented by a number of letters and other documents giving instructions, making grants of materials, or describing the progress of the works.[2]

It is only in the last period of the accounts, from 1 November 1528 to 24 October 1529, that items occur which seem to be directly relevant to the fate of the bells of St. Frideswide's. The accounts for this period survive in two versions. The first is a copy made by Twyne 'Out of the Journall or booke of the Expences of all the buildinges of Christchurch Coll: Oxon: which I had of Mr Pore of Blechinton'.[3] Hearne copied Twyne,[4] Gutch printed Hearne,[5] and *Letters and Papers of Henry VIII* reprinted extracts from Gutch.[6] None of them reproduced the totals of the fortnightly 'pays' copied by Twyne.[7] But it is these totals which show that the 'booke' seen by Twyne covered the

---

[1] The accounts formed the basis of Mr. Michael Maclagan's valuable discussion of the building of the college in *V.C.H. Oxon.* iii, 228–31. The only original account still in Oxford (Corpus Christi College, MS.565) was examined in detail by J.G. Milne and John H. Harvey, 'The Building of Cardinal College, Oxford', *Oxoniensia*, viii/ix (1943–4), 137–53. See also John H. Harvey, 'The Building Works and Architects of Cardinal Wolsey', *Journal of the British Archaeological Association*, 3rd ser. viii (1943), 50–9, esp. pp. 53–5, 58–9. The Cardinal College accounts still require a detailed analysis, which I hope to publish in due course.

[2] See *Letters and Papers Henry VIII* 4.i, No. 1499 (26); 4.ii, Nos. 2734, 3334, 4074, 4135; 4.iii, No. 5951; 5, Nos. 185, 577. The full texts of some of these and of other relevant documents are given in W. Douglas Caröe, '*Tom Tower*', *Christ Church, Oxford* (1923), 95–106 (Appendix A); see also Harvey, 'Building Works', 58–9.

[3] Bodl. MS. Twyne 21, pp. 350–7.

[4] Bodl. MS. Tanner 338, ff. 313–14 (formerly pp. 422–4).

[5] John Gutch, *Collectanea Curiosa* (2 vols., Oxford, 1781), i, pp. vii, 204–9.

[6] *Letters and Papers Henry VIII*, 4.iii, No. 6748 (8).

[7] Bodl. MS. Twyne 21, p. 354.

same period as the second version of the accounts for this period now preserved in the Public Record Office.[8]

Four entries in the accounts for this final period of the works, 1528–9, require detailed scrutiny.

    i.     'Item to James Flemminge, etc. for makinge scaffolds for the takinge downe of the old stepull     3s. 4d.'[9]

    ii.    'Item for 2 crowes for the carpenters to take downe the bells with, ponderinge 17 lb. – 2s. 1½d.'[10]

These entries show that the 'old stepull' was scaffolded prior to its intended demolition and that as part of these preparations the carpenters were provided with two specially-made crowbars, presumably so as to dismantle the wooden bell-frame in order 'to take downe the bells'. Most recent commentators have assumed, doubtless correctly, that these entries refer to Wolsey's intention to take down the steeple of the Priory church. Since the steeple survives, the scaffolds, although already prepared as the payment shows, can never have been used, their purpose thwarted by Wolsey's fall in October 1529. The bells were perhaps taken down, but there is no direct evidence to this effect, and it is not impossible that they remained undisturbed in the old steeple until 1545. It has usually been assumed that they were removed, partly to explain the amount of carpenter's work required in 1545 to prepare the steeple to receive the bells of Oseney, including Tom,[11] partly to explain the buttressed foundation in the cloister (above, pp. 67–72) as a temporary belfry intended to take the bells from the steeple. These arguments are to some extent circular. The work undertaken in 1545 may have been needed simply to adapt or rebuild the bell-frame in the steeple to accommodate the Oseney bells alongside some or all of the bells of St. Frideswide's. And the 'temporary belfry', if such it was, may have been as abortive as the scaffolds of the steeple.

    iii.    'Item to Will: Hobbs and Rich: Cooper for bringinge in of the bell frame in their drinkinge time    iid.'[12]

This entry shows that a bell-frame, not stated to be new but probably so, was brought in, i.e. presumably onto the site, under some press of urgency during the time of this account. 'In their drinking time' is a common phrase in Tudor building accounts. Such overtime was usually rewarded by an extra payment, which is how the 2d. should be regarded here. Another example in these accounts is the 12d. paid to the masons working on the tower at the E. end of the hall, 'in rewarde for their diligence in applienge of their labour . . . on Saturday after their houre accustomed to leave worke'.[13] Entry iii should probably be taken at face-value as referring to a new bell-frame, cut and fitted ('framed') elsewhere, taken down, and brought onto the site for erection in its intended place. It does not seem possible that it can refer to the movement of the bell-frame from the old steeple.

---

[8] P.R.O., SP1/55, pp. 221–38; abstracted in *Letters and Papers Henry VIII*, 4.iii, No. 6023. This sequence of copying and the relationship of the MS. copied by Twyne to that in the P.R.O. was established by Michael Maclagan, *V.C.H. Oxon.* iii, 230, note 25.

[9] Bodl. MS. Twyne 21, p. 351.

[10] Ibid. p. 352.

[11] Bodl. MS. Top. Oxon. b.16, *passim*; cf. *V.C.H. Oxon.* iii, 231.

[12] Bodl. MS. Twyne 21, p. 351.

[13] Ibid. p. 353.

iv.     'Paide to Tho: Hewister for carriage of earth and rubbell from the fayre gate
        and the newe stepull ... clvi loads at a peny the load, by computation
        13s.'[14]

This entry provides a number of problems. The 'fayre gate' is presumably Tom
Gate, but since 'the great tower over the gate' was already by December 1526 'as high
erect' as the completed lodgings to either side,[15] the earth and rubble carted from it in
1528–9 cannot have been from its construction, but must rather have been carried away
from a dump nearby. This assumes that the equation of the 'fayre gate' with Tom Gate is
valid, but this is not necessarily so. The 'new stepull' seems clear enough, but tells
nothing of its location and character. What is the meaning of 'stepull' here? Entry i,
discussed above, might seem to suggest that the word could mean to the compiler of
these accounts just what it means today, the spire of St. Frideswide's. But could it also
mean a relatively low, tower-like, buttressed belfry, for that is what it has got to mean if
the 'new stepull' is to be taken as a reference to the belfry for which the foundation in the
cloister seems to have been intended? The early uses quoted in *O.E.D.* show that the
primary meaning of 'steeple' is a tall tower, often containing bells, or such a tower
together with a spire or other superstructure; by the mid-16th century and perhaps the
late 15th, it could mean a spire, or, as a text of 1578 puts it, a 'poynted steeple'. Entry i
may well therefore refer not just to the spire, but also to the tower of St. Frideswide's,
and this explains why the bells were also to be taken down, for the bell-chamber is in the
tower, below the spire. But the idea of height, loftiness, is always contained in 'steeple'
and it must therefore be a real question whether the 'new stepull' of Entry iv can ever
have been applied to the relatively low structure set on the foundation in the cloister,
especially at a moment when the masons were working overtime on the tower at the E.
end of the hall. Measuring *c.* 55 by *c.* 60 feet in plan this tower, for such is the word
used,[16] can never have been intended to be less than 100 feet in height, and would have
dwarfed a temporary bell-tower immediately to the E. (Fig. 33).[17] Is it possible that the
'new stepull' refers not to a temporary structure such as that in the cloister but rather to
a new permanent bell-tower for Wolsey's new foundation? Daphne Hart's conjectural
drawing of Cardinal College in Howard Colvin's *Unbuilt Oxford* omits a bell-tower, but
Wolsey must have intended one, if only to complete his college as King's College,
Cambridge, should have been completed by the building of a great bell-tower to house
the bells presented by Henry VI.[18] It is most unlikely, on the evidence of other Tudor
buildings, that the great gate, now Tom Gate, was originally intended to take the bells.
This leaves only two possibilities, the tower E. of the hall, or another tower, possibly
detached, as at King's, whose site is now lost. For the integrity of Wolsey's plan, the
tower E. of the hall provides an obvious solution. Although its immense size in plan may
be an objection, it was a problem which G.F. Bodley overcame in 1876–9, when he raised
it into a bell-tower on the assumption that this was the place Wolsey had intended.[19]

---

[14] Ibid. p. 350.

[15] *Letters and Papers Henry VIII*, 4.ii, No. 2734.

[16] Bodl. MS. Twyne 21, p. 353, reads 'towre', *not* 'Town' as printed by Gutch, p. 207.

[17] For the suggested reconstruction of the temporary bell-tower, suggesting a maximum height of some 45 to
55 ft., see above, pp. 68–71 and Fig. 33.

[18] Howard Colvin, *Unbuilt Oxford* (1983), Fig. 7; for King's see below, n. 22.

[19] *V.C.H. Oxon.* iii, 233; *R.C.H.M. Oxford*, 33. For the appearance of the tower at the E. end of the hall as it was
in 1566 (and presumably more-or-less as it was left at the finish of Wolsey's works in 1529), see John
Bearblock's original drawing in Thomas Neele's verse dialogue composed for Queen Elizabeth's visit to
Oxford that year, now Bodleian, MS. Bodl. 13, f. 5ᵛ, reproduced here as Fig. 86 by kind permission of the

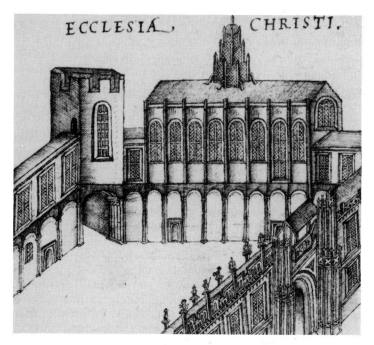

Fig. 86.   Christ Church in 1566, looking S.E. and showing the tower at the E. end of the hall on which work was being hurried on in 1529: see pp. 207–8 note 19. (Bodl. MS Bodley 13 f.5$^v$, reproduced by permission of the Curators of the Bodleian Library.)

The siting of a temporary bell-frame in the cloister immediately beside the tower E. of the hall is perhaps an additional point in favour of this tower as the site of Wolsey's 'new stepull': nobody moves bells further than is necessary, as the sites of bell furnaces within many an excavated church now show.

The 'new stepull' may of course have been on some adjacent site, but the foundations in the cloister can never have been intended to take the permanent bell-tower of Wolsey's new college, overshadowed as any bell-frame here must always have been by Wolsey's new tower at the E. end of the hall. Economy of argument, and the integrity of Wolsey's plan, should perhaps bring attention back to 'Bodley's Tower', as the place intended for the bells of Cardinal College.

In summary, the evidence of the building accounts seems to be as follows:

Bodleian Library. Bearblock's drawings were engraved by Hearne in 1713, re-issued by Whittlesey in 1728, and photolithographed by Guggenheim in 1882. They were reproduced again for *Queen Elizabeth's Oxford, 1566* (The Bodleian Library Calendar for 1983) with a useful introduction, and are conveniently available as Bodleian Library Filmstrips 338.1 and 338.2. The Bearblock drawing of Christ Church is also reproduced by W.G. Hiscock, *A Christ Church Miscellany* (1946), 199, where Chapter XX, 'The Buildings' (pp. 198–218) provides a particularly clear and appropriately illustrated account of the building history of Christ Church: Bodley's works are described on pp. 204–5. Another view of the tower E. of the hall, from the opposite direction, is given in the painting of Christ Church from the S.E. which appears in the background of Sampson Strong's posthumous portrait of Wolsey, painted in 1610–11 (Fig. 87). The tower is battlemented, as in Bearblock, and appears to be lower, but a close comparison shows that in both views the bases of the embrasures are approximately level with the hall parapet.

1. Wolsey scaffolded the spire and tower of St. Frideswide's and prepared to take down the bells, intending to demolish the whole (Entries i and ii).

2. Wolsey's fall halted the demolitions (as it did the works) in October 1529. The spire and tower were not taken down and there is no evidence that the bells were actually removed.

3. A new bell-frame was brought onto the site in some haste during 1528–9, probably to take the bells to be removed from St. Frideswide's. Without knowing when the bell-frame arrived during the year, we cannot be certain whether it had been erected before the works were halted in October 1529, but it seems likely that it was and that the foundation in the cloister was intended for it (Entry iii). But there is no evidence that the bells were ever transferred to this new frame,[20] and nothing to show that they were ever removed from the tower of St. Frideswide's. The bell-frame in the cloister may well have stood, complete, or more-or-less so, for sixteen years from 1529 to 1545, until demolished in the works of 1545–6 which saw the great tower and spire of St. Frideswide finally preserved and restored for the housing of the bells of Frideswide and Oseney.

4. A good deal of earth and rubble was taken away from the college some time during the year, apparently from two places, from a dump near the 'fayre gate' and from 'the new stepull'. It seems possible that 'the new stepull' refers to a new permanent bell-tower, rather than to a temporary structure. The most obvious site for this steeple is the tower at the E. end of the hall, 'Bodley's Tower', and the proximity of the site of a temporary bell-frame in the cloister supports this view. The haste with which the works were being pushed on in 1528–9, not least the works of the chapel (especially its roof) and of the tower E. of the hall, suggests that works for a permanent bell-tower would also have been in progress. The use of the word 'stepull' to describe what is also called a 'tower' in the accounts may be a reflection of changing names as the works developed, or may simply reflect a still unfixed terminology (cf. 'fayre gate'). The descriptions used by different compilers of the account, or presenters of the bills which were finally incorporated within it, may also have varied. The simplest and most probable solution is to believe that Wolsey intended the massive and otherwise unexplained tower at the E. end of the hall to be the great bell-tower of his college (Fig. 86).

Something further needs to be said on this last point, which represents a return to a Victorian interpretation which has been out of favour in recent years. The older view was well put by the *Oxford Journal* of 21 October 1876 in describing the work involved in the completion of the supposed belfry:[21]

> The difficulty arises from the great width of the basement line of work left by Wolsey. To build a tower in proper proportion to this basement line would mar the effect of the present Cathedral tower, which, probably, in the original design was to have been removed. Under the circumstances, therefore, a suitable tower will be constructed over the belfry in fair proportion to the surrounding buildings, and without destroying the old basement lines.

---

[20] In 1530 a series of payments for 'The costs of the bell tower' were included as a separate heading in a book of receipts and expenses for the fifth year of Cardinal College: *Letters and Papers Henry VIII*, 4.iii, No. 6788. There is no indication whether these payments refer to the tower over the crossing of St. Frideswide's or to a temporary bell-frame in the cloister.

[21] I am most grateful to Mavis Batey for kindly providing the text of this quotation.

The purpose of the tower defined by this immense lower stage is nowhere explained in sources contemporary with its construction: it is simply 'the tower at the east end of the hall.' The Victorians, who knew the structure before Bodley's works, seem to have had no doubt that it was intended to be a bell-tower. In taking this view they were apparently influenced by the scale of the existing work and all that this implied for its intended form. More recent views, influenced by the developing study of collegiate buildings usually conceived on less magnificent lines, and by the recognition and study of the contemporary design for a detached campanile at King's College, Cambridge,[22] have veered away from this interpretation. The idea has thus emerged that Wolsey's tower E. of the hall may have been intended for a muniment room and audit chamber (as suggested below by Mavis Batey and Catherine Cole, pp. 211–12), while his probable intention to provide a bell-tower would have been reflected in the construction of a detached campanile beside his new chapel on the N. side of the quad, perhaps (like Wolsey's tower of 1492–c.1509 at Magdalen) on the street-frontage of St. Aldate's.

Lavish as was Wolsey's endowment of his college, it seems unlikely that so large a tower as that E. of the hall would have been needed solely to provide access to the hall and to accommodate archives and audits, although these latter functions might easily have been contained within a tower designed to serve several purposes. There are other difficulties. The idea of a detached campanile is not supported by contemporary written evidence (the 'newe stepull' of 1528–9 need not carry this implication in default of other evidence) or actual remains. At King's the remote site of the original campanile may have been a particular solution to the peculiarly difficult sub-soil conditions in that part of Cambridge, where it would have been wise to keep so heavy a structure at some distance from the chapel, and distinct from it in both foundations and standing walls if differential settlement was to be avoided.[23] A detached campanile may even be an anachronism in the 1520s. The integration of all the elements within a single complex seems more likely at this time in a completely new building, not least when the scale and comprehensiveness of Wolsey's intentions are taken into account.[24]

---

[22] H.M. Colvin (ed.), *The History of the King's Works*, i (1963), 271–2, Fig. 29, Pl. 20. In fact, as Howard Colvin shows, Henry VI's intention in his so-called 'will' of 1448 was for the building of a tower attached to the W. side of a cemetery cloister, itself lying detached from and to the W. of the chapel. Henry's intended plan for Eton was very similar, although there the tower, also detached from the chapel, would have lain directly N. of the nave (ibid. 285, Fig. 31). Neither of these plans was in fact carried out, at least as regards the towers, and are unlikely therefore to have influenced Wolsey's ideas for his college. Had they done so they might have inclined him towards the integration of his tower in a claustral layout. What actually happened at King's was the construction of a temporary bell-tower detached from the chapel and about 70 ft. to the W., as fully discussed above, pp. 69–70, and illustrated in Fig. 32. This temporary tower might well have been known to Wolsey and his advisors and have influenced the construction of the temporary bell-tower at Cardinal College, but it seems most unlikely to have been an influence on Wolsey's plans for a permanent structure.

[23] P.V. Addyman and M. Biddle, 'Medieval Cambridge: Recent Finds and Excavations', *Proceedings of the Cambridge Antiquarian Society*, lviii (1965), 74–137, esp. pp. 100–3. It seems unlikely, however, that these considerations would also apply to Eton.

[24] I am grateful to Howard Colvin for reading the typescript of this article, but responsibility for errors is of course my own. As he suggests, the next stage is to undertake a detailed study of the standing fabric of the tower.

# The Great Staircase Tower at Christ Church

By MAVIS BATEY and CATHERINE COLE

SUMMARY

*The Christ Church Hall staircase, one of Oxford's finest pieces of architecture, was built in four stages over a period of 350 years. Cardinal Wolsey fell from power before the tower above it was completed, and his intentions for its use are uncertain. The Victorians, who commissioned G.F. Bodley to build the tower over the staircase, were convinced the Founder had intended it as a bell-tower. The base and fenestration of the building are Wolsey's; the beautiful fan-vaulting, the work of William Smith, was added c.1638; and the layout of the staircase was altered by James Wyatt in 1801 at the same time as he was building the great staircase at Fonthill.*

When Cardinal Wolsey fell from power in October 1529, three sides of his magnificent new Oxford College were already almost complete with the exception of the S.E. corner where 'the new steeple' (as his workmen called the tower), which was at once to provide covered access to the old cloisters and a handsome entrance to the Hall, was unhappily far from finished. Christ Church has not the advantage of King's in Cambridge where specific instructions were left in the Founder's will for the completion of his College. What would have been the final form of Wolsey's 'Cardinal College' with its superb chapel on the N. range of the quadrangle, and what the final disposal of the surviving monastic buildings, has led to much speculation. The tower, which remained as an unroofed shell for over a hundred years, was clearly thought by Wolsey to be an essential part of the College, as just before his disgrace the masons were paid overtime to try and complete it before the winter.[1]

The entrance arches and fenestration were in place, but without, as yet, any internal structure within the tower. The design of the windows, shorter by one light on the S. side, suggests that a stone staircase might have been built against this wall mounting to a landing and a second short flight of steps, with a gallery leading through the Tudor entrance door to the large ante-Hall which, at Christ Church, took the place of the usual screens passage. New College and Magdalen both have upstairs halls which are reached by a stairway leading straight up from the quadrangles in a very functional way. King's College and Eton were planned with stair-turrets leading to upstairs halls, libraries and chambers; Eton having seven such turrets or towers in the main quadrant. The Cardinal would certainly not have intended the whole space to be given up to the grand ceremonial approach to Christ Church Hall that Wyatt finally made. It is possible that Wolsey, following earlier precedents in Oxford and Cambridge, intended the upper

---

[1] *Collectania Curiosa*, ed. J. Gutch, Oxford, Clarendon Press (1781), 207. For full transcripts of the accounts cf. above, pp. 206–7.

Fig. 87.   Enlarged detail from portrait of Cardinal Wolsey by Sampson Strong (*c.*1610) showing his college in the background. The staircase tower, seen level with the hall, may have been reduced at this time.

floors of the tower for his muniment room and audit chamber.[2] The turret stair in the S.E. corner of the tower would have provided entirely private access.

After the Cardinal's disgrace, and in spite of his piteous entreaties, his 'poor college in Oxford' went through a critical period. Wolsey had intended to provide a foundation of 167 persons, but only the Dean and a small number of the proposed Canons, the necessary staff of the Priory church then being used as a temporary chapel, were, as yet, in residence. Nevertheless, these persons and the servants to support them had to be provided for, and this provision was grudgingly afforded by the King who had it in mind at first to destroy the Cardinal's college in its entirety. From this course he was dissuaded, and after more than two years of financial anxiety and stringency, Henry consented to reprieve the college and to refound it under the title of 'King Henry VIII's College' with limited funds and no provision for undergraduates. So matters continued until 1545, when the college was again surrendered; and in 1546 it was refounded on a smaller scale, a little over half the number intended by Wolsey. St. Frideswide's having been made a cathedral when the See was moved from Oseney to Oxford in 1545, the new foundation became both a cathedral chapter and an academic college.

---

[2] The earlier muniment and treasury towers generally had stone floors to guard against fire. The unusual size of the staircase tower would have made this difficult unless internal supporting walls were provided. This was the solution arrived at in 1646–8 when the black and white paved floor illustrated by Rowlandson was inserted.

The new Christ Church was lavishly endowed by the King, and could expect a yearly grant of £2,200 with an immediate grant towards necessary building repairs; but all the money was earmarked for the Dean and canons and for maintaining the cathedral. There was no surplus for new building, which largely accounts for the lack of major building activity during the rest of the century.[3] The two main projects undertaken were the extension of the college's boundary wall (paid for by Dr. Tresham) and, in 1578–82, the substitution in stone of the wooden wall erected by Wolsey's masons at the W. end of the truncated Priory church, and the construction of the fine W. window shown in Loggan's engraving.[4] The most noticeable gap in the college's requirements was a proper staircase to the upstairs Hall, the only approach being the stone staircase which led from the kitchens to the ante-Hall, for this had already been constructed by Wolsey's masons. Since funds were perpetually low, no attempt was made to remedy this utilitarian but adequate state of affairs.

It must have been these kitchen stairs that gave way in 1566 under the press of the crowd surging up to see Queen Elizabeth and the court watching plays in the Hall. The Queen sent her surgeon and the Vice-Chancellor to cope with the accident, in which three people were crushed to death while the play went on. The Queen herself did not, of course, go up the back stairs from the kitchen: special arrangements had been made for her to get up into the Hall. The College, according to Wolsey's statutes, had been designed for the reception of the monarch and his eldest son and entourage, and it was first used in this way for Elizabeth's visit in 1566. The whole of the E. range was intended as royal apartments and there were no canons' lodgings there until the 17th century. The royal apartments consisted of several separate chambers which could be thrown together by opening folding doors 'after the manner of Palaces'.[5] These rooms on the upper storey probably opened onto a long gallery on the western side, terminating on the S. by the wall of the staircase tower.

It is not clear whether any direct connection was intended with the Hall from the royal apartments, which were probably planned to be entirely self-contained with their own kitchen, reception chambers and eating rooms. Entertaining the monarch with plays in the Hall would not have been envisaged by Wolsey. This became an essential part of later royal visitations, the blueprint for which was made in Cambridge in 1564 when arrangements for orations, disputations and college plays were laid down for the Queen. The play chosen for Queen Elizabeth by Christ Church was Palamon and Arcyte, with magnificent stage scenery and a royal box on the stage.

The accounts of 1566 show how the college solved the problem of getting the Queen from her upstairs apartments into the Hall when there was no staircase. An opening (which is still visible) was made in the wall at the end of the eastern range and several carpenters worked for eight days to erect an aerial walkway to the Hall, similar to the carpenters' work galleries so popular in Tudor gardens. Women were paid for decorating the wooden supports with garlands and ivy.[6] There was no mention of how the Queen got into the Hall on her return visit in 1592 (beyond the Vice-Chancellor making provision that nobody else should kill themselves on the public stairs), so that

---

[3] Jane E.A. Dawson, 'The Foundation of Christ Church, Oxford and Trinity College, Cambridge in 1546', *Bulletin of the Institute of Historical Research*, lvii (1984), 208, and *History of Oxford University*, ed. James McConica, (1986) iii, Chapter 8.

[4] Christ Church Archives, Disbursement Books, 4 Qr 1581–82: xii.b.24f and 1 Qr 1582–83: xii.b.25 f 15ᵛ, under Reparations intrinsicall.

[5] C. Plummer, *Elizabethan Oxford* (O.H.S. viii, 1887), 123, 177.

[6] W.G. Hiscock, *A Christ Church Miscellany* (1946), 167.

the gallery, which is described as narrow and of fine workmanship, might have been more permanent than the usual external carpenters' gallery structure[7] and have been left in position for the next grand occasion. When the Dean moved into the Deanery in the extended N. end of the E. range, and a canon into the S. end, there must have been considerable alterations in the former royal apartments and the tower door was therefore probably blocked early in the 17th century. Thomas Ravis, who was Dean from 1596–1605, was almost certainly responsible for the new Deanery, and he also tried to make improvements to the hall access by putting up a sloping roof or 'pentie' to cover the entrance and a few years later, in 1609, new lead was laid 'upon two arches over the hall stairs', presumably over this sloping roof over the back stairs entrance to the hall.[8]

It was Brian Duppa, however, who became Dean in 1629, who was to make the real improvements to the Hall staircase. A one-time Fellow of All Souls, the new Dean stood well with Laud and was greatly favoured in royal circles. When Laud became Chancellor of Oxford he was much concerned by the slovenly and neglected condition of many of the chapels, and vigorous efforts were made by the colleges to rectify this abuse. George Garrod, visiting Oxford in 1636, remarked upon the success with which Laud's wishes were carried out.[9] In Christ Church the new Dean and his canons were faced with a peculiarly difficult situation. The cathedral was cold, draughty and dilapidated, with the pavement so uneven that worshippers tripped on the stone. For help Duppa and his enthusiastic Treasurer, Samuel Fell, turned to Inigo Jones's master-mason, Nicholas Stone, whose influence and popularity were then strong in Oxford and the neighbourhood. Stone employed his own skilled craftsmen and some of the regular college workforce to repair the cathedral and make it more suitable for a college chapel. Victorian critics derided as monstrosities the great gates which he devised to shut off the draughty W. end of the cathedral from the Dean and Canons at their daily services, but his efforts brought about a considerable improvement, according to the fashion of the times.[10]

After the work in the cathedral Duppa and Fell set about making improvements in accommodation by undertaking the necessary completion of Peckwater Quadrangle and the virtual rebuilding of the lodgings in Canterbury Quadrangle. The Great Quadrangle, however, still lay desolate, almost as Wolsey's masons had left it, with piles of stones and rubble littering the ground; cattle straying in from the unfenced northern end were often to be seen grazing in what the Cardinal had planned as the grandest show-place in Oxford. The festivities celebrating King Charles's visit in 1636 were conducted without any improvement in the state of the Great Quadrangle or access to the Hall, where he was entertained with the usual plays. This was a shameful contrast to what the King had seen at St. John's where the impressive Canterbury Quadrangle had just been completed by Laud's munificence.

At that time Christ Church, led by the poet William Cartwright, was called 'a nest of singing birds', and it is from these men that we learn much of the hopes and frustrations of the college during Duppa's term of office.[11] They were of course aware that improvements to College buildings, unlike those of the cathedral, could only be paid for by benefactions. The work in Peckwater and Canterbury quadrangles had been

---

[7] Ibid. 166.

[8] Ibid. 207.

[9] A.J. Taylor, 'The Royal Visit of Oxford in 1636', *Oxoniensia*, i (1936), 153.

[10] Christ Church Archives, Disbursements 1631–2 (in Receipt book 1631); Walpole Society Publications, vii, 92; A. Wood, *History and Antiquities of the University of Oxford*, (ed. Gutch), iii, 462.

[11] R.C. Goffin, *Life and Poems by William Cartwright 1611–1643* (1918).

paid for entirely by members of the college, but to provide further funds for the Great Quadrangle the poet feared 'a god must needs be sent'. It was bad luck that the nation had been subscribing for the restoration of St. Paul's and in 1634 Cartwright appealed, in *The Imperfections of Christ Church*,[12] for help for the College:

> Two sacred Things were thought (by judging souls)
> Beyond the Kingdomes Pow'r, Christchurch and Pauls,
> Till, by a light from heaven shewn, the one
> Did gain his second Renovation.
> And some good Star ere long, we do not fear,
> Will guide the Wise to offer some gifts here . . . .
> And if no succour come the Time's not far
> When Twill be thought no College, but a Quar.

The College got its succour in the form of the young Paul Bayning, 2nd Viscount Sudbury, the grandson of a prosperous ship owner, who was one of the founders of the East India Company. When he was 13 his father died possessed of a very large real estate and personal estate of £153,000. Paul was placed under the guardianship of his maternal grandfather, the Earl of Dorset, whose Chaplain Duppa had once been and through whose offices he had been appointed Dean of Christ Church. Paul Bayning was only at Christ Church from 1632–3, but this was the time when Duppa and the College Treasurer, Samuel Fell, were launching the appeal for the restoration programme. In 1638 a list of Benefactors was issued (now lost); Bayning's name would certainly have figured on it, as according to the eulogies[13] written at his death by the Christ Church poets he had already given rich gifts to the library and a considerable sum to the rebuilding of Canterbury and Peckwater quadrangles. Bayning died in 1638 after a journey abroad and, according to Canon Strode, there had already been 'rich legacies in foreign lands assigned'. Another Christ Church poet, Thomas Norgate, applauded his desire to complete Wolsey's intended buildings in his dying legacies as well as in his lifetime:

> For though no Founder of the place, yet must
> We say, thou rays'dst our Buildings out o' the Dust.
> Thou didst bequeath 'em their Nativitie;
> And they doe Glory their New-Birth from Thee.

The new birth would have been the completion of Wolsey's Great Quadrangle, including the N. range, and the cloisters of which elements already existed. Of this plan the staircase tower would form an integral part, being the continuation of the passageway from the quadrangle to the cathedral, and, because the need for an adequate staircase to the Hall was so pressing, it was natural that the work should start here. Cartwright had spoken of 'towers that thunder do provoke', and it was the roofless E. tower that Wood recalled as a child living in Merton Street. A noble fan vault was accordingly erected above the new staircase which was to be a climax for the intended vaulted cloister.

There is some ambiguity about the date at which this fan vault was actually built. Anthony Wood (*History and Antiquities of the University of Oxford*, p. 456) says 'that fair porch

---

[12] MS text, B.L. MS Add. 22602, f.26 b; Bodl. MS Rawl 696, select passages.

[13] A pamphlet, published in 1638, entitled *Death repeal'd by a thankful memorial sent from Christ Church in Oxford celebrating Paule, 1st lord viscount Bayning*.

Fig. 88.   William Smith's fan-vault of *c*.1638. Engraving by T. Malton shortly after Wyatt's alterations to the staircase.

or avenue leading up to it [i.e. the Hall] all most curiously vaulted and supported by one pillar only was built about the year 1630'. Elsewhere (*City of Oxford*, i, p. 192) Wood later states that 'Dr Fell built the arch to depend as it is now', and again 'then for the place where we go up into the Hall which was open on the top and a confused way of building and scarcely any steps, he [Fell] made it with the help of one Smith an artificer of London, who made the arch to depend as it is now'. Other writers have adopted this as a statement that the arch was built when Fell became Dean and have dated it as *c*.1640.

The confusion probably arose because Wood observed Fell's signature in the accounts and assumed that he was signing as Dean, which he became in 1638, rather than as Treasurer, which he had been since 1611. Fell was certainly behind all the building work, and as early as 1634 the Provost of Queen's highly commended him for his skill and contrivance in building, adding that the Dean of Christ Church would not have known how to proceed but for him.[14] George Garrod makes no mention of a new staircase in Christ Church when he visited Oxford in 1636, and the most likely date for the Staircase is 1636–1638.[15] Duppa was Chancellor of Salisbury and very familiar with the graceful central pillar of the chapter-house, which may have suggested to him the 'exquisite arch' supporting the fan-vaulted ceiling. He was also at that time tutor to the young Prince of Wales, and the presence of the Prince of Wales's feathers on the carving is another indication of his connection with the work.

In 1637 Nicholas Stone was once more concerned with Oxford, for he is credited with the design of St. Mary's porch being erected in that year. His advice was doubtless sought by Christ Church on the choice of a mason to carry out their great new project. Wood mentions 'one Smith' as the builder of the fan vault, probably quoting a reference in the Christ Church account books to 'Smith, an artificer of London'. This information is meagre, but there are good reasons for identifying the artificer as William Smith, who was Warden of the Masons' Company in 1640, an office held by Stone himself in 1633 and 1634.[16] Since both men were active on the livery of their guild and must have known each other well, both as people and as craftsmen, it is likely that Stone recommended William Smith to the College, judging him capable of carrying out their work.[17]

There is another very good reason why Christ Church would have made this choice. The Baynings' London home and place of business was in the parish of St. Olave's Hart Street, and in this church they were married, buried and had their children baptised. To this church William Smith also belonged and was commemorated by a tablet on the wall of the S. transept, which recorded his death in 1646 and his standing as a citizen and freemason of London.[18] The Smith tablet was destroyed in the Blitz but the prominent Bayning monument survives. When Laud was Bishop of London, and urging the rehabilitation of London churches, St. Olave's was restored in 1632, and there may have been the same benefactor-craftsman relationship between Bayning and Smith as at Christ Church. To any member of the Bayning family dealing with Paul's last wishes

[14] *The Diary of Thomas Crosfield*, ed. F.S. Boas (1935), 13 Dec. 1634.

[15] Hiscock op.cit. note 6, 201, n.3, says that Wood stated (*Hist. & Ant.* ii, 447) that Fell's work began about the year 1638; but the College accounts (missing until 1640) show that work on the canons' houses began only in 1641. This seems to show that the first part of the building programme was the work on the tower. Payments recorded in the accounts would only be made after the work was finished.

[16] Masons' Co., Warden's Account Book 1620–1706 (MS 5303/1).

[17] Other Smiths have been suggested, but Robert Smith who worked at St. John's died in 1635, and the two John Smiths who worked respectively at Cambridge and on the King's works were pre-eminently carvers and not masons capable of carrying out the Ch. Ch. work.

[18] William Smith married in 1612. His first son William was born in 1619 and his second son Robert in 1620 (*Harlean Soc. Publications: Register Section*, xlvi).

Fig. 89. *Left*: Interior of the Great Western Hall from John Rutter, *An Illustrated History and Description of Fonthill Abbey* (1823). *Right*: The Christ Church Great Staircase and the succession of gothic arches depicted by C.L. Bundt, painter to the King of Prussia in his *Views of the Most Picturesque Colleges in the University of Oxford* (1845).

concerning his College, the choice of a mason with such close connections with their church would surely recommend itself. Paul Bayning's young widow married, only a year after his death, the 5th Earl of Pembroke, whose family had both preceded and succeeded Laud as Chancellors of Oxford.

The erection of a large stone vault as late as 1638 has often been regarded as anachronistic: though other, smaller, stone vaults were being built in college gateways and over the porch at St Mary's at this time, London taste had moved towards the use of plaster rather than stone, and it was a plaster vault which was chosen for the nearly contemporary roof of the Convocation House. Duppa, however, was carrying out Wolsey's plans and would, therefore have to use stone.[19] Recently the walls of the Staircase have been cleaned revealing some interesting marks, which the college mason, Mr. Tony Walker, felt were at just the right height to indicate the platform put up by Smith to work on the fan vault.

When Christ Church became King Charles I's headquarters in the Civil War Parliament met in the Hall and the King received foreign ambassadors there. With the elegant staircase approach now completed, Wolsey's vision of a College which 'excelled not only all colleges of students but also palaces of princes' was beginning to take shape. No further work was undertaken in the Commonwealth, however; the cloister was abandoned, and the timber acquired for the new canonries to complete the N. range of the quadrangle was used for firewood by the Puritans. No written description of the staircase built underneath Smith's fan vault has survived, but it is later illustrated in one of Rowlandson's drawings.[20] This shows a typical wooden staircase of the period rising to a low first-floor level where a new floor paved with the then fashionable black-and-white paving-stones had been constructed to cover the greater part of the surface of the tower, with the exception, as we learn from Williams's plan of 1733, of the passageway into the cloister.[21] To accommodate this floor, three of the windows on the E. face of the tower had been shortened by one light. In 1654 Evelyn described an 'ample hall as one goes up the stairs', and Rowlandson shows it being used as a private dining room.

The staircase was transformed by James Wyatt at the beginning of the 19th century. Malton's print showing the completed work (Fig. 88) is dated February 1802 and it is most likely that the major part of the renovation was undertaken in the Long Vacation of 1801. Wyatt had already worked on Canterbury Quadrangle, fitting out the Old Library rooms, at the Deanery and in the Hall itself before he received the Staircase commission. His son Benjamin was up at Christ Church in 1795, giving him every opportunity to study the College architecture in detail. He was also working on William Beckford's Fonthill Abbey, his most daringly picturesque Gothic fantasy, at the same time. His Christ Church work was merely Gothic fancy-dress by comparison, but the two commissions inspired each other. From Christ Church Wyatt took the hammerbeam roof and fan vaulting to heart in his designs for Fonthill (Fig. 89, left). At both places, in his customary way, he revelled in opening vistas. At Christ Church the wainscotting at the W. end of the Hall[22] had been removed to achieve this and, as seen from Tom Quadrangle, there is a succession of gothic arches leading down to the darkness of the lower kitchen stairway (Fig. 89, right). The entrance to the Hall was changed, the 'ample room' as seen on Rowlandson was sacrificed in order to give the grand sweep up the

[19] The detail of the fan vault was criticized in the *Archaeological Journal*, lxviii (1911), 18, but to support this large span on a single pillar is surely something of a *tour de force*.
[20] *Rowlandson's Oxford* by Gibbs (Arthur Hamilton, 1911): Dr Syntax dines in Christ Church.
[21] William Williams, *Oxonia Depicta* (1735–7).
[22] Ch. Ch. MS Estates, 144, 27.

stairs, and the arches on the windows were raised to give a feeling of additional height as in the Fonthill great staircase.

Wyatt used Taynton stone, and the places where the 17th-century stairs were filled in are clearly visible as being more yellowish than the rest of the Headington stone. Pugin and other Goths greatly admired Wyatt's work on the Hall staircase, which they felt was the right complement to William Smith's survival Gothic, hailing it as a great challenge to work under the last spontaneous manifestation of its art. The staircase tower now combines original Wolsey Gothic (the marks of the masons he used at Whitehall can still be seen on the external spiral staircase),[23] Smith's Laudian Gothic, Wyatt's picturesque Gothic and Bodley's Victorian Gothic. When Gilbert Scott surveyed the cathedral in 1869 and found that the bells were too heavy for the spire he recommended that they should be removed to a new tower above the staircase.[24] The College felt that they were actually piously carrying out the Founder's intentions when Bodley built 'Wolsey's belfry', but it is clear now that Dean Liddell had not even as much information about Wolsey's overall plans as we now have.[25] Lewis Carroll was probably nearer the truth when, in *The Vision of the Three T's*, the Founder returned to view the Victorian restoration of his College and collapsed moaning into Mercury, his betasselled cardinal's hat left floating on the water.

---

[23] R.H.C. Davis, 'Mason's Marks', *O.A. & H.S. Reports* No. 84 (1938), 83.

[24] Ch. Ch. Archives. MS Estates 143, 231: Private Report of George Gilbert Scott on the Cathedral of Christ Church, Oxford.

[25] The term tower (*turris*) and steeple are interchangeable in the Ch. Ch. building accounts, but the Victorians must have taken the reference to the 'new steeple' (i.e. the Staircase tower) as indicating a belfry. The most likely place for Wolsey's bell-tower would have been beside his new chapel as had been proposed for King's College, Cambridge. [But cf. Martin Biddle's different conclusions above, pp. 205–10.]

# St. Frideswide's Monastery: Problems and Possibilities

## By John Blair

SUMMARY

*This final paper reviews the evidence for the Anglo-Saxon minster at Oxford; its churches and cemeteries; the process of the Romanesque rebuilding; and the locations of St. Frideswide's grave and shrine. An early precinct, pre-dating the creation of the town, may have been laid out along the edge of the gravel terrace, its main church sited on a bluff overlooking a now-lost channel of the Thames; possibly it included St. Aldate's church as well as the church on the later Priory site. Radiocarbon evidence shows that the cemetery existed probably by the 9th and certainly by the 10th century; the balance of probability favours the establishment of a minster here in Frideswide's own day. The minster was apparently given to Abingdon Abbey in the early 11th century, re-founded as a house of canons in 1049, and finally reformed as an Augustinian priory c.1120. The Romanesque church and cloister were probably laid out by Prior Robert c.1140–50 (in an extension to the precinct obtained by diverting the town wall) but built in slow stages. The E. cloister range, choir and N.E. chapel existed by 1180, when Frideswide's relics were translated; the canons then took a new decision to build both transepts with W. and E. aisles, producing curious anomalies in the ground-plan as the church was completed during the 1180s and 1190s. The square four-bay N. chapel, possibly part of an ensemble recalling the Holy Sepulchre, housed Frideswide's relics from 1180 onwards; the shrine was moved slightly in 1289, but remained in the N.E chapels until the Dissolution. This location may perpetuate the original grave site on the central axis of the Anglo-Saxon church, which probably lay on the N. side of its Romanesque successor. The replacement or supplementation of pre-Conquest minster churches by Romanesque conventual churches is discussed in the light of this and other cases.*

ACKNOWLEDGEMENTS

This paper owes much to the other contributions and to discussions with their authors. Martin Biddle, Sarah Blair, Ralph Davis, Brian Durham, Richard Gem, Richard Halsey, Richard Morris, Julian Munby, Christopher Scull and David Sturdy read it in draft and made many useful comments. I would especially like to thank David Sturdy for his patience in debating hypotheses which often differ sharply from his own; the disagreements which remain are clear, but amicable.

## OXFORD BEFORE THE TOWN

Oxford was a fortified late Anglo-Saxon town, listed in the Burghal Hidage.[1] Evidence is growing that some of the formally-planned burghal towns existed well before the age of

---

[1] The best summaries of the extensive literature are in E.M. Jope, 'Saxon Oxford and its Region', in D.B. Harden (ed.), *Dark-Age Britain: Studies Presented to E.T. Leeds* (1956), 234–58; T. Hassall, 'Archaeology of Oxford City', in G. Briggs, J. Cook and T. Rowley (eds.), *The Archaeology of the Oxford Region* (1986), 115–34.

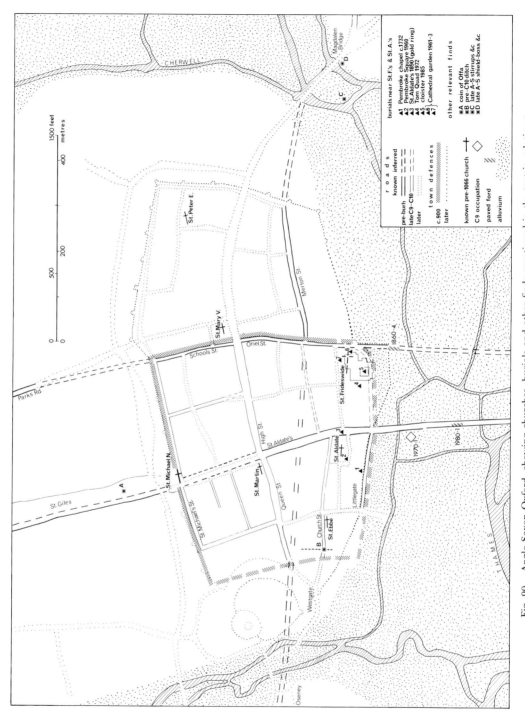

Fig. 90.   Anglo-Saxon Oxford, showing churches, burials and other finds mentioned in the text in relation to possible pre-*burh* features.

Alfred, but not, so far, for Oxford; indeed, such archaeological evidence as we have suggests that the rectilinear grid of streets and the enclosing bank were laid out *de novo* around the year 900.[2] If there was an 8th-century minster on the site of St. Frideswide's, the town must have been established around or beside it: we need to consider the topography of Oxford before Oxford. Fig. 90 shows the street-plan of the *burh*, in so far as it can at present be reconstructed, in relation to possible older features.

The southwards-projecting tongue of the gravel terrace on which Oxford stands is a classic Upper Thames settlement site, likely to have seen human occupation from the Neolithic period onwards. For the same reasons, it is a place where river-crossings and intersections of through-routes can be expected. One W.-E. track, from Wytham and Binsey to Headington and Shotover, crossed the gravel terrace well to the N. of Oxford (above, pp. 6–10 and Fig. 1). The course, and indeed the very existence, of another W.–E. route further S., through the site of the town, remains uncertain. Topographical anomalies, notably the sharp bend of High St. between St. Mary the Virgin (at the presumed original East Gate) and Magdalen Bridge, suggest a drastic re-alignment when the town was laid out. Any earlier route is likely to have been nearer to the edge of the gravel terrace, perhaps (as suggested in Fig. 90) running eastwards from Oseney through the area to the N. of Church St.,[3] following Jury Lane and Merton St., and joining the later road at Magdalen Bridge.[4]

Better-defined are the routes from N. to S. The funnel of St. Giles, where the Woodstock and Banbury roads converge on the North Gate of the town, was to all appearances created for this purpose: before the 10th century these roads, and perhaps others parallel with them, may well have continued southwards to separate Thames crossings.[5] Activity from the 8th century onwards on the line of St. Aldate's, the main crossing and perhaps the original 'oxen-ford', has been demonstrated archaeologically.[6] The northwards continuation of this route, through the site of Oxford and along the Woodstock Road, may explain the coin of Offa found at the Martyrs' Memorial (Fig. 90, site A).[7]

The obvious candidate for a 'pre-town' continuation of the Banbury Road towards the Thames is Parks Road, which can be projected southwards, along Schools St. and Shidyard (now Oriel) St., as an intramural road on the E. side of the primary town. The former existence of a major route here receives strong support from early 12th-century writs allowing the canons of St. Frideswide's to block up an intramural road bordering their precinct and to control a gate in the town wall (below, pp. 236–7): the Parks Road – Oriel St. alignment now stops at the N. boundary of the precinct, but it once continued southwards to a former gate in the wall flanked by the Corpus Christi bastion, due E. of

---

[2] One indication of the date of origin may be the penny of Edward the Elder found lying on primary road metalling in New Inn Hall St. (B. Durham in *C.B.A. Group 9 Newsletter*, x (1980), 158).

[3] Church St. itself cannot be the line of a pre-burghal route, since it crosses a ditch filled by *c*.1000 (below, note 77).

[4] A bridge over the Cherwell ( *(of) cere willa bricga*) existed by 1004 (*Cart. Frid.* i, 8). Two groups of late Anglo-Saxon military equipment (Fig. 90, sites C and D) have been found to the S.W. of Magdalen Bridge: see W.A. Seaby, 'Late Dark Age Finds from the Cherwell and Ray', *Oxoniensia*, xv (1950), 29–43. Another possible line for the early route (albeit through the marshy flood-plain) is slightly further to the S., over Milham bridge and causeway (Wood, *City*, i, 412–14).

[5] David Sturdy (pers. comm.) suggests, on the basis of a detailed analysis of deeds, surveys, maps etc., that there were as many as four medieval N.–S. routes through North Oxford.

[6] B.G. Durham, 'Archaeological Investigations in St. Aldate's, Oxford', *Oxoniensia*, xlii (1977), 83–203; Idem, 'The Thames Crossing at Oxford', *Oxoniensia*, xlix (1984), 57–100. Cf. R.H.C. Davis, 'The Ford, the River and the City', *Oxoniensia*, xxxviii (1973), 258–67.

[7] *Oxoniensia*, xvii–xviii (1952–3), 106 note.

the Priory church (Fig. 92).[8] South of the gate, this road crossed a former river-channel by a paved ford uncovered during building work in 1863 (below, p. 229 and Figs. 91–2). The date of the ford could be anything from Roman to late medieval (in 1266 Henry III ordered a ford below St. Frideswide's Priory to be deepened and dug out),[9] but at least it shows that St. Aldate's was not the only Thames crossing, and need not necessarily have been the oldest.

This evidence suggests a context for St. Frideswide's before the *burh*: on a favoured settlement location, at an intersection of routeways and between two Thames crossings. The prospect of a *burh* established around an older minster church need cause us no problems. In mid to late Anglo-Saxon England, minsters were among the most important foci for urban growth;[10] several Roman towns re-used as *burhs* contained minsters before that re-use took place,[11] as did some other non-Roman burghal sites.[12] In this respect there is a striking resemblance between Oxford and Wareham, which also encapsulates a pre-burghal minster (Lady St. Mary) on the river which forms its southern boundary.[13]

## THE CHURCH IN ANGLO-SAXON OXFORD

Like most large towns in southern and eastern England, Oxford abounded in churches by *c*.1130.[14] This proliferation may be a distinctively post-1050 phenomenon,[15] and the small Oxford churches known to be older were all in a special category, serving the urban *curiae* of substantial rural landlords:[16] St. Martin (Abingdon Abbey),[17] St. Ebbe (Eynsham Abbey),[18] St. Mary the Virgin,[19] and possibly St. Peter-le-Bailey.[20] St. Aldate's, where the case seems rather different, is discussed below (pp. 233–5).

There were also, apart from St. Frideswide's itself, two pre-Conquest churches of

---

[8] The bastion is in the angle between the S. town wall and its return southwards to enclose the E. side of the Priory precinct. Its function to defend a postern is proposed by B. Durham in *C.B.A. Group 9 Newsletter*, xii (1982), 156–9. Shidyard St. still ran to the bastion in 1299, when a house on its E. side was said to be 'at the head of the high altar of St. Frideswide': H.E. Salter, *Survey of Oxford*, i (O.H.S. n.s. xiv, 1960), 212, tenement SE 93.

[9] *Cal. Pat. Rolls 1258–66*, 663.

[10] See for instance J. Campbell, *Essays in Anglo-Saxon History* (1986), 140–6; J. Blair, 'Minster Churches in the Landscape', in D. Hooke (ed.), *Anglo-Saxon Settlements* (1988), 40–50.

[11] E.g. Winchester, Gloucester, Chester.

[12] E.g. Hereford, Wareham.

[13] See plan in *Archaeol. Jnl.* cxl (1983), 53.

[14] For the general context see C.N.L. Brooke, 'The Missionary at Home', *Studies in Church History*, vi (1970), 59–83, and D. Keene, *Survey of Medieval Winchester* (*Winchester Studies*, ii, 1985), ch.5. For histories of individual Oxford churches see *V.C.H. Oxon.* iv, 369–412.

[15] E.g. All Saints: *Oxoniensia*, xxxix (1974), 54–7.

[16] These are most fully discussed by D.A. Sturdy. 'Topography of Medieval Oxford' (unpub. Oxford B.Litt. thesis, 1965), esp. Appendix 6. For parallel cases see M. Biddle (ed.), *Winchester in the Early Middle Ages: an Edition and Discussion of the Winton Domesday* (*Winchester Studies*, i, 1976), 334–5, 340–2.

[17] In 1034 Cnut confirmed to Abingdon land at Lyford (Berks.), with the *monasteriolum* of St. Martin and the adjacent *praediolum* comprising the *haga* or *curia* in Oxford where Æthelwine had lived: *Chronicon Monasterii de Abingdon*, ed. J. Stevenson (Rolls Ser. iia, 1858), i, 439–42.

[18] St. Ebbe's served the *curia* given to Eynsham by its re-founder Æthelmær at the beginning of the 11th century, by which time it was probably already in existence (*Eynsham Cart.*, ed. H.E. Salter, i (O.H.S. xlix, 1906–7), p.viii); it is almost certainly mentioned, though not by name, in Domesday Book (*V.C.H. Oxon.* i, 397).

[19] In 1086 St. Mary's, which belonged to Earl Aubrey's land, had two houses attached to it (*V.C.H. Oxon.* i, 396); the parish later included Littlemore (*V.C.H. Oxon.* iv, 390).

[20] Later claimed as a chapel of the W. Oxfordshire minster church of Bampton (*Curia Regis Rolls*, ii, 143), possibly because it served a *curia* attached to Bampton rectory manor.

greater importance, with entries in Domesday Book which suggest minster status.[21] St. Peter-in-the-East was a wealthy church, with suburban land in Holywell in 1086 and a large extra-mural parish including the chapelries of Wolvercote and St. Cross;[22] its Romanesque crypt includes a late version of the *confessio*, presumably for displaying an important relic.[23] St. Michael-at-the-Northgate, incorporated in the northern defences, had priests with houses in the town in 1086.[24] With its three minsters of St. Frideswide (perhaps originally St. Mary, see p. 235 below), St. Peter and St. Michael, Oxford conforms to the normal pattern of Mercian towns, a distinctive feature of which was the possession of several minsters.[25]

The seniority of St. Frideswide's cannot be taken for granted. By analogy with other burghal towns it might be argued that St. Peter-in-the-East, with its apostolic dedication,[26] is the genuinely early minster, St. Frideswide's being founded in the immediate post-Viking period to house a saint's body translated from some other location. The obvious parallels are the translations of St. Oswald from Bardney to Gloucester and St. Werburgh from Hanbury to Chester, both into new minsters founded by the lady Æthelflæd.[27]

In the case of Frideswide's relics, however, the hagiographical tradition completely fails to support such an interpretation. The later communities at Chester and Gloucester never tried to disguise the source of their relics through false hagiography: they were proud of their acquisitions, and honoured Æthelflæd as a benefactor. The Lives of St. Frideswide, by contrast, locate her activities firmly in Oxford, though with episodes at Bampton and Binsey.[28] The 12th-century belief that her body still lay in her original grave, under the floor of her church (below, p. 247), points in the same direction. It is hard to believe that all memory of a translation of the relics from some rural minster to Oxford, presumably under royal patronage, could have been so totally displaced by a spurious story. The most reasonable interpretation of the evidence is that the historical Frideswide was genuinely associated with a pre-Viking minster at Oxford.[29]

[21] A possible fourth case is the college of St. George in the Castle, for which a pre-Conquest origin has been suggested: see J. Cooper, 'The Church of St. George's in the Castle', *Oxoniensia*, xli (1976), 306–8.

[22] *V.C.H. Oxon.* i, 413, 415; *V.C.H. Oxon.* iv, 398. The church lands comprised the whole township of St. Cross (where there were market-gardeners in 1086), and a small farm at Wolvercote.

[23] *R.C.H.M. Oxford*, 143–7. Excavations inside the church in 1968 revealed a stone church overlying a stone and timber church, which in turn overlay earlier domestic occupation: D. Sturdy pers. comm., and *Oxoniensia*, xxxvii (1972), 245.

[24] B. Durham, C. Halpin and N. Palmer, 'Oxford's Northern Defences', *Oxoniensia*, xlviii (1983), 14–18, 33–5; *V.C.H. Oxon.* i, 397.

[25] A useful recent discussion of this phenomenon is in A.M. Pearn [Bennett], 'The Origin and Development of Urban Churches and Parishes: a Comparative Study of Hereford, Shrewsbury and Chester' (unpub. Cambridge Ph.D., 1988).

[26] Cf. dedications listed R.K. Morris, *The Church in British Archaeology* (C.B.A. Research Rep. xlvii, 1983), 35–8.

[27] A.T. Thacker, 'Chester and Gloucester: Early Ecclesiastical Organisation in Two Mercian Burhs', *Northern History*, xviii (1982), 199–211; these and other translations are also discussed by D. Rollason, 'The Shrines of Saints in Later Anglo-Saxon England', in L.A.S. Butler and R.K. Morris (eds.), *The Anglo-Saxon Church: Papers . . . in Honour of Dr. H.M. Taylor* (C.B.A. Research Rep. lx, 1986), 36–40.

[28] Blair, 'St. F.' If the lives contain any clue to an earlier location of the relics, this can only be Bampton or Binsey. In the case of Bampton, the spurious localisation of miracles in a place 12 miles away, where St. Frideswide's claimed no rights and which had a minster church of its own, would be odd in the extreme (Christopher Hohler's observation, pers. comm.). The simplest and most natural interpretation of the Bampton episode is that it is, in a generalised sense, a true reflection of events in Frideswide's own day, though a posthumous translation of her remains from Bampton to Oxford cannot be completely ruled out as an alternative explanation.

[29] As suggested Blair, 'St. F.', 88–91, where a possible early connection between St. Frideswide's and Eynsham minster is noted.

ST. FRIDESWIDE'S MINSTER, 1002–1139: THE HISTORICAL EVIDENCE

The two earliest references to St. Frideswide's community and relics are almost contemporaneous: the entry *Đonne resteð Sancta Fryðeswyð on Oxnaforda* in the early 11th-century resting-place list,[30] and Æthelred II's charter of 1004 making reparation for the burning, two years previously, of 'a certain minster situated in the town called Oxford where the most blessed Frideswide rests' (*monasterium quoddam in urbe situm que Oxenford appellatur ubi beatissima Frid' requiescit*).[31] It is generally assumed that St. Frideswide's was at this date a house of canons, though in fact the text leaves unclear the nature of the community which the *monasterium* housed.

According to a narrative in the Priory's late medieval Cartulary, 'this church with its possessions was given to a certain abbot of Abingdon by a certain king' before the Norman Conquest; the canons were driven out, and the monks enjoyed their possessions 'for a few years' (*per annos aliquot*).[32] Another, apparently independent, narrative tells the same story: the original nuns were succeeded by secular clerks, and when these had been expelled because of their laxity (*ob eorum insolentiam*) the monks of Abingdon held everything for some time (*per aliquot tempora*), and were later suspected of having stolen Frideswide's bones.[33] That this tradition may have some substance is suggested by the note *[F]reoðeswyðe [uirg]inis* which appears under 19 October (the traditional date of Frideswide's death) in an early to mid 11th-century martyrology from Abingdon Abbey, the earliest known reference to the saint in any liturgical text.[34]

The Abingdon episode, then, must be taken seriously. The minster could have been reformed in the late 10th century as a cell of Abingdon, though if so it is odd that Æthelred's charter makes no reference to the fact, and survives in the St. Frideswide's rather than the Abingdon archive. It seems more likely that St. Frideswide's still housed canons in 1002–4, and was annexed to Abingdon for some probably quite brief period during the reigns of Cnut or his successors. If the Abbey lost all rights over it before the Conquest, the absence of any reference in the Abingdon Cartulary is not particularly surprising.

The St. Frideswide's Cartulary narrative goes on to say that by the beneficence of a certain king the canons' property was restored to them.[35] This statement makes sense of an otherwise puzzling annal for 1049 in an early 14th-century Rochester chronicle, noting the 'institution of canons' at St. Frideswide's.[36] The 'Monastic Reform' was not an exclusively one-way process: monks' property could sometimes revert to clerks, and early 11th-century kings and nobles saw nothing wrong in re-founding minsters for the benefit of communities of canons, sometimes following the Rule of St. Chrodegang.[37] It

[30] F. Liebermann, *Die Heiligen Englands* (Hannover, 1889), No. 46; D.W. Rollason, 'Lists of Saints' Resting-Places in Anglo-Saxon England', *Anglo-Saxon England*, vii (1978), 65, 93.

[31] *Cart. Frid.* i, No. 2.

[32] *Cart. Frid.* i, No. 3.

[33] Blair, 'St. F.', 117.

[34] Corpus Christi College, Cambridge, MS 57; see M.R. James, *A Descriptive Catalogue of the MSS in the Library of Corpus Christi College, Cambridge*, i (1912), 118. Michael Lapidge notes (pers. comm.): 'The entry for Frideswide has been copied in the left-hand margin by an Anglo-Saxon scribe (i.e. writing Anglo-Saxon minuscule), datable on palaeographical grounds to the middle of the 11th century, not I think later.' I am very grateful to Alan Thacker for drawing my attention to this important piece of evidence.

[35] *Cart. Frid.* i, No. 3.

[36] B.L., MS Cotton Nero D.2 f.98 (printed *Flores Historiarum*, ed. H.R. Luard, i (Rolls Ser. xcva, 1890), 568): *Eodem etiam anno institutio canonicorum Sancte Fredeswide de Oxonia*. This MS is a version of the standard *Flores Historiarum*, but the only one to contain the St. Frideswide's entry.

[37] For other cases see J. Blair, 'Secular Minster Churches in Domesday Book', in P.H. Sawyer (ed.), *Domesday Book: a Reassessment* (1985), 120–3.

is perfectly possible that St. Frideswide's had reverted to the crown, and that Edward the Confessor restored it in 1049 as a house of canons. Domesday Book shows 'the canons of St. Frideswide' holding their land in King Edward's day and in 1086.[38] Both the Cartulary narrative and Henry I's 'foundation charter' for the Augustinian community say that the minster had pertained to the king's chapel,[39] which suggests that it was among those regarded by the early 12th century as 'royal free chapels'.[40]

After 1100 royal minsters became prime candidates for re-foundation as houses of Augustinian canons, support for whom centred on Henry I's court.[41] The Cartulary narrative describes Henry's gift of St. Frideswide's to his chaplain Master Wimund, who ejected the seculars and gathered regular canons there (evidently from Holy Trinity Aldgate).[42] William of Malmesbury, a first-hand witness, says that 'only a few clerks remained there, who lived as they pleased, so Roger bishop of Salisbury gave the place to Wimund, a canon of excellent learning and no mean holiness'.[43] These stories are not necessarily incompatible, since Roger could have organised the reform of this royal minster as viceroy rather than as a private patron. But he seems to have had some previous involvement in the management of its endowments, for in 1113 × 16 he exchanged parcels of land beside St. Frideswide's church with Abbot Faritius of Abingdon.[44] The context for the reform of the minster is clearly the court circle to which Roger, Faritius (formerly Henry I's physician) and Wimund all belonged.

Wimund's canons were probably installed c.1120,[45] and received a royal confirmation then or soon afterwards.[46] They did not, however, escape from Roger of Salisbury: despite two vice-regal writs in which he protected their property, he found it necessary as he lay dying in 1139 to restore 'whatever I had taken from them unjustly'.[47]

[38] V.C.H. Oxon. i, 397, 409; V.C.H. Bucks. i, 243. The Oxfordshire entries lack T.R.E. data, but the entry for the Buckinghamshire manor of Over Winchendon notes the canons' tenure T.R.E.

[39] Cart. Frid. i, Nos. 4–5.

[40] Cf. Blair op. cit. note 37, 137; J.H. Denton, 'Royal Supremacy in Ancient Demesne Churches', Jnl. Ecclesiastical Hist. xxii (1971), 289–302. It may well be significant that Wolverhampton, another 'royal free chapel', was also appropriated by Roger of Salisbury (below, note 49).

[41] See Blair op. cit. note 37, 138, and J.C. Dickinson, The Origins of the Austin Canons and their Introduction into England (1950), which includes (pp. 113–15) an earlier discussion of the re-foundation of St. Frideswide's.

[42] Cart. Frid. i, No. 4. For Wimund, about whom we know nothing else for certain, see D. Knowles, C.N.L. Brooke and V. London, The Heads of Religious Houses (1972), 180. The evidence for colonisation from Aldgate is that house's own chronicle: see The Cartulary of Holy Trinity Aldgate, ed. G.A.J. Hodgett (London Record Soc. vii, 1971), 2, 228.

[43] Gesta Pontificum Anglorum, ed. N.E.S.A. Hamilton (Rolls Ser. lii, 1870), 316.

[44] Chron.Ab. op.cit. note 17, ii, 76 (RG, ii, No. 1128): a ratification by Henry I of this exchange.

[45] The canons' traditional foundation date of 1122 first occurs in the 15th-century Cartulary narrative (Cart. Frid. i. No. 4; another 15th-century copy of this text is in B.L. MS Harl. 79 f.1ᵛ). However, in the early 13th century Malmesbury's narrative was re-worked by Roger of Wendover as an annal for 1111 (Flores Historiarum, ed. H.O. Coxe, ii (1841), 188; Matthew Paris copies this (Matthæi Parisiensis . . . Historia Anglorum, ed. F. Madden, i (Rolls Ser. xliva (1866) 215–16). If Wimund reigned as prior for 19 years, as stated by Cart. Frid. i, No. 4, he must have been installed by 1120, since he was dead by 1139 (Oseney Cartulary, ed. H.E. Salter, ii (O.H.S. xc, 1929), No. 794). In 1122 the house subscribed to the bede-roll of Vitalis abbot of Savigny in the form T[itulus] Sanctae Trinitatis et Sanctae Fridesvidae Oxinefordensis, which it would scarcely have done if the house had not already been regularised (A. Clapham, 'Three Bede-Rolls', in Memorial Volume to Sir Alfred Clapham: Archaeol. Jnl. cvi suppl. (1952), 49). Henry I's three 'foundation charters', Cart. Frid. i, Nos. 5–7 (RG, ii, Nos. 1342–3, 1345), can only be dated by the witnessing of the chancellor Ranulf (1107–23). The precise dates of Augustinian foundations are often far from clear-cut, and in this case it is possible that Wimund held the minster for some time as a royal clerk before colonising it from Aldgate.

[46] Cart. Frid. i, No. 5.

[47] E.J. Kealey, Roger of Salisbury (1972), document Nos. 12, 17, 29, 30, 31. Cf. comments in ibid., p. 122, on Roger's ambiguous relations with St. Frideswide's.

Roger was a great architectural patron,[48] whose patronage may well have benefited St. Frideswide's; but he was also a minster pluralist in the time-honoured tradition of Spirites, Regenbald and Ranulf Flambard, in this respect a distinctively 11th-century figure.[49] After 1139 the canons, freed from his clutches, were ruled by a new and scholarly prior, in all respects a distinctively 12th-century figure: Master Robert of Cricklade.[50] Despite the civil war which came to their very doors, the early 1140s must have seemed to offer them a fresh start.

## THE TOPOGRAPHY OF THE MINSTER PRECINCT

### The configuration of the site

The S. edge of the *burh* corresponds roughly with that of the gravel terrace. West of St. Aldate's the line of Church Street marks a natural break of slope, from which the gravel slopes gently downwards to the S. (from 60.60 m. to 54.27 m. O.D.) into the marshy floodplain over which the Dominican Friary was built in the 13th century.[51] On this side of the town, therefore, there was no abrupt drop from the gravel terrace to the Thames.[52]

The configuration of the terrace-edge to the E. of St. Aldate's, where St. Frideswide's Priory stands, seems to have been rather different. Natural gravel has been located under the cloister at 59.40 m. O.D. (Fig. 17), and under the Latin Chapel and E. end of the N. choir aisle at 58.90 m. (Figs. 38, 42).[53] While the natural surface of the gravel did not survive in any of these exposures, and had evidently been lowered slightly under the N.E. chapels,[54] it is clear enough that the church and cloister occupy an essentially flat expanse of gravel. From the N. wall of the S. range, however, the modern ground-level falls southwards from 59.50 m. O.D. in the cloister walk to 58.35 m. at the N. wall of the Meadows Building (see section at bottom of Fig. 92). Excavations for the foundations of that building in 1863 revealed that the ground had been made up over a much more dramatic fall of level (Figs. 91–2). The clerk of works in charge of the project reported removing made ground to a depth of *c.* 20 ft.; further N.,

[48] R.A. Stalley, 'A Twelfth-Century Patron of Architecture', *J.B.A.A.* 3rd ser. xxxiv (1971), 62–83.

[49] Kealey op. cit. note 47, Nos. 26, 27, 28, shows that he had also appropriated prebends at Salisbury, the royal minster at Wolverhampton and the recently-reformed minster at Cirencester. For the annexation of minsters by earlier generations of royal clerks see Blair op. cit. note 37, 132–8; Campbell op. cit. note 10, 149–51.

[50] Blair, 'St. F.', 80, notes 8–9. Robert came from the Augustinian house at Cirencester, which had lately been controlled by Roger of Salisbury (see note 49); he may have come to Oxford at Roger's instigation.

[51] Natural gravel has been observed at 60.60 m. on the N. frontage of Church St. (*Oxoniensia*, xxxvi (1971), 5); at 59.22 m. (with ploughsoil) on the city wall line just S. of the W. end of Church St. (Ibid. xxxv (1970), 17); at 58.55 m. (with topsoil) at Littlegate 60 m. S. of St. Ebbe's church (Ibid. xxxvii (1972), 144); and at 53.80 to 54.27 m. (under alluvium) in an area around 200–300 m. S. of St. Ebbe's church, on the Blackfriars site, where it is interpreted as marsh rather than river-channel (Ibid. l (1985), 135. For the topography of this area see T.G. Hassall et al., 'Excavations in St. Ebbe's: Part i', *Oxoniensia*, liv (1989, forthcoming), where the N.–S. section illustrated as Fig. 3 may be compared with the present Fig. 92.

[52] An observation made by David Sturdy in 1957 indicates that St. Ebbe's church overlies the fill of 'a small stream which cut deeply into the edge of the gravel terrace' (Sturdy op. cit. note 16, i, 81; Sturdy informs me that the stream ran S.W.). However, the terrace has been observed to the S. of this (see note 51).

[53] Above, pp. 81, 87. Sturdy's observation of natural gravel in Cuttings **1** and **2E** at 2.10 m. below the Latin Chapel floor (61.00 m O.D.), and in Cutting **5** at 1.70 m. below modern ground-level in the angle between the choir and N. choir aisle (60.60 m O.D.), can both be calculated at 58.90 m. O.D.

[54] Sturdy found somewhat modified loamy topsoil in Cutting **5** (above, p. 88: **5**.4); but the gravel which it overlay was 50 cm. below the gravel observed in the cloister, and since a natural downwards slope from S. to N. is unlikely the topsoil in Cutting **5** was probably redeposited after a lowering of the gravel surface.

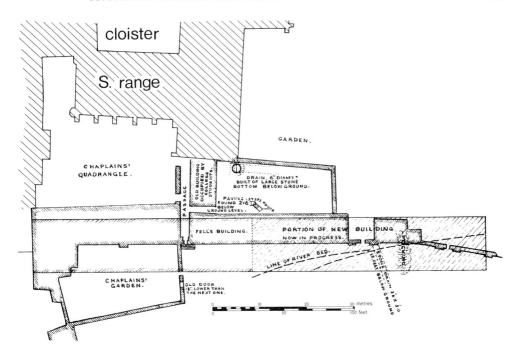

Fig. 91. Discoveries made during the construction of Christ Church Meadows Building, 1863: Conradi's plan (from *Proc. Oxford Archit. and Hist. Soc.* n.s. i (1860–4), opp. p. 218), with scale and outline of cloister and S. range added.

when digging about 2 ft. 6 in. below the present level of the ground I noticed some paving (Bladon stone) . . . and five steps leading down from the level of the paving, about 3 ft. 3 in. in the direction as shewn on the plan. At the foot of these steps a space about 5 ft. long and as wide as the steps (viz. 2 ft. 9 in.) was paved, forming a landing, and enclosed in front by a well-worked stone 8 in. high. From here a piece of masonry was carried along parallel with the line of Fell's Building . . . . [F]arther east, at the depth of nearly 20 ft., we had to remove made-up soil before we came to solid ground. The very mud we removed contained several matters of interest . . . . When we removed the last layer of this made-up soil the water rushed in . . . . From all circumstances connected, and from the section of our digging, there cannot be much doubt that we had come upon one of the old river beds or ditches on the outside of the old city wall. . . . About twenty-five yards from where we found the steps, and sixteen feet below the present ground, we came upon a large, well-constructed drain, 3 ft. 6 in. wide and 3 ft. high. . . . Between this drain and the east end wall of our Building we found some rough pitching right across the river bed, and on one side a large curb-stone . . .; and the first glance upon the curb-stone tells one that for a considerable time it had stood wear and tear from carts and other vehicles.[55]

A river-channel (surviving residually as the Trill Mill Stream) is indeed the obvious explanation. If the pitched-stone ford was 16 feet below present ground-level it lay at *c.* 53.30 m. O.D. – exactly the level of the late Anglo-Saxon paved ford found at the St.

[55] Mr. Conradi in *Proc. Oxford Archit. and Hist. Soc.* n.s. i (1860–4), 218–19 and figure opposite 218. The accumulation of material found in this operation (itemised Ib., 222 note) was not excavated stratigraphically, and included human bones, late medieval worked stonework, pottery, and 'portions of encaustic tiles, fourteenth century'; among the latter were presumably the tiles reported on above, p. 110, and below, pp. 259–63.

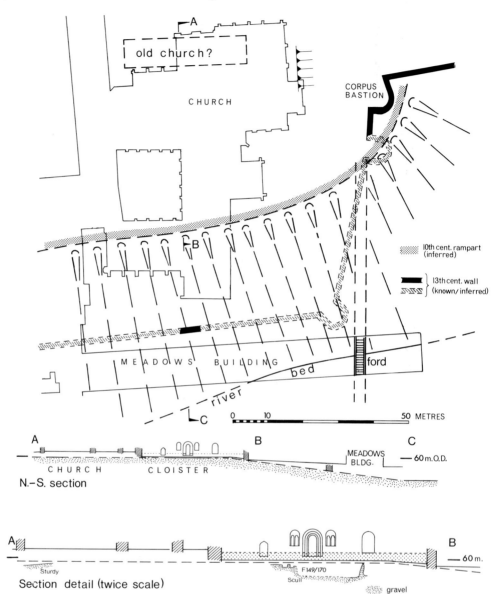

Fig. 92. *Above*: Suggested natural configuration of the Priory site, incorporating data from Fig. 91 (inferred line of later city wall after B. Durham). *Below*: Sketch sections from N. to S. through the church, cloister and Meadows Building site, showing the fall in levels from the S. range to the river-bed, and the late 12th-century levelling down of the cloister. Natural gravel encountered by Sturdy further E., in the Latin Chapel, is projected onto the section.

Aldate's crossing in 1981;[56] the alluvial deposits found outside the S.W. corner of Tom Quadrangle, and under Merton Grove,[57] may have been fill-layers in the same channel. There are also indications that the edge of the gravel terrace curves back northwards on the E. side of the Priory. Under the end wall of the choir the gravel surface steps down (presumably artificially) by about a metre from W. to E. (above, pp. 87–90 and Fig. 42); further eastwards the modern level falls appreciably, and 60 m. N.N.E. of the cathedral, in Corpus Christi quadrangle, loam has been observed to a depth of 4 m. below the modern surface without any exposure of natural gravel.[58]

What emerges from this evidence is that the configuration of the site, now softened after centuries of alluviation, dumping and levelling,[59] was originally more dramatic. On the S. and S.E., the ground fell from the cloister to the river-bed by 6 metres across a distance of some 40 metres; any Anglo-Saxon church on the site would have appeared from the river to be raised up on a bluff or promontory, especially if the channel curved around its E. side. Some major Anglo-Saxon ritual monuments, both pagan and Christian, were deliberately placed on headlands and promontories overlooking water;[60] could St. Frideswide's minster have been among them?

*The precinct, cemeteries and churches*

At the time of the Augustinian reform the precinct was in the extreme S.E. corner of the walled town, bounded by an intramural road (below, p. 236), and there is every reason to suppose that this relationship had persisted since the original laying-out of the *burh* (cf. Fig. 94). The Oxford Danes who fled to the minster in 1002 to escape the citizens must have been inside rather than outside the wall, and Æthelred's charter in any case describes it as *in urbe situm*.[61] The early 12th-century Life of St. Frideswide ('Life A') says that her monastery was founded *in urbe Oxinefordia*, a phrase which Robert of Cricklade ('Life B') re-casts as *infra urbis ambitum*.[62]

One of Sturdy's reasons for not believing that the 12th-century Priory occupies an earlier monastic site is what he claims to be evidence that it lies outside the 10th-century town: the lack of material remains, 'coupled with the prospect that the site lies outside the Saxon defences, requires us to consider other locations for the church that housed Frideswide's relics in about the year 1000' (above, p. 91). But given that the bank and ditch must have run S. of an urban *curia* including St. Ebbe's church (above, p. 224), and given too that the 13th-century town wall between Westgate and Littlegate was found at one point to overlie earlier domestic occupation,[63] Sturdy's proposed line for the

---

[56] Durham 1984 op. cit. note 6, 84, Fig. 14.

[57] D. Sturdy, 'Recent Excavations in Christ Church and Nearby', *Oxoniensia*, xxvi/xxvii (1961/2), 20–25; T.G. Hassall, 'Excavations in Merton College', Ibid. xxxvi (1971), 34–48.

[58] *Oxoniensia*, xxxviii (1973), 273–5. In 1989, excavation by A. Millard and the OUAS against the Corpus boundary wall, due E. of the N.E. corner of the Latin Chapel, augured to a depth of 57.71 m.O.D. without reaching gravel.

[59] As Sturdy points out (above, pp. 76–7), the sharp fall at the edge of the terrace has been much reduced by massive levelling-down in Tom Quadrangle and the roadway outside.

[60] Cf. M. Biddle, 'Archaeology, Architecture and the Cult of Saints in Anglo-Saxon England', in Butler and Morris op. cit. note 27, 22: 'The crypt at Repton . . . stands on a bluff above the River Trent . . . the king was buried overlooking the floodplain in just such a way as the dying Beowulf instructed Wiglaf (!) to build his memorial mound on a promontory by the sea.' Minsters seem to have been built on the N. banks of river-channels with a remarkable frequency (the early Northumbrian monasteries of Jarrow, Monkwearmouth, Bywell and Seaham, for instance). The point is well made by R. Morris, *Churches in the Landscape* (1989), 111–12.

[61] *Cart. Frid.* i, No. 2.

[62] Blair, 'St. F.', 96, 104.

[63] *Oxoniensia*, xxxvii (1972), 141–3; Hassall op. cit. note 51.

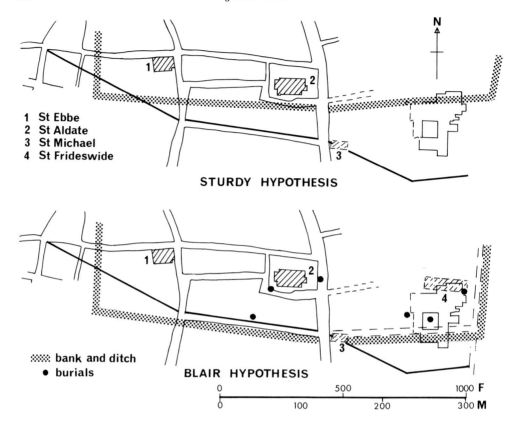

Fig. 93.   The S. side of Anglo-Saxon Oxford: two hypotheses. (For the burials cf. Fig. 90 and p. 223.)

original southern defence is surely too far to the N. (see the two versions in Fig. 93). The only evidence for it is the slight depression in the natural gravel (falling only 20 cm. from S. to N. across the width of the Latin Chapel) encountered in the 1963 excavations (above, p. 78 and Figs. 36, 38), which seems far too slight to be interpreted as a defensive ditch. In the light of the abrupt drop into a river-channel immediately S. of the cloister, common-sense suggests that the builders of the town would have taken advantage of the topography by scarping the natural river-bank and building a wall or bank along its top, leaving the Priory site on the inner side.[64] Sturdy's trenches were too small, and the site too disturbed, for his failure to find Anglo-Saxon structures to have any weight as negative evidence. Given the 9th- to 10th-century burials, and the early 11th-century floor-tile, described elsewhere in these reports, it seems perverse to entertain serious doubts that the Augustinian Priory stands on the site of its predecessor.

If the minster existed before the town, then so, presumably, did some kind of monastic precinct. Analogy with other minsters suggests that this precinct was probably

[64] Exactly this conclusion is reached by Hassall et al. op.cit. note 51 in relation to the southern defense further W.: 'Either there was no S. rampart in St. Ebbe's and the Trill Mill Stream was considered a sufficient obstacle, or alternatively the rampart followed the N. bank of the stream'.

larger than the premises of the 12th-century canons.[65] Hints – no more – pointing in this direction come from finds of human burials, and from possible relationships between St. Frideswide's and other churches on the southern edge of the town.

Graves from a large cemetery earlier than the Romanesque buildings have been found by Scull, Hassall and Sturdy (Figs. 14–15, 90, 93–4). Scull's excavation in the cloister found sequences of up to four superimposed burials, yielding calibrated radiocarbon dates which prove that the cemetery existed certainly by the 10th and probably in the 9th century (above, pp. 60–2 and Table 9). The two burials on beds of charcoal found by Hassall in the N.E. corner of Tom Quadrangle also appear (though on less stringent radiocarbon evidence) to have been 9th- or 10th-century.[66] In the cloister only the latest (i.e. 12th-century) graves included burials in stone cists, which seems elsewhere to be a distinctively 12th-century practice (above, p. 63); the similar cist-graves found by Sturdy are therefore probably quite late, only slightly earlier than the walls of the Romanesque E. end which cut through them (above, p. 91 and Figs. 42–3).

For topographical reasons the cemetery presumably cannot have extended much further to the S. or E., but its westwards limit is unknown; at least one other grave has been found in Tom Quadrangle.[67] Anglo-Saxon minsters sometimes had enormous cemeteries, later invaded by urban development;[68] some finds of stray burials are worth considering in this context, even though they are a long way W. of the Priory church and on the other side of the main road (Figs. 90, 93). It is hard to know what to make of the 'great Numbers of human Skeletons . . ., some 16 Feet deep, many with their Feet inverted to the South', which were found while digging the vault under Pembroke College chapel in 1732.[69] Christian-orientated burials have, however, been found by Pembroke College gate;[70] more important, a burial in a stone coffin under the road on the E. side of St. Aldate's churchyard, opposite Tom Gate,[71] was accompanied by an elaborate 11th-century plaited gold finger-ring (below, pp. 263–6 and Fig. 104).

St. Aldate's church is first mentioned (as *monasterium quoddam Sancti Aldadi episcopi venerationi consecratum*) in the second quarter of the 12th century, when it was held in equal halves by a priest named Nicholas and by two brothers and 'clerks of the town', Robert and Gilbert.[72] This pattern of ownership, characteristic in the late 11th and early

---

[65] See Blair op. cit. note 10, 48–50.

[66] T.G. Hassall, 'Excavations at Oxford, 1972', *Oxoniensia*, xxxviii (1973), 270–4. (For calibrations of the radiocarbon dates from these burials see above, p. 61 Table 9.)

[67] *Proc. Oxford Archit. and Hist. Soc.* n.s. i (1860–4), 220.

[68] Cf., most dramatically, Aylesbury: D. Allen and C.H. Dalwood, 'Iron Age Occupation . . . Aylesbury, 1981', *Records of Bucks.* xxv (1983), 1–8.

[69] A. Wood, *The Antient and Present State of the City of Oxford*, ed. J. Peshall (1773), addenda p. 29. ('In digging the Vault of Pembroke College', which probably refers to the chapel, built 1732.)

[70] *Oxoniensia*, xxv (1960), 134.

[71] The burial must, therefore, have lain almost directly opposite the E. end of St. Aldate's church, a position likely to have been an especially honorific one (Martin Biddle's observation). Burials in stone coffins are rare before the 12th century, and given the opulence of the finger-ring this one must have been of high status.

[72] *Chron. Ab.* op.cit. note 17, ii, 174–5. According to this narrative the brothers became monks at Abingdon *temp.* Abbot Ingulf (1130–59), taking their half of the church with them, but the canons of St. Frideswide's obtained Nicholas's half by trickery in the early 1150s. 'Half of St. Aldate's church' appears in Henry I's charter (*Cart. Frid.* i, No. 5), but since it is absent from the earliest papal confirmations this must (applying the argument of p. 5 note 12 above) be dismissed as an interpolation. Probably the first genuine reference in the St. Frideswide's material is in a papal confirmation of 1158 (*Cart. Frid.* i, No. 23), where it appears as *quicquid habetis in ecclesia Sancti Aldati*; this would be consistent with the Abingdon story if the canons acquired their half of the church 1154 × 8. However, Eugenius III confirmed St. Aldate's to Abingdon (*Chron. Ab.* ii, 192, 196). Properties between St. Aldate's church and the city wall later paid rents to Abingdon, to St. Frideswide's or to the church itself, suggesting that this block had been divided between the two monasteries (Sturdy op. cit. note 16, ii, 42).

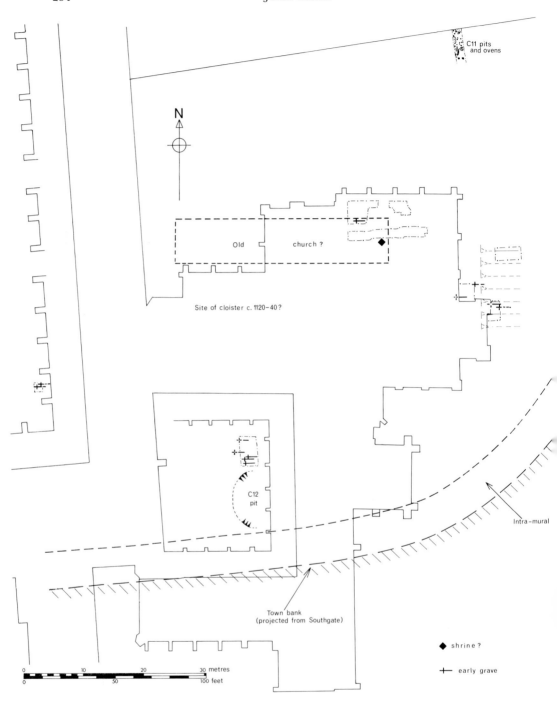

Fig. 94. The site before the Romanesque buildings, showing projected intra-mural road and known pre-Priory burials.

12th centuries of ex-minster property appropriated by individual canons,[73] may be a clue that St. Aldate's had once belonged to the community at St. Frideswide's.

It is becoming increasingly clear that important minsters often, perhaps usually, had two or more churches, and that these were frequently set out on axial alignments.[74] If, as suggested below (pp. 239, 250), the Anglo-Saxon minster stood on the site of the N. transept and N.E. chapels of the Priory church, St. Aldate's, and St. Ebbe's further W., would lie on much the same topographical axis, on the crest of the scarp but not in conformity with the main street-axes of the town (Figs. 90, 93). The early 12th-century Life of St. Frideswide mentions an 'original' dedication to the Holy Trinity, St. Mary and All Saints, possibly a garbled memory of two or three churches of which St. Mary's, where the saint was believed to have been buried, was the predecessor of the Priory church.[75]

The possibility raised by this line of argument is that the S. side of pre-urban Oxford consisted of a large ecclesiastical precinct, traversed by the two N.–S. routes and containing two or more churches[76] aligned along the terrace-edge. The S.E. and E. sides of this precinct would have been defined by the natural topography; its northern boundary could be the early W.–E. route proposed above (p. 223), while a possible candidate for its western boundary is the ditch found to the W. of St. Ebbe's church across the line of Church Street, filled in by the 10th century (Fig. 90, site B).[77] The constraints imposed upon the subsequent planners of the *burh* by their need to respect this established enclosure would be complex, and may explain why the topography of the S. half of the town seems so much less regular than that of its N. half.

### The early 11th-century church

St. Frideswide's seems to have been one of the relatively few major churches rebuilt under royal patronage in the early 11th century.[78] Æthelred II's charter says that the minster was 'renewed by me and mine' (*a me et a meis constat renovata*) after the burning of the Danes in 1002,[79] and 12th-century tradition ascribed to him the church inherited by the first Augustinian canons. William of Malmesbury says that 'the sanctuary was purified by the king's repentance and the monastery restored',[80] and Robert of Cricklade adds that Æthelred 'enlarged the perimeter of the basilica' (below, p. 247). Malmesbury believed that the pre-1002 church had had a tower, in which the Danes hid,[81] and miracle stories of the 1170s mention a tower which may have survived from the pre-Augustinian buildings (below, p. 248). Such analogies as we have suggest a church on the model of St. Mary's at Dover, with aisleless nave, central tower and N., S. and E. *porticus*.[82]

---

[73] Cf. Blair op. cit. note 37, 127–31.

[74] See Blair, 'St. F.', 89 note 46, and the examples discussed on pp.257–8 below.

[75] Blair, 'St. F.', 89.

[76] It is not impossible that St. Ebbe's is also an early church; but its recorded history is very different, and see note 52 above.

[77] *Oxoniensia*, xxxvi (1971), 3–6; Hassall et al. op.cit. note 51.

[78] Cf. R.D.H. Gem, 'A Recession in English Architecture during the Early 11th Century', *J.B.A.A.*, 3rd ser. xxxviii (1975), 32.

[79] *Cart. Frid.* i, No. 2.

[80] Loc. cit. note 43.

[81] *De Gestis Regum Anglorum*, ed. W. Stubbs, i. (Rolls Ser. xca, 1887), 213.

[82] See R. Gem, 'Church Architecture in the Reign of King Æthelred', in D. Hill (ed.), *Ethelred the Unready* (B.A.R. British Ser. 59, 1978), 105–14.

What architectural changes, if any, resulted from the grant to Abingdon Abbey and the re-foundation in 1049 is unknown. The only pre-Conquest ecclesiastical object so far recorded from the site is a relief-decorated floor-tile, the best artistic parallels for which are provided by pennies of the late 1030s(below, pp. 259–63 and Figs. 102–3). Such tiles have been found exclusively on late Anglo-Saxon monastic and cathedral sites, including Coventry where they may be associated with work of Leofric and Godiva in the 1040s. The Oxford tile provides a hint of high-level patronage at a similar date.

## THE AUGUSTINIAN PRIORY BUILDINGS

### The formation of the Augustinian precinct

Changes to the environs of St. Frideswide's during the first half of the 12th century are implied by a series of royal documents, the earliest of which is a writ of Henry I allowing the canons 'to enclose the road next the wall and the wall of Oxford itself, as far as their land extends, for the enlargement of their yard' (ut includant viam iuxta murum et ipsum murum de Oxenn', quantum terra sua extenditur, ad incrementum orti sui).[83] This writ (witnessed by Roger of Salisbury and William d'Albini) cannot be dated closely and may even be addressed to the pre-Augustinian community, but its most probable context is the creation of a precinct for the first Augustinians.[84] Henry I's 'foundation charter' (before 1123) confirms the licence to enclose the road by the wall, and further allows the canons to 'enclose or block all gates of the whole Priory' (do eis viam iuxta murum civitatis Oxenf' quantum extenditur terra eorum; et volo quod predicti canonici eandem viam includant, et concedo quod iidem canonici claudere possint vel obstruere omnes portas totius prioratus).[85]

An unmistakable implication of these texts is that the pre-1122 minster was bounded on the S. or E. side, or on both, by an intra-mural road (the counterpart of St. Michael's St. on the N. side of Oxford, and characteristic of burghal towns generally) along which traffic passed. The canons were to absorb this road and cut off all access to it, creating a fully-enclosed precinct. What seems to be archaeological evidence for the same operation, but defining the N. side of the precinct, was found by Sturdy's 1961 trench on the N. side of the Cathedral Garden: dense 11th- to early 12th-century occupation features comprising post-holes, pits and kilns were overlain in the early to mid 12th century by a boundary wall with a new road on its outer side (compare Fig. 94 with Fig. 97).[86] It may have been because the intra-mural roads along the E. and S. sides of the precinct had been closed off that this new road, outside its N. boundary, was needed. The environs of the secular minster, surrounded by the traffic and bustle of urban Oxford, required adaptation to the stricter lifestyle of the Augustinians.

That the town wall cramped the canons' precinct somewhat is suggested by the recognition, in 1136 × 40, that they had long enjoyed (ab antiquitate usi sunt) the rights of holding their gate in the city wall within their enclosure built for their use, and of erecting and maintaining buildings over the wall so long as they kept those sections of it in repair (habeant . . . portam suam in muro eiusdem civitatis infra clausum monasterii sui ad

[83] Cart. Frid. i, No. 514 (RG ii, No. 1344).

[84] The exchange in 1113 × 16, between Roger of Salisbury and Abingdon Abbey, of different plots of land by St. Frideswide's church (above, note 44), may be connected with these transactions.

[85] Cart. Frid. i, No. 6 (RG ii, No. 1343).

[86] D. Sturdy, 'Excavations in Christ Church', Oxoniensia, xxvi/xxvii (1961/2), 30–1 and Fig. 8.

*proprium usum suum edificatam, necnon aisiamentum ipsius muri ad superedificandum et eorum edificia sustentandum, ita quod loca per eos superedificata reparent et ad aisias suas reficiant.*[87] The need to have buildings in so inconvenient a position must have been a compelling one; it suggests that the church, the essential focus of the community, already lay very close to the wall (cf. Fig. 94).

The implications of this text contrast with the 13th-century line of the town wall, running south-eastwards from Southgate to pass well to the S. of St. Frideswide's cloister (Figs. 90, 92).[88] Given the evidence for a major change of levels further N., on the line of the S. (refectory) range, it is hard to avoid concluding that the wall still followed this northern line in 1136 × 40, but was later diverted to allow more room on its inner side. Precisely when this diversion occurred is uncertain, but the laying-out of the cloister must have rendered it highly desirable, if not essential. The vaulted basement of the E. range, running at least 22 m. southwards from the chapter-house, would have projected through the old rampart onto the river-bank beyond, with the refectory perched awkwardly along the very line of the rampart. The new town wall would have facilitated the levelling or terracing of the former river-bank between it and the refectory, the basement of which may have lain at external ground-level on this outer side.

### The first Romanesque church and cloister

The starting-point for analysis of this complex building must be the two parts of it on which it has been possible to reach broad agreement. Halsey argues from stylistic evidence that the E. range of the cloister must date from the late 1140s or 1150s, and the chancel from *c.*1165–70 (above, pp. 160–7, 133–4). I accept his evidence as conclusive, and Sturdy essentially agrees (pp. 91–4) though with a preference for slightly earlier dating. There is therefore a consensus that the E. range and chancel both date from the priorate of Robert of Cricklade (before 1139–1174 × 80). Robert was a notable scholar, and moved in circles interested in artistic patronage.[89] If he found old or makeshift buildings at St. Frideswide's he is unlikely to have been satisfied with them, and would have been well-placed to plan and see through a fully-fledged Romanesque scheme of conventual buildings.

It is also common ground among the present authors that the completed Romanesque church has peculiarities which must reflect the constraints of a simpler and earlier plan. The intrusion of the slype into the third bay of the S. transept (pp. 92–3, 147–50),

---

[87] *Cart. Frid.* i, No. 12 (*RG* iii, No. 637). The right of the canons of St. Frideswide's to have the use of the city wall, and a gate in it, is cited as a precedent in a late medieval Chichester text: see W.D. Peckham, 'Dean Croucher's Book', *Sussex Arch. Colls.* lxxxiv (1945), 16, 32. I am grateful to David Palliser for this reference.

[88] The line of the 13th-century town wall shown on Fig. 92 is Brian Durham's reconstruction, from his forthcoming report on the southern defences of Oxford. At present the only archaeological evidence for it between South Gate and the Corpus bastion is a short length of wall immediately N. of the Meadows Building, with a weathered N. face, observed in a contractors' trench in 1974 (Oxfordshire County Museum PRN 6296). This is almost certainly identical with the 'piece of masonry ... parallel with the line of Fell's Building' observed by Conradi (above, p. 229).

[89] For Robert see note 50 above. There are intriguing hints in the use of giant-order elevations at St. Frideswide's and Jedburgh (above, p. 155), and in a possible Scottish parallel for the chapter-house painting (below, p. 269), at an Anglo-Scottish cultural milieu with links to the well-developed architectural school of the Severn valley. Robert was interested in Scottish hagiography, and visited Scotland at least once. The gift of Piddington to St. Frideswide's by Malcolm king of Scots *c.*1159 (*Cart. Frid.* ii, No. 786) reinforces this notion.

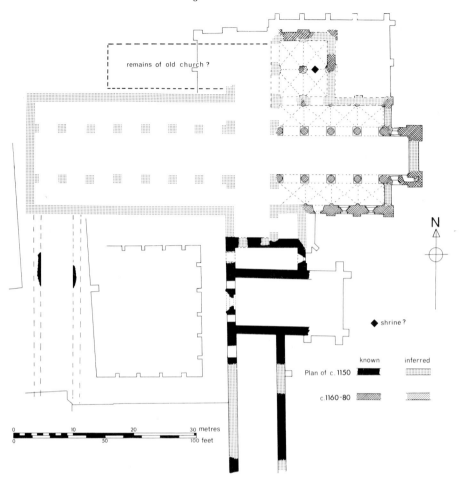

Fig. 95. The original Romanesque scheme: reconstruction of Robert of Cricklade's plan, and the parts completed during his priorate.

the clumsy arrangement adopted to provide the same transept with a W. aisle (pp. 149–52)[90] and the awkward junction between the E. aisle of the N. transept and the N. aisle of the chancel (pp. 139–46, 242–4) all betray the modification of a plan which included unaisled transepts, one and perhaps both of which were of two bays only.

When this church was built, and indeed *if* it was built, is more problematic. Halsey assumes that Robert's cloister and choir were added either to Æthelred II's church of 1002–4 or to an Augustinian church of the 1110s or 1120s (pp. 117, 120). Sturdy, who denies the existence of a pre-Conquest minster on the site, opts for the latter alternative and proposes a symmetrical church with stepped transeptal chapels (pp. 91–3 and Fig. 43A). There is, however, a third and perhaps more likely possibility: that a new church was planned and laid out *c*.1145–55, together with the cloister, but only built in slow stages (Fig. 95).

---

[90] Though Sturdy believes that it was never built (above, p. 92).

The view that Prior Robert accommodated his cloister and choir to an existing church has to contend with two difficulties. First, Scull's 1985 excavation showed that the cloister was built over what had previously been waste ground used for quarrying gravel and burying rubbish. The big pit (F149/170) contained pottery of the early to mid 12th century; the turf-line over its sunken backfill was cut by burials, themselves deposited when the area was still far from level and contained a gully (F140) running W.–E. under the chapter-house (Figs. 15, 17). The laying-out of the cloister must therefore post-date these burials, and it is clear that 'none of the claustral buildings was begun much before the middle of the [12th] century at the earliest' (above, p. 65). In other words, the existing chapter-house front belongs to the first claustral buildings on the site, set out c.1150. Since the canons, whom William of Malmesbury had praised for the regularity of their life, can scarcely have lived for thirty years without a cloister, the first Augustinian cloister must have been somewhere else. It does not inevitably follow that their church too was in a different position, but the circumstance tends to point in that direction.

Secondly, no Anglo-Saxon church other than the very grandest would have been large enough to take the cloister and chancel as additions to its nave and crossing without substantial further remodelling, including the addition of aisles. Fully-fledged Romanesque churches were scarcely ever built in this fashion: the piercing of arcades through standing walls, common in lesser churches, was an impracticable way of creating complex internal elevations with triforia and clearstories. The new style represented an ideology basically opposed to the retention of old buildings: they were rarely worth bringing up to date and, as many recent excavations have shown, architects preferred a *tabula rasa*.[91] Once the decision to rebuild had been taken it was often convenient to do so on a slightly different site, leaving the old church in use until part of the new one was ready, and when Anglo-Saxon minsters and cathedrals were replaced by Romanesque ones this was normally what happened (below, p. 257).

If Prior Robert inherited pre-Romanesque buildings, the setting-out of a new church and cloister in such a way as to leave the old ones temporarily in use is exactly what we should expect of him.[92] To build the E. range and chancel first would be quite logical if it enabled the canons to be re-housed domestically and liturgically before demolition of their old quarters commenced.[93] But the chapter-house, slype and chancel were built to suit a church with unaisled two-bay transepts, and the canons had to live with the constraints thus imposed on the plan as their church progressed during the next two decades and their ideas became grander (compare Fig. 95 with Fig. 97).

If this interpretation is correct, it follows that the old church is likely to have been somewhere on the N. side of the new one. Prior Robert's cloister, built over what had once been graveyard and more recently a waste area, impinged on the old town wall and occasioned its re-alignment further S.: a general southwards expansion of the monastic

---

[91] Cf. R. Gem, 'The English Parish Church in the 11th and Early 12th Centuries: a Great Rebuilding?', in J. Blair (ed.), *Minsters and Parish Churches* (1988), 23; idem, 'England and the Resistance to Romanesque Architecture', in C. Harper-Bill et al. (eds.), *Studies in Medieval History Presented to R. Allen Brown* (1989), 129–39.

[92] The development of the Augustinian abbey of Haughmond (Salop.), as revealed by excavation, provides a close parallel for the sequence proposed here. A small, older church had a little cloister added to it c.1130, probably at the time of regularisation; then, c.1170–90, new ranges were built around a much bigger cloister enclosing and burying the old claustral ranges and the nave of the old church, the E. arm of which underlies the S. transept of its successor. See J.J. West in *Med. Arch.* xxiv (1980), 240–1.

[93] At this stage access from dormitory to choir would probably have been down a temporary night-stair on the external E. face of the E. range, and through the small doorway, now blocked, in the S. wall of the choir (above, pp. 124–5).

Fig. 96.   The S. jamb of the chapter-house entrance, showing how the original work of *c*.1150 was extended
downwards to the new ground-level after the 1190 fire (cf. Fig. 92, bottom).

buildings seems indicated. An early 12th-century cloister on the S. side of a pre-
Conquest church could have delayed the building of the nave and N. transept, which
need not, on Halsey's chronology, have begun until around the time of the translation of
the relics in 1180.

The architectural evidence points clearly enough to the building of the transepts
and crossing-tower during the 1180s, and the completion of the nave in the years
immediately following the 1190 fire and Alexander Neckam's sermon (above, pp. 133–5
and Figs. 60, 97). The easternmost bay of the chancel poses special problems, however:
its footings are integral with those of the N. choir aisle (Fig. 42), yet the awkward
junction between the side windows and the arcade responds (Fig. 56), and the use of
keeled shafts in the external blind arcading of the buttresses, suggests work subsequent
to the main building of the chancel. Perhaps the most likely explanation is that this bay
was reconstructed on its old foundations during the 1190s, to provide the chancel
(already a generation old) with an up-to-date visual focus.

The chronology of the S. and W. claustral ranges is uncertain, but there was
evidently a significant lowering of the garth and cloister walks towards the end of the
Romanesque campaigns (see section at bottom of Fig. 92). The fire-stained mid
12th-century masonry of the chapter-house entrance starts 115 cm. above the present
floor-level in the E. walk, being continued downwards with jambs and bases of
*c*.1190–1200 (Fig. 96). This work, presumably carried out after the 1190 fire, involved
not merely repair but a wholesale reduction of levels: the chapter-house front is

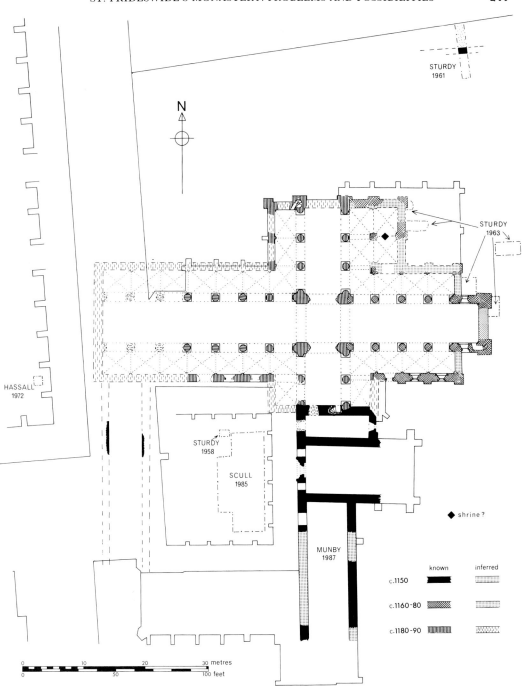

N

STURDY
1961

STURDY
1963

HASSALL
1972

STURDY
1958

SCULL
1985

◆ shrine?

MUNBY
1987

|  | known | inferred |
|---|---|---|
| c.1150 | | |
| c.1160-80 | | |
| c.1180-90 | | |

0   10   20   30 metres
0        50        100 feet

Fig. 97.   Reconstruction of the plan of the church and cloister as completed *c*.1200. (cf. Fig. 60).

unnaturally heightened so that it is impossible to see through the windows which flank the entrance, or even to see the figure painted on one of their jambs.[94] Likewise, the threshold of the original dormitory entrance is now 110 cm. above the floor of the E. walk (above, .p. 186 and Figs. 79–80). Clearly the cloister walk floor-level as conceived *c*.1150 was 110 cm. higher than the present floor, and therefore only 40 cm. below that of the church.[95] This earth-moving operation of the 1190s may have been connected with the construction of the S. range, the outer wall of which was presumably built up from the old river-bank: lowering the cloister garth would have gone some way towards evening out the natural fall, as well as providing material for building up the levels southwards.

## THE NORTH-EASTERN CHAPELS

The chapels in the angle between the N. choir aisle and E. transept are a strikingly idiosyncratic feature of the Romanesque and later plan. Since they almost certainly housed St. Frideswide's shrine, they are especially important in the present context. Thanks to the analyses of Halsey and Morris, and above all to Sturdy's excavations, it is now possible to interpret their development with some confidence. The following discussion uses the pier numbering system shown on Fig. 35 (p. 77), and should be read in conjunction with this plan and with Figs. 36 and 98–100.

### *The late 12th century*

The footings of the Romanesque precursor to the Latin Chapel are interpreted by Sturdy (p. 94) as a one-bay chapel projecting eastwards from the northernmost bay of the transept aisle. Halsey (pp. 143–6), however, sees them as the N. and E. walls of a square, four-bay chapel, vaulted on a central square pier with corner nook-shafts (II.4).

Only excavation in the Lady Chapel could settle the point, but there are some powerful arguments in support of Halsey. The plain voussoirs above the 13th-century arch between piers II.3 and II.4 are best interpreted as the remains of an earlier arch (above, p. 143), making it unlikely that there was solid walling here in the Romanesque period. Similarly, Sturdy's footing **2W** L, which he interprets as the N.E. corner of an earlier transeptal chapel (above, p. 83), might more convincingly be read as the corner of an isolated square footing under pier II.4. Perhaps most persuasively, the excavated footings and standing components of the N.E. chapel conform in their alignments and bay-divisions to the chancel, not to the transept (above, p. 140), and this seems incompatible with a 'pre-Latin Chapel' planned as a mere appendage to the chancel aisle.[96]

The hypothesis of a square, four-bay chapel will be accepted for the rest of this

[94] Martin Biddle's observation. The floor of the chapter-house was presumably also lowered, as indeed is suggested by the height of the internal blind arcading surviving at the W. end of its N. wall.

[95] In the early 1870s J.C. Buckler noted (B.L. MS Add. 27765E f.69ᵛ) that 'the evidence of changes repeatedly made by the builders, from a high to a low level of pavement, and back again to a midway line of floor, has lately been laid open to view on two sides of the cloisters, the north and the south, and were of a nature to explain clearly how from time to time the levels had been varied'.

[96] Sturdy claims that the N. wall of the 'pre-Latin Chapel' was integral with the N.E. corner buttress of the N. transept (above, p. 94, and cf. Fig. 36). However, the excavated evidence would be exactly the same if an originally free-standing N.W. corner buttress for the chapel had been subsequently incorporated into the transept buttress.

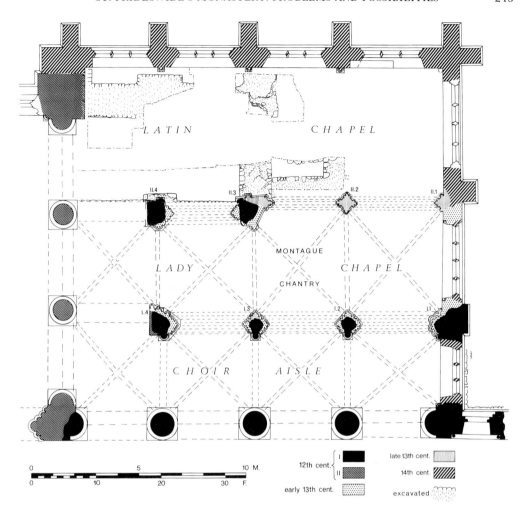

Fig. 98.   Plan of the N.E. chapels in their final medieval form, showing footings found in the 1963 excavations.

discussion. It follows from it that the chapel was built with the chancel, before the decision had been taken to add aisles to the transepts. Probably it was separated from the N. chancel aisle by solid walling, and from the projected aisleless transept by a pierced wall or by square piers like II.4 (cf. above, p. 146). As originally conceived it would have been self-contained and isolated, and its undercroft-like form even suggests the possibility that the main chapel was raised above it on an upper floor.[97] On Halsey's chronology it seems likely that the chancel and chapel, but not the transept, were complete by the translation of Frideswide's relics in 1180.

---

[97] I am grateful to Julian Munby for pointing out the interesting parallel of Chichester Cathedral, where the 'chapel of the Four Virgins', square with a central column, was built *c.*1210–20 to replace the N. transept apse (see *V.C.H. Sussex*, iii, 108–9 and plan after p.112). It had an upper chamber containing an altar of St. Edmund the Martyr, and although a generation later than the Oxford chapel it reinforces the possibility that this too may have had a chapel above.

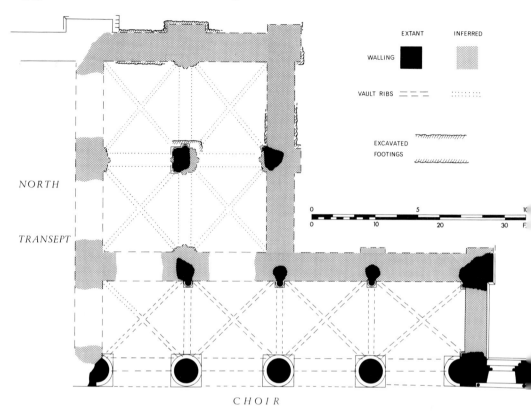

EXTANT     INFERRED

WALLING

VAULT RIBS

EXCAVATED
FOOTINGS

*NORTH*

*TRANSEPT*

0        5        1(
0      10      20      30   F

*C H O I R*

Fig. 99.   Reconstructed plan of the N.E. chapel in its original state, before the E. arcade of the N. transept was inserted.

The concept of an altogether grander church with aisled transepts, probably adopted as the cult prospered during the late 1170s or 1180s, changed the whole character of the N. chapel. The building of the columnar arcade (I.5-III.5) absorbed the two western bays of the chapel, together with the westernmost bay of the chancel N. aisle, to create an E. aisle for the N. transept. The obvious reason for the mis-match between these bays is that the new arch between piers I.4 and I.5 was thinner than the solid wall which it replaced, and had to conform to the rhythm of the transept arcade (cf. Fig. 62); the N.W. quarter of the vault in the westernmost bay of the choir aisle was therefore rebuilt to a grossly distorted profile, its rib (onto pier I.5) spanning a greater distance than the other three (cf. above, p. 145). The two eastern bays of the chapel, too, would have become more integrated with the body of the church, assuming almost the character of a second aisle. If the chapel had been built to house the shrine of 1180, this rather enclosed setting seems to have been quickly modified to cope with the flood of pilgrims recorded over the next two decades.[98]

[98] See H. Mayr-Harting, 'Functions of a Twelfth-Century Shrine: the Miracles of St. Frideswide', in H. Mayr-Harting and R.I. Moore (eds), *Studies in Medieval History Presented to R.H.C. Davis* (1985), 193–206.

*The 13th century*

The Lady Chapel was built *c*.1230 along the N. side of the N. chancel aisle (above, pp. 169–75). Its westernmost bay, a re-modelling of the S.E. bay of the original square chapel, is slightly narrower than the other two bays, which were not restricted by earlier structures. The arcade (I.1–I.4) between the Lady Chapel and the choir aisle, replacing the aisle wall, marks the final stage in the integration of the original N. chapel with the body of the church.

The footing of the Lady Chapel N. wall, with a buttress or wall-stub opposite pier I.1, was found by Sturdy (**2E**.G, above, p. 85 and Fig. 36). To interpret this feature as a wall-stub makes sense of the otherwise puzzling shaft II.3.C, with its early 13th-century base, on the S. side of the Latin Chapel. This shaft may well be re-used (the explanation favoured by Morris, p. 178 above), but if not it shows that the E. wall of the 'pre-Latin' chapel was pierced for an arch; this arch could have led into a small square chamber (perhaps a tomb-house or sacristy?), its E. wall represented by the northwards projection on **2E**.G, in the angle between the remains of the old chapel and the new Lady Chapel.

The next stage was the extension eastwards of the 'pre-Latin' chapel by two bays (or by one bay if the small square chamber already existed) , which were divided from the central and eastern bays of the Lady Chapel by a two-bay arcade (II.1–II.3). Morris considers that the piers of this arcade may be of *c*.1290, though surmounted by capitals and arches of the later Latin Chapel work (above, pp. 175–8). A short section of the E. wall of this late 13th-century chapel remains bonded with pier II.1 (Fig. 72); the line of its N. wall remains uncertain, but can most probably be associated with the robber-trench-like feature **3**.E found by Sturdy (Fig. 36).

*The 14th century*

The two northern bays of the original chapel were removed, together with the 13th-century eastwards extension, to make way for the unified building now known as the Latin Chapel (Figs. 74, 76). A likely context for its construction is the chantry which the canons established for Bishop Burghersh in 1338 as a *quid pro quo* for permission to appropriate Churchill rectory. The chantry ordinance, dated January 1338, provides for masses to be celebrated 'by one of our brethren before the altar of the Blessed Virgin Frideswide constructed in the conventual church of our house';[99] the following August a licence was issued for the dedication of 'certain altars newly constructed in the conventual church of St. Frideswide'.[100] If 'St. Frideswide's altar' adjoined the shrine it must have been somewhere near the Montague chantry (below, p. 252), and the establishment of new altars may reflect more extensive building works. A connection between Burghersh and the Latin Chapel is strengthened by the 14th-century tiles bearing a fork-tailed leopard (Fig. 50 No. 18), the Burghersh arms, which were re-used in its early Tudor floor (above, p. 104 and Figs. 37, 47). The construction of the Latin Chapel during the summer of 1338, to house the Burghersh and other chantries, would accord with the architectural parallels in the 1320s and 1330s adduced by Morris (p. 182 above).

---

[99] Linc. Reg. VI ff.124$^v$–125 (*et* [error for *coram*?] *altari beate Fredeswide virginis in ecclesia conventuali domus nostre predicte constructo*). Cf. *Cal. Papal Letters*, ii, 383.

[100] Linc. Reg. V. f.563. The canons had a licence to consecrate three further altars in 1344 (Linc. Reg. VII f.56$^v$).

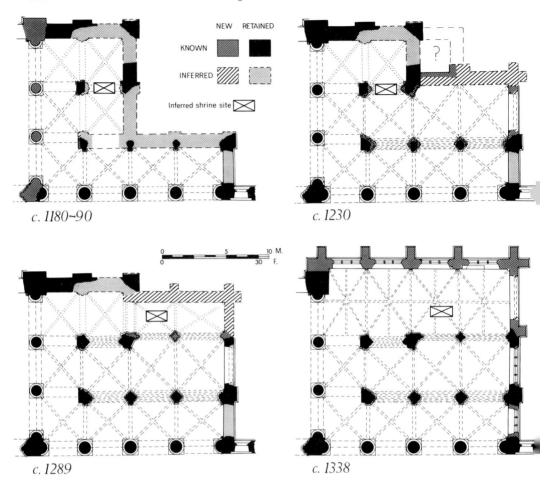

Fig. 100.   The N.E. chapels: development plans (second and subsequent phases).

## THE LOCATIONS OF ST. FRIDESWIDE'S GRAVE AND SHRINE

### Before the Romanesque church

Frideswide's relics are first recorded at Oxford at the beginning of the 11th century
(above, p. 226). Between then and the 12th-century references to her grave, the church
experienced many vicissitudes. There was a rumour in the early Augustinian community that Frideswide's bones had been stolen by the monks of Abingdon, and the
pains taken to refute this belief suggest that it may have been all too true.[101] We can be
far from confident, therefore, that the grave which the 12th-century canons venerated
was really an 8th-century feature.

[101] Blair, 'St. F.', 116–18.

The artless early 12th-century author of 'Life A' merely says that Frideswide 'was buried in St. Mary's church on the south side' (*sepultaque est in ecclesia Sancte Marie in australi parte*);[102] he was probably drawing on some earlier source, and in itself the tradition may well be genuine. Prior Robert of Cricklade's re-working of this passage in 'Life B' is more explicit:

> The blessed virgin was buried in the basilica of the spotless Virgin Mary mother of God, on the south side, beside the bank of the River Thames. The site of the basilica remained thus until the time of King Æthelred, who, after the burning of the Danes who had fled thither [i.e. in 1002], enlarged the perimeter of the basilica as he had previously vowed. It was undoubtedly done in this way, for the grave, which had previously been on one side [*or* on the south side?], came thenceforth to be the middle. (*Sepulta est beata virgo in basilica intemerate semper virginis Dei genitricis Marie in parte australi prope ripam fluminis Thamesis. Sic enim se tunc habebat situs basilice usque ad tempus regis Athelredi, qui, combustis in ea Dacis qui confugerant illuc, basilice ambitum sicut ante voverat ampliavit. Hinc nimirum actum est, quia sepulchrum, quod ante fuerat in parte, medium extunc esse contigit.*)[103]

It is important to note the element of inference in this passage: Robert deduces that the church must have been enlarged around the grave, because he assumes that the latter has never moved and must reconcile the tradition of a southwards position with his own knowledge of an axial one. Even if Frideswide really was buried on the S. side of her church, the validity of Robert's deduction depends on the dubious proposition that the 'grave' known to him was genuine.

Nonetheless, the passage throws light on the immediately pre-Augustinian arrangements. Robert must have known by personal observation, or on first-hand testimony, of a church which he believed to be Æthelred's. The church in question must have been significantly older than the Augustinian re-foundation, only some twenty years before Robert's arrival, and it is a reasonable conclusion that it was indeed the church of 1002–4. On its central axis lay a spot which was venerated as 'St. Frideswide's grave' and which was presumably marked by some kind of monument, probably a flat slab; it is even possible that a slab laid on the grave by the first Augustinians, or by their patron Roger of Salisbury, still survives (below, pp. 266–8 and Fig. 105).

A later narrative describes how the 12th-century canons opened the grave and found an empty stone coffin; suspecting a ruse to foil relic-thieves they dug deeper, and found bones which were identified as Frideswide's by a miraculous extinction of the excavators' candles.[104] This story may be accurate enough as an archaeological report, even if its outcome is painfully contrived. At this date only very important graves had stone coffins, and it seems likely enough that this one had formerly contained bones thought to be Frideswide's. A buried stone coffin with its cover-slab level with the floor would be quite appropriate for a local saint before the late 12th-century fashion for translations (cf. below, p. 268).

The bones thus found were presumably those subsequently enshrined. Fragments were taken away, either on this occasion or in 1180, and are later recorded among the relics at Winchester, Reading and Waltham.[105]

---

[102] Ibid. 101.

[103] Ibid. 116.

[104] Ibid. 116–18.

[105] Winchester: Biddle op. cit. note 16, 320–1 n, and Keene op. cit. note 14, 1406, 1440. Reading: *V.C.H. Berks.* ii, 70. Waltham: B.L. MS Harl. 3776 f.33ʳ⁻ᵛ (relic-list including *os de Sancta Fritheswida* given by Peter, first sacristan of the regular canons, in the time of Prior Ralph [1177–84]). I am grateful to Nicholas Rogers for the last reference.

*Between the 1170s and 1289*

In 1180 the bones were translated into a raised shrine at the instigation of Prior Philip, who had recently succeeded Robert of Cricklade. The prelude to the ceremony, and the numerous miracles which followed it, are recorded in a treatise written by Prior Philip and extant in a manuscript of *c*.1200; this throws a certain amount of light on the setting of the grave and shrine.[106]

Three pre-translation miracles are included as evidence of divine approval. All involve emissions of light from the grave, in one case 'from the fabric of the tower of the glorious virgin's church', and in another (dated to some eight years before the translation, i.e. to *c*.1172) in the form of a golden column rising from the grave to above the top of the tower.[107] On Halsey's chronology (above, pp. 124, 133) it is most unlikely that the Romanesque crossing-piers were complete by 1172, let alone the tower which they support: the tower mentioned in these stories must have been something older. Since the choir and N.E. chapels are the only parts of the present church likely to have existed by the early 1170s, the possibility remains open that 'the glorious virgin's church' was substantially still Æthelred's, and distinct from the half-built conventual church. However, Prior Philip's account of the 1180 translation describes the archbishop of Canterbury entering 'the same glorious virgin's church', lifting the bones from the grave and putting them straight into a feretory,[108] which suggests that the grave and the subsequent shrine site were by then under one roof, or at least in connected buildings.

Thirty of the post-translation miracle stories mention specific foci of Frideswide's cult, and make it clear that in the 1180s two such foci existed: the empty grave, and the feretory containing the bones. Fifteen miracles[109] are said to have occurred at the grave (*ad* or *super sepulcrum, ad* or *super tumulum*), which in three cases[110] is specifically described as the place where the bones had formerly lain or from which they had been translated. In eight cases[111] the petitioners are said to have spent one or more nights by the grave, and in six[112] to have prostrated themselves upon it. One witness saw 'a lady of wonderful beauty and dignity go around the grave with anxious care, asperging and then wiping one by one the faces of all the invalids who lay there' (*cum igitur nocte super beate virginis sepulcrum oraret . . . , vidit dominam quamdam mire venustatis et gravitatis, singulorum qui ibidem decumbebant infirmorum ex ordine facies aspergentem et postmodum extergentem, sepulcrum sollicite circuire*).[113] The fifteen miracles[114] which involve the feretory (*coram feretro, ad feretrum, ante feretrum*) show a slightly different pattern. Only three[115] are associated with nocturnal vigils; two[116] happen while the feretory is being carried in procession, and two others[117] while services before it are in progress. One petititioner offers a candle at the feretory, and two others return thanks there after their cures.[118]

---

[106] Bodl. MS Digby 177, printed *Acta Sanctorum: Octobris: VIII* (1853), 568–89. Miracles are cited here according to their numbers in the *Acta Sanctorum* edition.

[107] Nos. 5–7.

[108] Blair, 'St. F.', 119.

[109] Nos. 9, 10, 11, 13, 17, 18, 19, 20, 31, 33, 34, 37, 70, 76, 78.

[110] Nos. 10, 13, 31.

[111] Nos. 10, 13, 17, 31, 37, 70, 76, 78.

[112] Nos. 9, 11, 18, 20, 76, 78.

[113] No. 76.

[114] Nos. 8, 12, 21, 35, 38, 42, 44, 45, 46, 62, 64, 77, 82, 106, 109.

[115] Nos. 35, 77, 106.

[116] Nos. 38, 45.

[117] Nos. 12, 62.

[118] Nos. 8, 44, 46.

The impression given by these stories is that the normal *locus* for invalids spending long-term vigils in the church was the grave, whereas the main liturgical focus of the cult was the feretory. The locations of the grave and feretory within the church are nowhere mentioned, unless a clue is provided by the miracle story which involves 'a great crowd of people entering the church by the north side' (*vidit copiosam plebis multitudinem a parte aquilonari ecclesiam ingredi*).[119]

Later documentary evidence shows that the site to which the feretory was moved in 1289 was near the old one, and was almost certainly in the N.E. chapel (Fig. 100 and below, pp. 251–2); it follows that the site of the feretory between 1180 and 1289 was probably also in the N.E. chapel. This probability is made near-certainty by the unusual square plan of the original chapel, which must have had some special liturgical purpose and was probably built before 1180 (above, pp. 145–6, 242–4). Unless the feretory was raised up in a first-floor chamber, Sturdy's suggestion that it stood under the arch between piers II.4 and II.3, in the space where Prior Sutton's tomb was re-sited in the 17th century,[120] seems reasonable, in which case the excavated footing **2W.K**(2) might be interpreted as its base (above, p. 83 and Fig. 36). This arch was remodelled *c.*1230 as part of the Lady Chapel work (above, pp. 173–5), perhaps to give the shrine a more imposing setting.

Where, then, was the grave? Before speculating on this problem it is worth considering some parallels for the simultaneous veneration of raised feretory and empty grave. It was an established belief that earth long sanctified by a holy corpse retained the saint's *praesentia* despite removal of the physical relics, and there are well-attested English cases of graves still venerated centuries after their contents had been translated to new liturgical or architectural settings.[121] 'Tombs' marked the former resting-places of St. Cuthbert's body at Lindisfarne, Chester-le-Street and the pre-Conquest cathedral of Durham; the original graves of St. John of Beverley and St. William of York also had cenotaphs.[122] The best example is St. Swithun's former grave at Winchester, which was marked by a cenotaph even after the new cathedral of the 1090s, where the relics themselves were enshrined, had left it eccentrically placed outside the N. wall of the nave; thereafter 'a long sequence of monuments and chapels . . . preserved the precise location and alignment of the saint's grave to the end of the Middle Ages'.[123]

But translation did not necessarily involve removing the relics to a new location: sometimes they were merely elevated on a shrine-base over the original grave, confining in a single monument the physical remains and the spot which they had hallowed. St. Swithun's relics, at an earlier stage in their history, are again a good instance: between 974 and 1093 the reliquary evidently stood on a raised structure above the grave, the focus of a special memorial building at the W. end of the Old Minster.[124] Two cases where such an arrangement is suggested by surviving physical evidence are the early 13th-century shrine of St. Wita at Whitchurch Canonicorum (Dorset) and the mid 13th-century shrine of St. Bertelin at Ilam (Staffs.).[125] At Whitchurch the shrine-base

---

[119] No. 46.

[120] Wood, *City*, ii, 175.

[121] See Biddle op. cit. note 60, 3; examples are Jarrow (Ibid. 8); possibly Derby (ibid. 7–8); and Wells (W. Rodwell, 'From Mausoleum to Minster: the Early Development of Wells Cathedral', in S.M. Pearce (ed.), *The Early Church in West Britain and Ireland* (B.A.R. British Ser. cii, 1982), 49–59).

[122] H.D. Biggs, E. Cambridge and R.N. Bailey, 'A New Approach to Church Archaeology', *Archaeologia Aeliana*, 5th ser. xi (1983), 92–3.

[123] Biddle op. cit. note 60, 25.

[124] Ibid. 22–4.

[125] The following comments are based on personal inspection of both shrines in 1988. For Whitchurch see also *R.C.H.M. West Dorset* (1952), 263 and Pl. 210.

supports a stone coffin which, with its marble cover-slab, appears to be an older under-floor tomb (cf. below, p. 268). The Ilam shrine-base encloses an obviously older slab, coped and probably hog-backed, which was trimmed in the 13th century to allow the panels of the base to fit neatly around it. Both structures imply a concern to preserve the monument which had covered the relics before their elevation, imbued like the grave itself with borrowed sanctity.

The miracle stories provide no evidence that St. Frideswide's grave and shrine were near each other, but neither do they contain anything which excludes the possibility that the relics were raised above the grave. Such an arrangement would have been compatible with invalids prostrating themselves on the grave, for the feretory would probably have stood on a table supported by columns or arches. The distinction in the stories between grave and feretory is one of context, but not necessarily of location: suppliants keep vigil around the grave, fixed and at floor-level, whereas liturgy focusses on the feretory, elevated and portable.

A fruitful approach to the location of the grave may be to consider whether it is likely to have influenced the siting of the feretory. In Æthelred's church, if we are to believe 'Life B', the grave lay on the central axis. The lack of any suggestion that the relics were ever axially placed in the Romanesque church, either above or below ground, is therefore a fact requiring explanation. Sturdy suggests that the grave was in the projecting, easternmost bay of the existing Romanesque choir, which he interprets as a relic-chapel screened off behind the high altar (above, pp. 93–4). This idea starts from the assumptions that the choir conforms to the axis of the older church, and that the sort of architectural setting which became normal for major raised shrines is equally likely to have been built around a floor-level grave. These assumptions are dubious, especially since the shrine probably stood in the N.E. chapel after 1180. It would have been a reasonable enough suggestion, in the absence of evidence to the contrary, that the relics were translated *into* a shrine behind the high altar from a grave elsewhere; to propose the opposite movement seems much less convincing.

An alternative possibility is that the Anglo-Saxon and Romanesque churches were so placed in relation to each other that the central axis of the former ran through the N. transept of the latter: in other words, the church moved around the grave and the grave determined the position of the shrine, which was accordingly on the N. side of the church as existing after 1180. Good analogies are Lyminge, where St. Æthelburh's grave in the N. *porticus* of the old church adjoined the S. wall of the later church, built along its N. side; and Durham, where St. Cuthbert's grave on the central axis of the pre-Conquest church was later marked by a cenotaph in the garth of the Romanesque cloister.[126]

This hypothesis would be consistent with the archaeological evidence discussed above (pp. 237–40), and would help to explain what is, for a major shrine in a high medieval setting, an abnormal arrangement. There are good Anglo-Saxon parallels for shrines on the N. sides of churches,[127] but at Oxford the arrangement cannot, on the clear evidence of Life B, pre-date the 12th century. Although some post-Conquest shrines in N. transepts may perpetuate Anglo-Saxon arrangements, others evidently resulted from the rebuilding of the church on a more southerly axis in the way suggested here for

---

[126] *Archaeol. Jnl.* cxxvi (1969), 259, and Biddle op. cit. note 60, 8, for Lyminge; Biggs, Cambridge and Bailey op. cit. note 122, 91–7, for Durham.
[127] Biddle op. cit. note 60, 11.

Oxford.[128] At Bury St. Edmunds, for instance, the Romanesque church was built to the S. of the earlier round church containing Edmund's relics, which was left attached to the E. side of its N. transept in a position exactly equivalent to the N.E. chapel at Oxford.[129] In short, the position of St. Frideswide's shrine is more easily explained if we assume that it stood over her former grave than if we assume that it did not.

*Between 1289 and the Reformation*

On 10 September 1289, the old feretory was placed inside a new and more precious feretory near the former site ( . . . *translatum est vetus feretrum Sancte Fritheswythe Oxonie, et cum honore quo decuit collocatum est in novo et pretiosiori feretro in eadem ecclesia, et prope situm quo prius fuerat collocatum, quod quidem feretrum diu ante fuerat preparatum).*[130] It stood on a sumptuous shrine-base of Purbeck marble, the major pieces of which were found in a well-lining in 1875 and reconstructed;[131] the discovery of more pieces in 1985 is reported above (pp. 48–9, 191 and Fig. 29).

Since the piers of the two easternmost arches between the Latin Chapel and Lady Chapel (II.1–3) date from around 1290, it is a reasonable proposition that the chapel to which they belonged was designed to house the shrine of 1289 (above, p. 245). If the feretory stood in one of the bays of this chapel, or under one of the arches, it need have been no more than 15 or 20 feet from its inferred position since 1180 – indeed *prope situm quo prius fuit collocatum.* An important reason for building a new chapel, and for moving the shrine slightly, may have been to provide more prime grave-spaces for the rich and favoured, such as the clerk Thomas de Blewbury who was buried in 1293 *iuxta feretrum Sancte Fredeswide.*[132] In its turn, the replacement around 1338 of what was probably a cramped and irregular structure with the uniform, elegant and roomy Latin Chapel may reflect a growing pressure to fit tombs and altars into the space around the shine, Burghersh's chantry being only the most important (above, p. 245).

In 1346, Lady Elizabeth Montague established her chantry 'in our monastery, in the Lady Chapel, next St. Frideswide's feretory' (*in monasterio nostro, in capella beate Marie, iuxta feretrum Sancte Frideswide*).[133] Since the Montague chantry provides the most explicit evidence for the position of the shrine, locating it is of some importance. Lady

---

[128] Examples of this are Whitchurch Canonicorum (see note 125), Bampton (J. Blair, 'St. Beornwald of Bampton', *Oxoniensia*, xlix (1984), 50–4), and Rhoscrowther (*Archaeologia Cambrensis* 6th ser. xv (1915), 385–9). The matter is, however, a complex one, for there seems to have been a late 12th- and 13th-century fashion for putting *new* shrines in N. transepts. St. Hugh's request to be buried in the N.E. transept of Lincoln Cathedral (D.A. Stocker, 'The Mystery of the Shrines of St. Hugh', in H. Mayr-Harting (ed.), *St. Hugh of Lincoln* (1987), 89–124, esp. 111), may reflect a special preference for locating the tombs of revered bishops in eastern transepts (David Stocker's suggestion, lecture 1989), but this explanation cannot apply to shrines such as St. William's at Rochester (ex inf. Sarah Blair). Some north-side shrines may be part of the same phenomenon as north-side Easter Sepulchres, reflecting a concern to imitate the Tomb of Christ. More work is needed on this problem.

[129] R. Gem and L. Keen, 'Late Anglo-Saxon Finds from the Site of St. Edmund's Abbey', *Proc. Suffolk Inst. of Arch. and Hist.* xxxv (1984), 1–2.

[130] *Annales Monastici*, ed. H.R. Luard, iv (Rolls Ser. xxxvid, 1869), 318. In the preceding years gifts had been made to the work of the new feretory (*Cart. Frid.* i, Nos. 237, 585).

[131] J.C. Wall, *Shrines of British Saints* (1905), 64–71; N. Coldstream, 'English Decorated Shrine Bases', *JBAA* cxxix (1976), 17.

[132] Linc. Reg. I, f.75; the abstract in *Reg. Sutton*, iv (Linc. Rec. Soc. lii, 1958), 92, mistranslates *feretrum* as 'window'.

[133] *Cart. Frid.* ii, 10. For Lady Montague, who died in 1354, see Ibid. 1–17 and *Complete Peerage*, ix, 82.

Montague's tomb now stands under the arcade between the Latin and Lady Chapels, in the second arch from the E. (II.2–II.3; see Fig. 98). Although the excavations showed (above, pp. 84, 96, Fig. 36) that this tomb stands on a medieval sub-base (**2E**.C), the tomb itself shows clear signs of disturbance, notably in the poor fit between the side panels and the top slab, in the absence of a plinth-course, and in the clumsy tile packing under the S. side of the chest. Wood recorded a first-hand tradition that the tomb, originally surrounded by railings, had been moved in Dean Duppa's time from a position on the opposite side of the Lady Chapel.[134] The fine carvings on its end panels, now hard to see, suggest that it was meant to stand in an open space where it could be viewed from all sides, and the centre of the same Lady Chapel bay seems the most likely original location. The vault of this bay is richly decorated with censing angels, the paint and technique of which resemble the painted decoration on Lady Montague's tomb.[135] Whatever the exact position of the tomb, it is surely in this bay that the Montague chantry should be located.

From this it follows that in 1346 the feretory stood either in the Lady Chapel (W. or E. of the Montague chantry), in the second bay (counting from the E.) of the N. choir aisle, in the second bay of the Latin Chapel, or exactly where the Montague tomb now stands. The last two alternatives are consistent with the evidence already discussed, and have a further point in their favour: the centrepiece of the second window from the E. in the N. wall of the Latin Chapel, directly opposite the Montague tomb, is a figure of Frideswide herself, flanked by St. Catherine and St. Margaret.[136] Viewed from the choir, this image of the patroness in the company of other holy virgins would have formed a suitable and effective background to her shrine.

Sturdy suggests (above, pp. 95–6 and Fig. 37) that the shrine stood in the Latin Chapel but S. of the central axis, with an elaborate tile pavement defining the liturgically important area to its W., and with a screened-off area behind it in the easternmost bay. This off-centre position can be explained on the hypothesis that the shrine stood on the central axis of the narrow late 13th-century chapel, and remained undisturbed when the much wider Latin Chapel was built around it. This interpretation seems on the whole best, and is adopted in Fig. 100. It remains possible, however, that the shrine stood directly under the arch II.2–3, the footing **2E**.C now under Lady Montague being in fact the foundation of the shrine-base.

Two further pieces of late medieval evidence have a bearing on the location of the shrine, though neither is very explicit. First, the large Perpendicular tomb under the easternmost arch between the Latin and Lady Chapels (II.1–2) is surmounted by a timber loft (Figs. 76, 101), usually interpreted as a watching-chamber for the guardian of the relics.[137] If this interpretation is correct it confirms that the shrine stood somewhere in this part of the church, though the loft has open sides to N., S. and W. Secondly, in 1473 the will of Thomas Bloxham requests burial in St. Frideswide's, 'near the feretory of the same, between the altar there towards the choir and Dr. Boteler's tomb' (*iuxta*

---

[134] Wood, *City*, ii, 173 says explicitly that the tomb had stood under the arcade between the N. choir aisle and Lady Chapel, opposite its present location. This passage, however, is a re-working of an earlier and more ambiguous statement, where Wood recalls the archdeacon telling him in 1661 that it stood 'on the N. side of Christ Chur. quire in the middle betw. 2 pillars, about the place where the singing men sitt. It was railed in with Iron grates . . . ' (T. Hearne, *Liber Niger Scaccarii* (1728), 575).

[135] Ex inf. Martin Stancliffe.

[136] *R.C.H.M. Oxford*, Pl. 99. Doubt has been cast upon the locations of these windows, but the glass fragments found by Sturdy (above, pp. 100–2) show that they are original to the Latin Chapel, and there is no reason to think that the figures have been transposed.

[137] *R.C.H.M. Oxford*, Pl. 90.

Fig. 101. The S.E. corner of the Latin Chapel: mid 19th-century lithograph, showing the stalls formerly under the E. window (cf. p.100 and Figs. 44, 76) and the 'watching-loft'. (Bodl. G.A. Oxon.a.67, No. 115. Reproduced by permission of the Curators of the Bodleian Library.)

*feretrum eiusdem inter altare ibidem versus chorum et sepulturam doctoris Boteler).*[138] This is tantalising, but impossible to interpret until more evidence for the surrounding tombs and altars comes to light.


## The Reformation and after

The bizarre adventures of St. Frideswide's relics between the 1530s and 1560s are well-known. James Calfhill's pamphlet of 1562[139] recounts the death and burial of Catherine Martyr in 1552, the ejection of her bones from the church during Mary's reign, and his own efforts to return them to seemly Christian burial. On demanding to see where Catherine had been buried he was 'taken to Frideswide's tomb, and the former grave was pointed out not far from that place, on the N. side of the church' (*ad Fridesuide tumulum adducimur, atque non longe ab eo loco, in parte templi septentrionali, sepulchrum quod fuit, ostenditur.*[140] It appears, though Calfhill does not say so, that after the destruction of the shrine the relics had been buried: Cardinal Pole had ordered the removal of Catherine's body because it lay so close to Frideswide's (*quoniam iuxta corpus sanctissimae Fridesuidae iacebat corpus Catharinae*),[141] polluting the holy relics. On the other hand, the grave cannot have contained the relics in 1561, for Calfhill later found them in two silk bags and buried them, mixed with Catherine's bones, 'in the upper part of the church towards the east' (*in superiore fani parte ad orientem spectante*).[142] One wonders whether the *Fridesuide tumulum* might not have been the original grave from before 1180, still venerated as a holy spot in its own right.

This conjecture aside, Calfhill's explicit statement that the tomb was on the N. side of the church is useful in the present context. It must, however, be added that there is an independent source for these events which could be held to point in a different direction. Bartolomé de Carranza, who conducted the Marian visitation of Oxford, returned to Spain and in 1562 was tried for heresy. Eager to demonstrate his Catholic zeal, he recounted his actions on discovering that the wife of the great heretic Peter Martyr 'had been buried in the *capilla mayor* of the collegiate church of Oxford next to a saint's body' (*estava enterrada en la capilla mayor de la yglesia colegial de Oxonia junto a un cuerpo santo*).[143] The significance, if any, of this passage hinges on the term *capilla mayor*, which in recent Spanish usage means the chancel, or eastern chapel beyond the choir.[144] Whether 16th-century usage was so precise as to suggest that Carranza was thinking specifically of the chancel of St. Frideswide's, rather than the eastern arm in general, is unclear. If so, the fact can merely be recorded as in apparent conflict with the other evidence.

During the century after 1561 the site of the shrine seems to have been forgotten. Anthony Wood, who clearly had no reliable information, says in different places that the feretory was placed 'on the north side of the quire, somewhat distant from the ground',

---

[138] P.R.O. PROB 11/6 f.66ᵛ.

[139] J. Calfhill, *Historia de Catharinae uxoris D. Petri Martyris Piisimae Exhumatione, ac Eiusdem ad Honestam Sepulturam Restitutione*, in C. Hubertus, *Historia Vera de Vita . . .* (1562).

[140] Ibid. 202.

[141] Ibid. 199ᵛ.

[142] Ibid. 201ᵛ–202ᵛ.

[143] *Documentos Historicos*, ed. J.I. Tellechea Idígoras, iii (Madrid, 1966), 26; see also . . . . . Salazar de Miranda, *Vida y Sucesos Prósperos y Adversos de don Bartolome de Carranza* (Madrid, 1788), 27. For both these references I am extremely grateful to Glyn Redworth.

[144] Cf. G.E. Street, *Some Account of Gothic Architecture in Spain* (1865), 17. I am grateful to Howard Colvin for this reference.

and 'on the north side of the high altar'; elsewhere he calls the 15th-century watching-loft 'St. Frideswyde's repository', and reports without contradiction a belief that Lady Montague's tomb and effigy commemorated the saint.[145] Numerous drawings and engravings of the watching-loft between the mid 18th and mid 19th century are captioned 'St. Frideswide's shrine', a view which seems to have prevailed until the rediscovery of the fragments of the 1289 shrine. By then it was believed to have stood 'somewhere in the North Choir Aisle of this Church', probably a deduction from the Montague chantry deed.[146] No genuine tradition, therefore, is represented by the modern slab inscribed FRIDESWIDE which is set in the Lady Chapel floor beside the Montague tomb.

*Some implications of the grave and shrine sites*

On the evidence presented above, the following conclusions may be suggested:
(a) The house preserved a tradition that Frideswide had originally been buried on the S. side of her church.
(b) The church which the 12th-century canons believed to have been Æthelred II's work of *c*.1004, and which survived until the Romanesque rebuilding, contained on its central axis a site identified, whether rightly or wrongly, as Frideswide's original place of burial.
(c) This spot, which continued to be venerated as her grave after the first translation, lay within the church as existing in 1180.
(d) The 1180 shrine stood 'near' the spot later occupied by its successor of 1289, and therefore somewhere on the N. side of the Romanesque choir. The unusual square chapel in the angle between the N. transept and N. choir aisle was almost certainly built to house it.
(e) Since it seems improbable that the relics would have been moved from an axial to a non-axial position within the Romanesque church, the most likely reason for the position of the 1180 shrine is that it was raised over the supposed grave site, which was regarded as holy because of its long contact with the saint's bones.
(f) It follows from points (b) and (e), if both are accepted, that the central axis of the late Anglo-Saxon church passed through the N. transept and N.E. chapels of the Romanesque church.

THE PAROCHIAL ALTAR OF THE HOLY CROSS AND THE 'JERUSALEM CHAPEL': A CLUE TO THE PRE-ROMANESQUE CHURCH, AND SOME ANALOGUES

At this stage one more strand of evidence may be woven into the argument: the parochial attributes of the Priory, considered in the light of some analogous cases of pre-Conquest minsters with parochial functions which were replaced by Romanesque conventual churches.

St. Frideswide's, like other regularised ex-minsters, retained direct control over an urban parish, first mentioned (for purposes of locating a tenement) in a deed of *c*.1180.[147] Parochial duties, presumably discharged during the 12th century by the

---

[145] Wood, *City*, ii, 165, 166 note, 173; Hearne loc. cit. note 134.
[146] H.G. Liddell, *St. Frideswide: Two Sermons, Preached . . . 1880, . . . 1889* [not publ.: Bodl. 11113 e. 10(1)], 19.
[147] *Cart. Frid.* i, No. 99.

canons or their curates, were formalised in 1225 when Bishop Hugh de Welles established 'a vicarage in St. Frideswide's conventual church', with revenues divided between the vicar and canons.[148] Vicars were presented to 'the vicarage of St. Frideswide's parish church' in 1239/40, to 'the vicarage of St. Frideswide's church' in 1243/4, and to 'the vicarage of the altar of the Holy Cross in St. Frideswide's church' in 1249/50.[149] In 1298 the benefice was suppressed and all parochial functions and revenues transferred to St. Edward's, three reasons being stated: (a) the livings were both poor, and inadequate on their own; (b) the parochial offices of St. Frideswide's church and those of the canons had been celebrated 'not merely under one roof but in completely adjoining places, with no space between them worth mentioning' (*nedum sub eodem tecto sed in locis admodum vicinis sine notabili distantia*), causing mutual irritation and musical cacophony; and (c) the arrangement caused danger both to the canons through the opening of the church doors for visiting sick parishioners at night, and to the parishioners 'through the difficulty of having thence what their status requires'.[150]

Parish altars were often located in the naves of conventual churches, and it may be (as proposed by Halsey, p. 135) that this was the case at Oxford. But there is one clue which points in a different direction. The will of James Zouch (d.1503) requests burial 'under the myddell of the greet window yn the north part of the cross wynd yle in a chapell callyd chapell of Jh[erusale]m', and his tomb still remains against the N. wall of the N. transept.[151] The probability of a liturgical link between a 'chapel of Jerusalem' and an altar dedicated to the Holy Cross suggests some likelihood that the latter was also in the N. transept or N.E. chapels, the position which in any case best agrees with the statement of 1298 that it stood immediately next to the canons' choir.

This conclusion, coupled with the location of the shrine in the N.E. chapels, has two interesting implications. First, it suggests that the shrine and parochial altar may have belonged to an *ensemble* embodying some reminiscence of the Holy Sepulchre in Jerusalem, where the 12th-century church also includes the reputed hiding-place of the True Cross. The symmetrical and very unusual plan of the original N.E. chapels – a square containing four vaulted bays on a central column – becomes more explicable as an element in such an *ensemble*, which would presumably also have included a scaled-down rotunda associated with, or even serving as, the shrine.[152] Relevant in this context is T.A. Heslop's suggestion (below, p. 274) that the canopy over St. Frideswide's head on the late 12th-century Priory seal is copied from the bulls of the masters of the Order of St. John of Jerusalem, where it apparently represents the Holy Sepulchre (see Fig. 107). A programme of architectural symbolism likening Frideswide's shrine to the Tomb of Christ could well have originated in Robert of Cricklade's fertile brain, even if not realised until after his death.

Secondly, the location of a parochial altar near the shrine, and therefore on the N. side of the church, may provide a further clue to the pre-Romanesque arrangements. We have already noted possible indications that Æthelred's minster may have stood immediately N. of its successor; if it survived the initial laying-out of the conventual

[148] *Liber Antiquus de Ordinationibus Vicariarum Tempore Hugonis Wells*, ed. A. Gibbons (1888), 1; cf. *Rot. Hugonis de Welles*, i (Linc. Rec. Soc. iii, 1912), 182.

[149] *Rot. Grosseteste* (Linc. Rec. Soc. xi, 1914), 465, 481, 496.

[150] *Reg. Sutton*, vi (Linc. Rec. Soc. lxiv, 1969), 106–7.

[151] P.R.O. PROB 11/14 f.18ᵛ; H.F. Owen Evans, 'The Tomb of James Zouch in Oxford Cathedral', *Trans. Monumental Brass Soc.* ix (1952–62), 509–11.

[152] For copies of the Holy Sepulchre see R. Krautheimer, *Studies in Early Christian, Medieval and Renaissance Art* (1971), 116–30; see also note 128 above.

church during *c*.1140–55, and if the removal of the canons into a new choir during the 1160s left it exclusively for its pre-existing parochial functions, it is entirely likely that a parish altar would have been allowed to remain on its site when the shrine-chapel and enlarged N. transept finally obliterated it during *c*.1170–90.

This series of *ifs* is not so hypothetical in context as it may seem in isolation: the transformation of Anglo-Saxon minsters into 12th-century monasteries was rarely simple, and the kind of sequence just proposed was more the rule than the exception. To put Oxford in context it is worth citing some analogues:

(a) Some great Romanesque churches replacing lines of older and smaller churches were built directly over their predecessors, on the same axes (Glastonbury, St. Augustine's Canterbury),[153] but such cases may be in a minority. More often the pre-Romanesque church or churches had been differently sited and aligned, either to the N. or N.W. of their successors (Winchester Old Minster, Exeter, Rochester),[154] or to the S. (Wells, Peterborough, Lyminge, Durham, Haughmond, perhaps Abingdon and Hereford).[155] Bury St. Edmunds, where the vast late 11th-century church replaced heterogeneous pre-Conquest structures aligned along its N. side,[156] is a particularly telling parallel for St. Frideswide's.

(b) Where an Anglo-Saxon minster complex contained two churches, separation of monastic and parochial functions might be effected by rebuilding one as a fully-fledged conventual church and leaving the other for parish use. This certainly happened at Winchcombe,[157] and may be the true explanation of the pre-Conquest church which lay W. of Exeter Cathedral;[158] the arrangement at Lindisfarne, where the 11th-century or earlier parish church lies due W. of the Romanesque priory church,[159] is *prima facie* similar.

(c) Where a minster community was re-founded as a strict monastery, a new church might be built attached to, or near, the old one, which once again would be left for the use of secular clergy and parishioners. This happened after the Benedictine reform of Worcester in the 960s and the Cluniac reform of Daventry *c*.1108.[160] More relevant in the present context are Augustinian examples of the mid to late 12th century, involving

[153] H.M. and J. Taylor, *Anglo-Saxon Architecture*, i (1965), 253, 136.

[154] Winchester: Biddle op. cit. note 16, Fig. 9; Exeter: C.G. Henderson and P.T. Bidwell, 'The Saxon Minster at Exeter', in Pearce op. cit. note 121, 145–76; Rochester: Taylor and Taylor op. cit. note 153, ii (1965), 519.

[155] Wells: W. Rodwell, *Wells Cathedral: Excavations and Discoveries* (3rd edn., 1987); Peterborough: Taylor and Taylor op. cit. note 153, ii, 492; Lyminge and Durham: above, note 126; Haughmond: above, note 92; Abingdon: G. Lambrick, 'Buildings of the Monasteries at Abingdon from the Late Seventh Century to 1538', *Med. Arch.* xii (1968), 43, 51; Hereford: the cathedral obstructs the main W.–E. route through the town in such a way as to suggest that it has moved northwards: see R. Shoesmith, *Hereford City Excavations: II* (C.B.A. Research Rep. 46, 1982), 13–20, 74–83.

[156] Gem and Keen loc. cit. note 129.

[157] S.R. Bassett, 'A Probable Mercian Royal Mausoleum at Winchcombe, Gloucestershire', *Antiq. Jnl.* lxv (1985), 87.

[158] This is not the view of Henderson and Bidwell op. cit. note 154; but *two* aligned churches, the eastern always dedicated to St. Peter and the western to St. Mary, seems a more satisfactory hypothesis than their suggestion that the Anglo-Saxon cathedral was re-dedicated and assigned for parish use when the Romanesque one was built.

[159] See Taylor and Taylor op. cit. note 153, i, 398–9, and R.N. Bailey, E. Cambridge and H.D. Biggs, *Dowsing and Church Archaeology* (1988), 34, 83–5. A photograph of the early work in the parish church was published by P.F. Ryder in *Popular Archaeology*, June 1983, p. 41.

[160] C. Dyer, 'The Saxon Cathedrals of Worcester', *Trans. Worc. Archaeol. Soc.* 3rd ser. ii (1968–9), 34; M.J. Franklin, 'The Secular College as a Focus for Anglo-Norman Piety: St. Augustine's Daventry', in Blair op. cit. note 91, 97–9.

a new conventual church and cloister either attached to the E. end of the old church (Goring)[161] or free-standing a short way further E. (Bicester, Repton).[162]

(d) In some cases where a Romanesque church is known to have replaced the church or churches of a secular minster, a parish aisle or altar recorded in the later middle ages may represent a previously free-standing church with parochial attributes. A late Chester tradition relates that a church for St. Werburgh's relics was built in the 9th century against the E. end of the old minster of Sts. Peter and Paul there, which was re-dedicated to St. Oswald; if there is any truth in this story it suggests that the parish altar of St. Oswald, recorded in the nave of St. Werburgh's conventual church by the 13th century, perpetuates the memory and perhaps the site of the original church.[163] At Daventry, where the first Cluniac church had been built c.1108 against the 'parish church' (i.e. secular minster), parish functions were housed by the 15th century in a large S. aisle.[164] A particularly odd case is St. Martin-le-Grand in Dover, which absorbed under its roof the parish churches of St. Nicholas and St. John Baptist, each incumbent having his own high altar and distinct area within the church.[165]

These cases of minsters overshadowed or swallowed by large conventual churches may help us to understand the sequence at Oxford. Winchcombe, Exeter and Lindisfarne reinforce the suggestion that St. Aldate's may have been separated off, as a parish church, from the complex of which it had been an integral part; Goring, Bicester and Repton are cases of a mid to late 12th-century Augustinian community assigning its old church for parish use and moving to an up-to-date church and cloister nearby; Bury, Wells, Peterborough, Lyminge, Durham, Haughmond and Daventry illustrate a recurrent practice of building the new church directly alongside the old one; while Chester and Daventry show how an old church thus overshadowed might survive for a while but eventually vanish, its residual functions coming under the roof of the new church in the guise of a parish altar.

If we cannot at present prove that any of these things happened at Oxford, we can at least claim that the various hints and clues can be fitted into a wider context, and are consistent with the archaeological evidence from the cloister area which suggests a general shift southwards. Future archaeological planning should reckon with the prospect that an Anglo-Saxon minster church awaits discovery under the turf of the Cathedral garden.

---

[161] J. Blair, 'The Foundation of Goring Priory', *Oxoniensia*, li (1986), 194–7.

[162] Bicester: Blair op. cit. note 37, 136 note 161; D.A. Hinton, 'Bicester Priory', *Oxoniensia*, xxxiii (1968), 22–52. Repton: H.M. Taylor, *St. Wystan's Church, Repton: A Guide* (new edn., 1989); W. St. John Hope, 'On the Augustinian Priory of the Holy Trinity at Repton', *Derbs. Arch. Jnl.* vii (1885), opp. p. 154.

[163] Thacker op. cit. note 27, 203–4; *The Life of St. Werburge of Chester by Henry Bradshaw*, ed. C. Horstmann (E.E.T.S. lxxxviii, 1887), 151–2; *Chartulary of Chester Abbey*, ed. J. Tait, i (Chetham Soc. n.s. lxxix, 1920), 117–19.

[164] Franklin loc. cit. note 160.

[165] Canon Scott Robinson, 'The Old Church of St. Martin at Dover', *Arch. Cant.* xx (1893), 295–304.

# Notes

## AN EARLY MEDIEVAL FLOOR-TILE FROM ST. FRIDESWIDE'S MINSTER

The tile which is the subject of this note (now Ashmolean Museum Acc. No. 1970.552) was among the material found in 1863 during the construction of the Meadows Building, Christ Church (see above, p. 229 note 55). A tattered label stuck to one edge bears the number '39' pencilled over the original legend in faded ink. This is only legible in part, but appears to read ' . . . ]lett[ . . . / . . . ] New . . . . . . ] Ch 1863 . . . ./6' (characters in square brackets illegible). In the early 1950s David Sturdy noted this tile in a parcel, then stored in the S. transept gallery, labelled 'Tiles from foundations New buildings Ch: Ch: Mar. 1863'.

*Description* (Figs. 102–3)

The *fabric* is cream in colour and knife-trimmed to a silky surface on the sides of the tile. On the worn surface and through a few chips it is possible to see that the fabric has fired in places to a pale reddish-brown and that layers of this colour, sometimes including very thin brick-red bands, interleave with layers of cream to give a characteristic laminated effect to the core. Inspection under a ×15 lens shows that the cream bands consist solely of very fine sand particles, not resolvable at this magnification, and that the thin brick-red bands share this composition. The thicker, pale reddish-brown layers are composed of larger grains, easily resolvable at ×15, rounded or sub-angular, consistently *c.*0.05 to 0.1 mm. in diameter, and cemented together with little trace of a distinct matrix. The fabric is dense, hard, and well fired.

Fig. 102. Early medieval floor-tile from St. Frideswide's. *Scale 1:2.* (Drawing by Sarah Blair.)

Fig. 103.   Reconstruction of the pattern made by the early medieval floor-tile. *Scale 1:4.* (Drawing by John Blair.)

In *form*, the tile is square, each side measuring between 95 and 97 mm. on the face (slightly more than 3¾ by 3¾ in.) and 92 to 94 mm. on the back. The edges are bevelled slightly inwards from the face and smoothly cut, with sharp angles. The back is slightly uneven, but generally smooth; it is not keyed. The tile varies between 20 and 22 mm. in thickness.

The *decoration* on the surface is in relief, the outlines sharp and well-formed where not worn down. The pattern (which requires six tiles to complete it, Fig. 103) consists of tangentially arranged circles filled with 'crosses pommy' and separated by quatrefoils (Fig. 102). The circles consist of outer lines framing a lower and wider central moulding. The 'crosses' comprise an angular central element with four arms opening onto relatively large circular terminals. Both inside and outside the 'crosses', the field is sown with pellets. Between the circles, each element of the quatrefoils is elegantly lobed and brought to a fine point; each is filled with a line of two or possibly three pellets, the outermost smaller than the other(s).

The *glaze* is a rich dark-brown lead glaze. It fills all the recesses of the surface and originally covered the raised elements, where it has mostly been worn away. There is no attempt at polychromy. In places the glaze has run over the edge to form patches and thick bulbous drips of solid, very dark brown, almost black, glaze.

The *surface* of the tile is worn. The back and edges carry areas of both buff sandy (? original) and white mortar, showing that it was reused at least once. Traces of mortar on the surface may suggest that the tile was finally buried below a later floor or reused as rubble.

*Discussion*

The fabric, the use of relief decoration, the pattern, and the glaze all suggest that this tile is not an example (however uncommon) of the normal range of decorated later medieval floor-tiles,[1] but is rather a further example of the rapidly expanding group of early medieval relief-decorated floor-tiles. These now appear to comprise at least three broad styles or phases: an early and certainly pre-Conquest style, comprising at least two sub-groups, one of polychrome glazed tiles in a pale granular fabric ('Style 1a'), the other of apparently smaller tiles in a brick-red, sometimes laminated fabric ('Style 1b'); an intermediate style of larger and more elaborately decorated tiles, with one-colour glaze ('Style 2'); and a later, probably mid 12th-century group of 'St. Albans type', also large and with a plain glaze ('Style 3'). Since all three styles appear to ante-date the well-known series of medieval floor-tiles beginning in the later 12th century, it seems convenient to call these three styles 'early medieval', to distinguish them from the later series.[2]

The Christ Church tile, although not exactly matched by any other known tile, is apparently an example of Style 1, which is now known from Winchester,[3] St. Albans,[4] Bury St. Edmunds,[5] Canterbury,[6] York,[7] and Coventry.[8] The granular fabric characteristic of the reddish-brown layers of the Christ Church tile is very close to the fabric of some of the Winchester, Bury St. Edmunds and St. Albans tiles of Style 1a, but overall the tile is probably an example of Style 1b.

The individual elements of the pattern of the Christ Church tile are as difficult to place as the overall design. The concentric circles, displayed back-to-back, the quatrefoils, crosses 'pommy', and pellets cannot be paralleled individually, let alone in this arrangement, among the approximately 3,100 designs of the 14,000 or so later

[1] John Blair was the first to recognise the possible Anglo-Saxon origin of this tile. John Cherry, Richard Gem, Laurence Keen and Christopher Norton kindly commented on a drawing, but have not seen the tile itself; Mark Horton has seen the tile and commented on this note. Christopher Norton is not entirely happy with a pre-Conquest identification, noting that in his experience, in the present state of research, one or two anomalous tiles usually occur in any large group; he suggests a possible context for the pattern in the tile industries of the Penn group. Mark Horton, who has seen all the available tiles of Oxfordshire and Buckinghamshire, confirms that the fabric of the Christ Church tile is not comparable to any of them; he believes that it is characteristically Anglo-Saxon and also notes the thick drips of glaze on the edges as typical of Anglo-Saxon floor-tiles. John Cherry, Richard Gem, and Laurence Keen are prepared to accept an Anglo-Saxon date if the fabric and glaze are consistent with such an interpretation.

[2] This terminology of three 'styles' within an 'early medieval' series is proposed here for the first time. For previous publications of tiles in this series, see below, notes 3–8.

[3] J. Backhouse et al. (eds.), *The Golden Age of Anglo-Saxon Art 966–1066* (catalogue of British Museum exhibition, 1984), Cat. Nos. 142–3, with further references. The Winchester tiles will be published in M. Biddle and B. Kjølbye-Biddle, *The Anglo-Saxon Minsters at Winchester*, Winchester Studies 4.i (forthcoming 1990), and, with full technical discussion, in K. Barclay, *The Medieval Ceramics of Winchester*, Winchester Studies 7.i (in preparation).

[4] R. Gem and L. Keen, 'Late Anglo-Saxon Finds from the Site of St. Edmund's Abbey', *Proc. Suffolk Inst. Archaeol. and Hist* xxxv (1981), 1–30, at p. 23, Fig. 16, which also mentions the much larger series from the St. Albans excavations of 1978 and 1982–4. This will be published in M. Biddle and B. Kjølbye-Biddle, *The Chapter House of St. Albans Abbey* (Hertfordshire Archaeology, in preparation). For Style 2 tiles from St. Albans, see Backhouse et al. op. cit. note 3, Cat. No. 144; and for Style 3 tiles from the St. Albans chapter-house floor, G. Zarnecki et al. (eds.), *English Romanesque Art 1066–1200* (catalogue of Hayward Gallery exhibition, 1984), Cat. No. 552.

[5] Gem and Keen op. cit. note 4, 20–6, Fig. 15, Pl. I (colour).

[6] From the site of the Norman and later Archbishop's Palace: information kindly provided by T. Tatton-Brown.

[7] Gem and Keen op. cit. note 4, 24, Pl. II.

[8] M.A. Stokes, 'Late Saxon Tiles from Coventry', *Medieval Ceramics*, x (1986), 29–36.

medieval tiles in the British Museum collection.[9] The individual elements can, however, be found among the tiles of Style 1 of the early medieval series.

Addorsed semi-circles appear on tiles from York[10] and St. Albans;[11] concentric circles on another of the York tiles;[12] and pellets on three more of the York tiles,[13] and on some of the St. Albans tiles of Style 2.[14] Quatrefoils also occur on Style 1 tiles from Bury St. Edmunds[15] and Winchester,[16] but these are usually composed geometrically of the intersecting arcs of circles. By contrast, the individual leaves of the Christ Church quatrefoils have a more complex, sinuous outline. To some extent this results from the greater depth of wear near the margins of the (one surviving) Christ Church tile, but significantly it also arises from the outer ends of the leaves being formed of ridges which follow concentrically the outer curve of the addorsed semi-circles.

For possible parallels to the crosses 'pommy', it is necessary to turn to the patterns appearing on the reverses of late Anglo-Saxon silver pennies. The 'jewel cross' type of Harold I and Harthacnut, issued from early 1036 until late 1037 or early 1038, offers on the reverse a complex figure, the 'jewel cross', which consists of four round or oval 'jewels' radiating from a central circle or square. The latter is itself outlined by an outer circle appearing only between the arms or 'jewels'. Regional variations in die-cutting are reflected in slightly differing shapes of the 'jewel cross': in Harthacnut's type with right-facing bust (Variety R), round (as contrasted with oval) 'jewels' 'are usual at Canterbury and Oxford, but not at Winchester'.[17] Pellets, it is worth noting, form an element in the obverse design of the 'jewel cross' type, as of the preceding 'pointed helmet' type of Cnut and of the succeeding types of both Harold I and Harthacnut.

Although much remains to be discovered about the tiles of the early medieval series, the analogues of the Christ Church tile suggest that it is of pre-Conquest date and derives from another and as yet otherwise undefined group of 'Style 1b'. All the tiles of Style 1 have come so far from the sites or vicinity of major late-Saxon churches, and it seems probable that their function was to decorate the floor surfaces and steps around principal altars or shrines.

At Winchester, tiles of Style 1a and 1b are present before 980 or 993–4, at the latest.[18] At Coventry, Style 1 tiles are perhaps to be associated with the Benedictine house founded by Leofric and Godiva in 1043.[19] At Bury, they have been plausibly related to the masonry buildings erected after 1020.[20] If the analogy of the Christ Church tile with the 'jewel cross' coins of c.1036–7 is valid, a comparable date in the earlier 11th century is suggested.

---

[9] E.S. Eames, *Catalogue of Medieval Lead-Glazed Earthenware Tiles in the . . . British Museum*, 2 vols. (1980).

[10] Gem and Keen op. cit. note 4, Pl. II, Row 2, third tile; and another tile with similar addorsed spaced semi-circles in a frieze with ring-impressed borders above and below (drawings and photographs with the writers).

[11] Gem and Keen op. cit. note 4, Fig. 16, No. 3.

[12] Ibid., Pl. II, Row 1, third tile.

[13] Ibid., Pl. II, Row 2, fourth tile; and two other tiles (drawings and photographs held by the writers).

[14] Biddle and Kjølbye-Biddle op. cit. note 4.

[15] Gem and Keen op. cit. note 4, Fig. 15, No. 7, Pl. I, bottom row, second tile.

[16] Type D (Fabrics 1 and 2), e.g. Recorded find CG 1222: Biddle and Kjølbye-Biddle op. cit. note 4.

[17] Tukka Talvio, 'Harold I and Harthacnut's *Jewel Cross* Type Reconsidered', in M.A.S. Blackburn (ed.), *Anglo-Saxon Monetary History. Essays in Memory of Michael Dolley* (1986), 273–90. This suggested parallel between a design on a tile and one on a coin does not stand alone: several of the Winchester tile designs are exactly paralleled by reverse types of Cnut and Edward the Confessor. (Mark Blackburn confirmed the accuracy of this numismatic information, but must not be held responsible for the use made of it.)

[18] See above, note 3.

[19] Stokes op. cit. note 8, 29–30.

[20] Gem and Keen op. cit. note 4, 26.

The Christ Church tile is probably therefore the earliest physical evidence so far recognised for the presence of a major pre-Conquest church on the site of the Augustinian priory of St. Frideswide. It complements the evidence for earlier burials, notably those laid on beds of charcoal, recovered during the excavations of the last decade.

MARTIN BIDDLE and BIRTHE KJØLBYE-BIDDLE

## THE GOLD FINGER-RING FROM A BURIAL IN ST. ALDATE'S STREET, OXFORD

On 5 February 1903, a gold finger-ring was exhibited to the Society of Antiquaries of London that had been 'found about 1890 in a stone coffin in St. Aldate's Street, Oxford, when excavations were being made for a drain opposite the great gateway of Christ Church'.[21] In 1905 it was purchased by the British Museum (1905, 11–8, 1) and is No. 214 in Dalton's *Ring Catalogue* (1912).[22] Neither the British Museum Register nor the *Catalogue* contains any further information concerning its find circumstances. A seemingly very different account of its discovery by Bjørn and Shetelig in *Viking Antiquities* (1940)[23] turns out on closer examination to refer to a medieval gold ring found in Hertfordshire and may thus be ignored. Although it has been referred to and listed on a number of other occasions,[24] the St. Aldate's ring has never before been illustrated or discussed in detail.[25]

The ring (Fig. 104) is composed of six plaited rods tapering towards the ends, where they are beaten together into a narrow, plain band (parted in one place) which forms the back of the ring; its maximum external diameter is 2.6 cm., and that of the rods is 0.2 cm. The ring is in excellent condition apart from the break in the band, but this clearly took place in antiquity given that both ends are smooth even though one is straight and the other irregular in form.

Finger-rings of gold, silver or base-metal formed from twisted or plaited rods are known from England, the Isle of Man, Ireland and Scotland, as well as Scandinavia, in Viking-age contexts, in some later hoards and as single-finds. Indeed, the fashion for their use in the west is considered to be a result of Scandinavian settlement in Britain and Ireland.[26] Those as elaborately executed as the St. Aldate's example are relatively rare, characteristically made of gold and seemingly of 11th-century date.

The gold finger-rings of Viking-age type found in Scotland have recently received brief consideration in print;[27] those formed from plaited (as opposed to simply twisted) rods are present in two coinless hoards – one from the Hebrides and one from Stenness

[21] *Proc. Soc. Antiq. London*, 2nd ser. xix (1901–3), 221.

[22] O.M. Dalton, *Catalogue of the Finger-Rings . . .* (1912), 36.

[23] A. Bjørn and H. Shetelig, *Viking Antiquities in Great Britain and Ireland*, Part IV (H. Shetelig (ed.), 1940), 29.

[24] *V.C.H. Oxon.* i, 368, 371; *Oxoniensia*, xvii–xviii (1952–3), 109, No. 23; D.A. Hinton, 'Late Saxon Treasure and Bullion', in D. Hill (ed.), *Ethelred the Unready: Papers from the Millenary Conference* (B.A.R. 59, 1978), 135–58, at p. 156, No. 21.

[25] The drawing is by Eva Wilson, to whom I am particularly grateful for the time and care she expended on determining and recording the complex nature of the plait. I also wish to thank Leslie Webster of the British Museum for her assistance in the study of the ring and for discussing it with me.

[26] E.g. L. Webster, 'Gold Ring from Dane John, Canterbury', *Archaeologia Cantiana*, xcii (1976), 233–4.

[27] J. Graham-Campbell, 'An Unpublished Gold Finger-Ring of Viking-Age Date from the Isle of Skye, and New Light on the 1850 Skye Hoard', *Proc. Soc. Antiq. Scotland*, cxii (1982), 568–70.

Fig. 104.   Gold finger-ring of six plaited rods from St. Aldate's, Oxford. *Scale 1:1.* (Drawing by Eva Wilson.)

on Orkney Mainland.[28] A fine complex example like that from St. Aldate's is a single-find from Fladda Chuinn, off Skye.[29] None of these finds is precisely datable, but gold finger-rings of twisted rods are known from both early and late hoards, there having been one variant in the lost (late 9th- or early 10th-century) hoard from Gordon, Berwickshire[30] and another in the Plan Farm, Bute, hoard of *c.*1150.[31]

On the Isle of Man only one such gold finger-ring has been discovered, at Greeba in the parish of German.[32] It is, however, of the complex plaited type, as is a fine example from near Waterford in Ireland.[33] This is likewise a single-find, but recently another plaited finger-ring, of simpler construction, has been excavated in Dublin.[34] I am most grateful to Dr. Patrick Wallace for the following information concerning its construction and context (*per* D. Caulfield, 1/11/88):

> The finger-ring is made of three rods. It was found in a sod layer between two superimposed houses. The earlier house, FS12, plot 5, level 4 of Fishamble Street, had two coins: one an Athelstan *c.*925; the other an Athelstan *c.*930. Above this was the sod layer (?collapsed roofing material) where the ring was found. The house on top of this, FS18, plot 5, level 5, had an Eadred *c.*946–55.

The context for this Dublin ring suggests deposition about the middle of the 10th century, yet there exists the possibility that it had been concealed in the roof of a house

[28] S. Grieg, *Viking Antiquities in Great Britain and Ireland*, Part II (H. Shetelig (ed.), 1940), Figs. 58 and 62.

[29] Ibid. Fig. 58.

[30] J.A. Graham-Campbell, 'The Viking-Age Silver and Gold Hoards of Scandinavian Character from Scotland', *Proc. Soc. Antiq. Scotland*, cvii (1975–6), 114–35, see Pl. 14, 1.

[31] J.H. Pollexfen and G. Sim, 'Notice of the Coins Etc . . . found at Plan, in the Island of Bute', *Proc. Soc. Antiq. Scotland*, v (1862–4), 372–84.

[32] J. Graham-Campbell, 'The Viking-Age Silver Hoards of the Isle of Man', in C.E. Fell et al. (eds.), *The Viking Age in the Isle of Man* (1983), 53–80, at p. 80.

[33] J. Bøe, *Viking Antiquities in Great Britain and Ireland*, Part III (H. Shetelig (ed.), 1940), Fig. 72.

[34] E.g. ibid. Fig. 69; the Dublin ring is illustrated in P. Wallace, 'Dublin 988', *Ireland of the Welcomes*, xxxvii. 1 (Jan.–Feb., 1988), 17–25, at p. 24.

(FS12). It is thus necessary to extend the possible date-range for its deposition to 'the second quarter/middle of the 10th century'.

A similar simple (three-rod) plaited finger-ring, in a lead alloy, was recovered at 6–8 Pavement, York, from what would seem to be a late 10th-century context.[35] The gold finger-ring executed in the same manner from Hungate in York is, however, undated.[36] Rings of plaited wires are mentioned as having been excavated at 16–22 Coppergate, York, of which a complex lead-alloy example has been illustrated, but details of its construction and context are not yet available.[37]

For England, as a whole, it is premature to attempt a definitive list of plaited-rod gold finger-rings because previous authors have not always considered it necessary to distinguish the plaited from the simpler (and longer-lived) twisted varieties. In all at least 17 rings are on record,[38] but amongst these there is only one plaited example known for certain from a coin-dated hoard – the others being single-finds, with an apparent distributional bias to southern England. This hoard was deposited c.1068 near Soberton in Hampshire[39] – a date consistent with the limited Scandinavian coin-hoard evidence for plaited finger-rings which commences with the mid-11th-century Äspinge hoard from Skåne, Sweden (t.p.q. 1047).[40] As a result, Stenberger's central dating for three-rod types in Sweden was late 11th to 12th century, but more complex examples are there a rarity and undated.[41]

In conclusion, it seems reasonable to suggest at this stage of investigation that, whilst simple (three-rod) plaited finger-rings were introduced in Britain and Ireland in the 10th century, as demonstrated by the excavated examples from York and Dublin, the elaborately plaited rings of the St. Aldate's type were not current before the 11th century. In this light, the southerly distribution in England of twisted and plaited gold finger-rings suggests a fashion introduced under Danish rule. The most immediate parallels for the St. Aldate's ring are, however, those noted above from Ireland, the Isle of Man and Scandinavian Scotland. Finally, it is worth noting that plaited rings of this type are not known from 12th-century contexts in England, although a silver two-rod twisted finger-ring formed part of the Lark Hill hoard, from near Worcester, deposited c.1180.[42]

The deposition of such a gold ring of this date in a coffin in England appears highly unusual at first sight, given that only two examples of gold finger-rings are known from mid/late Saxon graves (in Exeter and Repton, Derbyshire) and both of these date earlier – to the 8th/9th centuries.[43] However, it is worth recalling that at least two others

[35] A. MacGregor, *Anglo-Scandinavian Finds from Lloyds Bank, Pavement and Other Sites* (Archaeology of York, xvii. 3, 1982), Fig. 47, No. 455.

[36] D.M. Waterman, 'Late Saxon, Viking, and Early Medieval Finds from York', *Archaeologia*, xcvii (1959), 59–105, see Fig. 10, 14.

[37] R. Hall, *The Viking Dig* (1984), 104, Fig. 122,d.

[38] Hinton op. cit. note 24, pp. 156 and 158; in this list Nos. 16 and 17 represent a single ring from 'West Bergholt, near Colchester', but Hinton omits two old finds, both plaited rings, from Suffolk (*Archaeol. Jnl.* vi (1849), 58 and Fig. 14), and from Ringmer in Sussex (*Archaeol. Jnl.* xv (1858), 96).

[39] No. 263 in M. Blackburn and H. Pagan, 'A Revised Check-List of Coin Hoards from the British Isles, c.500–1100', in M.A.S. Blackburn (ed.), *Anglo-Saxon Monetary History: Essays in Memory of Michael Dolley* (1986), 291–313; Dalton op. cit. note 22, No. 215.

[40] B. Hårdh, *Wikingerzeitliche Depotfunde aus Südschweden* (Acta Archaeologica Lundensia, Series in 4°, No. 9, 1976), Taf. 38, 4.

[41] M. Stenberger, *Die Schatzfunde Gotlands der Wikingerzeit*, i (1947), 137–8.

[42] J. Cherry, 'Medieval Rings, 1100–1500', in A. Ward et al., *The Ring from Antiquity to the Twentieth Century* (1981), 51–86, at p. 60, No. 112.

[43] J. Graham-Campbell, 'A Middle Saxon Gold Finger-Ring from the Cathedral Close, Exeter', *Antiq. Jnl.* lxii (1982), 366–7; M. Biddle et al., 'Coins of the Anglo-Saxon Period from Repton, Derbyshire: II', *Brit. Numis. Jnl.* lvi (1986), 16–34, the ring being from Grave 529, with coins of the 870s (see esp. pp. 25–6 and note 36).

amongst the group of 10th/12th-century twisted/plaited gold finger-rings (most of which are poorly documented, and some of which are from hoards) may have been deposited under the same circumstances: that from Hamsey churchyard, Sussex;[44] and that from Balmer, also in Sussex, which was first illustrated in 1824 around some finger-bones (although it is only described as having been 'ploughed up').[45]

J.A. GRAHAM-CAMPBELL

## AN EARLY 12TH-CENTURY PURBECK MARBLE GRAVESLAB FROM ST. FRIDESWIDE'S PRIORY

Among the worked stones found built into the E. wall of the choir in the 1870s are three fragments from the upper end of a Purbeck marble graveslab (Fig. 105).[46] It has a flat surface and a broad hollow-chamfer around the edge; it tapers slightly, and the width at the head end when complete would have been c.61 cm. The edges below the hollow-chamfer have coarse tooling, and the under-side is left rough. Carved in shallow relief on the surface are groups of concentric semicircles, the uppermost enclosing a rudimentary face, framing axially-placed concentric lozenges which may represent small crosses. The crudity of this surface decoration suggests the possibility that it may have been added locally to a slab sent blank from the quarry.

The design has obvious affinities with the slabs, usually dated c.1080–1120, on which groups of concentric lozenge and half-lozenge motifs form an over-all, vaguely cruciform pattern.[47] The semicircular forms are, however, exceptional, and the incorporation of a human face is still more so. So unsophisticated an idiom cannot be dated closely, but the general adoption of better-formulated cross patterns during the 12th century makes a date after the 1120s decreasingly likely for slabs of this type.

Much the most remarkable aspect of this monument is its material. The systematic production of architectural components in Purbeck marble is hard to trace back before the 1160s, when northern French influence, spread especially through Henry of Blois's patronage, stimulated a fashion for dark shafting.[48] Likewise, the first regular series of effigies and slabs in Purbeck marble are all of the 1160s onwards and show a restricted, south-western distribution,[49] though it is interesting that two of them have, like the Oxford slab, marginal hollow-chamfers at a date before this feature had come into

---

[44] Dalton op. cit. note 22, p. 36, No. 215a.

[45] T.W. Horsefield, *History and Antiquities of Lewes*, i (1824), 49, Pl. iv, 4, where the provenance is given as Bormer (= 'Borner' in Bjørn and Shetelig op. cit. note 23, p. 29, and Hinton op. cit. note 24, p. 156, No. 24). I am grateful to Fiona Marsden for help with this reference and the information that 'Bormer' is an archaic spelling for the modern 'Balmer'.

[46] J.C. Bucker records that the slab was 'found in the east wall, among the mason work of the latter part of the 13th century' (B.L. MS Add. 27765 E, f.98). It was illustrated in *R.C.H.M. Oxford*, Pl. 9, and is now on display in the City Musuem.

[47] See especially L.A.S. Butler, 'Minor Medieval Monumental Sculpture in the East Midlands', *Archaeol. Jnl.* cxxi (1964), 119 and Fig. 2A; F. Burgess, *English Churchyard Memorials* (1963), 92.

[48] J. Blair, 'Purbeck Marble', in J. Blair and N. Ramsay (eds.), *English Medieval Industries* (forthcoming); G. Zarnecki, 'Henry of Blois as a Patron of Sculpture', in S. Macready and F.H. Thompson (eds.), *Art and Patronage in the English Romanesque* (1986), 168.

[49] G. Dru Drury, 'The Use of Purbeck Marble in Medieval Times', *Proc. Dorset Nat. Hist. and Arch. Soc.* lxx (1948), 77–8, Pls. IX-XII; Blair, op. cit. note 48.

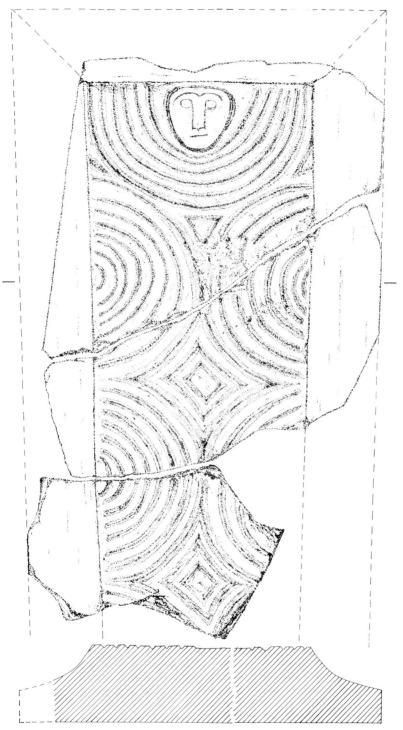

Fig. 105. Purbeck marble graveslab from St. Frideswide's. *Scale 1:6.* (Drawing by Sarah Blair.)

general use.[50] The existence of occasional Purbeck marble components of apparently early 12th-century date, and the appearance of one *Girardus Marbrarius* in a London deed of 1106,[51] suggest small-scale use of the material before the era of systematic production.

The Oxford slab, with its strange design and naive execution, must be a product of the craft in its infancy; it may well be the oldest surviving funerary monument in Purbeck marble. If it was made during *c*.1080–1130, it belongs to the last years of the unreformed community or the first of the Augustinians. Obtained from Corfe, or possibly London, at a time when there was no regular trade in Purbeck slabs, it must have been an exotic item indeed. Its presence at St. Frideswide's may well reflect the patronage of Roger bishop of Salisbury (above, pp. 227–8), whose architectural activities were concentrated in Wiltshire and Dorset and whose diocese included the Purbeck quarries.[52]

If the 'marble' of Corfe had already come to be thought of as a substitute for true marble, the slab was probably bought because it was appropriate to an exceptionally important tomb. It may not be too far-fetched to suggest that with this slab the Anglo-Norman canons marked the reputed grave of St. Frideside. St. Osmund's grave at Salisbury (1099) had a plain, coffin-shaped slab of Tournai marble, which was retained in the 13th century despite the elevation of the relics on a new shrine-base.[53] A more telling parallel may be the shrine of St. Wita at Whitchurch Canonicorum (Dorset), which incorporates a freestone coffin covered by a plain Purbeck slab, again with a hollow-chamfer edge moulding. The sides of the coffin and the edges of the slab below the hollow-chamfer are, as on the Oxford slab, rough-dressed: it appears that this originated as a below-floor tomb, raised up on the shrine-base around 1200.[54] The 12th-century excavators of St. Frideswide's tomb found 'an empty stone coffin' or 'the stone coffin empty' (*sarcofagum lapideum vacuum invenerunt*):[55] could this coffin, like St. Wita's, have been capped with a Purbeck marble slab?

JOHN BLAIR

## AN UNPUBLISHED 12TH-CENTURY WALL-PAINTING AT ST. FRIDESWIDE'S PRIORY

On the N. jamb of the mid 12th-century N. window of the chapter-house front, facing the cloister, one splendid fragment of the original painted decorative scheme remains, badly faded but still visible to the naked eye.

---

[50] Philip the Priest's effigy at Tolpuddle (G. Dru Drury, 'Early Ecclesiastical Effigies in Dorset', *Proc. Dorset Nat. Hist. and Arch. Soc.* liii (1931), 252–5); a coped slab in Winchester Cathedral, usually ascribed to William Rufus but probably for Bishop Henry of Blois, d.1171 (J.G. Joyce, 'On the Opening . . . of a Tomb in Winchester Cathedral . . .', *Archaeologia*, xlii (1869), 309–21).

[51] Blair, op. cit. note 48; *Early Charters of St. Paul's*, ed. M. Gibbs (Camden 3rd ser. lviii, 1939), No. 198.

[52] I am indebted to Dr. L.A.S. Butler for this suggestion. For Roger see R.A. Stalley, 'A 12th-century Patron of Architecture', *JBAA* 3rd ser. xxxiv (1971), 62–83.

[53] H. Shortt, 'Three Early Episcopal Tombs in Salisbury Cathedral', *Wilts. Arch. and Nat. Hist. Mag.* lvii (1959), 217–19. (I accept Shortt's argument that the plain Tournai slab is for Osmund, and that the low-relief Purbeck effigy with a metrical inscription is for Jocelyn de Bohun. *R.C.H.M. Salisbury I* (1980), 19–20 prefers, without serious discussion, an older view reversing these attributions.)

[54] Personal inspection, 1988; cf. *R.C.H.M. West Dorset* (1952), 263 and Pl. 210.

[55] Blair, 'St. F.', 117.

A man dressed in a long tunic stands with the head turned in profile to his left and the body turned only slightly in that direction. His right hand, palm inwards, points a little upward across his body; his left hand, palm upwards, gestures or points with thumb and first finger outstretched. The tunic is draped in the characteristic 'damp-fold' convention of much Byzantine-influenced English and English-influenced Continental work of the 12th century. Around his neck the front-opening collar or border continues downward around the fairly short front slit, a widespread but not particularly common style in the 12th century. The wide sleeves end in a similar narrow border or cuff ornamented with large dots or roundels. The medium-length slightly curly hair and large eyes can readily be matched in the once-splendid chapter-house decorations at Sigona in Catalonia, painted by English craftsmen in the 1180s or '90s.[56]

But the best parallels can be found in a group of manuscripts of the 1140s and '50s[57] comprising the Psalter of Henry de Blois or Winchester Psalter (Brit. Lib. MS Cotton Nero C IV), the Sherborne Abbey Cartulary (Brit. Lib. Add. MS 46487), the Littlemore Priory Anselm (Bod. Lib. MS Auct. D.2.6 ff. 156–200),[58] a Bestiary (Bod. Lib. MS Laud. Misc. 247 ff. 139–170),[59] and the charter granted to Kelso Abbey in 1159 by Malcolm of Scotland (Nat. Lib. of Scotland, Roxburghe deposit).[60]

The Anselm manuscript has been claimed to be 'the oldest surviving document of painting from the Oxford region' and recognised as having 'a certain stylistic relationship' with the 'magnificent seal of Godstow nunnery' and the fine lead font of Dorchester Abbey. Dr. Pächt compared it with an Austrian manuscript of Anselm and derived both from an earlier English prototype.[61]

The expanded letter-decorations of the Anselm measure no more than 7 × 10 cm., but their general character and, in particular, the expressive and variously gesturing hands are closely related to the St. Frideswide painting. Many heads are in profile, although this is not very common in 12th-century drawing, and the beaky nose and large eye are also frequent in the Anselm. However, the Anselm's twenty illuminations have no slit collars and only one appearance of wide cuffed sleeves.

The figure at St. Frideswide's stands 74 cm. high from the crown of the head, just cut off by a new jamb-stone inserted c.1890, to the lower thighs at the 12th-century window-sill level. A width of about 53 cm. of the composition remained in 1891, with part of a mock-masonry background which in fact followed the actual stonework. Only the rough red-lead underpainting remains, on a fragmentary thin plaster skin. All bright cloth-colours, flesh-tints and highlights, which may have been on a second thin plaster coat, have been lost. The painting's relationship with the conspicuous fire-reddening of the main wall-surface is not entirely clear. Presumably this was caused by the fire of 1190 which may have destroyed the wall-painting proper, and all the rest of the scheme on the other jambs and cloister walls.

On 29 June 1891 the skilful and determined Oxford antiquary H. Hurst made a full-size record drawing of the freshly revealed figure (Fig. 106).

DAVID STURDY

[56] W. Oakeshott, *Sigona, Romanesque Paintings in Spain and the Winchester Bible Artists* (1972), Pl. 52.

[57] F. Wormald, *The Winchester Psalter* (1973), 82–3.

[58] O. Pächt and J.J.G. Alexander, *Illuminated Manuscripts in the Bodleian Library, Oxford* (1973), 18, No. 154.

[59] Ibid., 14, No. 111.

[60] T.S.R. Boase, *English Art 1100–1216* (1953), 154 and Pl. 50a.

[61] O. Pächt, 'The Illustrations of St. Anselm's Prayers and Meditations', *Journal of the Warburg and Courtauld Institutes*, xix (1956), 68–83.

Fig. 106.    Wall-painting on the chapter-house front of St. Frideswide's: drawing by H. Hurst, 1891. (Bodl. MS
Top. Oxon.a.18 No. 14; reproduced by permission of the Curators of the Bodleian Library.)

## THE LATE 12TH-CENTURY SEAL OF ST. FRIDESWIDE'S PRIORY

There can be little doubt that the seal-matrix (Fig. 107) used by the Augustinian canons of St. Frideswide during the middle ages was made soon after the saint's translation in 1180. An accumulation of evidence points in this direction. To begin with, the size of the seal is large: 83 × 60 mm.[62] Arguably no institutional seal before the middle of the 12th century was on quite this scale, and even then only the grandest of religious houses, such as the Benedictine Abbey of St. Edmund at Bury, aspired to anything larger.[63] Locally, the dimensions of the slightly earlier seal of the Abbey at Godstow are directly comparable with St. Frideswide's, and may have prompted the Oxford canons to opt for this degree of ostentation.[64] Various features of the punctuation and lettering also suggest a date in the second half of the century. The use of a colon to emphasise certain word divisions was apparently disseminated by the second seal of King Stephen and the seal of Archbishop Theobald of Canterbury, both dating from the late 1130s;[65] however, it did not become common until the 1170s and '80s. Letter forms such as the uncial-derived M and A are also best explained as late features, as is the upward-turning curl on the final stroke of M and R.[66] In general aspect, the legend is quite like that on the seal of Bicester Priory, founded 1182–5.[67] It is even conceivable that the two matrices were cut by the same craftsman, who might well therefore have been locally based.

In its general style, the figure of St. Frideswide herself is hard to parallel. The most convincing comparisons so far discovered are the seal used by Henry II's illegitimate son, Geoffrey, while he was bishop-elect of Lincoln, and the seal of Constance duchess of Brittany and countess of Richmond. Both of these survive on charters datable to the 1180s, though the matrices may possibly go back to the previous decade.[68] On all three seals the design and disposition of the cloak and the long tight sleeves over thin arms, as well as other proportions, indicate a common aesthetic for which there is no compelling evidence earlier or later in the century.

One final aspect of the design, the canopy over the saint's head, may suggest an even more specific date, but it may also have an iconographical purpose. The curious roofline, which breaks from the horizontal into a semicircular arch in the centre and carries three domes, is very like that seen on the reverse of the lead bulls of the masters

[62] W. de G. Birch, *Catalogue of Seals in the British Museum*, i (1887), No. 3811; W. Greenwell and C.H. Blair, 'Durham Seals: Catalogue made by the Rev. W. Greenwell. . . . collated and annotated by C.H. Blair', *Archaeologia Aeliana*, 3rd ser. xv (1918), No. 3533.

[63] Birch op. cit. note 62, No. 2796; G. Zarnecki et al. (eds.), *English Romanesque Art 1066–1200* (catalogue of Hayward Gallery exhibition, 1984) [hereafter *ERA*], No. 356.

[64] Birch op. cit. note 62, No. 3209; Greenwell and Blair op. cit. note 62, No. 3489; R. Ellis, *Catalogue of Seals in the Public Record Office: Monastic Seals*, i (1986), No. M348; *ERA* op. cit. note 63, No. 357.

[65] For Stephen, *Regesta Regum Anglo-Normannorum*, iv, eds. H.A. Cronne and R.H.C. Davis (1969), Pls. i and ii; but cf. *ERA* op. cit. note 63, No. 332 for comments on the date and authenticity of this seal. For Theobald, Birch op. cit. note 62, Nos. 1173–1182, and A. Saltman, *Theobald, Archbishop of Canterbury* (1956), 225–6.

[66] H.S. Kingsford, 'The Epigraphy of English Medieval Seals', *Archaeologia*, lxxix (1929), 149–78, tabulates the various letter forms. His basic findings remain valid even though the analysis needs to be extended and refined in the light of subsequent researches.

[67] Birch op. cit. note 62, No. 2772; Ellis op. cit. note 64, No. M075. There is a photograph of the seal in *V.C.H. Oxon* ii, opp. 138.

[68] For Geoffrey, Birch op. cit. note 62, Nos. 1701–3; and see D.M. Smith, *English Episcopal Acta, 1, Lincoln 1067–1185* (1980), lx–lxi and notes. For Constance, Birch Nos. 6594–5; W. Farrer and C.T. Clay, *Early Yorkshire Charters*, iv (1935), 77 (and plate), 97; and v (1936), 352; also illustrated in C.H. Hunter Blair, 'Armorials upon English Seals from the Twelfth to the Sixteenth Centuries', *Archaeologia*, lxxxix (1943) Pl. XVb.

Fig. 107. The late 12th-century Priory seal: +SIGILLUM: ECCLESIE SANCTE FRIDESWIDE OXENE-
FORDIE:. *Left*: photograph of B.L. Seal Cast LXX.79 (reproduced by permission of the British Library). *Right*:
composite drawing by John Blair, based on the B.L. cast and the impressions illustrated *Cart. Frid.* i,
frontispiece. *Actual size.*

of the Order of St. John of Jerusalem. The obvious date at which this design would have
become known in England was during the visit of grand master Roger des Moulins early
in 1185, and this in turn suggests a date in the mid or late 1180s for Frideswide's seal.[69]

Frideswide herself is shown in an interesting guise. Given her supposedly royal
lineage, one would expect her to be crowned and, since she founded a monastery and
was (presumably) its first head, she should carry a crosier. Neither is the case.[70] The
only possible reference to her religious life is the open book in her left hand. In
11th-century England this attribute had been shown on bishops' seals, where it denoted
a gospel or mass-book.[71] Male and female conventual rulers in the 12th century also
carry a book, probably the monastic rule conveyed to them during the consecration

[69] Birch op. cit. note 62, Nos. 4508–9. Roger des Moulins came with the embassy of Patriarch Heraclius of
Jerusalem; see J. Riley-Smith, *The Knights of St. John in Jerusalem and Cyprus, c.1050–1310* (1967), 64, and R.W.
Eyton, *Court, Household and Itinerary of King Henry II* (1878), 263.

[70] For example, the first known conventual seal of Romsey, dating from the second quarter of the 12th
century (Birch op. cit. note 62, No. 3927; Ellis op. cit. note 64, No. M735), shows either St. Ethelfleda or St.
Merwenna with pastoral staff, and a closed book held against her stomach. This iconography, with the
addition of a crown, was current for Etheldreda of Ely by the 13th century (Birch op. cit. note 62, Nos. 3111–2).

[71] Seals of 11th-century English bishops shown holding books are: Wulfstan of Worcester, Anselm of
Canterbury (for both see T.A. Heslop, 'English Seals from the Mid Ninth Century to 1100', *Jnl. British Archaeol.
Assocn.* cxxxiii (1980), 12–13 and Pl. IIB and F) and Peter of Chester (J. Cherry, 'The Lead Seal Matrix of Peter
Bishop of Chester', *Antiq. Jnl.* lxv (1985), 472–3, and Pl. CVIb). On 12th-century English episcopal seals the
books does not appear as an attribute.

ceremony; but this is invariably shown closed.[72] Frideswide's seal does not fit into either category and is quite possibly left deliberately ambiguous to encourage the assocation of Frideswide with ideas of learning, perhaps even to represent her as a personification of it. Contemporary images of the Liberal Arts, such as the figure of Grammar on the west front of Chartres, and Philosophy or Wisdom the fountainhead of the Arts, were shown with this symbol.[73] In her right hand the saint holds a flower. This was a commonplace on ladies' seals at this period and is frequently adopted by the Virgin Mary. Frideswide's flower is probably too short in the stem to be regarded as either a sceptre or a 'virga', so that connotations of rulership and virginity cannot be specifically intended. Its presence here may indicate more general ideas of beauty, youth and flourishing success, and is perhaps stimulated by the plant metaphors used in association with Wisdom in Ecclesiasticus xxiv.12–17.[74] It introduces a 'natural' element to counter-balance the man-made book.

The most noteworthy feature is that Frideswide is shown enthroned. In general this pose was reserved for saints of high status. On English seals at this period, apart from universal saints such as Mary and Peter, only Alban and Edmund seem to have merited such treatment.[75] Lesser saints were usually represented standing. Even further down the scale St. Egwin of Evesham, for example, and St. Neot were shown in the presence of, and subsidiary to, a major figure – in both these cases the Virgin Mary.[76] This argues that communities were, in general, capable of a realistic appraisal of the importance of their patron saints. Indeed, the local patron might be omitted altogether from the major conventual seal. At Burton-on-Trent, Mary is shown seated alone on the Abbey's large seal, St. Modwenna is relegated to a small counterseal.[77] Interestingly the Burton seal depicts Mary alone, without the Christ Child. Instead she holds a book and a flower, rather in the same way that Frideswide does. It may be that an assimilation to the personification of Ecclesia is intended and, if it is, it is conceivable that such an association was also in the minds of the Oxford canons when they drew up the contract with the maker of their new seal.

At Oxford, the status implied for Frideswide by her enthronement is enhanced by the canopy placed over her head. There were several formulae current for showing a figure within a structure, but these almost always involved the depiction of supporting columns or side walls with doors and windows.[78] The exceptions are the reverse sides of

[72] For the tradition of abbots' seals see *ERA* op. cit. note 63, No. 365 (Hugh of Bury) and Birch op. cit. note 62, No. 2617–8 (Walter of Battle). As with abbesses (see note 70 above) a crozier was placed in the right (dexter) hand and a closed book held against the body with the left. The book is almost certainly the Rule of St. Benedict, given during the consecration service: see D.H. Turner, *The Claudius Pontificals* (Henry Bradshaw Soc. xcvii, 1971), 103.

[73] See most recently M. Warner, *Monuments and Maidens, the Allegory of the Female Form* (1985), ch. 9, and M. Evans, 'Allegorical Women and Practical Men: the Iconography of the Artes Reconsidered', in D. Baker (ed.), *Medieval Women* (1978), 305–328; also G. Cames, *Allegories et Symboles dans l'Hortus Deliciarum* (1971), illus. 6.

[74] See T.A. Heslop, 'The Virgin Mary's Regalia and Twelfth-Century English Seals' in A. Borg and A. Martindale (eds.), *The Vanishing Past* (British Arch. Reps. Internat. Ser. cxi, 1981), 53–62; and *ERA* op. cit. note 63, No. 337 (Isabella, countess of Gloucester) for the use of 'flowers' on ladies' seals. In the Vulgate the verses where Wisdom describes herself as a flourishing plant are Ecclesiasticus 24. 16–23.

[75] For example Birch op. cit. note 62, Nos. 3939–43 (St. Albans) and 4299 (Westminster, St. Peter), *ERA* op. cit. note 63, Nos. 349 and 351 (also ibid., Nos. 350, 352, 356).

[76] Birch op. cit. note 62, No. 3957 (St. Neots). Ellis op. cit. note 64, No. M314 (Evesham) is from the same matrix as Greenwell and Blair op. cit. note 62, No. 3464; see *ERA* op. cit. note 63, No. 355.

[77] Birch op. cit. note 62, No. 2778; Ellis op. cit. note 64, No. M137.

[78] For example Oseney (Birch op. cit. note 62, No. 3799), Canterbury (Birch, No. 1369–72; *ERA* op. cit. note 63, No. 358) and Peterborough (Birch, No. 3827).

the bulls of the masters of the Order of St. John of Jerusalem mentioned above as the probable source for Frideswide's canopy. As well as providing an argument for the date, this comparison also suggests another line of enquiry. It seems likely that the reverse of such *bullae* was thought to show the Holy Sepulchre with the body of Christ laid inside it.[79] The Sepulchre was, of course, the archetypal Christian burial site and one that was, as a consequence, widely emulated. It was also a major centre of pilgrimage. There are obvious reasons why these two factors would have had very positive and attractive connotations for the canons of St. Frideswide given the recent translation of their saint into a new shrine. But the canopy has not been copied unchanged: the central, arched element of the model has been enlarged. This may have been done for purely aesthetic reasons, but it can equally have been to lay particular stress on the idea of a dome. This may be taken to imply the covering of a ciborium or a tomb, or perhaps even of a large centralised building. While this does not constitute positive proof that Frideswide's body was actually placed in a centralised building or roofed architectural micro-structure,[80] it nonetheless indicates the degree of elaboration which the canons thought their patroness merited. They were clearly not alone in their admiration: both the popularity of pilgrimage to her shrine and the appearance of her name in contemporary calendars indicate that Frideswide's reputation had reached a very high level.[81]

T.A. Heslop

## CATHERINE OF ARAGON'S VISIT TO THE SHRINE OF ST. FRIDESWIDE

In a paper devoted to the shrine of St. Frideswide in the 12th century, Dr. Mayr-Harting drew attention to the fact that it was particularly visited by women.[82] It was perhaps natural, he adds, for women to favour a female saint. Certainly when miraculous cures there were recorded by Prior Philip at the end of the 12th century the cures of women outnumbered those of men by two to one. Moreover, while some of the cures related to adolescent girls (and none specifically to women in childbirth), one had been of a woman of Chadlington whom no-one had believed to be pregnant when she was. Again, visitors to the shrine had usually tried every remedy before resorting to the saint to seek a miracle. The chief clients who visited her in the late 12th century seem to have been drawn from knights, townsmen, upper peasantry and their womenfolk living within a circle of forty miles round Oxford.[83]

On 12 April 1518 the King's Secretary, Richard Pace, reported to Wolsey in London

---

[79] E.H. King, *The Rules, Statutes and Customs of the Hospitallers 1099–1310* (1934), opp. 34. Idem, *Seals of the Order of St John of Jerusalem* (1932) contests that this was regarded as a representation of Christ's sepulchre, but this is how the tomb is shown elsewhere, in particular by the Canons of the Holy Sepulchre itself in the 1170s; see G. Schlumberger, F. Chalandon and A. Blanchet, *Sigillographie de l'Orient Latin* (1943) Pl. V/9, and E. Baldwin Smith, *The Dome* (1971 edn.), Pl. 222.

[80] [cf. above, p. 256: EDITOR.]

[81] Lavish provision of feasts of Frideswide in the calendars of a group of English psalters from around 1200 is one of the reasons for attributing their production to Oxford. See N.J. Morgan, *Early Gothic Manuscripts: 1. 1190–1250* (1982), cat. Nos. 23, 28, 29. See also H. Mayr-Harting, 'Functions of a Twelfth-Century Shrine: the Miracles of St. Frideswide', in H. Mayr-Harting and R.I. Moore (eds.), *Studies in Medieval History presented to R.H.C. Davis* (1985), 193–206.

[82] Mayr-Harting op. cit. note 80, 197–8.

[83] Ibid., 195–204.

that it was secretly said that the Queen, Catherine of Aragon, was with child.[84] It was to prove her last pregnancy. A daughter, the Princess Mary, had been born in 1516,[85] but her three male children had none of them lived for more than a few weeks.[86] Pace prayed heartily to God that the child might be a prince, to the surety and comfort of the realm. The court from which he wrote was on 16 April at Abingdon. It was to move to Woodstock by the 18th.[87]

The Queen took the opportunity to visit Oxford en route, and to call on the former royal almoner to Henry VII who had preached at the funeral of Prince Henry (the first of her three baby boys) in 1511, Richard Rawlyns, warden of Merton. He entertained her to a meal, and recorded his enthusiasm for her prestigious visit in his own hand in the College Register, where he compared her to Juno and Minerva.[88] To this day a portrait of her (perhaps contemporary) hangs in the Warden's House, though not in the Lodgings where Rawlyns received her.[89] But her visit to Oxford was much more than a social occasion. She also went to the shrine of the saint in the Priory[90] and sought a miracle – a male heir for the Tudors. On the failure of the Anglo-Saxon princess to answer her prayers[91] hung the fate of the English Reformation.

J.R.L. HIGHFIELD

[84] *Letters and Papers, Foreign and Domestic, of the Reign of Henry VIII*, ed. J.S. Brewer et al., II, pt. ii, No. 4074. I am grateful to Dr. S. Gunn for this reference.

[85] *D.N.B.*

[86] The first had died in 1511. The second had been born in 1513 and a third in 1514, but 'lived not long after' (G. Mattingly, *Catherine of Aragon* (1942), 127).

[87] *Letters and Papers . . . of Henry VIII*, II, pt. ii, Nos. 4085, 4089. I owe these references to Dr. Gunn.

[88] *Registrum Annalium Collegii Mertonensis, 1483–1521*, ed. H.E. Salter (Oxford Hist. Soc. lxxvi, 1921), 477.

[89] Mrs. R.L. Poole, *Catalogue of Oxford Portraits* (Oxford Hist. Soc. lxxxi, 1926), ii. 45.

[90] See note 88.

[91] A stillborn girl was born in November 1518 (*D.N.B.*).

# Index

(NOTE: Counties are not indicated for places in Oxfordshire, cathedrals, and some other major places.)